IN EXTREMIS

'Rarely has a friend and colleague written such a brave and uncompromising testament to such a rare, brave and uncompromising woman. Would that a few more of us should be so blessed in our courage and our friends'
Shami Chakrabarti

'In Lindsey Hilsum, Marie Colvin has found, posthumously, the right biographer. She penetrates the war-zone of Colvin's life, and fetches her back in all her beautiful, brave complexity. This is a heartbreaking portrait that does not detract from the legend, but understands the compulsions which returned Colvin time and again to seek out the most dangerous places'
Nicholas Shakespeare

'One of the modern world's most experienced and admired foreign correspondents, Lindsey Hilsum, has now written a riveting, intimate and deeply moving account of the epic life of her late friend and colleague, Marie Colvin, who will be long remembered – not least because of Hilsum's fine work in this book – as amongst the great war reporters of her generation'
Jon Lee Anderson

'Superb. A fitting account of the life of one of the finest war correspondents of our time, written by another. I admired Marie greatly, and In Extremis showed me I was right to do so'
John Simpson

IN EXTREMIS

The Life of War Correspondent
Marie Colvin

LINDSEY HILSUM

Chatto & Windus
LONDON

7 9 10 8 6

Chatto & Windus, an imprint of Vintage,
20 Vauxhall Bridge Road,
London SW1V 2SA

Chatto & Windus is part of the Penguin Random House group of companies
whose addresses can be found at global.penguinrandomhouse.com

Penguin
Random House
UK

First published in the United Kingdom by Chatto & Windus in 2018

penguin.co.uk/vintage

A CIP catalogue record for this book is available from the British Library

ISBN 9781784740931

Printed and bound in Great Britain by Clays Ltd, Elcograf S.p.A.

Typeset in 10.5/15.5 pt Mercury Text G1
by Integra Software Services Pvt. Ltd, Pondicherry

Penguin Random House is committed to a sustainable future for
our business, our readers and our planet. This book is made
from Forest Stewardship Council® certified paper.

MIX
Paper from
responsible sources
FSC® C018179

In memory of Sarah Corp, another companion on the road

It has always seemed to me that what I write about is humanity *in extremis*, pushed to the unendurable, and that it is important to tell people what really happens in wars.

MARIE COLVIN, 2001

Fair Weather

This level reach of blue is not my sea;
Here are sweet waters, pretty in the sun,
Whose quiet ripples meet obediently
A marked and measured line, one after one.
This is no sea of mine, that humbly laves
Untroubled sands, spread glittering and warm.
I have a need of wilder, crueler waves;
They sicken of the calm, who knew the storm.

So let a love beat over me again,
Loosing its million desperate breakers wide;
Sudden and terrible to rise and wane;
Roaring the heavens apart; a reckless tide
That casts upon the heart, as it recedes,
Splinters and spars and dripping, salty weeds.

DOROTHY PARKER

CONTENTS

CONTENTS

PREFACE

The way we are living,
timorous or bold,
will have been our life.

Seamus Heaney

There was only one topic of conversation over dinner in Beirut that night: whether to find people smugglers to sneak us over the border into Syria and the besieged town of Homs. It was February 2012 and revolution was turning into civil war. The rebels who had hoped to overthrow the Syrian government were holding out in the Baba Amr neighbourhood of Homs as President Bashar al-Assad's forces pounded it with artillery.

The four of us had taken plenty of risks in our reporting lives. Jim Muir had been a BBC correspondent in the Middle East since the early 1980s, staying for years in Lebanon despite the threat of kidnap. Neil MacFarquhar, who had been brought up in Libya, reported from the Middle East for the *New York Times*. I had covered conflicts in Rwanda, Iraq, Libya and a dozen other countries. And then there was Marie Colvin of the *Sunday Times*. She wore a patch over her left eye, having lost the sight in it to a grenade fired by a government soldier in Sri Lanka a decade earlier. In 1999, as militiamen armed with guns and machetes threatened the United Nations compound in East Timor, Marie had refused to leave even though most other journalists had taken the last plane out. In the winter of the same year, she nearly perished in the freezing mountains of Chechnya as the Russians bombed the roads. She always went in further and stayed longer.

Not only was the bombardment of Baba Amr relentless, but the smugglers might kidnap us for ransom or to sell on to jihadists. For three of us, this was beyond our danger threshold, but Marie shrugged. 'Anyway it's what we do,' she said. And that was that. She would go in.

Fifteen months earlier I had been in London at St Bride's, the journalists' church on Fleet Street, when Marie gave an address at the annual service to commemorate those of our number killed during the year. 'We always have to ask ourselves whether the level of risk is worth the story,' she said, standing tall at the lectern, her rail-thin body encased in a black jersey dress, glasses on the end of her nose so she could read with her sole functioning eye. 'What is bravery, and what is bravado?'

Returning to my hotel after dinner that evening in Beirut, I wondered uncomfortably whether Marie was reckless or I was a coward. I had my reasons for not going to Homs – bad knees, an editor who thought the trip too dangerous, a book to write – but they were just excuses. Marie knew where the story was, and would stop at nothing to get it. My reporting on Syrian refugees in Lebanon was done and I flew back to London. Marie spent a few more days organising her trip before she and photographer Paul Conroy set off on the perilous journey by foot, motorbike and jeep, at one point crawling through a storm drain.

A few days later I got an email, sent by satellite phone. 'Made it to Baba Amr. Nightmare here but so anger making it's worth it. I'm supposed to be applying for an Iranian visa, but I have left my Iran contacts at home. Have you got a number for that nice (relatively!) woman in the Islamic Guidance Office?' Marie was already planning her next trip.

That Sunday I read her story about 'the widows' basement', as powerful a piece of war reporting as any by her famous role model Martha Gellhorn, who had covered the Spanish Civil War and the

D-Day landings. 'It is a city of the cold and hungry, echoing to explod-
ing shells and bursts of gunfire... Freezing rain fills potholes and snow
drifts in through windows empty of glass,' she wrote. 'On the lips of
everyone was the question: "Why have we been abandoned by the
world?"'

I had presumed that she was on her way home, but two days later,
I heard that she had returned to Baba Amr. I was angry with her. Why
take the risk a second time? She sent me an email saying she had
regretted leaving, and other European journalists were also in Homs
so she felt she had to be there too. It was so urgent, she needed to get
the story out before her paper on Sunday. We arranged a Skype call so
she could do an interview for Channel 4 News, where I work. We
spoke before she started the interview.

'Lindsey, this is the worst we've ever seen.'

'I know, but what's your exit strategy?'

Pause.

'That's just it. I don't have one. I'm working on it now.'

The following morning I woke thinking of a friend who had been
kidnapped and murdered in Baghdad. That could be Marie, I thought.
I was on the bus heading for work when a message came through from
a Spanish friend in Beirut whose journalist husband was also in Baba
Amr.

'I think something terrible has happened to your friend Marie.
Have you heard?'

* * * * *

The days that followed Marie's death merged into one another. A young
French photographer, Rémi Ochlik, had also been killed. The *Sunday
Times* was desperately trying to get Paul Conroy out – he was badly injured, as was another French journalist, Edith Bouvier. I subsumed my
grief and anxiety into talking about Marie on the radio and writing her
obituary for the *Financial Times*. I found myself thinking of when we
first met in 1998, after war had broken out between Ethiopia and Eritrea.

A dozen or so journalists, including Marie and myself, were in Djibouti, the hottest place on earth, eyeing up a rickety Ukrainian aircraft that had been ferrying out aid workers and businesspeople from the Eritrean capital, Asmara. It was the usual situation – all reasonable people were scrambling to get out, but 'a little bunch of madmen', the journalists, were trying to get in. A pair of Ukrainian pilots agreed to turn round and take us. Marie and I found ourselves walking together across the melting tarmac. Once on board we sat together and, as the plane taxied down the lumpy runway, we noticed two objects whipping past the window outside – our pilots' sweaty shirts, which they had hung on the wings to dry out and forgotten to put back on. We peered through the open cockpit door – yes, they were flying bare-chested. The aircraft lurched upwards and the TV gear that had been piled up, unsecured, at the front gradually slid down the aisle. Marie and I laughed so much we nearly fell out of our seats. We were like two schoolgirls with the giggles in class. It's my first memory of her. Of course I had seen her before, and knew her by reputation, but that was when we became friends, the time we couldn't stop laughing, thinking we might plunge to our deaths from the skies above the Red Sea.

For the next fourteen years we would meet on the road or at the Frontline Club, the foreign correspondents' hangout, near Paddington. She invited me to parties first at her flat in Notting Hill and later at the house she bought in Hammersmith, on the north bank of the Thames. Elegant in a black cocktail dress, she mixed vodka martinis, the house full of actors, poets and politicians as well as journalists. As the conflicts of the late twentieth and early twenty-first century proliferated, I felt we were partners in crime, the Thelma and Louise of the press corps. In April 2001 I heard that she had been shot in Sri Lanka. By the time I got hold of her she was in the United States, awaiting surgery on her damaged eye. 'I can't cry,' she said. 'And I need to because I keep getting messages from Tamils wanting to donate their eye to me.' The surgeon found a 6mm piece of shrapnel wedged against her optic nerve. The eye patch she wore from then on became her trademark, a badge of bravery.

She was famous now, sought after and showered with awards, but she grew thin and erratic. When I saw her in Iraq after the US invasion in 2003 her face seemed more deeply lined. One evening in London we shared a platform in front of an audience of human rights activists. An earnest young woman in the audience asked how we coped with the trauma of covering conflicts. It's a question foreign correspondents who go to war zones hate – are we really meant to bare our souls on a Thursday evening in front of an auditorium of strangers? Marie and I exchanged glances.

'Lindsey and I, we go to bars and we drink,' she drawled in the East Coast accent she'd never lost, and we got the giggles.

Sometimes it wasn't so funny. I was furious when she turned up two hours late and drunk for an interview with an Iranian activist in London that I had arranged. I forgave her, of course, because everyone forgave Marie – she had a charisma that made you excited to think she considered you a friend. I knew her in that easy way you know someone with whom you share adventures and the exhilaration of survival, when the bomb goes off just after you leave, or hits the empty building down the road missing you by a few yards or minutes. I only glimpsed the dark side, the broken marriages and post-traumatic stress that I knew afflicted her.

In the week after her death I found a photograph from 2002, the year after she lost the sight in her eye, showing the two of us in the rubble of the Palestinian refugee camp of Jenin, which had just been destroyed by Israeli bulldozers. In it, Marie is wearing a pale blue denim shirt and grey jeans, patch across her eye, notebook in one hand, pen in the other. I'm wearing a purple shirt and dark blue trousers. We look dusty and tired and happy, which is exactly what we were, united in a fierce journalistic urge to get the story and delighted to have run into each other. The pictures from that encounter are the only ones I have that show us together.

I had known her so fleetingly – dinner in Tripoli, a bumpy drive through the West Bank, a drink in Jerusalem – and now she was gone. There was so much I didn't know about Marie, things she had hidden from me, or that I had chosen not to see. What drove her to such extremes in both her professional and personal life? Was it bravery or recklessness? She was the most admired war correspondent of our generation, one whose personal life was scarred by conflict too, and although I counted her as a friend, I understood so little about her.

As grief subsided I thought of her no less often. She was always there, her ghost challenging me to discover all that I had missed when she was alive.

* * * * *

PART ONE
America

Chapter 1

DEAD MAN'S BRANCH

She had lived with bad dreams for many years, but nothing prepared Marie for the recurrent nightmare that plagued her after she was shot. As she drifted into sleep her subconscious re-ran what had happened, the fear and indecision never resolving, like a horror film stuck on a loop, repeating into infinity.

In the dream she is lying on the ground, seeing the flares, hearing the machine-gun fire and the soldiers' voices exactly as she heard them that pitch black night in Sri Lanka before the moon rose over the fields. These are her choices: she can stand up and shout, hoping they will see that she is white and female, obviously a foreigner. She can try to crawl away, knowing they will shoot at anything they see moving. Or she can lie still awaiting her fate. The decision will determine whether she lives or dies but nothing will undo what is about to happen. She cannot roll back time, nor can she push it forward. Stand up? Crawl away? Lie still? Stand up? Crawl away? Lie still? The choices repeat and repeat, a drumbeat of fear pounding louder and louder, as she lies paralysed.

In real life, it was hard to figure out exactly what was happening, although later she understood that it had been quite simple. The Tamils guiding her from the rebel-held part of Sri Lanka into government territory ran into an army patrol as they crossed the front line. Marie dropped to the ground as the bullets whined past, but her escorts fled into the jungle, back the way they had come. She lay there for about half an hour, alone and petrified, before making her fateful decision.

'Journalist! American journalist!' she shouted as she rose with her hands up. Suddenly her eye and her chest hurt with a pain so acute she could scarcely breathe. One of the soldiers had fired a grenade at her. As she fell, she realised that blood was trickling from her eye and mouth. She felt a profound sadness that she was going to die. Crawling towards them in the desperate hope they would stop shooting and help her, she shouted 'Doctor!' Maybe they would see that she was a wounded foreign civilian and not a guerrilla fighter. They yelled at her to stand up and remove her jacket. Somehow she managed to stumble forward, hands in the air. Every time she fell they shouted at her to get up again.

In the nightmare, time freezes before the shot is fired and her life passes before her. Scenes from conflicts she has witnessed flicker across her mind: the old man with rasping breath in the basement in Chechnya with the back of his head blown off by a Russian rocket; the body of a peasant dressed in a worn woollen suit that she came across under a bush in Kosovo; the young Palestinian woman she watched die from gunshot wounds in Beirut. The human body, fragile and broken. Her own body. The images re-run until she wakes, unrested, terrified, safe in her own bed but dreading the next night when she must live through it all again.

Marie Colvin went to Sri Lanka in April 2001 because no foreign journalist had reported from Tamil Tiger territory in six years. In nearly two decades of war, some 83,000 people had been killed. Barred by the government and mistrusted by the fanatical guerrillas fighting for independence, reporters had dared not cross the frontline, so the pitiful situation of Tamil civilians who bore the brunt of the violence had gone largely unreported. That was why she went. That was why she thought it worth the risk.

She was flown to New York for treatment. The surgeon said he couldn't save the sight in her left eye, but he would try to save the eye itself. Frantic with worry, her mother insisted that Marie come home to Long Island where she could nurse her, cook her the meat loaf she had loved as a child, ensure that she had everything she needed to recover. Marie's ex-husband flew in and he and her mother agreed that this time she would have to submit to their ministrations.

Why did she resist? To be looked after was surely exactly what she needed, but somehow it felt unbearable. As if it weren't bad enough to lose the sight in one eye, now she would lose her independence too. She wanted to stay at a fancy hotel in New York, to smoke, to have a cocktail, to spend time with her best friend Katrina, who would make her laugh. She needed to recover what she could of the self she had become in two decades as a journalist. It was sixteen years since she had left America. She had lived in Paris, London and Jerusalem and had travelled to conflicts all over the world, taking chances, beating the odds and earning her reputation as one of the toughest but most compassionate reporters in the world as well as the best and funniest company. That was who she was. She feared the waves closing over her, feared being subsumed by her family, by the cloying parochialism of her home town, by a promise of safety that would crush her essence. However desperate her situation, she could not let herself be pulled back to where she had started.

* * * * *

The town of Oyster Bay, on Long Island, where Marie spent her childhood and adolescence, was quintessential suburbia. The families in the Colvins' neighbourhood were America's new post-war middle class: teachers, small-business owners, government employees. This was the era when mothers stayed at home and fathers came back from work to a cigarette and a highball, a whiskey cocktail. They watched *Leave It To Beaver* and *The Donna Reed Show*, genial TV sitcoms about family life. It was Marie's father's claim to fame that his eldest sister, Bette, was a hostess on the quiz show *Beat the Clock*.

Marie, the Colvins' first child, was born on 12 January 1956, in Astoria, Queens, a restless baby who soon sprouted a head of thick, dark curls. America was changing fast. Dwight D. Eisenhower, re-elected that year, was the last US President born in the nineteenth century. Elvis Presley scandalised the nation with his hip-thrusts as he sang 'Hound Dog' on the *Ed Sullivan Show*. The Cold War was escalating: it was the year of the Suez Crisis and the Soviet invasion of Hungary. Marie's parents had more immediate concerns – Marie's mother, Rosemarie, struggled to get her and her brother, Billy, born the following year, up and down three flights of stairs in their apartment block. Now she was expecting again. Long Island, with its beaches, fields and potato farms, looked like a perfect solution. They found a new-build in East Norwich, adjoining the more upmarket Oyster Bay. By the time Michael was born, the family was settled in the house where Marie's parents would have another two children and spend the rest of their lives.

For Rosemarie this was a huge step up in life. She had been raised in the working class South Bronx in the lean times between the wars. Like many others in the area, her parents, Rose and James Marron, were of Irish descent. After her father died when she was just a few months old, her mother struggled with three children, becoming ever more religious and unyielding. Rosemarie had to work her way through Fordham Jesuit University where she trained as a teacher. 'I didn't feel I was ready for a relationship,' she recollects. 'I had to educate myself and had no help at home.' But when she met William Colvin – six foot tall, slim, confident, with dark wavy hair – she changed her mind. 'He was very kind and accepting of anything or anyone,' she says. 'I had grown up in a family that was dogmatic, but I wasn't that way. It was a great relief to meet someone who felt the same as I did.' This, she thought, was how she would like to bring up her own children: good Catholics, disciplined and studious, but tolerant and open-minded.

* * * * *

The Colvins were what Rosemarie called 'lace curtain Irish' – middle class and relatively privileged. Although Bill's father's side was descended from Scots, they saw themselves as Irish Catholic, and Bill

6

had attended Saint Augustine's Catholic High School. Writing for the school newspaper made Bill dream of becoming a journalist but in 1944, aged seventeen, he enlisted in the US Marine Corps. He was still undergoing training when the United States dropped atomic bombs on Hiroshima and Nagasaki. Posted to the Chinese port city of Tientsin – now Tianjin – on occasion he and his platoon 'tangled with the gooks', as he put it, when Communist units attacked US forces. After he left China in September 1946 he rarely spoke about his experiences but, years later, Marie would recall marching around, aged six, singing 'From the halls of Montezuma to the shores of Tripoli', the Marines' Hymn which her father had taught her. It seemed, she said, 'very romantic and exciting'. All her life she got along well with military men. Her father had a soldierly bearing and was determined that his children should uphold the high standards of behaviour he had learnt in the Marines.

After finishing his military service, Bill started to feel unwell. He had contracted tuberculosis in China, and had to spend two years at the US Marine Hospital in Queens. Journalism was not an easy profession to enter, and upon discharge he went for a safer option, training as a teacher at Fordham. When he met a tall, determined young woman five years his junior with red hair and an open face, one who shared his passion for self-improvement, he felt that at last everything was falling into place. Bill Colvin and Rosemarie Marron were married at St Luke's Church in the South Bronx. She wore a long white silk dress with a scalloped neckline and carried a bouquet of lilies. He was in a morning suit and striped cravat, his hair shining with pomade. They went to Bermuda on their honeymoon and started their family immediately.

Bill Colvin was a dedicated and, by all accounts, exemplary English teacher, spending his entire career at Forest Hills High School in Queens. He led a Boy Scout troop and was active in local politics, but he never lost his youthful passion for writing. Like millions of Americans, he responded to an advertisement in the *New York Times Book Review* for a correspondence course at the Famous Writers

School, in Westport, Connecticut, which promised to 'teach you to write successfully at home', holding out the possibility of 'financial success and independence' as a writer.

The application form he completed in 1967 reveals a lot about the father against whom Marie would soon rebel. His main ambition, he said, was, 'To be a good person, lead a full life and create something with beauty and meaning before I die.' Interests: politics and reading. Favourite classroom subjects: English and philosophy. Favourite writers: Walt Whitman, William Faulkner and Shakespeare. His chosen magazines and newspapers were *Good Housekeeping*, the Jesuit weekly magazine *America*, and the *Oyster Bay Guardian*. 'Maybe I just want to wrestle with eternal conflicts on paper,' he wrote in a piece about why he wanted to write, but more may have been revealed in a story he wrote about a teacher, who just happened to be called Bill. 'Society won't accept a man simply as a teacher,' he wrote. 'He must really be something else in order to justify his existence.'

* * * * *

Marie's sister Aileen, nicknamed Boo, was born in 1960. Four years later, just before Marie turned nine, Rosemarie gave birth to their fifth and final child, Cathleen, always known as Cat. Marie had taken little interest in the birth of her other siblings but she was enchanted by the new baby. The feeling never faded and from the moment she could toddle, Cat was Marie's shadow. As the eldest, Marie had a small room of her own on the first floor. Cat remembers lying in bed playing 'postage stamp kisses', a game her big sister invented. 'She would tell me a story about a place – Brazil, maybe, or China – with parties and dancing women or Amazon queens. Then she would give me as many kisses as hours it took to get there by plane to send me to my dreams.' Life for the Colvin kids took place largely 'down the hill' at the back of the house. Bill mobilised the fathers of the neighbourhood to dig out the sandy slope, shoring up the retaining wall at the top with old tyres and creating a flat play area at the bottom, where they planted ivy, honey locust and dogwood trees. The neighbourhood kids and Marie's siblings trailed in the slipstream of her enthusiasm. She was not only the oldest, but also tall, wiry, strong and game for anything. With her shock of dark curls and her determined manner, she commanded attention. 'She was the person to follow,' says her brother, Michael. 'I thought if I tagged along with Marie, everything would be fine.'

Their favourite game was Dead Man's Branch. 'We each had our own tree,' recalls Billy. 'You had to climb out along a branch to see whose would break first.' Invariably, it was Marie who pushed out farthest. If her branch broke and she took a tumble, she'd just pick herself up and find another branch. On the whole, though, the other kids would have given up long before she reached the flimsy end. The game appealed not only to Marie's physical bravery but also to her competitiveness: she liked to win. When the first snows fell, the neighbourhood fathers would carve out a snaking toboggan run which, when the grown-ups were safely out of sight, Billy would douse with water to ice it up so the toboggan went faster. When she was about ten, Marie careered full-tilt into an oak tree, breaking her nose and splitting open her forehead. She was taken to hospital, and ended up with a scar. It was one of the rare occasions when the Colvin children ran for help – their parents' rule was that you could come home in tears only if you were bleeding.

The sea was a constant in the Colvins' lives, just a bicycle ride away. In winter, when the bay froze at the edges, they would drift out on ice floes, daring one another to go out farther. In the summer, they would spend the whole day at the beach. They joined the Scouts and went camping at Planting Fields, a nearby park and arboretum, green and lush in the summer, sparkling with orange, red and gold by October. The leader of Marie's troop noticed that at the end of a hike, Marie would frequently be on her own, rather than sticking close to the others. 'She was not naughty, only curious and unafraid,' she noted later. 'Her dominant, courageous personality stood out even then.'

The centre of Oyster Bay comprised a handful of shops, a railway station, the council buildings, and that was about it. The loudest noise came from the gulls that lifted and hovered over the ocean. It was a safe place where everyone knew everyone and children wandered freely, but nevertheless the dangers of the world beyond Long Island hung over them. The elementary school Marie attended held periodic nuclear drills, in which the children were told to gather in the hallway, where there were no windows, and crouch against the walls. (How this was meant to save them in the event of nuclear war was unclear.) One day in November 1963, Marie arrived early to take Billy and Michael home from kindergarten, about a mile from the house. 'I didn't know what it was but I could see that something horrible had happened,' Michael recalls. 'She was crying so I started crying too as we walked.' The teacher had broken the news to Marie's class: President Kennedy had been assassinated.

For Bill and Rosemarie it wasn't just a question of remembering where they were when they heard the news. As mainstays of the local Democratic Party they had campaigned tirelessly for Kennedy. When he came to office in 1961, the Democrats, who had previously been the underdogs, gained control of the Oyster Bay Town Council, a sign of the new liberal mood sweeping America. Local politics gave Marie her first glimpse of power and corruption. Oyster Bay was a Republican bastion, the Grand Old Party in Nassau County reputed to be the most powerful in the country. The party chairman, Joseph Margiotta, drove a car with the licence plate GOP–1. Municipal hiring, promotions and contracts all went through him, and he was eventually convicted of collaborating in an insurance scheme to benefit his political cronies.

In 1965 a newly elected Democratic town supervisor sacked the town historian and appointed the 'young and dynamic' Bill Colvin. Marie's father did the job, unpaid and part time, for a year until he was appointed to a full time salaried position as county treasurer that required him to take a leave of absence from teaching. When he ran for election within the party, the kids were dragooned into making buttons in red, white and blue with the slogan 'Count on Colvin'. On his defeat, his loyal eldest daughter declared it 'a conspiracy'. In the evenings, after the children tumbled into the house, conversation round the dinner table frequently turned to politics. Marie heard her parents lamenting America's deepening involvement in the Vietnam War. She saw their despair when Robert Kennedy and Martin Luther King were also assassinated, and understood their disappointment when, in 1968, the Republican Richard Nixon was elected.

* * * * *

By 1969, Marie was attending Oyster Bay High, a public school in an imposing 1920s art deco building, its russet brick walls decorated with white limestone friezes above sash windows, just a hundred yards from the bay. Excelling in both arts and science, she went straight into the Honors Class. Sometimes her home experiments went awry, such as when she tried to incubate a duck egg by making a cradle out of a towel that she hung on a standard lamp in her room. That night, at around 1 a.m., the towel caught fire. Smelling smoke, Rosemarie rushed up to gather the children and take them on to the patio as the fire fighters arrived and the neighbours gathered to watch the drama. Marie had just started to keep a diary in which she recorded her verdict: 'DUMB!'

Marie's diaries reveal the preoccupations of most teenage girls: a close observation of who sat next to whom on the school bus, endless deliberation on the meaning of a particular boy's glance or greeting, and the urgent need to reject the red dresses with round collars that her mother chose for her.

2nd Jan 1969. Everyone is wearing pants. I've got to talk mommy into letting me do it, for honor's sake. I'm not sure I want to but I must.

A few days later, fashion interfered with her ability to play French horn in the school band.

6th Jan 1969. Wore pants. Blue dungaree bell bottoms. Hard playing instrument, pants are so tight.

By late spring, all the girls were wearing shorts to high school.

28th May 1969. Today I went to HS in shorts. So did everyone else. But mine were v short and v tight. Wore a vest and sandals too. When we got back was mommy mad. We had a mother to daughter talk about why I was doing this. She told me how pro-vocative I looked.

Provocative was, of course, exactly the point because Marie was trying to attract the attention of a boy called Jeff. Her parents, especially her father, were getting in her way. Despite being politically progressive, Bill's views on family remained traditional. He was the breadwinner, and – as the man of the house – exempted from the chores everyone else had to do. Although he supported his daughters' academic ambitions, he had little time for the women's liberation movement that was beginning to influence the protest culture of the time. Chafing against the limits he imposed, Marie had an unerring instinct for what would anger him most. 'The confrontations started when she was around twelve,' remembers Rosemarie. 'Marie knew how to push his buttons.'

Mass on Sunday at Saint Dominic Roman Catholic Church was a ritual for the Colvins, and no excuse for absence other than serious illness was accepted. The family was usually late because Bill and Marie had fought about what she was wearing. Rebellion gave her a certain satisfaction.

8th June 1969. To church. Wore mini. The mother and the father no like.

Marie who had received her first holy communion some years earlier, tried to get God on her side, offering Him her record collection and pledging to say an act of contrition every night if He made Jeff like her. 'Hope it works,' she wrote. (It didn't.) She worried that she was taller than most boys and that other girls were slimmer and prettier. In fact, she was growing increasingly attractive, with green eyes, pale clear skin that tanned easily in summer, an even mouth and two long curly curtains of hair like Carole King, one of the folk-rock singers she and her friends loved. But sometimes she couldn't fathom her own feelings. She knew she was cleverer than the boys, yet she longed for their attention. She relished the feeling of vanquishing her father when she outran him, chasing round the house in the wet grass – yet as much as she wanted to defy him, she also craved his approval. If a boy misbehaved at school, his punishment was to go and stand with the girls, as if that were the ultimate degradation. It was hard to make sense of it all.

* * * * *

Marie's diaries reveal a vivacious, intelligent, funny girl excited by the world around her. She read Tolkien, bought the albums of Steppenwolf, John and Yoko and the musical *Hair*, trained the dog, Piper, to sit, fibbed about coming second in an athletics meet when in fact she was unplaced, got grounded by her father for disobedience and joined the rest of America in collective excitement about the space programme.

> *12th March 1969. Apollo still in orbit, splashdown tomorrow. We may be on the moon in May!*

In the summer of 1969, she learnt to sail, a pastime that would be a passion all her life.

> *16th July 1969. I had the tiller most of the day. Did OK. The wind was great and we kept heeling – going really fast in the Sound. 17th July. Cindy and I went out alone … Boy was it fun … coming back in I made a perfect mooring … Ma saw me. A man on the dock said 'Look at those girls, they're good.' Julie says she thinks we made skipper rating. Wow!*

For nearly a year her drive for independence was channelled into one project: buying a boat. Her father put up a list of obstacles: she would need a life saving certificate and a safety licence, and to earn enough money to buy the boat herself. He told Rosemarie he thought this would take her a couple of years, which was fine, as sixteen would be a suitable age. Marie took this as a challenge. She got the life saving certificate that summer, began to work towards the safety licence and squirrelled away her babysitting money.

18th July 1969. Put $29 in bank. Now have $79.50!

By May of the following year, she had enough to buy a second-hand Sunfish, a two-person dinghy with a triangular sail. The whole family remembers the afternoon a man drove up unannounced with the boat on a trailer, Marie hopping from foot to foot at the front door, oscillating between triumph and nonchalance, her father not knowing whether to be proud or aghast. She was fourteen. She had taken five-year-old Cat into her confidence through the months of plotting. 'It was an impossible goal but she did it,' says Cat. 'That's what my childhood was like. She'd get you so excited. There'd be a build-up. It was like a conspiracy – every step of the way it was so exciting. And when the boat pulls up it's like "Wow!" To me she was invincible.'

* * * * *

Marie was on the hunt for causes. In January 1970 she wrote a story about three Martian scientists who speculate about whether there is life on Earth and conclude that there can't be because the atmosphere is laden with carbon monoxide from vehicle emissions. The piece ends with a plea from the author: 'Isn't it time we did something, Earthmen?' She avidly watched the documentaries of the marine biologist, Jacques Cousteau, and worried about ocean pollution. With her wild curls and determination to change the world she must have fitted right in with the environmental hippie crowd but she was becoming self-conscious about her image.

25th April 1970. Went to State U today. I'm now all hepped up about ecology. We really have to stop polluting the world or

there won't be any left. The place was loaded with groovy people.
Felt square in 'nice little loafers.' Shouldn't have worn them!

She started a recycling scheme, putting up notices telling people to bring their cardboard, newspapers, bottles and cans to the Colvin house. All fine, except she had omitted to tell her parents. 'She got the entire town to bring their junk to our yard,' recalls Rosemarie. 'We had to pack it all up. The whole family had to get involved.' Nonetheless, Rosemarie and Bill were generally happy to encourage their daughter's social conscience. 'The family boycotted meat for a long time because of the way the animals were being raised,' Cat remembers. 'We had salmon loaf, chicken and fish but no beef. We boycotted grapes because workers in California were being exploited, and Nestlé products for some reason I forget.'

Every day Marie walked along the school corridor past the portraits of half a dozen young men in uniform, former students who had been killed in Vietnam. Often, older students would be out on the lawn in front of the school with banners reading 'Stop the War' and 'Peace for All'.

8th May 1970. The school was protesting today. The whole
high school was out (just about) and they were either at home
or on the lawn at a rally. I joined them … Mom said I couldn't
but I did.

Although Rosemarie may have objected to her daughter skipping school to protest, from time to time she and Bill joined anti-war demonstrations themselves. 'Our community was very conservative and pro-war but we thought it was terrible and we communicated that to our kids,' she recalls. Another adult frequently out protesting was Sister Adrian Barrett, a radical left-wing nun based at St Dominic's. A small, round ball of a woman, just four foot eleven, Sister Adrian was known as 'Sister Sneakers' after the footwear she wore with her knee-length navy skirt. In the early 1960s she had been an activist with the civil rights movement. Now she chaired a social action committee, that gave food and toys to the poor and campaigned for low-cost housing. When she became chair of the Oyster Bay Democratic Committee she said it felt like joining an underground church, and on at least one occasion police had to escort her past a jeering crowd who opposed her activism. Marie became her right-hand girl.

In a very American version of the parable of the loaves and fishes, Sister Adrian was behind what became known as the Miracle of the Pies. A representative of the frozen food firm Mrs Smith's Pies called to say they had 10,000 perfectly edible pies deemed unsaleable because the crust was too dark. Thom De Jesu, another Oyster Bay High School student, remembers Sister Adrian and Marie organising the distribution. 'We were shlepping pies into trucks and they were giving them out to every church and soup kitchen in the neighbourhood,' he recalls. 'Any flavour you like as long as it's coconut custard!'

Sister Adrian took a group from Oyster Bay to Washington DC for one of the big anti-war marches on the Mall. Initially, Bill and Rosemarie said that at fourteen Marie was too young to go, but in the end they relented, partly because they trusted Sister Adrian and partly because it was increasingly hard to say no to their strong-willed eldest child.

* * * * *

After a decade and a half as a housewife and mother, Rosemarie went back to full time work as a teacher. All the children were at school now, and although they were by no means poor, the family could do with another salary. Bill ran for election to the town council. 'A community man, a family man, Bill Colvin understands people,' read the legend on a leaflet. A photo showed the Colvins holding hands in a chain as they walked across a lawn. Off to the left, not holding hands with anyone, is Marie, wearing a short white dress, her long thick hair framing her face. She is smiling and facing the camera, but her body is turned away from the rest of the family, as if she were about to go in a different direction.

Bill was not elected so went back to his teaching job. He was still council opposition leader but his political ambitions were waning. An application to teach in Australia went nowhere. The photo of the perfect family belied some uncomfortable realities. Marie tried to help Billy, who was dyslexic and doing badly at school, but he had become worryingly disruptive, bunking off to go down to the beach to drink beer, and not coming home until late. Rosemarie would go to bed, but Bill always stayed up, drinking whiskey and smoking, watching *The Dean Martin Show* or reading until everyone was home. After a few drinks, if he was in a good mood, he would take the kids outside to show them the Big Dipper and other constellations, but if they came back after their curfew, he would be furious. 'My relationship with Dad wasn't good,' recalls Billy. 'I'd sneak home at 2 a.m. and if I got caught he'd hold me against the wall yelling and screaming.' Marie was also clashing with their father. 'He was very strict. He had high standards. And she was a hippie,' adds Billy.

Aged fifteen and suffering from a heavy cold, Marie accidentally overdosed on a soporific flu preparation. Combing her room for other medication, the paramedics found birth control pills. Bill was furious; Rosemarie thought it an inevitable part of growing up. As long as Marie was doing well at school – and she was a consistent A plus student – her mother wasn't too worried, but Bill fretted that his daughter was going off the rails. When a youth in tatty jeans with long, straight hair drooping across his face called for her one evening, Bill took one look and asked his wife in horror whether she was really going to let their daughter go out with such a creature. Rosemarie went to see who it was and came back laughing – it was Thom De Jesu, the neighbourhood kid who had helped with the Miracle of the Pies and who Marie hung out with in High School and teen club. She and Thom dated briefly and when it didn't quite gel, remained friends. After school they would sit on the beach, smoke spliffs and talk about all that was wrong in the world. 'She liked the adventurous side of life,' recalls Thom. 'She had a strong backbone and a great thing about the downtrodden.'

Marie grew bored. Schoolwork was easy, her siblings irritating and Oyster Bay too small. At sixteen, she started to date a tall, lean long-haired boy who also loved to sail and who promised excitement. Chris Biggart's mother had moved to East Norwich with eight of her twelve children after their father died. Chris was frequently in trouble with the police for drink-driving, or driving without a licence. 'We were wild kids,' he says. 'Marie was always round because we were a party house. Her parents hated me. They thought I was a bad influence from the wrong side of the tracks.' Marie would shimmy down the tree outside her bedroom window to spend the night with Chris. 'It was her first big romantic, sexual thing,' says Thom. 'The Biggarts were tough guys. She was thrilled. She found them exciting, looser than her family. I was a bit jealous.'

Marie and Chris would go to Cagney's, a hole-in-the-wall bar at Pine Hollow, where she would dance to the jukebox and he would shoot pool. Sometimes they hitch-hiked into New York City to see bands and drink in bars, brandishing fake IDs so no one knew they were underage. They took LSD, smoked pot, sneaked into people's gardens late at night to go skinny dipping in their pools and had sex in a half-built house up the road, the tarp on the floor scraping Marie's back. On one occasion Bill stalked up to Chris's house, half a block away, burst into his room and caught them in bed together.

'Marie – home now!' he ordered, his voice cracking with fury. He yelled at Chris, jabbing his finger at him. 'Stay away from my daughter!' On another evening, Chris and Marie were in her bed when they heard her parents come home unexpectedly early. 'I ran out of Marie's house naked into the woods carrying my clothes,' recalls Chris. 'It was really bad.'

When she was in her twenties, Marie reflected in her diary that having sex in Oyster Bay was a kind of 'victory – a validation'. But she was more her father's daughter than either realised. Chris remembers that she was always reading and doing her schoolwork, her wildness tempered by self-discipline. And although her father's attitude to sex felt stultifying, at least her parents were honest. What she hated most was the small-town veneer of respectability she saw around her, the men who slept with prostitutes in the city and came home to their respectable wives, the politicians who doled out summer jobs to their friends' children, the hypocrisy of it all. She was determined to escape.

Thanksgiving with Rosemarie's side of the family, Christmas with Bill's. Easter egg hunts in the backyard. Frequent visits from Gommy, Rosemarie's devout, cantankerous mother. A week's summer holiday in upstate New York. Parties at home on St Patrick's Day and the Fourth of July. As Marie grew older, the reassuring rhythms of the Colvin family calendar began to pall. She and Billy would take a little drop of alcohol from each bottle in their parents' bar, and 'down the hill' became a place to drink and smoke. Marie covered her bedroom walls in black corduroy decorated with peacock feathers and bulrushes, and lay on her bed listening to folk-rock and protest music – Bob Dylan, Country Joe and the Fish, Leonard Cohen. Cat, who trailed around after her beloved older sister, says she never learnt any nursery rhymes but Marie taught her to sing every song on Joni Mitchell's album *Blue*. Marie took her along when her friends were hanging out, strumming guitar and smoking dope. 'I was a little flower child,' says Cat.

Relief came for Marie – as it would do so many times in the future – from sailing. She traded in the Sunfish for a Hobie Cat. Dozens of boats bobbed gently on the flat water of the bay but Marie would sail out into the open seas of Long Island Sound, and stay for hours. When the clouds darkened and the waves grew rough, others headed back to shore, but she would sail into the storm, relishing the rocking of the boat, the fight with the spinnaker and the possibility of capsizing, using her skill to right the craft as the waves crashed around her. Danger, she found, was thrilling.

When the sea calmed, she would stare at the huge houses half hidden by foliage on Centre Island, where the wealthy lived, secluded amongst groves of massive trees. Down on the shore she could see the grey-blue cedar-shingle mansion of the Seawanhaka Corinthian Yacht Club. One summer she got a job there as a waitress. With its oak-lined bar and an exclusive membership, Seawanhaka was the most prestigious club in the area. The yachts of the rich and famous could be seen roped to the moorings after a regatta. This was the closest Oyster Bay came to high society, and to Marie it opened up a lifestyle she had never seen before. She would come home with mangoes and lobster claws left over from the fancy weddings and fundraisers at which she had waited tables. She found that talking to the wealthy came as naturally as chatting with the janitor or other club staff. She was comfortable with everyone. This place was classy, she thought. More than that, it was a world away from the cramped house in East Norwich with Michael blasting The Who and Aerosmith at all hours, endless fights with her father, and her siblings squabbling over the household chores.

* * * * *

By her penultimate year at High School it was clear that, although she was still getting top marks, Marie was too rebellious to plough through, so she decided to go abroad for a year on a cultural exchange with the American Field Service programme. In later years she would portray this as an act of independence like running away to sea, but in fact her mother administered the local AFS chapter. Usually students in the programme went to stay with a family in Europe, but Marie applied to go to South America, a decision that counted as news in Oyster Bay – the local paper, *The Leader*, ran a story under the headline 'Marie Colvin Goes to Brazil', saying Marie had asked to be sent to a country 'with which she had the least cultural affinity'.

In January 1973, two weeks after her 17th birthday, Marie flew to Rio de Janeiro for a short Portuguese language course before joining Gilda and Oswaldo Bier and their three children, first in their beach house and then in São Leopoldo, a small industrial city founded by German immigrants in the far south of Brazil. On the plane, she felt nervous, worrying about what on earth she would say and how she would make herself understood. Gislaine, the daughter of the family, remembers Marie getting off the plane attired as if ready for the Amazon. 'She was wearing a green, rubberised cloak and rubber boots,' Gislaine recalls. 'She said she was dressed like this because in Brazil there were many bugs.' Within a few days they were laughing about it, and Marie began to understand that this adventure would be not quite as she had imagined. The diary she kept during her first few weeks with the Biers is a study in how bewildering and thrilling travelling by yourself at a young age can be. Everything is unfamiliar, exciting, worrying, worthy of note and comment. Oswaldo was a doctor at the local hospital and Gilda an artist. Although at fifteen Gislaine, nicknamed 'Nani', was younger than Marie she seemed more sophisticated and 'like an older sister'.

> *3rd February 1973. All the neighbors are excited to see me but I can't talk to them. They all kiss each other – so I follow. Tonight we went out with Nani's friends – I was the quiet extra girl. It seems to be the custom to just drive around and around, back and forth. At the center all the youth for miles around gather – really fashion dressed – on display. Even the guys dress to kill. It's strange – I don't miss home at all. I like this one better.*

Marie picked up immediately on the different attitude to sex in Brazil:

> *5th February 1973. The guys here go to whorehouses to get their sex – it's legal and socially acceptable. They date 'respectable' girls. This gives kind of a bad attitude towards sex – as though it's dirty, a desire to be hidden … They are incredulous about many things in the US. People living together before marriage is unheard of!*

She rapidly lost her nervousness and settled in with the family. 'I love them already,' she wrote. In Marie's eyes Gilda, a petite woman in her mid-thirties, several years younger than Rosemarie, with styled bouffant blonde hair, was unutterably glamorous. She straightened Marie's corkscrew curls and bought her tight-fitting shirts in the

Brazilian style of the time. Always highly conscious of her body and her weight, Marie was embarrassed to realise that she was fatter than the Brazilian girls and her baggy hippie trousers and loose tops made her look frumpy. She resolved to go on a diet.

The letters she wrote home have been lost, but she kept many that her family and friends wrote to her. The most welcome may have been from Cat, now aged eight: 'We had to write what we would do if we had a magic ship. I put, "I'd go to Brazil to see you". I miss you a lot. Do you miss me?' Letter by letter, Marie and her father began to repair the rift between them. His reveal an attempt to treat her as an adult, not the little girl she so resented him for wanting her to remain. 'Dear Rie,' he wrote. 'It's hard to believe you've been away almost four months. We miss you very much. There seems to be a gap in the family without you. We miss much of the day-to-day excitement you were so good at providing.' He wanted to know if Watergate was having any impact on the scene in Brazil. 'The court battle to get the White House tapes should make history – history that your children will study as a classic Supreme Court case of Nixon vs Congress and the people of the United States.'

In fact, Marie found that the people she was meeting had very different political views from her parents. Brazil was then under a right-wing military junta, and São Leopoldo was one of the most conservative cities in the country. 'Just about all of South America is pro-Nixon – according to everyone I meet,' she wrote, seemingly oblivious to the millions of South Americans she had not encountered. 'Kind of hard to get into political arguments yet, but I think it's time. They dig Nixon's anti-Communist stand.' Once or twice on the way to school she saw a horse and cart clopping along, a glimpse of the poverty beyond the middle-class suburb where the Biers lived. Here, she realised, everyone shared their emotions freely but rarely talked politics, just the opposite to back home in Oyster Bay.

While in Brazil, Marie attended Colégio Sinodal, a Lutheran High School, adapting to lessons in Portuguese as easily as she had adapted to living with a new family. 'She became a Brazilian!' says Gilda. The highlight of the year was something the old Marie would have scorned – the debutante ball. Carefully made up and dressed in a short, figure-hugging aquamarine silk dress and pearl earrings, she sashayed along the catwalk with the other debutantes and danced the waltz with Oswaldo. 'She was radiant, happy, as if in a fairy tale,' remembers Gilda. 'I think that night she convinced herself that she was a beautiful woman.'

Marie returned to Oyster Bay in December 1973. The passport photograph taken just before she left ten months earlier shows a round-faced girl with long, unstyled hair, wearing a white sweater with a knitted pattern around the neck. In the picture taken as she left Brazil, her hair has been cut and straightened, her eyebrows shaped and she is wearing a slim-fitting black turtleneck. The real difference, though, is her stance. Instead of looking passively at the camera, she has raised her chin and moved her head at a slight angle to her body. She looks both calm and defiant. This was a new Marie Colvin.

Marie had taken her Scholastic Assessment Tests (SATs) – effectively the entrance exam for university – in Brazil, and done so well she became a National Merit Scholarship finalist. There was no need for her to return to school for the last year, so she got a job at an advertising agency in New York, taking the train to the city every day. At this point she had set her mind on becoming a marine biologist, like Jacques Cousteau. The only problem was that she had missed the application deadline for college. In the spring of 1974 she drove to New Haven and explained to the admissions staff at Yale that it had been impossible to mail the forms from Brazil. It was the first of many occasions when missing a deadline proved no obstacle to Marie's success. She was accepted for entry in the fall.

* * * * *

Marie had grown up in the year away, and while her father didn't approve of her lifestyle, he couldn't curtail it. In the evenings and on weekends she would hang out with a high-school friend, Jerelyn Hanrahan, a thoughtful artistic young woman with an intrepid spirit to match Marie's own. All through her life Marie made close friendships with women and Jerelyn was the first.

In tight dresses and high heels they would hit the bars. They were eighteen years old, beautiful, unfettered and confident enough to use their sexual power to attract men and then leave them standing. Both had cars – Jerelyn's a big old Ford, Marie's a '67 Chevy Malibu. 'I remember driving along the shore road talking about guys then switching to politics,' says Jerelyn. 'Everything was equally important. Marie was addicted to the *New York Times* and would buy it every day.' They would make a bonfire on the beach and sit round talking about everything: their families, Watergate, sex, college, their hopes and plans. 'She thought Oyster Bay was a nowhere town,' says Jerelyn. Determined not to regain the weight she had lost in Brazil, Marie started to drink coffee instead of eating. 'She was fanatical about being in shape and obsessive about exercise,' recalls Jerelyn. 'She'd have twenty-five cups of coffee, drink alcohol, not eat and then have a stomach problem.' It was a pattern set for life.

At weekends, they waitressed at Seawanhaka. When their shift ended at 11 p.m., they'd take off their white uniforms and swim naked in the sea. Marie would strike out with her long, languorous stroke, turn over and look up at the stars. Other times they would drink Long Island Iced Tea cocktails in the bar with Walter, the blond mustachioed bartender. One night the three of them, slightly the worse for wear, staggered up to the top floor of the club, made a bubble bath and sat in it naked, giggling and quaffing a bottle of champagne. Walter said, 'I think I've died and gone to heaven.'

That summer, Marie and Jerelyn told their parents they were going to visit Jerelyn's sister in San Francisco, but their real plan was to travel on to Mexico. In Colorado, they heard a radio station advertising rides and hooked up with a slightly older woman who was driving down and wanted to share expenses. Clad in hiking boots, shorts and long-sleeved shirts, and with Jerelyn carrying a knife in her belt, they slung their backpacks into the car and set off. A few days into the trip, as they drove through Durango late at night, they hit rocks on the road: a classic bandit tactic for robbing cars. The driver managed to keep going far enough for them to escape, but the car's axle was broken, so they locked the doors and slept in the vehicle. The next day Marie and Jerelyn walked to the nearest town. Someone on the dusty streets of Velardeña told them of a doctor who spoke English, which is how they came to meet Dr Francisco Lozano, commonly known as Pancho. 'He must have weighed 300 lbs and he came to the door in suit pants and a white shirt,' remembers Jerelyn. 'He would sit and read, eating jalapeño peppers out of a can.' They slept in a dirt-floored room in Pancho's house, and the next morning, after being woken by a rooster who had somehow managed to scuttle in, took up the doctor's offer to show them the local silver mines.

The cliffs from which the metal was extracted were pitted with holes and criss-crossed with ropes and planks of wood. This was very primitive mining. Marie and Jerelyn watched a woman dressed in black walking past with five kids darting this way and that like small birds. Pancho said she was a homeless widow whose husband had probably been killed in a mining accident. It was a world of poverty and grind unlike anything Marie had seen in Brazil. 'Marie was very concerned about the workers, and kept asking how much they got paid, how many hours they worked,' says Jerelyn. 'She couldn't probe him enough. She kept saying, "I can't believe they only get 25 cents an hour. I just can't believe it."' Jerelyn thinks that some kind of alarm went off in Marie's head that day. 'I had never seen her ask questions like that before. I think it was the moment she became a journalist.'

Two years later, when studying at Yale, Marie wrote a travel piece for a journalism class about searching for 'the real Mexico' with Jerelyn.

Arriving in Chihuahua, our first night in Mexico, we strolled jauntily out for a Mexican meal and a look at the nightlife. Nervous glances began to get panicky after two blocks; men who passed turned to follow, catcalls came from corners and open doors, cars honked suggestively ... there wasn't another woman on the street ... friends who had travelled to Mexico had returned with glowing stories about how warm and open the local people were. They neglected to tell us all their friends had been male; we'd neglected to notice all the storytellers were also male.

That was typical of Marie. It never occurred to her not to do something because it might be unwise or dangerous, nor because as a woman she might face particular dangers. Such adventures, she realised when she began to write, were rich seams like the silver ore in the rocks of Durango. An eye for detail, the ability to conjure a scene and scant regard for her own safety were to become trademarks of her journalism.

* * * * *

Chapter 2

FATHER AND DAUGHTER

On her first day at Yale Marie found herself queuing for registration next to a girl with hair as hard to tame as her own. Katarina 'Kato' Wittich's family, half German, half Hungarian, atheist and bohemian, was very different to Marie's, but they had something in common: both were outsiders in the preppy world of the Ivy League. Just being female made them historical outliers – Yale had begun admitting women only five years earlier, in 1969, and 60 per cent of the students were men. Marie was at Silliman College, named after a nineteenth-century science professor. It felt ancient even if it wasn't, designed to impress on students the weight of tradition and the demand for academic excellence. The list of famous alumni included writers, Nobel laureates, Supreme Court judges, diplomats and dozens of other successful Americans from all walks of life.

Marie and Kato became inseparable bohemian twins. Slim and striking, Kato always in black, Marie in cinched-waist 1940s-style thrift shop dresses, they cut something of a dash on campus amongst the skirts and cardigans worn by most other girls. Sometimes they teamed up with Gerald Vitagliano, a freshman they had also met on day one, who was agonising about whether to come out as gay. All three were trying to forge new identities away from home. 'Marie had a tremendous fierceness and passion – it was hard not to fall in love with her,' recalls Kato. 'But I also saw the part of her that was tender and fragile and insecure and didn't know where she belonged.' Marie's scholarship didn't cover all her tuition, so she worked at the dining hall to cover some of her costs. She, Kato and Gerald would go dancing at Partners in New Haven, a gay bar that attracted a contingent of African-American transvestites, but not many Yalies. Some parts of New Haven were quite rough in those days, but that never deterred Marie.

In February, she met two seniors planning a trip to New Orleans for Mardi Gras, so she knocked on Gerald's door to persuade him to join them. He said, 'Don't be silly, I've got papers to write,' but she wore him down, and the four of them drove for twenty hours through Pennsylvania, West Virginia, the corner of Kentucky, Tennessee, Alabama and Mississippi to Louisiana, taking turns at the wheel, music blasting from the radio. They stayed with the mother of one of the seniors, went to dozens of bars and parades, got roaring drunk and threw confetti over one another. 'It was incredible fun and I wouldn't have done it without her,' says Gerald.

One day in the Silliman courtyard she got into conversation with Victor Bevine, an aspiring actor two years older than her, with dark brooding eyes and a soft, sensitive mouth. She offered to patch his jeans – rather a traditional feminine ploy for one so independent – but it worked. Victor was unsure about his sexuality but Marie was irresistible, pursuing him until he relented. She taught him a line from her favourite Brazilian song: *São demais os perigos desta vida/pra quem tem paixão* – the dangers of life are too great for those with passion.

They walked to Wooster Square in New Haven, sat on a bench and talked. Victor told her that his parents were divorced and he hadn't seen his father for many years. Marie said her experience was entirely the opposite. 'My parents are so in love with each other, I only hope that when they go, they go together,' she told him. 'I don't think they could live without each other.' Kato saw a different side. 'She didn't talk about her father much but it was clear that something there wasn't okay,' she recalls. 'It was about proving herself, defying any limitations put on her, which is what her dad was doing. He would say: "You can't do this, you can't do that." And she would feel: "Anything you say I can't do, I'm going to do better than anyone else."'

Victor introduced Marie to a school friend, Bobby Shriver, the son of Eunice Shriver, sister of the late President Kennedy. Marie was gliding into social circles not unlike those she had seen at the Seawanhaka Corinthian Yacht Club. 'If something scared or challenged Marie, she determined to conquer it,' says Kato. 'She decided that she was going to conquer privilege and power and get up there in those ranks.' Marie didn't see it like that. Bobby and his friends harboured dreams of being writers and journalists, which she found intriguing. Her new friends partied a lot, which she enjoyed and Kato did not. By the spring of her sophomore year the two girls had drifted apart.

Bobby was graduating that semester, so he threw a party at the Kennedy family home in Hyannis Port. He asked Marie to bring along another sophomore, Katrina Heron, who was on the fringes of their group. Fiercely intelligent and effortlessly good-looking, Katrina impressed Marie. With her WASPy New England background, she seemed very together, well read and confident, but the two women soon realised that they were similarly adventurous, yet full of doubts. Like Marie, Katrina had spent a year in Latin America, living in Mexico, and travelling to Guatemala and Belize. Both knew they had earned the right to be at Yale, yet somehow they felt they didn't belong. Maybe it was about being women, or the straitjacket of success into which they were now expected to fit. They both loved to run, so they went to the gym together, and tried out for the women's soccer team. (When Katrina made the cut but she didn't, Marie vowed to go to every game to cheer for her friend.) More than anything they shared a love of books. Katrina, who was studying English, introduced Marie to literature she had not previously read, ranging from the lesser known works of Jane Austen to contemporary fiction. 'She was a much faster reader than me, and would read more than one book at the same time,' recalls Katrina. It was the beginning of a lifelong delight the two took in recommending titles to each other and discussing them avidly, each feeling she hadn't really experienced a book until the other had read it too. They became soul-mates. It was a deep friendship that would endure.

Katrina also turned Marie on to country music. 'I would have an album by Bonnie Raitt or Emmylou Harris, and she would play it over and over,' she recollects. 'When the needle retracted, she'd go and get one of her endless cups of black coffee and put it back at the beginning. Every third time, I'd have to turn it over.' There was much dancing and drinking, many late night conversations listening to Patsy Cline and talking about love and the meaning of life, and adventures made more absurd by Marie's lack of a sense of direction and her inability to remember where she had left her keys. On one famous occasion, while Marie was driving her brother Billy's convertible, they ran out of pet-rol on the Long Island Expressway because Marie insisted that the temperature needle on the dashboard was the fuel gauge. Adversity made them giggle; they were a unit of two, bound together by confi-dences and laughter. Boyfriends came and went but they always had each other. Katrina was always Kim, and Marie was Rie. They shared each other's clothes and began to pick up each other's manner-isms and turns of phrase, as close as sisters.

Where Katrina was well organised, Marie was often chaotic but she had a way of dealing with practical details that irked or bored her – she simply ignored them. She rarely paid her library fines and was always behind on the administration of her student loans. Debts were an irri-tant in the back of her mind, not a real concern. As she rarely drove her old Chevy Malibu, she offered it to her brother Michael, who came up to New Haven to collect it during a cold spell. 'It looked like a VW Beetle because it was covered in snow,' he recalls. Marie handed him a baseball bat. 'I started smashing the snow and ice, and under every layer I came across a parking ticket! No wonder she wanted to get rid of it.'

* * * * *

Bobby and Marie came up with a plan for the summer after her soph-omore year: a clambake business on Cape Cod. Katrina said she was in. Determined not to rely on his famous family, Bobby called himself 'Robert Cotton' on the leaflets. They rented a sagging two-storey shingled house on a large sandy lot, shaded by trees, to accommodate themselves and a constantly changing cast of friends and helpers.

'We ran the business out of the kitchen – mammoth sacks of clams, briny bins of seaweed, stacks of tablecloths,' remembers Katrina. 'We left all the windows open all the time, rain or shine, to keep the air moving so it didn't smell like a fishery.' Marie threw herself into collecting firewood, cooking and schmoozing the guests. Her enthusiasm was part of the draw; she had always loved parties and now she was being paid to organise them. 'We hustled for customers, called up hotels and got them to give out leaflets,' says Bobby. 'We had a little truck and went to collect seaweed to steam the clams on hot rocks in the old-fashioned way. We did about three or four clambakes a week.'

Marie returned to Yale that autumn confident and happy. Any feelings of being an outsider that she might have harboured when she arrived two years earlier were long gone. She and Katrina were sharing an apartment on Dwight Street, just around the corner from the campus. Their friendship enabled Marie to think through her relationship with her parents. Both young women were pulling away from their families, trying to forge a new life in a new era in which women were rejecting the roles their mothers had lived and their fathers expected. Her mother understood that Marie was unlikely to settle for a conventional life, combining a decent but not all-consuming job with a family, but what did Marie's father, the benign patriarch and the person whose approval she craved most, expect of her? She didn't know, and while she wanted not to care, the question nagged at her. 'Her father was a lodestone for her,' believes Katrina. 'But I got the impression that she was in a stand-off with him.'

Marie's ideas were changing. She was no longer interested in becoming the next Jacques Cousteau, nor in pursuing her major, anthropology. Neither path was creative enough. She worried that it was too late to change to history or English, but Katrina convinced her that anthropology was an equally good background for journalism.

This was a time when reporters were heroes. In 1971 the Pentagon Papers, exposing how the US government had secretly escalated the war in Vietnam with the covert bombing of Cambodia and Laos, were leaked and published first in the *New York Times* and, when the government took out a federal court injunction against the paper, then in the *Washington Post*. The following year, Seymour Hersh uncovered the My Lai massacre, in which US soldiers killed more than 300 unarmed civilians in a Vietnamese village. Then there was the Watergate scandal, exposed by the *Post*'s Carl Bernstein and Bob Woodward – himself a Yale graduate – which had brought down President Richard Nixon. Bernstein and Woodward's book *All The President's Men* came out just before Marie went to college and in her junior year was turned into a movie starring Dustin Hoffman and Robert Redford. Journalists were the 'good guys' exposing official deception and dishonesty.

Bobby suggested that Marie try for a job at the *Yale Daily News*. Housed in an elegant red-brick building with mullioned windows, it seemed like another of Yale's impenetrable elitist institutions. Those who worked at the 'Yalie Daily' had been building up to it for years and often went on to work for America's top newspapers. Marie, it seemed, was too late to get in but, by a stroke of luck, that semester a group of students was launching the *Yale Daily News Magazine*. It was perfect. She reviewed theatre productions and films, ranging from a little known Czech play ('"Tango" explores the inevitability of revolution and counter-revolution: it also pays homage to the genius of Nietzsche, relying heavily on his philosophy for much of the dialogue') to the latest James Bond movie ('Cliché piles upon cliché, all of them wonderful') illustrated by five photographs of Bond girls in bikinis.

One highlight was attending a reading by the Beat poet Allen Ginsberg, whom she described as 'an unlikely prophet in a rumpled dark suit, button-down yellow shirt and striped tie, his neck encircled by a shining gold medallion'. Ginsberg read out 'found police poetry', excerpts from FBI documents obtained through a Freedom of Information Act suits that revealed a US government covert campaign against left-wing agitators. In an interview afterwards Ginsberg told Marie that official propaganda discrediting '60s activists had stoked disillusion in the current generation, providing 'the key to the cynicism and apathy of the '70s'. In an arresting simile, Marie wrote: 'Ginsberg is like a hoary Jewish grandmother, feeling the warm forehead of her sick child, trying to diagnose this new generation of Yalies.'

Marie herself was neither cynical nor apathetic, but her street protest days were nonetheless over. She needed a new cause, but she didn't yet know what it was. She just knew that journalism was the next thing she wanted to explore.

* * * * *

One evening in November 1976, Victor was visiting Marie in her Dwight Street apartment. He was in the bath when he heard the phone ring. *Late for the Sky*, the most recent Jackson Browne album, was on the turntable. When the last track came to an end, the needle crackled and bumped as the disc continued to revolve – Marie had not set it back to start the record again. Sensing that something must be wrong, he got out of the tub, dried himself and went to the living room, where he found Marie in tears, almost unable to speak.

'My father has cancer,' she sobbed. 'It's everywhere.'

Marie returned to Oyster Bay to find the family in turmoil. Billy, who had joined the Marines, was about to ship out to Okinawa. Michael had just gone up to college in Pennsylvania. Only Boo, then aged fourteen, and twelve-year-old Cat were still at home with their parents. Bill had been experiencing pain in his side since the summer, when he had lifted something awkwardly while building a patio, but thinking it was nothing, didn't go to the doctor until just before Thanksgiving. Tests showed that he had colon cancer, which had metastasised. In December, exploratory surgery revealed that the cancer had spread too far for further treatment. Marie went to visit him in the hospital, scarcely knowing what to say as the tall, strong authoritarian figure against whom she had defined herself lay helpless and shrinking. 'You have time to read now,' she said, trying to think of something, anything, to say that wasn't tainted by pity or fear. He looked at her. 'Yes,' he replied, and turned away to stare wordlessly out the window at the parking lot.

That Christmas, all the aunts and uncles and cousins from both sides of the family came to the house in East Norwich. Gaunt and weaker every day, Bill sat propped up in a sweater in his chair, the last act of the family man, presiding over Christmas gifts and games. He and Rosemarie had decided he would die at home, in the house where they had brought up their family and been happy. He spent time with each of his children, trying to encourage them, telling them to be brave when he was gone. Marie, carefree and without responsibilities, and about to turn twenty, was catapulted into adulthood, comforting her mother and looking after Boo and Cat, while feeling her way through the mist of her own sorrow. She told Victor she could no longer see him. By now he was deeply in love with her but still struggling with his sexuality; she couldn't handle the demands of the relationship and rejected the support he offered. Katrina was the one she relied on now. During the spring semester, she returned to Oyster Bay to see her father at weekends. A nurse visited him daily and his sister Aileen's husband, a trained navy medic, came to bathe him and attend to his personal needs every evening. At night Bill and Rosemarie talked about their life together and what lay ahead for her after he had gone. 'My mom and dad would be up most nights,' remembers Boo. 'By the end they talked every night all through the night. I would fall asleep listening to them.'

Bill Colvin died at home in East Norwich on 5 February 1977. He was fifty. His funeral was held at St Dominic's. Several of Marie's college friends, including Katrina and Gerald, drove down from New Haven. The local paper recorded that some 500 people attended – students and teachers from the school where he had taught for twenty-two years, scouts from the troop he led, fellow members of the Community Social Action Council, his colleagues in the local Democratic Party, dozens of relatives and friends of the family, including kids who had been at

Oyster Bay High with Marie. As a former marine, Bill was buried at the Pinelawn military cemetery, a few miles away.

Forty years later, Rosemarie cries when talking of her husband's illness and death. Theirs had been a wonderful marriage, she says. After his death, she was financially secure with his pensions and her earnings as a teacher, but part of her had died with him. Marie offered to suspend college for a year and stay in Oyster Bay to help her mother with the younger children, shouldering the responsibility that her father had always impressed on her as the eldest. But Rosemarie refused – she didn't want Marie to sacrifice her future. She was stoical. She worked and looked after Boo and Cat until they went to college, carried on with church and community activities, put one foot in front of the other every day. The house filled up with foreign students she invited to stay. She never succumbed to despair.

* * * * *

Back at Yale, Marie struggled to find meaning through her grief. Cat frequently came to stay, tagging along with her big sister as she had done as a little girl. Marie understood that her father's death marked an abrupt end to the luxury of adolescence that many of her fellow students enjoyed. She spent long nights talking to Katrina about her truncated, unresolved relationship with Bill. 'I think what she had been hoping was that some time in adulthood they would find each other again and everything would be okay,' says Katrina. 'She was devastated by the revelation that there wasn't going to be a way or a time to fix it.'

> *10th July 1977. My father's death has had such an influence on my life, I still don't realise the extent. But I watched a man go from a virile, happy man – a man with everything he wanted – and that was pretty much true, everything was the family, the family was the purpose to everything. Why go to work every day, save up your money, buy that house, buy that car, if there is no*

purpose? It has begun to seem meaningless to my mother since he left. He went from this to that cadaver, cold, calm with such a dignified peace – he was so righteous even in the coffin. 'I have lived a good life. I made people happy. And I did what I thought was right.' The last one – it is the essence of my father. I feel so weak-spirited when I think of him. Why should all the pettiness matter to me? But I did learn – LIFE IS TOO SHORT.

She realised that she didn't just *want* to become a journalist – she *had* to. Maybe she was channelling her father's frustrated dreams of writing, or maybe the shock of his death had given her the clarity to understand herself better. But the choices she made now would define the rest of her life, and the standards she set herself were her father's.

10th July 1977. There's so much I wanted to show him – prove myself to him. Somehow, he was and is still my standard. I did everything to make him proud. That's probably going to seem like, 'you say it now, now that he is gone.' And it's not entirely true – but it is necessary to make the statement so bald, because if I made him proud that was the main thing that mattered. Yes, I do have my own goals, and no, there is no chance I'll not persevere now that he's dead, but I did so want to make him proud ...

She took a class in the Politics of Journalism, writing a paper about the Cuban daily *Granma* and one critiquing the *Wall Street Journal*. In another class she practised writing TV scripts, basing some of her work on the reporting of ABC's Hilary Brown, one of the few women to cover the Vietnam War. But the course that changed her life was Non-fiction Writing, taught by the Pulitzer Prize winning reporter and novelist John Hersey.

Born in China to missionary parents, Hersey had covered the Second World War in Europe and Asia. He had written more than two dozen books and was famous for pioneering the use of fictional writing techniques in non-fiction while remaining clear about the essential differences between the two genres. Hersey was a reserved man, just over sixty when he taught Marie, the ultimate gentleman dressed in a tweed jacket with leather elbow patches, his thick white hair swept back from his brow. A Yale graduate himself, he picked only a dozen students in their junior and senior years for his course, many of whom went on to distinguished careers in journalism. He would assign readings as varied as Maxim Gorky's profile of Leo Tolstoy or a piece from Nora Ephron's *Crazy Salad*, as well as commissioning students to write stories that would be discussed in class. He talked about truth rather than balance, and was more interested in character and narrative than in the gathering of facts taught on basic journalism courses. A stickler for clear expression, he often referred to *Fowler's Modern English Usage* as he spent time with each student individually, correcting clumsy phrasing, and scribbling his comments in the margin in pencil in case further discussion with a student led him to change his mind.

Marie would always say that Hersey's *Hiroshima* was the best book on war she had ever read. Short and understated, and based on the reporting he did the year after the atomic bomb was dropped, it traces the lives of five Japanese civilians and a German missionary who survived and whose lives intersected. In an interview for the *Paris Review* in 1986, Hersey said it had been inspired by Thornton Wilder's novel *The Bridge of San Luis Rey*, which traces the interlocking stories of five people who are killed when a rope bridge gives way in Peru. 'That seemed to me to be a possible way of dealing with this very complex story of Hiroshima; to take a number of people – half a dozen, as it turned out in the end – whose paths crossed each other and came to this moment of shared disaster. So I went to Hiroshima and began right away looking for the kinds of people who would fit into that pattern,' he said.

Hersey does not dwell on the arguments for and against the atomic bomb nor the strategy behind its use, but allows the experience of individuals to reveal the human impact of political and military decisions. In sparse prose studded with tiny details, like a Japanese painting, *Hiroshima* conjures the terror and bewilderment of the atomic aftermath, starting with simple sentences describing what each of the survivors was doing at the moment the bomb fell. The survivors emerge organically like characters in a novel rather than subjects of a journalistic report, their stories woven together like a plot, remembered dialogue bringing events alive. 'My hope was that the reader would be able to become the characters enough to suffer some of the pain, some of the disaster, and therefore realize it.'

Hersey, however, was no fan of the fashionable 'New Journalism' practised by writers such as Norman Mailer and Tom Wolfe. The concept of the 'non-fiction novel', a term coined by Truman Capote to describe *In Cold Blood*, his bestselling 1966 book about a murder in Kansas, was in Hersey's view, dangerous. Making things up, as novelists do, would undermine the reader's belief in journalism, which had to remain pure. 'In fiction, the writer's voice matters; in reporting the writer's authority matters,' he wrote in 'The Legend on the License', a 1980 essay for *The Yale Review*. 'It is very simple … All we need to do is insist on two rules: the writer of fiction must invent. The journalist must not invent.'

Fired up as never before, Marie sought out Katrina after the first class with Hersey. She already knew she wanted to be a journalist – now she knew what kind of journalist. 'This is it, this is what I want to do,' she said. 'I want to tell these big stories in this way.' She became a disciple. Hersey's philosophy and methods were the principles that guided her journalism all her life. He told her that the physical act of writing was the only way to learn – there was no theory, only practice. Events, what people did, were of the essence, and the reporter was less of an artist and more of a carpenter, hewing a story from a tree, chipping away, sanding and polishing until it was perfect. It was for Hersey's class that Marie wrote the account of her and Jerelyn's trip to Mexico City the summer before she came to Yale. 'We descended, exhausted, cramped, still overwhelmed by the smell of the bus packed cattlecar tight including several chickens for passengers,' she wrote. Hersey commented in the margin, 'Overpacked phrasing. A little tortuous' but then praised as a 'nice touch' her phrase, 'bedraggled newspapers sold by the original recyclers'. Twice he criticised her for using clichés. At the end he wrote, 'I like the tough, honest realism, but no individual human beings emerge. Places, however, are evoked well.' Her later work, with its emphasis on individual stories in war, shows how much Marie took these lessons to heart.

* * * * *

Despite his entreaties, Marie couldn't go back into a relationship with Victor. After her father's death she was reluctant to get involved with any man. Then, just before the end of her junior year, she tangled with Gerald Weaver, known as Gerry.

A senior, a year older than she was, with brown eyes and a sceptical demeanour, Gerry was a history major who played football and boxed, and had his pick of girlfriends. After a wild party he and Marie ended up making love in Grove Street Cemetery, near the Yale campus. 'Marie had this sparkle in her eyes that said she was up for anything,' recalls Gerry. 'She was irreverent, bold, unconventional.' He found all that hugely attractive but, in the weeks that followed, he was unavailable, sometimes physically, always emotionally. His elusiveness tantalised her. They ran into each other at parties, dropped acid together, occasionally went to bed. It wasn't really a relationship, not even dating. She knew he had a girlfriend. She could act cool – that was essential in her circle at Yale – but Gerry was beyond cool, almost icy. Sometimes she thought that he was laughing at her. She felt awkward, as if she weren't sexy or feminine enough. 'Gerry – is it you or me that feels such a need to be constantly cool?' she asked, but he never got a chance to answer because she didn't send the letter in which she asked the question.

There was an edge of danger to Gerry. Katrina thought he was simply untrustworthy but to Marie he was mysterious. She was in ferment, not just because she could feel herself falling in love, but also because her father's death had left her raw and vulnerable. Her enthusiasm for journalism was consuming but that ache, that need not just to be loved but to be validated by a man, had not diminished.

10th July 1977. There are so many things I want to put my energy into, I often ask why I'm not happy completely without a man. Is it ingrained? My sense of self is not independent of men – I need their feedback. That old dichotomy, I want my liberty, I want to be free to create, be the free spirit, but at the same time I guess, I've admitted that I want security.

It was indeed a perennial dilemma. Marie would later learn about the female journalists of the 1930s and '40s who had struggled – and frequently failed – to combine the life of a war correspondent with maintaining a fulfilling personal life. Thinking about the issue now, aged just twenty, she was unknowingly echoing the words of Lee Miller, the great Second World War photographer who had been a muse to both Man Ray and Pablo Picasso before forging her own career. In 1938, as she struggled in an unhappy marriage, Miller wrote, 'I want to have the utopian combination of security and freedom.' Martha Gellhorn, who would become Marie's heroine, was one of the greatest reporters of her generation and yet was often referred to as 'Ernest Hemingway's wife' even though they were married for less than five years. Marie was part of a cohort of women, just a few years after the vanguard had breached the ivy-clad walls of America's elite universities, proving through hard work and native ability that they were equal to their male peers. Yet she craved tradition too. 'We were careful to say to ourselves that if we don't get married it's fine, but the romantic ideal was that you would find this wonderful man and marry and have children,' says Katrina.

In those days, Marie was resistant to much feminist thought. Pioneers of the new discipline of 'Women's Studies' were regarded as humourless and shrill, an image that repelled her. She didn't question the accepted view of what made a woman attractive, she just wanted to ensure that, whatever it was, she had it. Without downplaying her intelligence or ambition, she found ways of pleasing men, sometimes by being 'one of the boys', and at other times by flirting.

3rd July 1977. I will always be wary of men who believe in the importance of men being able to cry. Men who talk about being sensitive belong with hyper-feminist Yale women who will always dominate them. They are always the one or two males in a Women's Studies course because they can 'relate'.

Yet she would learn that her combination of sharp intelligence, fearlessness and a habit of hopping into bed with any man she found attractive puzzled a lot of men. Gerry was the first to say that he found her 'masculine'. Her insouciant bravery contradicted received ideas of what a woman should and could be. As the semester came to an end and Gerry prepared to graduate, Marie was unsure whether she would ever see him again. She tried to say goodbye, resolving to forget him and get on with her life under the assumption that the relationship – if it deserved such a title – was over.

In the unsent letter, she made a pledge.

10th July 1977. That's one thing I always did like about our relationship: no demands, no expectations. 'I do have one though: if I don't see you until we meet at a cocktail party when we're both fifty, 1) you will not have a paunch and 2) you will grab me and drag me off. Maybe by then I'll be cool. I promise I'll appear to be.'

* * * * *

Marie spent the summer in Oyster Bay trying to provide support to her mother, Cat and Boo. In September, she returned to Yale before the start of term to paint the interior of 33 Lynwood, the house that she and Katrina would share during their final year. Speckled with paint, she went for a quick drink at the student bar and got into conversation with

41

Dave Humphreville, a kind, thoughtful history major from Illinois who was at Yale on a football scholarship. They soon started dating. Dave didn't come from the Yale celebrity set Marie moved in, but that never bothered her. She loved his sincerity, quiet intelligence and comforting physicality. He was drawn to the way she rushed at life. 'She didn't seem to care what people thought about her,' he recollects. 'It was liberating. She wasn't class oriented. Some people in her clique thought I was a jock or something but she didn't care. She just laughed.'

Katrina and Marie were the glamorous seniors everyone wanted to know, and 33 Lynwood – a spacious if dilapidated townhouse clad half in slate and half in red brick on a tree-lined street – became famous for parties. 'Marie gave parties at least every week if not twice,' recalls Claire Enders, Katrina's cousin, who had just arrived at Yale. People would roll up around 10 p.m. and there would be plenty of cheap white wine, pot and often food, as Marie loved to cook. Beers would be stacked up in the snow on the porch to keep them cold and someone always had a bottle of Jack Daniel's. Marie was often the first and last on the dance floor as the Rolling Stones, David Bowie or new punk bands such as the Clash blared from the speakers.

She worked hard on her journalism, honing her skills with a light-hearted first person story about going hot air ballooning with Katrina and friends, that was published in the *Yale Daily News Magazine*, where she was now a staff writer. One night she took Dave to the seedy end of New Haven to spend ten hours at a tattoo parlour where the tattoo artist, known as Foxy, practised her craft on a biker and a pair of born-again Christians. It made for a colourful piece of writing. She tried to banish thoughts of Gerry, but it was difficult because he was now at Yale Law School and she still ran into him at parties. Dave was a much better bet, but she was still prey to the allure of the unattainable, the two men corresponding to the opposing sides of her nature, the good boyfriend and the bad, the one she could have and the one she yearned for despite herself.

In her last week at Yale, she spent her nights holed up in the library with her coffee pot, desperately darting about like the Mad Hatter

from one stack of books to another, finishing papers so she could graduate. She had missed all deadlines for scholarships, grants and fellow-
ships. Through the four years, however, she had developed something
of a philosophy, a combination of ambition and fatalism, as she
explained in a piece entitled 'Running Out of Time'.

Yale Daily News, Commencement, 1978.
It doesn't matter if you mess up, choose the wrong road, flop
in Vegas. What's important is to throw yourself in head first,
to 'go for the gusto.' And if you blow it, you blow it. What we
have to worry about now is success. Once you're successful, it
becomes embarrassing to make mistakes, and more difficult to
grab onto the nearest straw and hold on. You can always be a
star, so what's the rush?

And with that her college years were over, and she was ready for the
next adventure.

* * * * *

After graduation, Marie moved to New York to look for work as a
journalist. She spent a few weeks sharing a room in a seedy hotel in
Midtown with a friend from Yale, before finding a cheap sublet studio
on the forty-third floor of an apartment block in Hell's Kitchen, in those
days a down-at-heel area. It was painted white, with a parquet floor, a
double bed, a few plants and a 'picture postcard Manhattan' view.

*5th July 1978. I can do what I want with it and myself. Tomorrow
I scrub every surface, touch everything, make it clean, a surface
to write on, blank page in typewriter. I am alone – joy!*

Soon the constant buzz of traffic was as soothing to her as the sound
of the sea. Every morning she ran along the West Side Highway, glory-
ing in her anonymity and observing the homeless guy habitually

snoozing in the sunshine, his baseball cap shading his face. In between seeing friends from Yale, she sent out résumés and looked for short-term assignments to keep her going. She went to Philadelphia to interview the actor James Coco for the *Village Voice,* and learnt what any travelling salesman or peripatetic journalist knows: long days and nights alone in a hotel in a strange city are initially exhilarating and suddenly lonely. As the deadline for the piece approached she plucked her eyebrows and noticed she had drawn blood: 'Keep it down, calm face, punch walls, gritted teeth.'

Back in New York, every few weeks she would see John Schley, a Yale alumnus twenty years older whom she had met at a Harvard/Yale ice hockey game in her final semester. The scion of a wealthy New Jersey horse farming family, John dabbled in stocks and later in real estate. He always had money that he was only too happy to spend on taking her out for dinner in SoHo or the West Village. Once he invited her to a party at his parents' imposing country house – she didn't have anything suitable to wear, so they scrambled into the attic and found a grey silk gown that had belonged to his grandmother. Tall and slender, her lustrous hair tumbling down her back, Marie looked stunning. John was not Marie's usual type. He was shorter than her, socially awkward and somewhat inarticulate with no particular ambition. A mutual friend called him 'a case of arrested development', but his unqualified adoration was hard to resist. He wanted to marry her but theirs was not a sexual relationship, and she laughed when he proposed. Just as Gerry frequently failed to turn up when he said he would, making it clear that Marie was secondary to his other girlfriend, so Marie misused John, standing him up if she got a better offer. It was as if she were testing him, the way a child might test a parent, to see if he would love her unreservedly.

After they graduated, Katrina had moved to Texas to work on the *Dallas Morning News.* A few months later Marie flew down to see her and the two drove round the state playing country music on the radio, going to the rodeo, and laughing as usual. Back in the city, Marie would spend mornings in the reading room of the New York Public Library looking up the names of editors from papers ranging from the *Chattanooga Times* to the *Montgomery Advertiser*, applying for a position, any position, as a reporter, trying to find a way into 'journalism, this religion I want to enter'. Sometimes she wondered if she was deluded in her ambition. 'I am nobody,' she mused. 'Untrue. I don't accept that. Why? I feel potential within. But I do accept this may come to nothing.' She was ready to go anywhere but part of her felt she should stay near her mother, at least until both Boo and Cat had left home. She read constantly – *The Beautiful and the Damned, The Thorn Birds, The World According to Garp* – but the book that affected her most was Walker Percy's *The Moviegoer*. Identifying with the anti-hero, Binx Bolling, alienated from his own life until the moment he finds himself lying in a ditch contemplating a dung beetle, she found herself thinking that she too had had a moment of epiphany.

> *12th October 1978. For me, it was my father's death. It's as if my prior life had been lived unconscious; as if, looking back, it had been lived by someone else ... The realization that what mattered was being able to write, that I was scared to attempt it because of fear of failure; everything has always come so easy for me. To fail at anything else would not really be to fail; to fail at writing would be real failure. And to succeed the only success I would value.*

Earning little as a freelancer, she knew she should economise, but it was hard and she sank into debt. She got by until December, when a friend of her father's told her that Local 237, the New York City municipal employees' branch of the Teamsters union, was looking for someone to edit their members' newsletter.

* * * * *

Joe McDermott had been unconvinced when a friend from Long Island suggested he interview some girl who had recently graduated from Yale and who wanted to be a journalist. As a working class Irish Catholic union man, he was automatically suspicious of anyone from the Ivy League, but – aware that he had no idea how to edit a newsletter and needed someone immediately – he reluctantly agreed to meet her. 'She walked in and she was beautiful,' he recalls. 'She had this white Irish skin like the underbelly of a mackerel. And black hair. She had a great sense of humour and took over the interview. I hired her before she left the office.'

Marie was thrilled. She had always been attracted to tough guys and the International Brotherhood of Teamsters, the most famous US labour union, had a reputation for being the toughest of the lot. Jimmy Hoffa, the notorious Teamster leader, had been convicted of involvement in organised crime back in the 1960s but Richard Nixon commuted his sentence, allegedly in return for the union supporting his candidacy for President. Three years before Marie started working for Local 237, Hoffa disappeared after an aborted meeting with two Mafia leaders in Detroit. He was eventually declared dead, but the circumstances of his disappearance were never fully explained. Many of the union men Marie met were still loyal to Hoffa. To her mind, the Teamsters were intriguing, with the edge of danger that she craved.

After her interview one of guys she met said: 'Hey Marie, Joe tells me you have a nice telephone voice. Do you sing?'

'Can't sing a note.'

'You can't sing?'

'If I could sing I'd have a job.'

'How 'bout dancing? Can you dance?'

'Dance, I can.'

'Well, then let's go.'

And so, Marie twirled on the bright burnt orange shag rug in front of the man's huge black desk.

Marie described the encounter in her diary but made no comment. She had to adapt to this overwhelmingly male environment – the only other women working there were secretaries. Her colleagues called her 'little girl' and ostentatiously stopped telling dirty jokes when she entered the room, but according to Joe, Marie soon earned their respect by transforming Local 237's newsletter. She understood immediately that members didn't want dry pronouncements from union leaders but to see their own pictures and stories in print. For one issue she interviewed the men who raised and lowered the bridges over the waterways into the city. For another, she hung out at the stables with the hostlers who shod the horses for the New York City Police Department. ('Keeping New York's Finest on the Hoof' was the headline.) Soon, the rank and file were queuing up to have the young woman with the cloud of dark hair and the easy manner come and talk to them, take their photo, write their story.

Some of the union officials took a little longer to be convinced, not least Mickey Maye, the former leader of the Uniformed Firefighters Association. Six foot two inches tall, and weighing in at more than 200 lbs, he had previously been a prize fighter and had lost the last union election after punching his rival during a debate. When gay activists tried to gatecrash the annual firefighters' ball in 1971 he slugged a protestor, sending him tumbling down the escalator, and was prosecuted for assault. But he also had a heroic side, once being photographed rushing out of a burning building giving a baby the kiss of life. Loyal to Jimmy Hoffa and, as an Irish Catholic, a big supporter of the Irish Republican cause, Mickey was rumoured to be involved in arms smuggling to the Irish National Liberation Army, or working for the CIA. Twice Marie's age (as well as nearly twice her size), he was initially patronising, predicting that she would get 'knocked up' within two years and settle down. When she earned his respect for her intellect and hard work, Mickey expressed it in the only terms he knew by telling her she thought 'like a man'.

Now she had a job, she moved to Greenwich Village, to a studio apartment on Christopher Street, with a wheezing radiator and a view of the alleyway behind, a few doors down from the Boots and Saddle gay bar. She stocked her fridge with chicken, Grey Poupon mustard and champagne. Mickey carried her bed up the steps on his back, sweat pouring down his face. He might have been the toughest guy in the Teamsters but he couldn't say no when the 'little girl' asked for help. They went out to Rockaway in Queens to walk on a deserted beach, discussing Henry Kissinger's latest book, union negotiating tactics and relationships. He convinced her of the righteousness of the Irish nationalist cause, which her parents had never supported, but which Marie decided was not only a struggle for freedom but part of her heritage. (In later years, when trying to burnish her credentials with the leaders of liberation movements, she would hint that her father came from a long line of freedom fighters, a claim that had no basis in family mythology, let alone fact.) Mickey and Marie would frequently down a bottle or two of wine at lunchtime. In the evening, Joe would join them, and the 'Three Musketeers' would go to the Lion's Head, a dingy dive with a dark whiskey-coloured bar, conveniently located just across from Marie's new apartment and between the famous gay bar Stonewall and the offices of the *Village Voice*. The Lion's Head was a journalists' pub, its walls decorated with the jackets of books, many written by the clientele. The bathrooms were covered in graffiti – a plan to repaint sparked a popular rebellion. Known as an Irish pub for 'drinkers with writing problems', it stayed open till all hours, so reporters from the *New York Post*, the *Daily News*, *Newsday*, the news agencies and a dozen other papers would show up whatever time they came off shift. Marie was an instant hit there, and became a regular, always surrounded by men drawn to her dynamism and her looks – and who soon learnt that she could not only hold her own in any conversation but also drink them under the table.

Marie might have sounded confident at work and in the pub but that wasn't necessarily how she felt inside.

19th April 1979. I am scared because everyone around me expects me to succeed and I know how weak, flimsy I am … Joe is so sure I will 'make it', as if it's a 'fait accompli'.

For the first time, it occurred to her that being a woman might stand in her way. She was furious when the printer of the Teamsters newsletter referred to her as a debutante, and even angrier when she turned up to interview the commissioner for sanitation, and he said, 'How did you get into the Teamsters? You look like you should be writing fashion.' (Too late she thought of a good response: 'Well, *you're* in the right profession – sanitation.') But their assumptions pointed up her own dilemma – how was she to satisfy her ambition without negating her femininity? 'I want everyone to think I'm fun, but also to take me quite seriously, think me competent,' she mused in her diary.

> *22nd May 1980. For those of us who want to break out, be the bad girl, there are no role models, nor the chance of earning recognition à la Norman Mailer, James Dean, Marlon Brando. Something sexual, desirable in their rebellion . . .*

She could see that a sexually promiscuous female writer or journalist would be judged differently from her male equivalent, noting down a sentence she read in the *New York Times*: 'There's been a lot of sex and very little liberation.' The classic role model for a serious female writer was the bluestocking, and Marie was never going to be that. Reading *The Powers That Be*, David Halberstam's book about the relationship between political power and the media in America, she wondered how a woman could earn respect in the fiercely competitive male-dominated word of journalism, noting that he did not cite a single female voice covering (much less participating in) Vietnam, the McCarthy hearings, Watergate or any international crisis.

She wondered too if men simply saw everyone as victor or vanquished. Maybe this had influenced history? It was a question the Women's Studies students she had been so scathing about at Yale might have regarded as basic, but only now had it occurred to Marie.

The more she tried to fathom how men thought, the more she worried about her image as a woman. Sometimes she binged on cheese and crackers or ate a whole loaf of bread. Then she would curse herself, because she wanted to be slim and beautiful, to fulfil a vision of herself as both effortlessly gorgeous and clever. She didn't use the word in her diary, but she was showing the symptoms of bulimia. Only sailing lifted her out of herself. She, Cat and Rosemarie went on holiday to the Florida Keys where they rented a boat. Convinced that she knew where she was going, Marie piloted them so far south they thought they had landed in Cuba. There was much relief and laughter on realising the shore was just a southerly key.

1st April 1980. Sailing a wonder ... I forgot the feeling, working with and against the water, wind. As we leave, sunny, breezy. Five thirty black clouds and scary winds blow up fast ... I love the ocean. Calming, soothing, boundless, constant.

Without warning, she would find herself crying about her father, thinking that he had never really known her, and wondering if she had known him. She was angry with him for dying, and envious of the apparent stability and contentment he had enjoyed in his life. She knew that if she were ever to find fulfilment, it wouldn't be at the Teamsters. Listening to Joe talk of his passion for workers' education, and reading letters from union members signed 'Yours, in the struggle' she realised that this was not *her* struggle.

Katrina – 'the person most important to me in the world' – had recently moved to New York to join a small, independent technology magazine and was living just a block away in the Village. Her world, she thought, was the one she shared with Katrina. The two women were often in the Lion's Head together, and occasionally they went to Studio 54, a cavernous nightclub and disco famous for its theatrical sets and lights and its celebrity clientele. Claire Enders remembers seeing Marie dancing in 'a gold miniskirt and high sandals, her slim form lighted under disco balls and strobe lights with an aura round her pre-raphaelite curls'. For a moment music could drown out the questioning voice in Marie's head.

* * * * *

Wanting to 'write, talk, think about books', she started an evening class in Modern Fiction at the New School at New York University, taught by the writer and *New York Times* book critic Anatole Broyard, a slight, elegant man with dark hooded eyes, who often wore a cravat. Years later, after his death, it became known that Broyard hid his Louisiana Creole ancestry, choosing to pass as white. Certainly to Marie he seemed the ultimate insider. He singled her out from the other students, taking her for dinner at an Italian restaurant, where he regaled her with stories of fashionable writers he knew, including Norman Mailer and Anaïs Nin. In her notes on his classes she jotted down his citation of Freud's generalisation, 'Man responds to novelty, woman to habituation.' Although the course featured plenty of similar sexist assumptions, Marie found Broyard's company intellectually stimulating. Over a period of months, she came to see that their perceptions of the world were fundamentally different; while he was trying to write a novel in which events would be completed in a way that would never happen in real life, she had 'a fixation on fact'. She identified with Anna, the heroine of Doris Lessing's *The Golden Notebook*, who pins news clippings around the room. Copies of the *New York Times* piled up in her apartment. Her passion wasn't so much writing, Marie realised, but reporting.

It was time to move on, emotionally and professionally and it was the Lion's Head that would provide opportunities for both. One night she got talking to a friend of Joe's, an Irish American with dark wavy hair and a ready laugh. Paddy Sullivan worked for the *Daily News*. They were already quite drunk when he mentioned that he had a sailboat. 'She perked up,' he recollects. 'We had a couple more drinks and at about one or two in the morning we get in my new VW Beetle and go up to the North Bronx. It's pitch black, we get on the boat, go sailing, drop the anchor, wake up the next morning and have no idea where we are. Both of us. That started it.' Already in his forties and divorced, Paddy was an established reporter who had worked on the

New York Post and at the news agency United Press International (UPI). They shared not only a love of sailing, but an enthusiasm for reporting and the ability to consume industrial quantities of alcohol. Soon they were seeing each other most evenings, and spending nights at his place.

Mickey was heartbroken. He wept when she told him she was seeing another man. Marie returned to her apartment, overwhelmed with shame for abandoning him. With his polyester check suits, spilling ketchup over his hands in the diner, he didn't fit into the image she had of the life she wanted, but she felt that they had 'the same soul' and she had opened up to him in a way she never did with younger men.

24th July 1980. I have not cried, sobbed like this, since my father died. It's the same feeling as with Dad. Incomplete, he's gone and you can't say the final word.

* * * * *

Chapter 3

LOVERS AND MENTORS

As 1980 drew to a close, Marie sublet her apartment on Christopher Street and moved in with Paddy. Through him she met UPI reporters who steered her towards an editor who would consider her résumé and clippings. In early 1981, UPI offered her a job as General Assignment Reporter in New Jersey. Leaving the Teamsters was not without sadness, but her boss Joe McDermott encouraged her – he was sure she would have a glittering career. It didn't feel very glittering at first. Most afternoons she would travel more than an hour by train to the state capital, Trenton, an unlovely city where industrial plants were closing and the centre was deserted after dark. UPI was housed in two dingy rooms with battered linoleum floors off the newsroom of the *Trenton Times*. Marie worked an eight hour shift, sleeping in the bureau if there was a big story and refusing Paddy's offer of her cab fare, insisting on walking to and from Trenton station at all times of day and night.

Jonathan Landay, an eager young New Yorker with dark hair and chiselled features, always leaning forwards to emphasise a point, showed her the ropes. 'New Jersey was an incredible place to start your career,' he says. 'You had the mob, serious environmental issues, the beginning of casino gambling in Atlantic City and oil exploration off the New Jersey coast.' He remembers Marie as a quick learner and a good colleague, soon confident enough to staff the bureau alone. Working methods were defined by the technology of the time. The reporters were usually tethered to a landline, checking with the fire service and the cops for news and updates. Marie learnt to write in the brisk, clear way demanded by a wire service. She had to key her story into a tele-type machine, which would convert it into a long ribbon of perforated dots that, when fed through the machine, sent a signal to the newsroom in New York, where the story would appear as a paper copy, a telex. After editing, it would be put out on the wire so newspapers could pick it up for publication. She also had to adapt the story for broadcast. Trenton was the state hub so the reporter there would edit copy com-ing in from Atlantic City, Newark and the New Jersey State House to send on to New York. The wire machines clattered and it was always a rush to finish one story and start the next. In her first week, Marie pasted into her diary a telex from an editor entitled 'Today's Nitpicks' with precise instructions on the format for datelines, language to avoid ('more than' not 'over') and how not to get bogged down in the lede – the first line – if a higher court reversed a lower court judgement. This was the nitty-gritty of wire service writing, and the skills she learnt at UPI would stand her in good stead for the rest of her career.

Another colleague in Trenton was Willard Cook, a slim, blond young man with literary ambitions whom Marie had briefly dated when they met at a party in New York a few months earlier. It was immediately apparent to him that her boundless energy and ability to nail down the facts would make her a star reporter. 'She never screwed the story up. She was very accurate in her reporting,' Willard recalls. 'She cared about the news and she was very quick.' In those days, hundreds of American towns had daily papers, most of which subscribed to UPI and its rival, the Associated Press (AP). A reporter was judged by the number of newspapers that put his or her story on the front page. With a keen eye for a tabloid tale, Marie scored an early hit in August 1982 with a series of reports on Jojo Giorgianni, a quarter-ton rapist deemed by doctors too fat to sur-vive in his cell. Fascinated by the mob, Marie was keen to get out of the bureau to chase crime and corruption stories, but the demands of everyday news reporting got in the way of original features or investigations. She spent several dark, cold nights following the story of a state trooper who died in a caving accident, and occasionally managed to indulge her taste for the bizarre.

UPI, Paterson N.J, 8th October 1982

A self-proclaimed witch donned a white gown and shiny gold cape Thursday and cast a 'tax-cut spell' on the city of Paterson. Joyce Luciano, known as the 'official witch of Paterson,' was joined in her noon incantation by about 100 city residents and employees. The audience gathered around a table that Ms. Luciano set up in the city's public safety complex and lustily chanted 'Peace, Prosperity and Love,' at the urging of the blond witch.

It wasn't Anatole Broyard's modern fiction, but Marie was on her way. She went over her clips, fearing that they read like 'someone trying to sound like a newspaper writer'. But she was joyful: 'The feeling is – I did this!' And she was having fun. 'She had that infectious giggle,' says Willard. 'We would go out drinking until 2 a.m. and afterwards she would go back to work. She was very disciplined and had this stamina that was astonishing.' While the AP was somewhat strait-laced, UPI had a certain hipster panache. Like all newsrooms of the era, it was dominated by men, but Willard never noticed Marie being fazed. 'I heard about sexism from other women, but never a peep about it from her,' he remembers.

Paddy was working the night shift at the *Daily News*. 'She'd wake me up and we'd go sailing,' he says. She loved being with her 'sailor-man', as she called him, but she was restless. From time to time she would see Gerry Weaver from Yale and the old longings and insecurities would rise again, even though he was about to marry. It was hard to define what was wrong, but she craved a bigger world to match her appetite for life. 'I have too many excesses in me,' she thought. Eventually she told Paddy their relationship was over.

16th December 1981. I felt I was drowning, my thoughts, emo-tions dulled – any pain is better. Severance makes one think. It is the forcing of yourself over the brink.

* * * * *

After breaking up with Paddy, Marie moved back to her Christopher Street apartment. She thought she wanted to be alone, but soon start-ed dating a reporter who had recently moved to New York from the UPI Atlantic City bureau. John Rhodes was handsome, courteous, hard-working and considerate. He and her colleague Jonathan had made an art of stretching out one- or two-dollar bets all night in order to get free drinks at the Atlantic City casinos. All three loved to sail, and John's father had a sailboat at their family home in Connecticut. Marie and John spent a blissful New Year's Eve together and cele-brated her 26th birthday two weeks later in New York.

12th January 1982. Felt the pieces of my life beginning to fall into place. But also the need to stop waiting for the unknown but expected event, and to take charge.

She took John to Oyster Bay, and her mother dared to hope that maybe Marie might settle down. She and John liked doing the same things – galleries, movies, reading – and did the same job, yet, just as with Paddy, she couldn't shake off her restlessness. She loved John's 'inner surety' but when he said he loved her, she felt trapped again, like a caged animal, 'always pacing, testing the strength of the confin-ing bars'. Maybe she wasn't meant for relationships, she mused, and yet she was always in them.

That summer, Marie and John went on holiday to France, her first trip to Europe, and a chance to use the French she had learnt at classes in New York. She had always envied Katrina, who had lived in Paris briefly as a child, and who was, in Marie's eyes, more cosmopolitan as a result. Now she delighted in being 'awash in the strangeness' and pronounced herself 'in love with Paris'. She thought about the impression John and she might be making.

16th June 1982. John looking très Americain but quite handsome, tall, blond, shirt off-white Oxford cloth with pencil-line dark stripe, me feeling pretty in a flimsy summer dress … I think I could spend my life dressed in a white summer dress, a bottle of wine split with a man who thinks me beautiful, in the bottom of whose eyes I can see wonder, love, at least for the moment.

Her vision of the two of them as characters in a film was marred by worry about her weight. Back home no one would have regarded her as fat, but in Paris she felt like the clumsy American around the slim, impeccable French girls in their T-shirts and jeans short enough to bare the ankle. That was especially hard because she couldn't resist buttery croissants with jam for breakfast, washed down with bitter, strong coffee, followed by a long, slow four-course dinner with cheese and a bottle of Côtes du Rhône. They visited the usual tourist sites – the Eiffel Tower, Notre Dame, the Louvre – and although the military hardware on display at Les Invalides bored her, she tried to imagine the feelings of those who had carried the weaponry, and reflected on the grandeur of Napoleon as she visited his tomb.

They drove to Normandy to tour the Second World War battlefields and Allied cemeteries, and to visit the museum, where she lingered over the exhibit about the D-Day landings.

24th June 1982. Looking at all the photos and diagrams it kept striking me how it must have been to be one man alone in the invasion of June 6. Tons of bombs, tens of thousands of soldiers rushing through waves to shore being machine-gunned and dropping in the surf. In the battle plan, all the mass moves make sense – but to one person? I wonder if you can ever give up the individual desire to live, in the mass movement?

It was a question worthy of her journalistic mentor John Hersey and one she sought to answer all her life. She was already thinking like a war reporter. The role and feelings of the individual in the collective violence of war would become a major theme of her journalism.

They took the train to Avignon, made love frequently, and generally behaved like any young couple. She felt she was at a crossroads.

24th June 1982. I looked at him during the trip and our first night in Paris as the person I would spend the next years with, have children with, would go through the cities, countries, jobs with.

All through that holiday she dreamt of former boyfriends and events from years ago, as if subconsciously cleansing herself of the past while trying to work out whether she and John could have a future together. She made an effort to learn about international events, reading the *International Herald Tribune* every day and memorising facts about Europe.

28th June 1982. Lying in bed last night could actually look out of my window into the night sky and see one star. Thought it might be symbolic, so wished for a job in Paris.

John also made a wish but kept it secret. She was sure it had something to do with her. He began to type up his résumé. She wondered if living together, maybe in France, would be their joint project. They went on to London, saw a Shakespeare play at the National Theatre and friends of John's in Oxford. He made her a photo album-cum-scrapbook with tickets and wine labels stuck in as a memento.

In September 1982, Marie took Cat up to Yale – her baby sister was following in her footsteps. Boo was already at Harvard. Marie's own life was moving on. After eighteen months in Trenton, UPI assigned her to the metro desk in New York, but the company was in financial trouble, and in 1983, after being bought by two entrepreneurs in their mid-thirties from Nashville, it transferred all core operations from New York to Washington. Marie was appointed features editor on the foreign desk. UPI cut staff salaries but she didn't care – the job in Washington might be her first step towards an overseas posting, maybe in Paris. As for John, he had left UPI and taken up a job in New York with the *Daily News*. That was okay, Marie thought. They would see each other on weekends.

In the meantime her new job in Washington would bring her into the orbit of a man who would become her mentor, and whose extraordinary life extended beyond journalism and into the world of the Beat Generation and one of the most notorious crimes of mid-twentieth-century New York.

* * * * *

Nearly four decades earlier, around the time Marie's father enlisted in the Marines, Lucien Carr and his friend Jack Kerouac tried to board a merchant ship sailing out of New York towards Europe; they hoped to make it to Paris before it was liberated by the Allies. The first mate took one look at the young men, realised they were stowaways and threw them off the ship. A slender, handsome youth of nineteen with a blond moustache and a sardonic grin, Lucien was in his first year at Columbia University where he had introduced Kerouac to Allen Ginsberg and William Burroughs, who was a few years older. Together they became known as the Beats. Although never famous as a writer, Lucien was the charismatic central figure who held them together: 'Lou was the glue,' Ginsberg would later say. Lucien also defined their artistic creed in three aphorisms: naked self-expression is the seed of creativity; the artist's consciousness is expanded by derangement of the senses; and art eludes conventional morality. On the fringes of the group prowled a man in his thirties, David Kammerer, a friend of Burroughs, who had harboured a sexual obsession with Lucien since being his scoutmaster in St Louis back in the 1930s.

That night, after being chased from the port, the two young men went drinking at one of their regular haunts. Quite drunk, Lucien ended up walking alone with Kammerer on West 115th Street. According to Lucien, the older man tried – not for the first time – to sexually assault him. Lucien stabbed Kammerer with his scout knife, bound his hands and feet and dumped his body in the Hudson.

The case got huge media attention, with many editorial writers more sympathetic to the killer than the victim. The distinction between a sexual predator and a gay man was rarely made in the 1940s, and Lucien used his heterosexuality as a defence. Convicted of first-degree manslaughter, he served just two years at the Elmira Correctional Facility in upstate New York. On his release, the only job he could get was as a copy boy at UPI. By the 1980s he had risen to senior copy editor in the New York bureau. 'You heard that story immediately you walked in the door at UPI,' says Willard. 'Lucien carried the weight of the whole thing and was not very comfortable with it.'

You also heard the story of how Lou, as he was known, had provided the roll of yellow UPI teletype paper on which Kerouac wrote *On The Road* in 1951. (The roll was eventually bought for $2.4 million and occasionally tours museums as part of a Beat Generation exhibition.) All this was passed on as oral history; Lou himself rarely mentioned his past. Presumably aware of their curiosity, he kept a distance from young reporters, and, having gone on the wagon after his dissolute early life, didn't frequent the Lion's Head or other bars. He had suffered long bouts of depression and alcoholism; self-control was essential for his survival. Having given up smoking, he too would sit in the centre of the newsroom with a plastic stir-straw in his mouth as a cigarette substitute. Divorced from his first wife, the mother of his three sons, he lived in the East Village with his second wife, Sheila Johnson, an African American half his age. His son, Caleb, a novelist, later wrote that his father had physically and verbally abused his children, possibly in reaction to the abuse he himself had suffered at the hands of Kammerer, but this was not public knowledge in the 1980s when Lucien was at UPI.

Lou was never a reporter. His peculiar talent was to read thousands of words someone else had written and get the essence of the story in a flash. He could listen to a reporter's pitch and know instantly whether it was a story or not and how to tell it and sell it. His journalistic mantra was, 'Make 'em laugh, make 'em cry, make 'em horny', encapsulating the imperative to make the news exciting, not just informative. His oft-repeated criticism of young journalists' copy was, 'Why don't you put the second par first?' Slight but sinewy, with a bass voice that carried across the newsroom, Lucien had an aura that drew people to him and made young reporters strive for his approval.

While the other Beats were fêted as literary figures, Lou Carr was a footnote to their story, the beautiful troubled boy who fell by the wayside. He found redemption in being a mentor. Sometimes Ginsberg would acknowledge the debt at a poetry reading, but Lou often felt unappreciated. 'I've watched them get better and better and when they're great, say thank you, talk about how I've helped them and not mean a word,' he grumbled to Marie. But he took his role seriously. 'God put me on earth to be a catalyst,' he told her.

When the UPI's New York City office closed, many senior staff left, but Lou opted to join the enforced exodus to Washington. Although he and Marie were not yet close, they ended up sharing a two-storey townhouse in Adams Morgan, the nearest thing the US capital had to Greenwich Village. The third member of the household was Dan Chiszar, a reclusive character who later left journalism and joined the circus as a roustabout. The fourth was Lou's dog Pancho, a small wire-haired three-legged mutt who wore a red bandanna.

'Lou would sit in an armchair like King Lear, Pancho at his side,' remembers Susanne Ramirez de Arellano, a young Puerto Rican reporter on the UPI Latin America desk. 'I would sit at his feet, but Marie was always at his level.' The two young women would drink wine and whiskey and chain-smoke in the kitchen before coming into the living room to talk – or maybe more often to listen – to Lou. Susanne was glad Lou didn't drink, because at times she felt his mask of restraint was about to slip. 'He could turn 180 degrees from most wonderful erudite discussions of politics, poetry, the Beat Generation, and suddenly become angry if we didn't understand what he was saying. His voice would go really rough, like broken glass and cigarettes.' She was slightly scared of him. 'Marie could control Lucien. It was like when you're sailing and a big wave comes but you know how to buffet it.'

One evening, Lou took Marie to a tavern in Dupont Circle to meet some friends, who turned out to be William Burroughs and Allen Ginsberg. For her it was especially thrilling, because of the interview she had done with Ginsberg for the *Yale Daily News* back in 1978. As the evening wore on, she realised she knew one person in Washington who more than any other would want to be there with them, so she went to the phone booth. 'Gerry,' she said, 'I'm with William Burroughs and Allen Ginsberg. I told them about you and they say you must come on down and have a drink.' Fearing that another assignation with Marie – they had seen each other a few times since she moved to Washington – would precipitate the end of his marriage, Gerry reluctantly declined. A few weeks later Marie sent him a framed photograph of Burroughs, signed by Ginsberg – a gift that demonstrated her success as well as her generosity.

Day to day, Marie was pouring her energy into the new job, making it work, caring about it possessively, rising and falling emotionally on the day. The UPI office was above a metro stop where corporate Washington met the inner city. She and her colleagues sat around a large metal desk with box style computers. With UPI always about to go under, younger journalists got more responsibility than they might have been given elsewhere. It was often Marie's decision as to whether reporters needed to check their sources or do more research before their story could be put out on the wire. She enjoyed polishing prose and got satisfaction from seeing the stories she had edited published in the major papers, but it was all just a rehearsal for the big break she hoped was on its way.

She and Susanne talked long into the night about their ambitions, and their desire to emulate famous journalists such as Martha Gellhorn, who had reported the rise of fascism in Europe in the 1930s, and Oriana

Fallaci, who had been in the resistance against Mussolini before embarking on a career covering war and revolution. Marie and Susanne dreamt of having it all. 'We wanted to be superhero female journalists to show men we could do the same as them. But we also wanted the home and the flowers and the smell of the apple pie,' says Susanne.

In the spring of 1984, Marie and John joined her old Yale friends – Katrina and her boyfriend Chris Bartle, Dave Humphreville, Bobby Shriver and others – for a sailing holiday in Belize. They drank prodigious quantities of alcohol, argued about who was the better writer, Ernest Hemingway or Alice Walker, and got stranded on a sandbank from which they were rescued by local Rastafarians. Slipping back into her carefree student ways, and feeling nostalgic for her college romance with Dave, Marie grew impatient with John who was driving her crazy with his protectiveness, always saying 'Marie, be careful' and 'Marie, watch your hands' when they were sailing. She felt ugly – 'greasy hair, belly fat' – compared to Katrina – 'looking great in pink shorts, white T shirt'. More to the point, she thought Katrina and Chris seemed happy together. By contrast, she and John were becoming estranged. He was looking for stability, but she craved adventure.

Back in Washington, she and Jonathan Landay introduced Lou to their favourite pastime. 'I took Lou sailing for the first time and he fell in love with it,' says Jonathan, who had a Sailmaster 22 called the *Ananda*. Strong and wiry, Lou quickly learnt how to wrestle the boat into submission in turbulent seas, although he did suffer the occasional cracked rib. 'We'd go out in really rough weather,' says Jonathan. 'I remember keeling over and he just loved it.' In Lou, Marie had found a kindred spirit who didn't exhort her to be careful, who preferred the storm to the calm. Lou bought the same model of boat as Jonathan and christened her the *Ananda II*. She had a fibreglass hull with wooden brightwork and mast, so Lou and Marie would spend hours sanding and painting before heading out into the Chesapeake Bay, in fair weather or foul.

When Cat visited from Yale in 1984, they took her out for what was supposed to be a couple of days. 'It ended up being a week because we hit the doldrums and there was no wind,' she remembers. 'We were stuck out there with no electricity.' Lou told her the story of David Kammerer's murder and his prison years. Cat had initially found it hard to understand why her sister was hanging out with someone as old as their father would have been – even older than her previous boyfriends, but on that sailing trip she got it. 'He was so inspiring and charismatic,' she says. Katrina wasn't so sure. 'Rie,' she said on one of their long phone calls. 'I just fear you'll jump into this and spend a long time extricating yourself. You're very susceptible to guilt.'

Katrina had reason to fear for her friend. Lou had slipped off the wagon. One day after they had been drinking on the boat, he passed out. A storm came through, and Marie had to steer back into harbour alone and carry Lou ashore. It was the talk of the newsroom, a titbit that added more to Marie's mystique than Lou's. By now, everyone believed they were more than housemates. 'She was in her twenties and he was in his late fifties, but they were in love and I thought it was wonderful,' says Jonathan. 'But I knew that it wasn't going to last because she was young and ambitious and wasn't going to stay there for ever.' Allen Ginsberg asked Marie what she thought of Lou's drinking.

'He goes into rages sometimes. Have you seen those?' he asked.

'I'm afraid of them,' she replied.

* * * * *

Pearls around her neck, a loose shirt over tight jeans, Marie had a bohemian style all her own. Despite her agonies over dieting, she was slim and naturally elegant. Her abundant curls, cut now to fall just above her shoulders, were still the first thing anyone noticed about her, and then her intense green eyes. Heads turned whenever she walked into a room. 'It's hard to overstate how cool Marie was,' says Tim Golden, a recent graduate who had just joined the UPI Latin America desk. 'She was really bright in a funny, unpretentious and curious way. She knew every fun thing to do in whatever place it was. People wanted to be around her.' Tim also discerned a vulnerability that conflicted with

Marie's growing professional and social confidence. 'You had the sense that she wanted to be loved, but that there was something missing, maybe something that had to do with her father.' As a mentor, Lou was more overtly a father figure than other older men she had known. He noticed her ability to feel deeply but suspend emotion. 'Her brain has such a capacity to separate that you could tell her tonight she would be executed and she would still go out and have a great time,' he once said. It was true, Marie thought. Lou was able to help her examine her thoughts, cutting through what she characterised as 'the slick veneer' she gave them, 'the gloss that allows me to glide along, handle this crisis, that'. Lou's own feelings were complex. He grew prickly when Tim was around, sensing a rival for Marie's affections.

Tim and Marie talked about their ambitions. Although five years younger, he had already spent time reporting from the wars in Central America, the biggest news story of the day, his fluent Spanish and go-for-it confidence compensating for his youth and inexperience. Within six months, he left Washington for a reporting job in El Salvador with the *Miami Herald*. Marie felt left behind, approaching her thirties and stuck on the foreign desk. 'Shit, if you can do this, there's nothing stopping me,' she said to him as he set off. Sometimes she would snort a line of coke as a distraction when she couldn't cope with the decisions she knew she had to make. In mid-1985 she decided to clear the decks, finally telling John Rhodes what they both knew: their relationship was over. She couldn't be with someone who had 'no tragedy, no angst, no darkness'. But she understood the consequences of casting aside what had been the most stable relationship of her life.

18th May 1985. Sitting on bed, sunny day outside, tears tears, crying, for myself really. I've told John I don't want to see him ... I want a different life ... I'll never find anyone who loves me as unreservedly as John, is as good a person or as good to me.

With her eyes on the position of UPI Paris Bureau Chief, she took more French classes. In her application for the job she highlighted the knowledge of French history and politics she had gained at Yale, but possibly more persuasive to managers in a company that was spiralling down towards bankruptcy was her last sentence: 'I am single and own nothing that couldn't be fitted into a suitcase so I would be easy to move.'

The wish made on the star she had seen in the sky above Avignon came true; she got the Paris job. Her going-away party on 31 July 1985 was a wild, all night affair. Lou's dog Pancho sported a blue bandanna she had bought him for the occasion. She wore what Lou called her 'French drinking dress' and wrecked the baby blue Charles Jourdan shoes that she and John had bought on the Champs-Élysées. Her mother, who came along to the party, remarked to anyone who was listening, 'She's hard on shoes', while making coffee for those left at the very end. Rosemarie, unsurprisingly, had hoped Marie would stay with John, who she thought would look after her daughter. Lou and Marie, she commented somewhat acerbically, were 'both takers'. Marie ended up in Lou's room drunkenly confessing her love and asking why they weren't sleeping together. The newsroom gossip was wrong – their relationship was still chaste. In the morning, Lou took her to the airport, where, still drunk, she fell asleep.

'Wake up, Marie, or they won't let you on the plane,' he said.

* * * * *

4th August 1985. First day in Paris! I'm the Paris bureau chief. I've done it. Exultant.

In Paris, Marie found what she had sought in New York years earlier: female role models. The *New York Times* columnist, Flora Lewis, then in her late fifties, took Marie under her wing. 'She taught me the skill of drinking vodka martinis,' Marie later said. 'I thought, I can do this job – talk to contacts while drinking martinis. I was very enthusiastic. Then Flora in that gravelly no nonsense voice said, "Marie – you have to remember next morning what people have told you."'

Then there was Aline Mosby, aged sixty-three and still reporting for UPI, who had been the first American woman posted as a correspondent to Moscow. She famously interviewed Lee Harvey Oswald who, some years before assassinating President Kennedy, had tried to defect to the Soviet Union. In a long career at the news agency, Aline had also been posted to Beijing and Vienna. Petite in a Christian Dior suit, her grey-blonde hair elegantly coiffed, she impressed Marie, who initially stayed at her apartment, which had a spectacular view over the Seine and Notre-Dame. Marie noted the elegant furnishings – peach satin drapes on wooden rings, heavy antique wooden furniture, Russian icons inlaid with gold, paintings, bookcases, rugs. These were the spoils of the kind of international career she hoped to have. She noted down a cautionary tale about her new friend: 'When Aline in Moscow she dating Kosygin's son, showed up at a party function, drank something, drugged, woke up three days later in the gutter. Pictures in paper showed "Drunken US correspondent" and she was expelled.'

Aline helped Marie find an apartment on the Left Bank near the famous bookshop Shakespeare and Company. Just off a cobbled street, the building had wide stable doors opening out on to a tiny courtyard with impatiens and geraniums in pots. The older woman introduced her to the best *charcuteries,* taught her how to distinguish a so-so Burgundy from a good one, and took her to neighbourhood restaurants where Aline insisted on dicing the best steak into morsels for her Siamese cats, Natasha and Miaomiao.

Every day Marie walked across the bridge to the boulevard des Italiens where the UPI bureau was housed on the third floor of a grand but dilapidated mid-nineteenth-century block. Amongst the dusty cardboard files she found shards of glass from a recent bomb attack on an Israeli bank opposite – small acts of terrorism by far left groups would be regular news stories in the months to come. The telex machine clattered with copy from francophone Africa, and papers piled up under battered old green metal desks but the coffee machine worked and her office had floor to ceiling windows opening on to one of the city's four great boulevards so she was happy. Despite her youth, Marie discovered that it wasn't too difficult to assert her authority. She injected a sense of mission into the bureau, working long hard hours and sweeping others along in her enthusiasm. 'She was a great bureau chief,' said one. 'She supported her staff and always had our back.' The cheerful UPI drinking culture extended across the Atlantic, and with Washington DC six hours behind, deadlines were distant so there was no reason not to have a bottle of Burgundy with lunch at the nearby Pub de la Presse. When anyone had a birthday, they drank champagne and ate foie gras and cheese in her spacious office. The dollar was strong, and even those on a reduced UPI salary could live well in France.

Marie worried that her French wasn't good enough so she took more classes, watched French TV and read constantly – French novels, French history, French current affairs. She went to the opera, classical concerts and art galleries. In the mornings she ran along the Left Bank, and at night she looked out over the river scarcely daring to believe her good fortune.

26th September 1985. Seine black mirror smooth tonight, reflection of bridges play with each other, telescoped over each other. Lights on Notre Dame smoky, air heavy with fog.

She and Lou spoke almost daily. 'I love you and I miss you,' she told him. 'Paris is perfect except that you're not here.' He flew to Paris for a long weekend. Both were overcome by desire but she began to understand why he had been reluctant to sleep with her when they were in Washington: not only did he have prostate problems, but he was also suffused with guilt about his wife. Although they had both craved a physical relationship, it just didn't work, so they drank more vodka, seeing Paris and each other through a veil of alcohol. Lou said he would get a divorce and move to Paris. Marie demurred – he would have nothing to do there. Sometimes she thought she would like to have children with him; she imagined little green-eyed blonde girls, but she was beginning to feel herself pulling away. 'He's anti-social, but I still love the bright lights, dancing. I want to ride in an open sports car up the Champs-Élysées at dawn. That's not Lucien.'

In December, she flew to meet him in San Juan, Puerto Rico from where they would sail to the US Virgin Islands. Both knew that this trip would define their future, together or apart. Lou talked of staying married to Sheila but being with Marie, then of divorcing Sheila to marry Marie but her being free to sleep with other men who could provide her with the sexual satisfaction he could not. They drank piña coladas, smoked cigarettes and played Marie's favourite Patsy Cline songs. From time to time Lou would fly into a drunken fury. 'I love him drinking but fear what we now call his rampages,' Marie wrote. In the back of her mind was the unmentionable fact that he had once killed a man. For both, the easiest thing was to revert to the old relationship: teacher and student. After one argument she stormed off to the beach. He followed her with a writing pad. 'You can hide from me but not from this,' he said. 'There's an acorn of genius in you. I know and I'm never wrong. You have to stop being Marie the party girl. You have to be a journalist for a while, but you can't stop there or you'll end up with a handful of ashes. I'll make a novelist of you.' One day they sailed straight into a storm, courting the danger and excitement that had brought them together, but Lou was tired, and couldn't hoist the sail quickly enough. His age was showing, and Marie had no patience.

After he returned to Washington and she to Paris, she called him to say that it was over. Lou sent her a dozen red roses and begged for another chance. She felt guilty as Katrina had predicted. The balance of power had shifted – they were no longer mentor and mentee, but a younger woman gliding into the future, leaving the older man behind. Late at night, as the moon rose over the Seine, she sat in her apartment reading Graham Greene's *The End of the Affair*. It was distressingly close to the bone. Love affairs always end, she thought, and the worst part is when you can see it coming.

* * * * *

Her new best friend in Paris was a reporter for the *New York Times*. Judith Miller was eight years older, but Marie felt an immediate bond, describing her as 'pretty, very analytical mind' but also noticed she had 'edges so sharp'. If you found Marie at a party or diplomatic reception, you found Judy, and vice versa. One French *député* fell in love with them both. Bored with the round of French political intrigue and minor terror attacks, Marie and Judy used the excuse of a feature about the truffle season to drive to the countryside. All the way there they talked about the stories they would really like to be doing: the hostage crisis in Lebanon, aircraft hijackings, the war between the Soviets and the Western-backed *mujahideen* in Afghanistan. Living in France was fun, but they hadn't become journalists to do stories about pigs snuffling in the forest. At dinner a curious waiter asked what two single American women were doing in such a remote part of *la France profonde*. When they explained he looked at them in some astonishment. '*Mesdames,*' he said, '*Les Americaines* do not understand the nobility of the truffle.' That, they thought through their laughter, was undeniably true.

At Christmas, they decided to hold a party at Judy's apartment, inviting diplomats and officials and even a couple of ministers. Marie showed up in the early evening. 'Where's the tree?' she asked. Judy said there hadn't been time to buy one. 'But you can't have a Christmas party without a tree!' Marie said, and as caterers laid out the food, she dragged Judy down to the Marais, where they bought the only tree they could find, and heaved it back through the snow. Of course it was too big to get into the apartment, so Marie borrowed a saw from the concierge's husband and cut it down to size. When the guests turned up an hour later, the branches were still bare. 'We decorated the tree as an activity,' recalls Judy. 'The French officials and ministers were very stiff, but a large amount of alcohol was drunk and they said it was a most unusual Christmas party.' Buoyed up by their success, the two women went out for a nightcap after the last guest had left, not returning until the early hours. The next morning the concierge pointed out that Judy and Marie had unwittingly locked the caterers, as well as the concierge and her husband, inside the apartment. The husband had climbed out of a window and slithered down a pole to retrieve a spare key and free the others.

Paris, with its round of concerts, cocktails and interviews with politicians and businessmen was a lot more fun socially than Washington had been. Marie took a trapeze class for a story and decided to carry on with the lessons as a cool way of keeping her weight down. In her diary she noted what the well dressed women she knew were wearing; Aline, who covered the Paris fashion shows remained her icon of good taste. They went underwear shopping together, and Aline encouraged Marie to discard her practical American sports bras for the satin and lace of La Perla, with silk panties to match. Marie started to buy expensive clothes, whether or not she had enough money in the bank. Her mother came to visit and Marie took her round the sights. Rosemarie was impressed by how well her daughter spoke French, and how she seemed to know so many diplomats and government officials.

On her 30th birthday, Marie's colleagues presented her with a chocolate cake and she spent much of the day shopping with Aline, but that evening she was alone. Growing nostalgic and sorry for herself, she played a tape of her favourite country and western songs that John Rhodes had sent.

12th January 1986. 30 years old. Sad sad sad ... Too fat for my jeans, double chin in the mirror and cellulite cheeks. Alone ... Why do you think I always drive so hard through life leaving bodies? I can't feel, I stop feeling. I am not afraid, I don't feel for more than a moment ...

Lou didn't answer when she called. Like Gerry Weaver and Mickey Maye before him, he had accused her of being unwomanly. 'You are your father's son. That explains a lot, why you are such a boy-girl,' he said. Marie had tried to explain that she had always felt different from other girls, who she thought went at things in a roundabout way while she liked to tackle problems head on. Maybe that was why men thought there was something wrong with her, she mused. Maybe they were right. She was abandoning Lou in the same way she had Mickey, Paddy and John. How could she be so unhappy and still feel heartless? Lou had said to her, 'You'll never be in love. That's sad.' Sometimes she wondered if he was right.

20th January 1986. What is this hardness in me? This falseness? I so want to love. But in love and alone I feel lonely. I want him there and I hate that feeling. In love, with him there, I get claustrophobic. I want out after the first rush.

In February, Lou came for a final visit. They hired a car and drove to the Loire Valley, Marie increasingly irritated by his dropping cigarette ash in chic hotel rooms and telling her she was 'middle class' for caring about such things. It was, she thought, undeclared warfare. After he returned to Washington she called to tell him that this time her decision was final: it was over.

There was no new man to distract her; a new story was what she needed. The following month, she got the break she'd been waiting for. King Hassan of Morocco was celebrating his quarter century reign and had invited journalists to witness the celebrations. It was Marie's first trip to North Africa and she arrived trembling with anticipation, clutching a copy of Elias Canetti's *Voices of Marrakesh*. The waiter who brought her coffee at the Semiramis Hotel was careful not to catch her eye: 'We were both embarrassed at my femaleness,' she wrote. When she took a taxi into town, the police followed to see what she was up to – she wasn't sure if it was because she was a woman, a journalist or just a foreigner.

3rd March 1986. Drove through crowds of women veiled up to their dark eyes, wearing djellabias *that at times were nothing more than burlap covers, others satin with embroidery ... got to Djema el Fna, square at center of city, bustle ... Men with snakes, owls, one led his monkey on a leash up to shake my hand, wizened black skin, tiny knuckles.*

The reporters were taken to the palace, and Marie filed her story on the preparations for the celebrations, describing the phalanx of guards in red uniforms holding lances and the banqueting tables laden with silver trays of sweets and nuts. One of the Moroccan journalists invited her to a nightclub, where she watched a snake charmer coil a huge cobra round the neck of an American tourist. She was not surprised when the journalist came on to her, but she was taken aback by his chat-up line: 'I must tell you that I love my king. Morocco is very blessed to have such a king.' The visiting press corps went to a reception at the American Embassy and on to a cocktail party hosted by a French countess at the Villa Taylor, where Churchill had once entertained Roosevelt. It was there that Marie met the *Sunday Times* correspondent David Blundy. When she told him she worked for UPI, he responded, 'Oh, a real journalist.' And so began one of the most consequential relationships of her life.

David, then forty, was something of a legend amongst British journalists. He had covered conflicts in Northern Ireland, Central America and the Middle East as well as famine in Ethiopia and government-sponsored killings in Zimbabwe. Usually dressed in jeans and a leather jacket, David had a shambolic demeanour that belied the sharpest of minds – he ferreted out details that others had missed and had the ability to make interviewees say far more than they had intended. While trying to give the impression of doing very little, he was in fact a highly conscientious reporter. A charismatic figure, with tall, dark good looks, he had a knack for making a woman think she was the centre of his world for the time he focused on her. Usually, that was not very long. Despite his reputation as a heartbreaker, a 'girl in every port' type, women forgave David because he was funny and had a boyish vulnerability that made them want to look after him. Men were also drawn to him, not sexually, but because he was good at banter – self-deprecating in the British way, witty and entertaining.

The day after the royal ceremony, the international reporters were taken to the airport for a trip into the Sahara, a chaotic journey of endless confusion and delay during which the plane flew to the wrong airport and everyone's luggage got lost. This was Marie's first experience of one of journalism's more ridiculous rituals: the press trip organised by nervous and incompetent government minders trying to herd a group of rebellious reporters on an un-newsworthy visit to a model factory or farm. When the plane landed at an airstrip in the desert, the reporters were told to get on a waiting bus. David put his leather jacket on the seat next to him – Marie picked it up, slung it over her shoulders and sat down. The highlight of that day's tour turned out to be a chemical factory, where the two found themselves laughing hysterically as earnest reporters from state-run Third World news agencies filmed boards of switches and noted down endless details on phosphate production. Marie and David found everything hilarious; they were, as she put it, in 'matching madcap moods'.

At the small town hotel where they stayed that night another reporter told Marie about David's long term girlfriend, Samira Osman. Marie wasn't bothered: she was thinking of telling David that she knew she had met her match – and she was right, though not in the sense of having found a life partner. Marie and David were like twins. They shared not only a sense of humour but a way of rushing at the world, of lighting up a room and dazzling everyone in it. Both would do almost anything to get the story, or to have a night of fun, damn the consequences. And they moved on quickly, fearing being trapped if they stayed still too long. Theirs was less like meeting and more like looking into a mirror and seeing the other's reflection.

The next day the Moroccan government took the reporters to a military base deep in the desert. It was Marie's first trip in a helicopter. An Austrian reporter lent her his Walkman so as they swooped over the sands of the Sahara she could drown out the roar of the rotors with Dire Straits and Bruce Springsteen, while watching the crescent-shaped dunes and cloud shadows below. A jeep took them on to the base, where a colonel offered them a whole roasted goat and took questions on the Polisario, the rebel force claiming the Western Sahara. Exhausted, caked in dirt, a scarf wrapped round her head and wearing goggles for the return journey, Marie was as happy as she had ever been. At the beginning of the trip, while the other reporters swapped war stories, she had felt like the little girl in their midst. Now she was one of them. Back in Marrakesh, she filed her stories from the desert trip, showered and changed into a white dress and green sweater. David joked that he didn't recognise her now that she was clean. In the evening, the two of them drank whiskey late into the night and, inevitably, ended up in bed. She had a strong sense that her life was about to change.

* * * * *

While Marie was in Morocco, Colonel Muammar Gaddafi had been holding an international conference in Libya to establish a 'fighting international revolutionary force' to combat the United States. Gaddafi would be its sponsor and leader, President Ronald Reagan its prime target. The Libyan leader, who had seized power in a coup in 1969, saw himself as the guiding light of a global struggle against imperialism. Reagan, who called Gaddafi 'that mad dog of the Middle East', believed that the Libyan leader was trying to assassinate him. Israel was also in the Colonel's sights – he had provided weapons and forged passports for deadly terror attacks at the Israeli airline check-in desks at Vienna and Rome airports, carried out by the radical Palestinian Abu Nidal Organisation in 1985. The Guide, or the Brother Leader, or the Universal Theorist, as Gaddafi variously styled himself, was constantly threatening to attack US warships operating in the Gulf of Sidra off the Libyan coast. Under maritime law, international waters start 12 nautical miles from a country's shore, but Gaddafi decreed that the 'line of death', beyond which he would allow no foreign ship to pass, was at 62 nautical miles. On 23 March 1986 a US battle group of aircraft carriers, cruisers, frigates, destroyers and 250 aircraft crossed the line, claiming they were carrying out a 'freedom of navigation' operation. In fact, the Americans were provoking Gaddafi, because they wanted to demonstrate the force of weaponry that he would face if he continued his terror attacks. The following day the Libyans fired SA-5 missiles that they had recently bought from the Soviet Union, and used aircraft to intercept US fighter jets. In the land and sea skirmish that followed, thirty-five Libyan seamen were killed with no American losses.

Marie, who had just returned to Paris from Morocco, was amongst a group of foreign journalists invited to Tripoli three days later. At last she was where she wanted to be: on the biggest story in the world. At the airport, the journalists were served tea under a banner proclaiming, 'We are the natural and historical contradiction to America as an imperial power.' A poster showed President Reagan's face against a desert background and a skeleton, with the caption, 'The barbarian Reagan is a necrophiliac, because his approach suffocates humans.' The local colour she observed at the airport and on a quick walk in the street was enough for Marie's first story, but what every editor wanted was an interview with Gaddafi. Judy Miller, who had previously spent three months in Libya, but had not managed to get a visa on this occasion, had given Marie her list of contacts, including those closest to the Brother Leader. It was well known that Gaddafi was more likely to give an interview to a female reporter – the younger and prettier the better – but he was predatory, frequently propositioning the women who interviewed him. Marie was undeterred. David Blundy had just flown in and was fulminating because he knew Gaddafi was more likely to talk to Marie than him. She kept calling Gaddafi's aides, and after five days her persistence was rewarded.

The summons came at 3 a.m. A car arrived at the hotel, and Marie was driven through the empty, dark streets of the Libyan capital to Gaddafi's fortified compound, Bab al-Aziziyah. A far cry from the Bedouin tent in which he pretended to live, his bunker was surrounded by high concrete walls and guarded by Russian-made tanks. His female guards, wearing tight camouflage uniforms, pistols holstered on their hips, glowered at Marie as they led her downstairs to a tiny dark den with imitation wood panelling, a thick curtain separating it from a bedroom and bathroom. Marie was in his inner sanctum. After a few minutes he entered dressed in a grey padded flight suit, sockless feet peeking from lizard skin slip-on shoes.

'I am Gaddafi!' he announced.

'No kidding!' Marie thought.

He sat down beside her on an upholstered sofa. 'Soft Arab music and a sweet aroma filled the air,' she wrote in an article later. 'An aide arrived with two cups of espresso coffee and two glasses of a sweet milky almond drink.' She noticed that Gaddafi was wearing French cologne. At the end of the interview, during which he had said he was ready to hit US targets anywhere in the world and described the conflict between the US and Libya as being like the Crusades, he put his hand on her thigh and asked if he could see her again, as if this were a date. 'Why don't you call me?' said Marie.

A few days later an aide did just that and Gaddafi came on the line to say he wanted to speak to her again. This time the meeting was a little weirder, and more menacing. When she arrived at the bunker, a white dress and a pair of little green shoes had been laid out for her on a chair. She refused to put them on, saying they were too small. Gaddafi then strode in, locked the door and put the key in his pocket. Marie had always paid attention to people's clothes, but Gaddafi was the most extraordinary dresser she had ever seen. He was wearing a red silk shirt, baggy white and silver striped pants and a gold cape. Every time she asked about the tension with the US, he turned her tape recorder off and put his hand on her knee, saying he was tired and wanted to talk about something else. He told Marie that Libya had had nothing to do with the bombing of La Belle discotheque in Berlin the previous week, in which two American soldiers and a Turkish woman had been killed. US intelligence said it had intercepted a congratulatory message sent by telex from Tripoli to the Libyan Embassy in East Berlin. 'Libya never had anything to do with this bombing,' said Gaddafi.

Marie asked what he felt about the coming US attack, which everyone now saw as inevitable. 'Who told you that?' he asked. Somewhat nonplussed, Marie said, 'I heard it on the BBC.' Gaddafi immediately sprang up and turned on the radio which was tuned to the BBC World Service, as if the idea of an American attack were new to him, even though no one in Tripoli was talking of anything else. He rambled on about Arab unity, the Palestinian cause and his 'Third Universal Theory', a political philosophy based on on his musings and obsessions. In a reversal of the normal situation where the interviewee brings the interview to an end, it was Marie who, after several hours, said she really had to leave, and made her escape.

The interview was front page news in America and across the world. Cat, who was still at Yale, remembers her friends rushing into her room saying, 'Your sister's on the radio!' Their mother, who was at a teachers' convention in Philadelphia, was less than happy when she turned on the TV and saw Marie in a city everyone expected to be bombed in the next few hours. Dave Humpreville, her old boyfriend from Yale, heard her and called Katrina, who was simultanously delighted to hear of her friend's success and concerned for her safety. Suddenly, Marie Colvin was not an anonymous news agency reporter, but the brave woman who had interviewed Muammar 'mad dog' Gaddafi as American warplanes revved their engines on the tarmac.

Marie – who would earn a reputation for being generous to other reporters – gave David Blundy the details of her encounters with Gaddafi for his stories. On the night of 14 April, the two of them were with Hugh Dunnachie, the British consul, at his villa in Tripoli, known amongst reporters as the House of Shame, because it was the only place you could get a drink. She had told one of Gaddafi's aides where she was, and at 1.30 a.m. the villa's phone rang with the news that US planes were bombing the eastern city of Benghazi. A raid on Tripoli was expected at any time. Marie called Gaddafi's office but there was no reply. Half an hour later, according to David's account, 'The windows and doors rattled in the British consul's residence, chandeliers shook and the building itself trembled as thirteen F-11 fighter bombers and three radar-jamming planes swooped in low over the sea.' Marie, David and Hugh climbed up to the roof to watch the tracer fire and listen to the anti-aircraft guns which pounded for at least 15 minutes after the raid was over.

'Everyone rushed into the streets,' wrote Marie in her despatch for UPI. 'We tried to get back from the consul's residence to the hotel where the journalists were based. Gaddafi's Revolutionary Committee guards poured into the streets.' Officials told the journalists that

Gaddafi's adopted daughter, Hana, had been killed in the raid (a story that persisted for twenty-five years until it turned out that she was alive and well and studying medicine). He himself did not appear in public until two days later when, dressed in a white naval uniform with gold epaulettes and five bands of military decorations on the left breast pocket, he sat in front of a large map of Libya and gave a TV address. Marie's special access seemed to have run out, and she was bussed with all the other journalists to see a chicken farm and other sites that had been hit in the US raid. She had never worked so hard in her life, filing three or four stories a day in a chaotic atmosphere where the Libyan armed forces randomly fired anti-aircraft batteries in case there was another raid, and journalists never knew from one hour to the next if they were going to be fêted, detained or expelled.

Eventually, they were all told they must leave before the end of April, but a few weeks later Marie returned to see Gaddafi again. 'Summoned into sanctuary, usual scramble of guards who run, hurrying you along for no reason, everyone conspicuously armed,' she noted in her diary. This time Gaddafi was attired in a navy blue ski suit tucked into black Italian mid-calf boots, aquamarine stripes on the sleeves. 'What is this, that you did not warn me that they were going to bomb my house?' he asked her. She replied that she didn't have his private phone number, and that when she had called his office, no one picked up. He began to speak in Arabic to his assistant, a young woman called Fatiya, who started to cry. 'This is ridiculous, you can't blame Fatiya,' said Marie. Offhandedly Gaddafi squeezed Fatiya's breast – more evidence of his casual *droit de seigneur* attitude. Fatiya, Marie noted, didn't react.

Gaddafi said he had in fact known that she had tried to call him and was grateful. He seemed to think Marie had been trying to warn him rather than get a reaction for a story. Had she heard him mention her on television? he asked. She was baffled, until she remembered that a few days after the raid Gaddafi had said that although Reagan hated him, the American people loved him, and the proof was that 'an American woman' had called to warn him of the raid. She realised he had been referring to her. 'I didn't use your name because Reagan would have you killed if he knew,' said Gaddafi.

* * * * *

Marie's Gaddafi interviews were UPI's scoop of the year, but they couldn't halt the demise of the company. There was talk not just of pay cuts and redundancies but complete collapse. Marie and Judy Miller co-authored a piece about Gaddafi for *Rolling Stone* magazine, and Marie cast around for new opportunities. Then David Blundy had an idea. Rupert Murdoch, who had bought *The Times* and the *Sunday Times* in 1981, had decided to modernise production by cutting hundreds of unionised printers' jobs. After a move from Fleet Street to Wapping, where the papers would be produced by fewer staff, the printers went on strike. With Prime Minister Margaret Thatcher hell bent on crushing the unions, the journalists were divided between 'refuseniks' who joined the printers, and others who crossed the picket line. As the dispute dragged on, the *Sunday Telegraph* offered David a highly paid position as its Washington correspondent. Why didn't Marie try out for his old job at the *Sunday Times*? he suggested. He would give her his 'black book' of contacts and she would be set. With her solid news agency experience and a bulging portfolio of frontline stories from Libya, she was well qualified. Despite her Teamsters background, she had no interest in the British battle between Mrs Thatcher and the unions – she just wanted to report the Middle East. Stepping into David's shoes seemed like destiny.

On leaving the *Sunday Times* after sixteen years, David left a wry note to colleagues that ended: 'I will miss the Middle East (with the exception of Iraq, Jordan, Libya, Sudan, Israel and West Beirut – Morocco was all right). I know that I have left it in more slender and probably more competent hands than my own. Colvin is good, but you don't have to use words like "stunning" and "gosh" when you read her copy from Libya (much of it culled from a piece of my own as I remember). I wish you all the best, even Colvin who is taking over my job, my flat, my car, my computer, my new crystal glasses and is about to enter into a meaningful relationship with Samira.'

Marie started at the *Sunday Times* in September 1986. She delayed by a week so she could fly to Boston to be a bridesmaid at Katrina's wedding to Chris Bartle. Her best friend seemed to have it all – marriage and an editing job at the *New York Times Magazine*. But Marie's life was looking pretty exciting too. She was following not just David Blundy but famous war correspondents from earlier generations. Martha Gellhorn's friend, Virgina Cowles, had been the *Sunday Times* correspondent during the Second World War. The paper's star reporter in Vietnam had been Nicholas Tomalin, famous for writing 'The General Goes Zapping Charlie Cong', one of the first pieces to reveal the casual way US forces killed civilians. Tomalin himself had been killed by a Syrian missile in 1973, while reporting the Yom Kippur war. The paper had a reputation for hard-hitting investigations, both domestic and international. In her diary, which she had neglected during the long, busy months in Tripoli, Marie wrote briefly of a goodbye dinner in Paris.

23rd September 1986. Moved to London Monday night, tired, new job at 'Sunday Times' Tuesday morning. New Agnes B dress, big newsroom, felt out of place but proud.

She was off to Beirut on assignment the next morning.

* * * * *

PART TWO
Middle East

Chapter 4

THE PATH OF DEATH

Marie's instructions on landing in Beirut were to walk out of the terminal and 'stride manfully' up a hill until she saw a driver named Abed who would, it was hoped, have her name or at least know she was from the *Sunday Times*. He would be easy to recognise because he was small and balding with a moustache. 'Must be a zillion in Lebanon,' she mused, as she sat in the hotel in the Cypriot city of Larnaca, waiting for her flight. 'Fear I have not set this up well.'

In September 1986, Beirut was the most dangerous city on earth. Five months earlier, the British journalist John McCarthy had been kidnapped on his way to the airport where Marie was about to land. The American University of Beirut lecturer Brian Keenan was abducted around the same time. The bodies of another two AUB lecturers had been found at the edge of the city, and two weeks before Marie arrived another two American teachers were kidnapped. The division between the Christian East and Muslim West Beirut was only one fault line; the conflicts within West Beirut were equally deadly and twice as baffling, with seemingly endless militia, factions and sects pitted one against another. Westerners were kidnapped to be exchanged for political concessions or money to buy weapons. If you were taken, you had no idea how many years you might spend locked in a basement while your captors bargained with your life.

Marie was nervous, about both her own safety and her ability to understand and explain the story. From her hotel room in Larnaca, she rang Katrina and talked for so long that the hotel desk interrupted to say the call had cost £97. Both women were aware that this was the beginning of the rest of Marie's life, the moment she had been waiting for, when she would succeed or fail, survive or perish. The idea was too big to contemplate so they talked about clothes and holiday plans. Katrina said, 'I don't want to get off, then you'll be 3,000 miles away again. I love you.' On the plane Marie wore her 'New York subway face', trying to look bored, slightly absent. A man from the Commodore Hotel, where journalists normally stayed in Beirut, met her at Arrivals – 'Miss Mary Colvin? Come with me' – and led her to where Abed was waiting. A reassuring character in his late fifties he took his responsibilities seriously. He told Marie, 'You are the only American in West Beirut. That's why I will stay with you all the time, everything you do.' They drove past the pancaked US Marine headquarters, blown up three years earlier, and down bombed out streets where buildings had caved in, dirt piled up and kids played in the gutter wearing only their underwear, to the Summerland Hotel. The Commodore – famous for its parrot, Coco, who would imitate the sound of an incoming artillery shell from his cage in reception – was now too dangerous: firefights had recently broken out right in front of it.

Marie walked into her room, opened the curtains and saw an anomalous tableau: the ruined city as backdrop to a massive blue swimming pool, frequented by 'fat tanned white-haired men with stretch marks and beautiful women with black one-pieces cut to their hip bones to reveal perfect cheeks, tanned and glimmering'. This was Beirut, a playground for wealthy Gulf Arabs, a place of both chadors and bikinis, a city where the region's sects and religions had been blown apart and roughly reassembled like crazy paving, mismatched and broken.

The destructive energy of a dozen or more Middle Eastern conflicts was concentrated in these few square miles. At the heart was the battle between Palestinians and Jews for control of Israel, to the south. In 1982, Israeli forces had invaded Lebanon to push out the Palestinian

Liberation Organisation, which had been carrying out terror attacks against Israeli targets across the world. Although the PLO leader, Yasser Arafat, and his closest associates, had left Beirut, the Israelis had remained, allying themselves with armed Lebanese Christians. Iran and Syria, both ardently anti-Israeli, sponsored two local militia, Hizbollah and Amal, both comprised of members of the minority Shi'ite Muslim sect. It was Hizbollah that had attacked the US Marines, who had been in Beirut to monitor the PLO withdrawal, and who were hated across the region as allies of the Zionists. Lebanon's Sunni Muslims also formed armed groups, as did the Druze, a minority Muslim sect. Alliances shifted all the time, territory was won and lost, and outsiders found it increasingly hard to fathom who was fighting whom, let alone why.

Abed drove Marie to the headquarters of various armed groups to get press passes, all the while explaining the geography of war. 'This is Amal controlled, this area is Hizbollah – see that woman?' Marie spotted a young woman in a red beret toting aloft a machine gun. 'She is well known in Beirut, she drove her car into an Israeli post,' said Abed. Before they had finished their sandwiches in a café on the corniche, Abed jumped up. 'Okay, we're going,' he said abruptly and pushed Marie into the car. He had seen a man who might have been sizing her up for kidnapping. 'I don't like it when a person walks by first away from me, then back toward me, then away again,' he explained. They drove off past three small boys squabbling over an open flick knife.

Marie conducted interviews with politicians and militia leaders, crossing the Green Line, the informal border that separated East from West Beirut, relying on Abed for everything. She made the embarrassing mistake all Western women make once, extending her hand to shake that of a pious Muslim man, only to see him to bow slightly and place his hand over his heart. Abed explained that the man would touch only women within his family. Amongst the press corps, the talk was all of kidnappings. David Hirst, the *Guardian* correspondent, said that the idea of spending two years chained to a radiator had given him the strength to fight his way out of a car he'd been bundled into the previous week. 'If I'd been James Bond I'd have done it differently,' he said. Kidnapping was not the only danger, of course. Asked if Beirut made him depressed, Jim Muir, the tall, blond, ascetic-looking BBC correspondent, listed the friends who had died in the previous few months. Next to such battle-hardened journalists, Marie felt young and inexperienced. They taught her never to say 'Israel' but 'Dixie', in case spies or stray militiamen heard her discussing the reporters' frequent travel to the Jewish State, which could make them a target. She slept with her window open to hear the shelling, her short-wave radio tuned to the BBC World Service, in case news broke in the middle of the night. She was picking up the habits of the war reporter.

Filing for a Sunday newspaper, she realised, was very different from working for a wire service. She relished the fact that she no longer had to stay close to a phone or telex, because she didn't need to send copy every time she got a snippet of news. She had thought it would be great to interview people at length, to spend time and understand things in detail. But the need to be first with the news was now replaced by the pressure to be original. As she had a full week to find a story, her editors expected something exclusive that they couldn't read on the wire or in the daily papers. Her first despatch was from the port city of Tyre, where a UN force was trying to keep the peace between the Israelis, who occupied part of the area, and sundry militia. Amal and Hizbollah both said their main enemy was Israel but they were too busy fighting each other to take on the Israelis effectively. Posters of Ayatollah Khomeini of Iran were everywhere; fanaticism was on the rise. Marie's attempts at explaining the constellation of militia groups were confusing but the story came to life when she wrote about people she had met.

Sunday Times, Tyre, 28th September 1986
On the way back to Beirut from Tyre, I gave a ride to a young Amal fighter, Neemeh Ahmad Amin. He proudly lifted his Rambo T-shirt to show eight bullet holes left by an Israeli machine gun. 'Rambo was just a movie,' he said. 'We are the real Rambos.'

In the US, Marie would never have been allowed to write in the first person. American editors insisted on phrases such as, 'this reporter saw' or 'a reporter saw' rather than 'I saw'. British newspaper writing was less formal. Stuck between her American training and the new more conversational style, Marie felt insecure. After filing the Tyre story, she decided she hated what she had written. 'Maybe I can't write anymore. I just didn't pull it together,' she thought. Drinking late, sleeping three hours and getting up early to write just before the deadline, she had not left herself enough time to perfect her prose. She remembered David Blundy, late at night in Tripoli, scribbling the structure of his piece in his notebook. She envied the lightness of touch with which he wrote. The following Friday night, with four hours to deadline, she stuffed herself on fruit, whiskey, wine, cheese and hummus. When she eventually filed her story, she hated it. The next day the *Sunday Times* said the telex hadn't got through; she had missed the deadline. She was distraught.

At night she dreamt sometimes of David and sometimes of Katrina, the people she loved and admired most. At last she was living the life she had craved, but she was full of doubt that she was up to the task.

* * * * *

Marie had had little time to settle in David's flat in Highgate, north London, because she was on the road so much of the time. In December 1986, Saddam Hussein's government invited a small group of reporters to see how Iraq was winning the war with the Islamic Republic of Iran. In fact, neither country would prevail, but after six brutal years the Iraqis had recently repulsed an Iranian incursion into the Fao peninsula to the south-east of the city of Basra, so they felt confident enough to take foreigners to see their fixed positions. This would be Marie's first experience of conventional warfare.

One of the other reporters in the pack was a correspondent for the *Daily Telegraph*. Patrick Bishop had until recently worked for the *Sunday Times*. He had spotted Marie when she first arrived in London but his attempt at chatting her up over the photocopier had been less than successful. 'She was polite but distant, to say the least,' he recalls. Patrick, then thirty-four, was also from Irish Catholic stock, but quite the proper Englishman – an Oxford graduate with tousled dark hair and crinkly eyes, given to wearing a rumpled jacket over his jeans. Having covered the Falklands War, Patrick fancied himself as a bit of a military expert, which he thought might come in handy for impressing Marie.

Once in Baghdad, Marie and Patrick were amongst about a dozen reporters escorted to Basra, where they were briefed by Saddam Hussein's generals, before being taken by road to the front line. The two armies had dug in on either side with several hundred yards of no man's land in between. Muddy trenches were wreathed in barbed wire, heavy armour lined up behind – it looked like a scene from the battle of the Somme. 'We will kill anyone who comes to our land,' the Iraqi soldiers said to the reporters, obediently following the script laid down by their superiors. 'We are so happy to kill all Iranians.' Rows of barefoot Iranian prisoners of war, many with bandaged shrapnel wounds, some of them teenagers who had been sent in Ayatollah Khomeini's 'human waves', were made to kneel down on the road for the journalists to inspect. The French TV correspondent demanded to see bodies. The German journalist kept muttering darkly about Iraqi 'secret weapons'. Patrick, ever the boy reporter, was explaining for Marie's benefit the difference between a Soviet-made T-55 tank and the more up-to-date T-72 model, as the thud of shelling continued some distance away.

'A lot of banging goes on, but mostly it's not dangerous,' he reassured her. 'You have to know the difference between outgoing and incoming fire.' It was all outgoing, he explained until he heard a louder crash. 'But that's incoming!' he yelled as he dived for the ground. The shell was, indeed, incoming but had landed half a mile away. Patrick was the only person grovelling in the dirt. Marie stood there, seemingly unfazed, looking down at him quizzically as he scrambled up and brushed himself off. 'I thought, I've had it now,' he recalls. 'No chance of impressing her after this. So for the rest of the trip I was having these fantasies that maybe with any luck the jeep we're in will be hit and I'll be able to drag her from the flaming wreckage!'

Like Patrick, the Iraqi soldiers appeared overwhelmed by an unstoppable male urge to show off in front of women. The moment they saw Marie and the other female journalist in the group, the gunners in the heavy machine-gun division, who had been sitting quietly in their fixed positions watching battery-powered TVs and smoking, started firing. The Iranians, a few hundred yards away, fired back and for a few minutes it appeared that the presence of two women had reignited the war in an area that had been quiet for months. 'Everyone else stiffened and thought this was an alarming development but Marie didn't seem bothered,' remembers Patrick.

Marie and Patrick celebrated New Year's Eve with a couple of American reporters at a vast dance hall in Basra where Iraqi soldiers on furlough mingled with belly dancers and prostitutes. Loud music blasted out and everyone joined in the dancing and drinking. Relieved simply to be alive, the Iraqis were letting off steam, and welcomed foreigners in their midst. As midnight was about to strike, everyone rose, but instead of singing a traditional Iraqi song or 'Auld Lang Syne', for some reason no one could explain the crowd burst into an enthusiastic rendition of 'Happy Birthday to You'. Convulsed with laughter and on the brink of falling in love, Marie and Patrick sang along. Why not? It was a wonderful, weird beginning to 1987.

* * * * *

Being a female journalist in the Middle East had its advantages. Marie became fast friends with Lamis Andoni, a Palestinian American reporter, who was also on the trip to Iraq. Although the same age as Marie, Lamis was sometimes mistaken for a teenager, because of her slight build and sweet face framed by dark hair. People who read her byline frequently assumed she was a man, because it didn't occur to them that a woman – especially an Arab woman – might be reporting from the frontline. Lamis explained to Marie that the Middle East was a land of families and tribes where a lone woman was regarded as a curiosity. 'They think I'm just a cutie-pie going around. Arab women have to work harder to get respect,' she said. She advised Marie to dress conservatively and talk about her family. The only problem with being female, Lamis told her, was that if you got a good interview, people would accuse you of sleeping with someone to get it. Still, Arab men often felt protective of women reporters, invited them to tea and talked more freely than they might with a man.

In early January the Iranians began a fresh assault on Basra. Night after night the city was shelled as the residents cowered in basements after dark and tried to leave by whatever transport they could find in the morning. Much to their frustration, the journalists were confined to Baghdad, watched over by Ministry of Information minders who had been instructed not to let them get wind of any Iranian success on the battlefield. Rumours of Basra's fall began to circulate but no one could confirm it. Lamis had an idea: maybe if they dressed like Iraqi women, she and Marie could catch a train to Basra and see what was going on. Marie, who spoke no Arabic, would have to remain silent, but that was okay, Lamis had Iraqi relatives and more or less spoke the dialect so she would do the talking. Marie thought it a brilliant plan. As the cold of the Baghdad night clung to the concrete city, the two women dressed warmly in sweaters and long, dark skirts and stuffed a few belongings into small handbags of the type Iraqi women carried. Marie pinned a headscarf tightly over her curls and, before dawn, she and Lamis sneaked out of the hotel.

Lamis, unfortunately, had lost her voice, so was not sounding as confident as she had hoped. They took a taxi to the station, bought tickets to Basra and jumped on the first train, but as it pulled out of the station, the other passengers all yelled, 'Get off!' Lamis and Marie realised they were on a train full of soldiers heading for the front, so they had to hop off. The next train was crowded and lively, and of course, handbags and headscarves notwithstanding, people could tell there was something different about them. Lamis stuck to her cover story. 'I'm travelling to Kuwait, we're going back to my family,' she croaked in her hoarse voice. The other passengers looked suspiciously at the tall, slim woman beside her. 'Is she foreign?' they asked. 'Oh yeah, she's my sister-in-law, married to my brother,' said Lamis. Marie couldn't understand a word of the conversation but was impressed by Lamis's innocent-looking face. She was a good liar, Marie thought, and that was essential if they were going to succeed.

The train chugged slowly through the desert, past rows of ragged date palms and small nondescript settlements of cement houses until they drew into Basra, quiet in the afternoon. Few cars, let alone taxis, were on the road, but Lamis managed to flag down an empty bus. The driver stared at her in disbelief when she said they wanted to go downtown. 'You're crazy! Who goes into the city?' he said. 'Everybody is leaving or in hiding.' Lamis invented a story about looking for her son, and eventually the driver agreed to drop them somewhere near the Sheraton Hotel, the only place they could think of as a destination, and which happened to be on Shatt al-Arab, the waterway which marked the front line. Deserted, rubble-strewn streets passed by the window as the driver quizzed the tiny woman with the funny accent, and her silent companion. What were they really doing there? The government had told Iraqis to trust no one because Iranian spies could be planted anywhere. In the end he pulled up to the side of a potholed street. 'You girls are crazy. I don't believe you,' he said. 'Get out.' So there they were in the middle of Basra at dusk, alone and unprotected, waiting for the shelling to start.

After about 15 minutes, the first rockets crashed around them. Luckily a businessman who had been sleeping in his office took pity and ushered them into his basement. 'I think this is how Germany must have felt in the last days of the Second World War,' he said. Eventually, they made it to the Sheraton. Burnt-out cars littered the road leading up to the hotel. The hotel windows had been shattered and the swimming pool was full of shrapnel and rubble from a recent strike on a nearby bar. A dead horse lay next to a bomb crater. The guards outside looked incredulous when Lamis said they wanted a room for the night, and took them to the basement where the Swiss manager and other hotel staff were sheltering.

'Ah, you're the journalists,' they said. 'The army is looking for you.'

The military allowed them to stay the night – there was really no choice. At one point a shell slammed into the hotel but by good fortune did not explode. The next morning Marie and Lamis returned to the station, which was heaving with soldiers and refugees, kitbags, suitcases and crying children piled up on the platforms, but there was no sign of a train. Eventually, Lamis agreed to pay a man who was driving towards Baghdad to take them. The hotel had nothing to eat but uncooked white beans so she and Marie were delighted to stop at a kebab stall where bus drivers ate, before jumping into the car. Luckily soldiers at the checkpoints didn't usually ask for women's papers, and it was deemed rude to peer too closely at a man's female relatives inside a vehicle, so Marie and Lamis shrank down into the back seat, scarves across their faces, and no one asked about them. The first driver arrived at his destination and passed them on to another until, eventually, they found themselves back in Baghdad, bone-tired, buzzing with adrenalin, but safe and with a story that no other journalist had been able to get.

Sunday Times, Basra, 25th January 1987
In Basra, they say the day belongs to Iraq; the night to Iran. Iraq's second city is under siege, and Iranian shells slammed into houses for the 17th successive day yesterday … Everywhere there are tales of tragedy. One soldier was crying as he described how three friends had gone out to telephone home when the bombardment appeared to ease on Wednesday. All three were killed by a shell.

In a piece about being a female correspondent, Marie described the trip in a matter-of-fact way:

Sunday Times, Basra, 1st February 1987
When the shells started falling in Basra and I had no cover, I just felt stupid for getting myself into yet another mess – that this time I might have gone too far. The fear hits later, you really

do get weak in your legs. But we got the story that the town was besieged but not falling. And we got into the city because we were women, and routinely subject to less scrutiny … Lamis and I were congratulated on our return by the male members of the press corps. We had got a good old-fashioned scoop, and there's no question, you use any means you can to do so.

Lamis has a different recollection. She says that the male reporters scolded them for 'queering the pitch' for everyone, grumbling about 'feminine wiles' as if no male reporter had ever taken advantage of journalism's old boy network or the assumptions contacts might make because of their gender. Marie either believed or found it politic to say there was no issue.

The Iraqi officials were furious that two reporters had slipped their grasp – for ministry minders, losing a reporter was potentially a sacking offence. Marie and Lamis were not allowed to leave the country, and feared being imprisoned. News of their misdemeanour went up the chain and came to the attention of an important visitor: Yasser Arafat. Lamis took Marie along to meet the PLO Chairman, whom she knew well, and managed to convince him that he should put in a good word for them with the government. Theirs was a positive news story, one that dispelled damaging rumours of Basra's fall. It worked. Marie was allowed to fly to Kuwait for the Arab League Summit, while Lamis left on Arafat's plane.

Marie exhaled. She had got away with it.

* * * * *

More than 300 operations were carried out under general anaesthesia, the remainder under local or without anaesthesia. The overall operative mortality was 3.2 per cent. Despite the deprivation, many patients survived severe and complicated wounds because they were quickly brought to the hospital, provided with adequate quantities of fresh blood for transfusion, and sound surgical principles were followed.

Dr Pauline Cutting's academic paper 'Surgery in a Palestinian Refugee Camp' gives the dry facts and figures of the courageous, terrifying work that she and her colleagues carried out amongst Palestinians in Beirut for two years from 1985. For a few months in early 1987 the story riveted the British public. Since the founding of the state of Israel in 1948, the refugees had lived in a square kilometre called Bourj al-Barajneh in southern Beirut. The word 'camp' was a misnomer, employed by both the Palestinians and their Lebanese hosts to indicate that this was only temporary and that one day – *inshallah* – the refugees would return to the homes from which the Israelis had driven them. The last of the tents had been removed in the 1960s to be replaced by two- or three-storey breeze block houses separated by winding alleyways fringed by open drainage channels flowing with filthy water and sewage. Fighters from Yasser Arafat's PLO lived amongst the civilians. It was an overcrowded shanty, where people lived in poverty and now in fear.

Since October 1986 Bourj al-Barajneh and other camps had been besieged by the Shi'ite militia, Amal, which Marie had come across on her first trip to Lebanon. The 'War of the Camps' was a conflict within the wider war in Lebanon. Amal controlled several suburbs of south and west Beirut. As an anti-Israeli force, it was broadly pro-Palestinian. However, its main backer, Syrian President Hafez al-Assad, wanted to control the Palestinians. The armed men within the camp remained loyal to the PLO leader, even though he had been forced out of Lebanon several years earlier. Assad wanted to replace the camp leadership with Palestinians loyal to him, and Amal was his tool.

Most British newspaper readers had long ago given up on the internecine complexity of Lebanon's civil war, but it was easy to grasp the fact that an English surgeon, Pauline Cutting, and a Scottish nurse, Suzy Wighton, had volunteered to live in this hell, sending out regular bulletins and cries for help by radio-phone. They described 15,000 people on the brink of starvation, children reduced to eating cats and dogs, women being shot by snipers and their own desperate attempts to save lives. A team from ITV's *News At Ten* had managed to sneak in and film children crossing no man's land under sniper fire to bring medical supplies into the camp. It was dramatic, heart-rending stuff but no other foreign correspondent had managed to penetrate the siege. The British doctor and nurse had become the sole source of information for the outside world.

In March, Marie returned to Beirut with the photographer Tom Stoddart. At first they tried to talk their way into Bourj al-Barajneh, with no success. Eventually, they located an Amal commander who was susceptible to bribery. If they paid him a few hundred dollars, he would order his men to hold fire for the one minute it would take Tom and Marie to run across no man's land and into the camp. He would do the same 24 hours later, so they could run back along the same route.

Tom was only three years older than Marie, but more experienced in war zones. They talked about the danger. On the one hand they had secured a way in. On the other, they couldn't inform the Palestinians of their arrival, so there was the possibility that even if Amal didn't shoot them, the PLO might. They knew it was possible to get in – and, equally important, to get out – because the TV team had done it, but they decided not to consult the *Sunday Times* foreign desk on their plan, because they expected they would be told it was too dangerous. Back and forth they went, trying to assess the risk. Tom knew this trip might yield extraordinary pictures. Marie had a burning urge to tell the story of the siege, and to prove herself – to her editors, to her peers, to herself. So they decided to go for it.

Abed, the driver Marie had worked with on her first trip, took them to the edge of the camp, north-east of the airport. In the early afternoon, at the exact time agreed upon with the Amal commander, they made a dash for it. In the minute it took to cross the desolate landscape, it felt as if time had stood still. Deserted tower blocks surrounded the camp with Amal snipers perched like malevolent falcons at the windows. 'It was terrifying,' recalls Tom. 'We had to run about 50 metres across exposed open ground. We held hands so if one was shot the other could drag them to safety.' It would have been easy to trip and fall on the damp, red earth, studded with tussocks of grass.

'Not far now. Keep going ... nearly there,' they gasped as they ran, their own rasping breaths loud in their ears.

The Palestinians had built up earthworks to protect the camp. Breathless, Marie and Tom crested the berm and ran straight into a unit of PLO fighters. Luckily they were not on guard but sitting around drinking tea. Amazed that two journalists had taken such a risk, they guided Marie and Tom to the offices of Fatah, Arafat's faction of the PLO, which sent a message to Pauline who rushed from the hospital with Suzy. Pauline was skinny, exhausted and fraught from months under siege. She had rings from sleepless nights around her dark eyes and her hair hung straight and stringy down her cheeks. Her world had shrunk to the confines of the camp, and she was struck by how well these envoys from the outside world looked in comparison to her and everyone around her. 'Marie was vibrant and bubbly and had an extraordinary presence about her,' she remembers. 'She was likeable and funny and interested in everybody she met.' Red-headed Suzy, always coughing from an undiagnosed ailment, thought the journalists looked 'high on adrenalin and anxiety'. As a young Western woman, blown in from the world beyond the siege, Marie became an object of great attention as she and Tom were led through the broken concrete labyrinth, past houses wrecked by battle, their facades crumbling, windows broken, walls scarred by bullets, rockets and grenades. They picked their way along the edge of bomb craters, skirting open sewers and broken water pipes, passing children playing in the rubble, old men in chequered keffiyeh headdresses and stalls selling a few miserable vegetables.

The top two floors of Haifa Hospital had collapsed under Amal shelling, so the staff, including Pauline, worked and slept in the basement. By day, they stacked up the mattresses to make room for patients. Rain leaked through the roof and ran down the stairs; the windows, which were all broken, had been sandbagged. A mountain of garbage and hospital waste had accumulated outside, attracting rats. Pauline, the only qualified surgeon, led a team of six Palestinian doctors. They and the nurses, foreign and Palestinian, struggled to deal with diseases of poverty and hunger as well as the daily gunshot and shrapnel wounds. They were also in great danger themselves. Pauline had received death threats. Amal militiamen would shout across the front line that they were going to starve the camp and then storm in and slaughter everyone. Foreigners would not be spared.

Someone found some tinned fish and tomatoes and cheese but, reluctant to eat scarce supplies, Tom and Marie said they weren't hungry and ate no more than a few mouthfuls. Just before they went to bed the camp was shaken by a huge explosion accompanied by a red flash – a crude TNT bomb thrown in by besieging militiamen. Suzy clutched Marie by the jacket; she was battle hardened but this one had made everyone jump. Tom slept inside the hospital in a room running with rats, while Marie went with Suzy to stay at the house of a nearby family, who plied them with sweet tea. The two young women stayed up late as Suzy told Marie about life in the camp: how the wife of Mustafa, the young man in whose house they were staying, had been shot, how two of his brothers had been hit by shrapnel as a mortar impacted just outside their house, how the pregnant women would run to avoid bullets.

They woke at 7 a.m., after light, much to Marie's annoyance, as she had wanted to be out by six to watch the Palestinian women set off down what had become known as the 'Path of Death'. Every morning just after dawn women would dash down the track, running the gaunt-let of Amal snipers positioned above, to buy food outside the camp. It was a game of Russian roulette. Sometimes the snipers shot the women when they tried to leave. At others they let the women leave, but stole the food from them as they tried to get back in. And when they felt like it, the snipers allowed the women to go and buy the food and then picked them off on their return.

Marie refused breakfast in her haste. Suzy wrote in her diary: 'Marie chafing to find Tom and stomping on up the road when Mustafa stopped to find out how many had been injured at the exit. She continued to march on up the road as greetings were exchanged, and both Mustafa and I signalled to each other that she may get shot doing that.' Eventually, they found Tom and reached a place where they could watch the terri-fied women rushing down the track. A hundred yards away they saw a traffic jam along the airport road. That was the war in Beirut – utter terror juxtaposed with the banality of everyday life.

Suddenly a commotion broke out: a woman had been shot. Haji Achmed Ali lay bleeding in the dirt some 20 metres from the relative safety of the camp. Despite being hit in the head and the abdomen, she was still alive, feebly moving her arms. The men tossed out a rubber hose for her to grasp so they could pull her in but she couldn't reach it. Others talked of staging a firefight as a diversion, but they knew Amal was wise to that trick and would probably shoot again. The young woman lay there for half an hour, in the stultifying heat. Suddenly, three other women with sacks of food appeared at the far end of the 'Path of Death' and – ignoring the cries of the crowd that they should take cover – ran screaming into the camp.

Sunday Times, Beirut, 5th April 1987
Their terror broke the stalemate. It is the women who are dying and it was women who tired of men's inaction. Two raced from cover, plucked Achmed Ali from the dust and hauled her to safety. She was tumbled onto a stretcher and carried through the streets to the camp hospital … a man ran alongside the stretcher, with his hand on her face to staunch the blood flowing from the bullet hole near her nose.

'She looked dead when I got to her: dilated fixed pupils, blood everywhere, over her face and thighs,' wrote Suzy in her diary. At the hospital, Pauline and the other staff were ready but there was little they could do. Marie looked on, one hand over her mouth, as they wiped away the blood and dirt and tried to resuscitate the young woman using a manual respirator. She had never seen anything like this before. She observed the scene and took notes. 'You could see the shock in her face, but she was very calm,' recollects Tom. 'I didn't detect any fear in her.'

Sunday Times, Beirut, 5th April 1987
Though her hair was clotted with blood, Haji Achmed Ali seemed younger now that she had been cleaned. Her body was soft and shapely. She wore two tiny gold earrings. Someone opened her fist and cleaned out the handful of blood-soaked dirt she had clenched in her pain.

The hospital didn't have enough fuel for an operation, so a group of women took the unconscious young woman by stretcher to the edge of the camp to flag down a car on the airport road so she could be treated at a better equipped hospital in the city. Yet Pauline knew it was a hopeless case. 'Her brains are out. She's going to die,' she said. Fifteen women had lost their lives this way; 22-year-old Haji Achmed Ali would be the sixteenth. She explained to Marie that the angle of the bullets' entry proved that she was shot from above, where Amal had positions, not from inside the camp – anti-Palestinian propaganda always said that the PLO shot their own people. While Pauline had been trying to save the young woman's life, Suzy had been writing a letter to the Queen. 'Every day we hope that this day there will be no more injured, but already before 7.30 a.m. one woman was shot in both legs. As I write this, an explosion has occurred 100 yards away from me – some sort of rocket, I think, and 120mm mortars,' she wrote. 'Please, if you can exert any influence to halt this, even just to allow the International Red Cross into the camp to bring medicines and evacuate the wounded we would be most grateful.'

Marie interviewed more patients in the hospital, including another woman who had a broken femur, and was speaking vehemently and gesturing with her arms.

'What's the matter with her?' Marie asked Pauline, who was translating from Arabic.

'She wants you to tell the world her story,' said Pauline.

It was time to leave. Marie hid the letter to the Queen and Tom's film in her underwear, and they ran for it. The Amal commander and Abed were waiting for them on the other side. To Marie and Tom's relief, the commander didn't search them or ask questions about what they had been doing. He had his money and just wanted them to leave. He did, however, give them the benefit of his opinion, telling Marie that his men were entirely innocent, and that the stories of women being shot were just Palestinian propaganda. Abed drove them across the Green Line to Christian-held East Beirut and they left that night for Cyprus. Marie wrote furiously on the ferry. She knew this was the most important story of her life so far. Her description of the killing of the young woman, and Tom's pictures, would have an impact.

That Sunday the paper splashed her story across the front page under the headline 'War on Women'. The piece began:

Sunday Times, Beirut, 5th April 1987
She lay where she had fallen, face down on the dirt path leading out of Bourj al-Barajneh. Haji Achmed Ali, 22, crumpled as the snipers' bullets hit her in the face and stomach. She had tried to cross the no man's land between the Palestinian camp and the Amal militiamen besieging it to buy food for her family ...

The facts were clear and brutal – no hedging or sourcing as Marie had seen it with her own eyes. She told the story not just of the woman who had been killed but of others who had been injured, adding: 'The war on women includes Dr Cutting. Amal has passed death threats to her.'

'She knew the story was not about fighting, nor about politics and the Palestinian question but about women being murdered,' says Tom. 'The girl who died – her name was up front. It was very personal.' Three days later, Syrian forces took up positions around Bourj al-Barajneh and ordered their proxy, Amal, to stop sniping. The following day the International Committee of the Red Cross was allowed into the camp, bringing several more journalists with them. The militia was ordered back. In a few days the 'War of the Camps' was over.

It is impossible to say whether it was the *Sunday Times* story that brought to an end the 163-day siege of Bourj al-Barajneh, but the story was undoubtedly part of the mounting pressure on President Assad.

His plan for Amal to break the PLO, first by besieging the camps, then by occupying them, had been thwarted. The Lebanon War's calculus of cruelty was worked out far from the dingy, battle-scarred alleyways of Beirut. Assad was in turn sponsored by the Soviets, and Mikhail Gorbachev, the then Soviet leader, was susceptible to Western pressure. The *Sunday Times* was an influential newspaper. 'I think it was the most important story I ever did,' says Tom, who in a career of nearly five decades went on to take pictures in Bosnia and many other war zones. 'Those six frames of the girl lying on the path made a huge difference. It was one of the few times where being in the right place at the right time with a great reporter convinced people. It was tangible. It stopped the siege and saved lives.'

A few weeks later, Marie and Tom went to see Pauline, now safely at home with her parents in Maidenhead. 'We owed them a great debt of gratitude. I think they helped save our lives,' Pauline says. 'I think without the story coming to the fore, the camp was going to be overrun and everyone killed.'

The 24 hours she spent in Bourj al-Barajneh had a huge effect on Marie. The image of the young woman lying on the path, her lifeblood seeping into the dirt, never left her. Haji Achmed Ali had reminded her of Cat – the earrings she had noticed were similar to a pair she had given her younger sister. Years later she would talk about that day in the camp, and about the horror and fear she saw amongst the Palestinians there. She was proud of her story, believing that it had made a difference. As a Sunday newspaper journalist she had the time to get right into the middle of whatever situation she was reporting on, a variation on the famous war photographer Robert Capa's maxim, 'If your pictures aren't good enough, you're not close enough.' Other journalists might remain at the margins, filing from relative safety, but not Marie – she would get up close. She would not write about herself, but her journalism would be distinguished by the intensity of her personal experience.

* * * * *

Marie was now a fixture in the nomadic family of journalists covering the Middle East: war between Iran and Iraq, the eccentric exploits of Colonel Gaddafi, kidnappings in Lebanon and the growing conflict between Israel and the Palestinians. Many reporters had retreated to Cyprus after Beirut became too dangerous. Colleagues from London and Paris would join them there, drinking and talking, usually while waiting for a hostage release. But their favourite place was the American Colony in Jerusalem, a rambling Ottoman-era palace with thick, pale peach-coloured stone walls, which had been bought by a utopian Christian community in the nineteenth century and later converted into a hotel. Val Vester, an Englishwoman who married into the family who owned the Colony, had moved there with her husband in 1963. Her aunt was the First World War era British diplomat and archaeologist Gertrude Bell, so she had her own history in the region, and she continued to run the hotel after her husband's death. She was proud of its reputation as a neutral place, situated on the Green Line between Palestinian East and Jewish West Jerusalem. Marie loved to sit and read in the Colony's shady courtyard, with its orange trees and pots of geraniums, where T. E. Lawrence and Graham Greene had also found refuge from the heat and bustle outside. She and Val, then in her seventies, became friends. Journalists were on first name terms with the Palestinian staff and everyone knew Ibrahim Zeghari, the barman. Marie loved the camaraderie of the Colony's half-lit below-stairs bar – between the courtyard and the pool, warmed by an open fire in winter, always cool in summer – an exotic version of the Lion's Head in the Village, back in New York.

Whenever Marie was in London, Patrick Bishop courted her assiduously. He admired her ambition and sharp mind, and how she never turned down a challenge. She, in turn, admired his writing, the way he could conjure a phrase or a sentence with an elegance that often eluded her. His dry, clever British wit made her laugh, and he had a certain gentlemanly charm. He loved her American 'peppiness' as he put it, the way she threw herself into reporting or a dinner party or anything she found fun. If he thought of an idea for a holiday or a story, she would rev him up and make it happen. Some of her *joie de vivre* rubbed off on him. He knew about history and painting and all the cultural things that mattered to her, quite apart from the fellow feeling they got from being on the same beat as journalists. They would spend their evenings sparring about books and politics, sometimes just the two of them, sometimes with friends. It was liberating for Marie to be with someone who shared her sense of adventure, but with whom she felt secure. Part of that may have been because they had similar backgrounds. His father had also been in the military. Both had four siblings and came from middle-class families who placed a strong emphasis on education and aspiration. She came from a suburb of New York, he from a suburb of London. Both had acquired an elite education through intelligence, hard work and the social mobility of their time.

She thought about her previous lovers: the older men she had surpassed, Gerry Weaver who had never loved her, John Rhodes who was so suitable yet never made her catch fire. Patrick was her equal. She knew that with their similar dark curls and green eyes they looked quite dashing together – the kind of young couple you notice walking arm in arm along the street or sitting at a bar. He was a romantic figure in her mind – a handsome man, a writer and an intellectual, but with an elusive quality. He said he loved her, but on some level he was unavailable. After a while, she decided that their relationship should be exclusive. 'I can't sleep with you, I'm in love with someone new,' she told a boyfriend in Jerusalem as she kissed him one last time before skipping back to London. As a Brit, Patrick seemed rather repressed to her American way of thinking, but he was also Irish in a familiar way, and he loosened up after a drink or two. 'We shared that conviviality, the corny things attributed to Irish Catholics that are largely true,' remembers Patrick.

The couple were frequently to be found at the Groucho Club, which had opened a couple of years earlier in Soho as a haunt for writers, actors and other creative types who eschewed London's stuffy Gentlemen's Clubs but wanted a venue to drink and talk and put the world to rights.

Their other haunt was 192, a Notting Hill restaurant that had become popular with film stars and the media crowd. Both places had been founded by the architect Tchaik Chassay and his wife, the interior designer Melissa North, who quickly absorbed Marie into their social sphere. With her gift for friendship and her boundless social appetite Marie could have been at parties and dinners every night of the week. 'London fell in love with her,' says Emma Duncan, another journalist. 'She had this vigour, this palpable life force.' Olivia Stewart, a film-maker, remembers Marie as 'enormous fun – you were dragged along to everything. She extended that feeling you have at university with the gang, the parties, the high jinx.' On one occasion, she recalls, Marie even got one of her *Sunday Times* editors to do backflips over the sofa.

When Katrina came to London to visit, she found Patrick charming. 'He seemed fascinated by Marie,' she recalls. 'Not being an American, there was a certain glamour about him and they appeared extremely compatible.' London friends, though, knew that behind the charm, Patrick could be feckless. He had nearly married at least once, but hadn't been able to muster the commitment. Still, if anyone could get him to settle down, it would be Marie, and the couple were clearly besotted with each other. Oscillating between London and the Middle East, comfortable in both places, Marie began to harbour dreams – maybe Patrick was the kind of man she had longed for when she and Katrina were at Yale, a man who understood her need for independence, but with whom she could put down roots and have a family.

* * * * *

On 8 December 1987, an Israeli truck crashed into a queue of cars in the Gaza Strip, killing four Palestinians. The next day demonstrations erupted – Palestinians believed it was no accident but collective punishment, retaliation for the stabbing of an Israeli a few days earlier. Israeli paratroopers were sent to Gaza but the young men of the refugee camps felt they had nothing to lose and refused to surrender. Tension had been building for years, as Israel took more Palestinian land for Jewish settlements, and the Palestinian leadership, exiled in Tunis, jetted around the globe denouncing Israel rather than address-ing the needs of youths who had been born in camps in the Occupied Territories. The youths met Israeli bullets with stones, and rioting spread to the occupied West Bank. The first Palestinian uprising or intifada had begun.

Marie and Patrick, now very definitely a couple although not living together, spent that Christmas in London, and New Year on a beach holiday in Trinidad. By the time they returned it was apparent that the crisis in the Middle East was going to be headline news for the year to come. The *Sunday Times* was happy for Marie to move to Jerusalem, where Patrick had just been appointed the *Daily Telegraph* Middle East correspondent. Marie was thrilled: not only would she be at the heart of the story, but she was with the man she was now sure she loved. In Jerusalem, she found a small nineteenth-century stone house built by the British banker Moses Montefiore in Yemin Moshe, a neighbour-hood of cobbled streets and olive trees on the Green Line, overlooking the Old City. It was a romantic place to live, just down from a windmill Montefiore had also built. By April 1988 they were installed in their new home, as the First Intifada intensified.

Marie's reporting was scrupulously fair and always first hand. She had grown up regarding Palestinians as terrorists. Plane hijackings and other terror attacks were often on the news when she was a child, and her grandmother had dithered about a trip to the Holy Land – as she called it – in 1974 after two massacres at Jewish settle-ments in the West Bank. In a 1979 diary, Marie had mentioned a press conference in which Arafat declared support for the Iranian Revolution. She saw it as 'weird' that 'modern, civilised 6 o'clock news is filmed at terrorist headquarters'. But now, having spent time with Lamis, a fierce advocate of the Palestinian cause, and having seen for herself the suffering of Palestinians in the refugee camps of Beirut and under Israeli occupation in the West Bank and Gaza, she had a more nuanced understanding. With no fixed ideology nor political certainties, she quickly overcame any preconceptions she might have harboured.

Most weeks, Marie would spend several days in the West Bank, usually with a photographer or a couple of other reporters, to witness battles between Palestinian youths and the Israel Defense Forces. What was at first alarming soon became routine: Palestinian youths used stones and marbles, often in slingshots, to taunt young Israeli soldiers, who shot back with tear gas and live fire. The Palestinians always came off worse. Funerals would turn into protests and so it would roll on, violence ebbing and escalating, the world transfixed by the desperation of a Palestinian generation who saw no future and an Israeli authority using ever more draconian tactics to maintain control. Through Uzi Mahnaimi, an Israeli journalist based in London for a Hebrew newspaper, Marie had made good government contacts. Some of her best stories came from leaks. One week she investigated a claim that Israeli soldiers had beaten four Palestinian youths senseless and buried them alive, interviewing people exhaustively until she had multiple eyewitness accounts. The next, she got hold of a secret Israeli military report showing that soldiers had been obeying orders to beat Palestinians and break their bones.

The reporters covering the conflict grew accustomed to tear gas and to hiding behind walls to watch the daily battles. In some ways, it was a game and both sides knew the rules. If you shouted 'Sahafi, sahafi!' ('Journalist, journalist!'), the Palestinians would do their best to provide protection. In the pre-internet era, the Palestinians could not communicate directly, and so wanted Western journalists to show the world their situation. The IDF, for its part, would try to deter journalists from going to the West Bank, but they knew they couldn't stop them: the country had a tradition of free speech, allowing the Israeli media and human rights organisations to criticise government policy and the behaviour of the military.

War may be hell, as the cliché has it, but life was fun – at least for Marie and her cohorts. Competitors by day and comrades by night, most of the journalists based in Jerusalem were in their thirties, trying to make a name for themselves, swapping sometimes tall tales of near-misses and derring-do over wine and whiskey in the Colony bar, laughing late into the night, falling into bed with each other, waking ready for another adventure. Marie had started to smoke heavily, partly because it was sociable and partly to stop herself from eating and putting on weight. She was drinking a lot, but who wasn't? With David Blundy now covering the wars in Central America, she made new friends amongst the 'hack pack'. Often she was the only woman in the group, but that just added to the fun. She was more herself than she had ever been – this would remain the part of the world that animated and intrigued her more than any other, and the people she met there would become lifelong friends.

One Thursday Marie and Tim Phelps of the Long Island paper, *Newsday*, drove into the West Bank. Their car had yellow Israeli licence plates but they tried to blend in to avoid trouble, approaching Israeli checkpoints as settlers did with a traditional Jewish kippa on the dashboard, which they replaced with an Arab keffiyeh in Palestinian areas. They made it to the town of Hebron, where Israeli soldiers were trying without success to enforce an all-day curfew. Black smoke from burning tyres was billowing into the air when Marie, in the passenger seat, saw a teenager running out from behind the barricades. A rock suddenly smashed through the windscreen, hitting her in the face and breaking her nose. 'It was one of a dozen such incidents that day,' she wrote somewhat casually in her story for that Sunday. 'It belied the Israeli complaint that journalists create incidents. The boy who threw the stone probably believed he was throwing it at a Jewish settler.'

Tim was solicitous but Patrick, who took Marie to the hospital that evening, was less sanguine, yelling at her that she was stupid for running such risks. He couldn't see why she always had to go to the most dangerous place – ever since they had met in Iraq he had doubted her ability to assess danger. Bravery was one thing, recklessness another. Their relationship was getting rocky. The elusiveness that had attracted her now made her angry. 'You're leading a double life, seeing your friends, playing the happy drinking bachelor to them,' she told him in a diary entry she probably never showed him. 'You want a girlfriend so someone's there when you come home, not someone to share your life with.' Patrick told her he regretted his 'Celtic unrelia-bility', but Marie was unreliable too, often failing to turn up as planned, or arriving several hours late. He was jealous when she stayed out, or seemed too friendly with other men. Both were unfaithful at different times. The attraction was irresistible, but, like magnets, once turned, they repelled each other with equal force. Their professional competi-tion grew bitter. Sometimes he would put her down in public, as if he saw himself as intellectually superior, humiliating her in front of their friends. They would have furious rows; ashtrays would fly. Marie accused him of refusing to talk about their relationship, of seeing eve-rything intellectually, of not loving her enough. 'Mom didn't raise me to be a victim,' she thought. But after the storm had passed, they would make up. A fight followed by a passionate reunion answered Marie's desire for drama and excitement, as if theatrics made for a life less ordinary. For Patrick, it was a Catholic ritual: sin, remorse, confession, repentance and redemption. A pattern had been set.

When Patrick happened to be in New York later that year, Marie got Cat to meet him in a bar. 'All the men wore freshly pressed suits but there was one in a rumply linen jacket so I knew that must be him,' Cat recalls. 'I really liked him a lot.' Marie's mother also met him when she came to Jerusalem on a visit. Initially, Rosemarie was nervous, fearing terror attacks, but after taking a bus tour to Bethlehem with a group of Latin American tourists she was full of how exciting it had been to meet Palestinian Christians. She could see that her daughter loved Patrick and was in her element. Patrick grew to love Rosemarie, seeing her as wise and strong, bearing the burden of the family after Bill had died, but the turbulence between him and Marie never ceased – with him, Marie had sailed into another storm. After a particularly bad row in Jerusalem, she got on a plane to London, saying she had had enough. Full of remorse, he followed her. They went for dinner at 192. As the evening wore on, they drank more wine and all was forgiven. They had been together about two years, but despite the rows, they remained endlessly fascinated with each other, passionately drawn together. They would try again and do it properly this time.

* * * * *

Marie Colvin and Patrick Bishop were married at St Dominic Church, Oyster Bay, on 19 August 1989. She was thirty-three; he was thirty-six. Marie was travelling almost up to the day, so Cat and Rosemarie, with input from Katrina, were left to organise everything according to Marie's instructions. She wanted a reception with a marquee outside on the bay, an oyster bar and a country music band. Cat bought her a veil, but Marie was determined to wear the silk gown her mother had worn to be married to Marie's father. She tried it on only a couple of days before the ceremony, but it fitted perfectly, the scalloped neckline, fitted waist and full-length, flared skirt flattering her long, lean figure. Pure white in her mother's day, the gown had aged to a delicate honey colour. She pinned back her dark curls, placed a string of white pearls round her neck and carried a bouquet of ivory and pink roses. Katrina – whose own marriage had recently collapsed – was matron of honour, while Cat and Boo, Marie's London friends Emma and Olivia, and Patrick's sisters were bridesmaids, wearing calf-length turquoise Laura Ashley dresses patterned with pink flowers in the unflattering fashion of the time. Patrick wore a morning suit with a white rose in his buttonhole. His family flew in from Ireland and Britain. Dozens of Marie's friends and relatives arrived from the US and beyond. Even David Blundy came, and most of the gang from the American Colony in Jerusalem. The reception was held on the lawn of a family friend's house sloping down to the ocean, with waiters bearing oysters on silver platters like something out of *The Great Gatsby*. It looked like the wedding of any middle-class suburban American couple who had splashed out to make the big day perfect.

Why did Marie opt for such a traditional wedding in Oyster Bay, a place that stood for the values she said she despised? 'It was truly an act of faith to marry Patrick,' believes Katrina. 'She threw herself in as only she was capable of doing.' Maybe, in the frenzy of her life in the Middle East, with its thrills and dangers, and the volatile nature of the relationship itself, Marie was trying to recreate something from her past that might provide the security she craved. 'At some level Marie was just an American girl who had those dreams,' says Judy Miller. 'There was part of her that always yearned for that.'

The night before the wedding, Patrick was drunk and maudlin, confiding in his friends that he was not at all sure he was doing the right thing. In his heart he knew that he was not ready for marriage, and was bound to disappoint his bride. 'One of the things that Marie took from her childhood was this memory of a perfect marriage,' he said nearly thirty years later, as he looked back on their life together. 'Her parents were madly in love until the day her father died. After that her mother never looked at another man. It was a pretty high ideal of love and marriage that she got from her upbringing.'

Joe McDermott, Marie's old boss from the Teamsters, was pleased to be invited to the wedding but didn't enjoy the day. 'It was a beautiful wedding but I just couldn't see this surviving. He wasn't impressive. It didn't make sense.' Marie's mother liked Patrick, and felt comfortable with his family, but even she had doubts about what Marie was doing. 'I was surprised she married anybody,' she says. In the British tradition, the best man, Patrick's friend Nick Glass, was affectionately rude about the groom, referring to his 'nomadic circuit of the watering holes of the world', and imagining the happy couple with children – 'an episcopate of little Bishops'. He quipped, 'This at least is one Middle East dispute that's finally been settled.' Then he quoted Yeats, the couple's favourite poet:

I have spread my dreams under your feet,
Tread softly because you tread on my dreams.

The guests drank champagne and danced as the sun set over the bay. Mellow from alcohol and sunshine, they stripped off their clothes to swim, the Americans leaping in naked while the uptight Brits retained their underwear. Marie and Patrick were preparing to honeymoon in Amagansett, on the other side of Long Island; they would spend the

Marie with her father Bill, probably in 1958

JANUARY 2 4

Every one is wearing pants. I've got to talk Mommy into letting me do it, for honor's sake. I'm not sure I want to, but I must.

I am going to tell Mom about the plg. for God.

I saw Jeff today. He saw me, but seemed awkward. I smiled, but no sign of recognition. Wonder why. Wish hed show he likes me. Does h.D.A.R. due tomorrow. On the bus, stood on the stairs. Jeff was on the bus, but didn't see me.

In January 1969, just before her 13th birthday, Marie started to keep a diary. This is her second entry

Marie (third row up, fifth from left), aged seven, in her elementary school photo

Marie's father used this photo in his campaign for local office, 1971.
Left to right: Marie, Michael, Rosemarie, Bill, Cat, Boo, Billy

Before (top) and after (bottom) Marie
went to Brazil, aged seventeen

Marie as a debutante in Brazil with
Oswaldo Bier, 1973

Lack of title represents a last apartm...

"The señoritas want a room? Hotel Grande, señoritas. Muy bueno. The best in the city. Real cheap, señoritas. Special, just for you..."

We descended, exhausted, cramped, still overwhelmed by the smell of the bus packed cattlecar tight with several chickens for passengers, unnerved by hairpin turns taken at 60 by a nodding driver. The usual confused mass which greeted every bus arrival in Mexico surrounded us. From all sides came offers of greasy sausages on street spits, grimy sweets cooked by fat señoras and hawked by their youngest, bedraggled news- papers sold by the original recyclers, the most expensive sleazy hotel rooms in town. All at a specialprice - "For you, only..." Turtlelike with our top-heavy knapsacks, we pushed through the crowd. Jeralyn, my travelling companion, followed listlessly. Drained by the tourists' special affliction, pale, she didn't care where we stayed as long as the bathroom wasn't down the hall.

Mexico on $5 to $10 a Day had long since been discarded. The recommended hotels were defunct or doubled in price, res- taurants were expensive and tourist-filled. Anyway, if we spent that much, we'd have to leave Mexico in two weeks. We were out to see the 'real' Mexico, not the Mexico of the tou- rist brochure with its tanned smiling faces, gleaming umbrella- dotted beaches, and peasants looking poor but proud in color- ful garb that had gone out with Montezuma. The Acapulco Hil- ton was for Americans to meet Americans; you could do that at

An article Marie wrote for John Hersey's class at Yale, 1977. Hersey's comments – 'overpacked phrasing', 'nice touch' – are in pencil in the margins

The staff of the *Yale Daily News Magazine*, 1977. Marie is standing, third from left

Marie sailing off Belize with her lifelong friend Katrina Heron and
Katrina's then boyfriend Chris Bartle, May 1984

At UPI's Washington newsroom, 1985. Lucien Carr is in the
foreground, while Marie types to his left

In August 1989 Marie married Patrick Bishop in Oyster Bay, Long Island

Marie wore her mother's wedding dress to marry Patrick. Katrina was matron of honour,
and the bridesmaids wore exquisitely unflattering Laura Ashley dresses

All her life Marie was famous for giving great, wild parties

Marie and Katrina at Katrina's wedding to Winter Mead, summer 1994

Marie on the beach in Cyprus, 1988

Amman, Jordan, 1991. On the bus out of Baghdad the previous day, Marie overheard a French journalist talking about a lover, and realised this lover was her own husband, Patrick

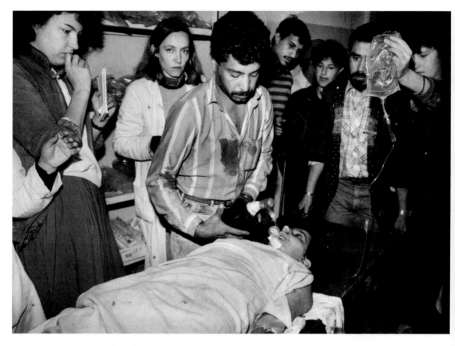

Beirut, 1987. Marie (far left) and Dr Pauline Cutting look on as a Palestinian nurse, Hussein al-Adawi, tries in vain to save the life of Haji Achmed Ali, who was shot by snipers in Bourj al-Barajneh camp

Tunis, 1988. Interviewing the Palestinian leader Yasser Arafat

first day sailing with Marie's old flame, Paddy Sullivan, who had his boat moored at Sag Harbor.

Everyone joined in a rousing chorus of 'Wild Thing' by The Troggs. On Marie's insistence, three times the band played 'Crazy', the Willie Nelson song made famous by Patsy Cline.

> *Crazy, I'm crazy for feeling so lonely*
> *I'm crazy, crazy for feeling so blue*
> *I knew you'd love me as long as you wanted*
> *And then someday you'd leave me for somebody new.*

* * * * *

Chapter 5

IN A MAN'S WORLD

In the eighteen months before her marriage, Marie had been thinking more about the kind of journalism she wanted to do. While Patrick saw himself as a writer on military matters, she wanted to follow in the tradition not just of John Hersey and Martha Gellhorn, both of whom drew out the stories of the victims of war, but also of Oriana Fallaci who had made a career of in-depth interviews with world leaders. Indira Gandhi, the Shah of Iran, Ayatollah Khomeini, Henry Kissinger – Fallaci had interviewed them all. She flattered and charmed her subjects by studying in depth their lives and thoughts, and then relentlessly probed their weak points. Marie was fascinated by Arab dictators who were vilified in the West, curious to understand not just the nature of their power but also what motivated them as people. Having already interviewed Muammar Gaddafi, she turned her attention to the PLO Chairman, Yasser Arafat.

After Lamis had introduced her to Arafat in Baghdad, in the wake of their adventure in Basra, Marie was determined to get to know him. In the US and Britain, he was widely regarded as a terrorist. The news was dominated by the beginning of the end of the Cold War, as Gorbachev introduced policies that hastened the collapse of communism. The Middle East was a sideshow. But Marie saw that as an advantage because the field was not too crowded. It was a prescient decision, enabling her to build up her contacts and make her mark before the fate of Israel and the Palestinians rose to the top of the agenda again.

Arafat rotated between a number of bougainvillea-covered safe houses in Tunisia where he lived in exile, always expecting an Israeli assassination attempt – in 1985 Israel had bombed the PLO headquarters just outside Tunis, hitting his living quarters, but he had been sleeping elsewhere. Marie was often the only woman hanging out with PLO officials at the Tunis Hilton as their wives and children had been despatched to the safety of Kuwait or Cyprus, and very few women had official positions in the organisation. Everyone slept by day because Abu Amar, as Arafat was known, worked at night and frequently summoned his aides at 2 a.m. or later. Marie would join PLO officials and bodyguards, sitting up all night, sipping coffee, smoking endless cigarettes and listening to stories of their former lives in Palestine and Beirut, as well as complaints about Arafat, who drove everyone crazy with his prevarication and his ability to ensure that no one knew quite what he was thinking. Partly for security and partly to keep them all guessing, he rarely scheduled meetings or trips.

On Marie's first visit to Tunis she spent several weeks waiting, seeing one aide and then another, unsure who – if anyone – had the power to decide whether she would get an audience with the Chairman. One of her best contacts was Bassam abu Sharif who had taken part in terrorist attacks while a member of an extremist faction and been severely disfigured by a letter bomb sent by Mossad, the Israeli intelligence agency. The two of them spent many evenings drinking whiskey and talking into the early hours. Waiting for the interview Bassam promised would come in the end, Marie made a half-hearted attempt to learn Arabic and read a lot about the Six Day War of 1967, which had enabled Israel to seize Palestinian land. Eventually one night she got a message: 'Abu Amar wants to see you.' A car was waiting to whisk her through the darkness to the villa where he was working. She walked in through a fug of smoke, past a crowd of uniformed men with machine guns and revolvers at their hips, and into a brightly lit room where she saw 'a small, obsessive figure' with 'bulging eyes behind oversize black-rimmed glasses'. Arafat had five days' beard growth under a prominent lower lip. It was hard to see what made him so powerful, as he had no apparent charisma. 'He sat behind a desk in a scruffy room laden with symbols, rather like a medieval painting,' she wrote later. 'Behind him was a mural of Jerusalem's golden dome of the Haram al-Sharif, the Muslims' third most holy place in the city he claimed as the Palestinian capital.' His desk sported the Palestinian flag and a two foot high pile of papers. The TV in the corner was playing *Tom and Jerry* cartoons.

It would be the first of more than twenty encounters. The Palestinians were always nervous; after all, many of their number had been assassinated by Mossad. Journalists were always suspect. But Marie put in the time so that the officials felt they were friends not just contacts. She had a way of making Arafat feel comfortable, and he liked female company, but that didn't mean she was soft in her interviewing technique. Sometimes her questions angered him but he respected her dedication to learning about the Palestinian cause. Knowing that many Palestinians identified with Irish Republicans, she exaggerated her Irish Catholic roots and sympathies. He grew to trust her, even telling her about his childhood in Egypt – despite the Egyptian accent with which he spoke Arabic, he usually burnished his credentials by implying that he had been brought up in Jerusalem. Like other journalists, she analysed his diplomatic manoeuvres and parsed his ambiguous statements about terrorism, but she was amongst a select few who were allowed to travel on his plane, and so was able to observe him up close.

An aide always carried a pot of honey, because the Chairman liked five teaspoonfuls in hot milk, as well as honey drizzled on the cornflakes submerged in tea he had for breakfast every day. While his aides all drank and smoked, Arafat did neither. His uniform was a source of great speculation in those days. The golden pin on his chest was shaped like a phoenix, which he said symbolised the Palestinian people who would rise again. His black-and-white keffiyeh headscarf was always neat and pressed, draped carefully over his right shoulder in the shape of the future state of Palestine. Marie solved the riddle of why the uniform itself varied. Whenever his aides travelled, they would be under instructions to pop into an army surplus store and pick up a uniform in his size. That way he had an inexhaustible but subtly changing supply. She noticed that he always travelled with four cheap leather suitcases: one for the crisply laundered uniforms, the second for his fax machine, the third for documents and the final one for a blanket so he could curl up for a catnap whenever he needed. These were details of Arafat the man that neither his fans nor his detractors had previously observed.

Marie's access to Arafat had been noticed by the *New York Times*, who commissioned a 5,000-word magazine cover story. Arafat was about to announce the Declaration of Independence, a historic document that implied for the first time that the PLO recognised the State of Israel and was ready to negotiate. The plan was for Marie and a photographer to follow him on his travels around the region as he explained the Declaration to other Arab leaders. One afternoon by the American Colony pool, Marie asked Alexandra Avakian, a young freelance photographer who had recently arrived in Israel, if she would like to take the pictures. Flattered and excited, Alex called an editor she knew on the paper and within 10 minutes had the assignment. It was, said Marie, a secret – not even Patrick knew. He did, however, have an inkling that something was afoot so he and a Bolivian journalist, Juan Carlos Gumucio, cornered Alex as she left the hotel, saying they knew Marie was up to something.

'I can't tell you,' said Alex. She happened to be carrying a book about Gaddafi.

'Aha!' they said, grabbing it from her. 'You're going to Libya!'

'Not true,' she replied.

In fact it was true, although Alex didn't know it. She and Marie flew to Rome and from there to Tunis where they hung around with Arafat's aides for ten days. Marie told Alex that she had to learn to drink Scotch. 'I hate Scotch,' said Alex. 'You have to, it's like the Russians and vodka, if you want access you have to drink,' responded

Marie. Late one night they were told to grab their passports and go to the hotel front desk, from where they were taken to a villa where Arafat was staying, armed men positioned in the surrounding trees for his protection. By then Marie was accustomed to the ways of a guerrilla army in exile, but Alex's heart was pounding. Arafat questioned them separately about the project, and, once satisfied, he instructed that they should be lodged in the villa. For a few days they stayed there, sometimes taking meals with Arafat, until without warning an aide asked for their passports and, giving them scarcely enough time to grab film and clothes, hustled them into a red Mercedes and drove them to another house. It was just before midnight; the palm trees rustled in the dark. They changed cars and caught up with Arafat's motorcade heading to the airport. He had borrowed a plane, plus pilot, from Saddam Hussein, but no one would tell them where they were bound.

As the plane took off, Arafat's secretary, Samira, handed him some papers that he marked in red ink. Marie noticed his small, neatly manicured hands. It was hot in the plane; everyone was sweating. Marie and Alex started to guess where they were going. 'I don't think it's Baghdad because we're flying so low,' mused Marie. 'Maybe it's somewhere else in North Africa? Maybe Egypt?' After an hour the plane started its descent. As they landed, Arafat turned to Marie. 'Have you been to Tripoli before?' he asked.

Colonel Gaddafi did not come to meet his guest. The PLO delegation was taken to a beachfront villa. In the morning Alex was allowed to take pictures as the Chairman ate his customary cornflakes and worked on his papers, but he was growing moody. Tension ran through the delegation like an electric current. After a while Arafat dismissed Alex, and his aides briefly tried to confiscate her film. The day wore on. It grew hotter. Arafat had a nap in the afternoon while his guards lounged around the TV, weapons dangling, watching *The Muppets* in Arabic. Rumours circulated that Gaddafi was not in Tripoli but in Sebha, in Libya's far southern desert. Leaving Arafat waiting like this was an insult, made more embarrassing by the presence of a journalist and a photographer. By the next day the Palestinians had had enough.

In the late afternoon Marie and Alex were told to gather their things. The Chairman was leaving. The two of them climbed into a vehicle with Samira, who was hiding behind Yves Saint Laurent sunglasses, and set off for the airport. Halfway there, another vehicle careered up alongside them, madly honking its horn and gesturing that they should pull up. 'Quick, get into my car! The Colonel has asked for you!' said the Palestinian fighter in the car, looking straight at Marie. Alex saw a look of fear pass across Marie's face, and she grabbed Alex's thigh. 'Whatever happens, don't leave me alone with him,' she said. Marie knew that Gaddafi would press her for sex – Alex's presence was the only way of avoiding the danger. At Gaddafi's downtown barracks, Bab al-Aziziyah, they were ushered past a phalanx of female bodyguards and into a cavernous anteroom where a much more cheerful Arafat was sitting, dressed in his uniform, pistol at his hip. After a while, Gaddafi walked in, resplendent in robes. He greeted Arafat and then turned.

'Mary,' he said – neither Gaddafi nor Arafat ever learnt to pronounce Marie's name – 'What are you doing here?'

'She's with me,' said Arafat. Marie thought it sounded as if he were boasting that she was on his arm at a London première.

'What happened to your nose?' asked Gaddafi.

The scars from her encounter with a Palestinian stone-thrower were still evident, but Arafat launched into an entirely fictitious version of the story in which the culprit was not a Palestinian but an Israeli settler. After a few more minutes of surreal chat, the two leaders disappeared for their meeting. Later that evening, Marie and Alex learnt that they had been unwitting participants in a feint. Angry about the delay to their meeting, Arafat had wanted Gaddafi to think that he was leaving and so had very publicly sent them towards the airport. It worked. Gaddafi, fearing that Arafat would go, had quickly called to say the meeting was on. Marie had become not only a spectator, but also a bit player in the theatre of Arab politics.

They flew to Algiers where Arafat was to announce the Declaration of Independence to the Palestinian National Council, the parliament in exile. One evening they were with other journalists at a villa where

Bassam abu Sharif was staying, when suddenly the lights went out. 'On the floor!' shouted Bassam. 'Now!' The PLO was on edge, expecting an Israeli attack at any time, and this could be it. For 45 minutes they lay motionless before the lights flickered back on – it had been a power cut, a false alarm.

* * * * *

A few months later, the attack was for real. Marie had agreed to work with Anthony Geffen, a young documentary producer, on *The Faces of Arafat*, a film about Arafat for the BBC and the US network HBO. Anthony knew Marie was the key to access, so he put up with her unreliability: she never seemed to understand that the camera operator, sound and light technicians and producer needed her to turn up when she had said she would. She and Anthony were in one of the Tunis safe houses, talking to Arafat off camera, when a small explosion shattered the windows. Everyone in the room dived for the floor as Arafat was whisked away – he was on a plane out of Tunis in less than half an hour. Some months later, a senior Israeli intelligence official mentioned the incident to Anthony. 'We didn't want to kill Arafat then,' he said. 'We just wanted to frighten him.'

They waited in London for the main interview. When word came that they should fly back to Tunis, Anthony took a taxi to meet Marie in the morning pulling up just as she rounded the corner, slightly dishevelled, after a night out partying. They rushed to Heathrow with a cameraman, missed the plane, but made it to Tunis the following day. The Chairman, they were told cryptically, was going 'to the land where there is no Coca-Cola'. After a few more hints and a process of elimination, they realised he was heading for China. Going with him would be expensive, but, Anthony decided, the only way to nail down the access. Bassam arranged papers for them as part of the Palestinian advance party and off they set. The subsequent days were an extraordinary example of how journalists operated before the era of routine metal detectors, computerised passport checks and strict runway security. At Frankfurt, they thought the trip might be aborted before it had started as Bassam decided to buy a set of kitchen knives for his wife. It seemed unwise as he would have to get them through security and his photo – under a different name – was on a poster of 'Wanted Terrorists' in the airport. But no one made the connection, or worried about the knives, so they got on the plane.

Driving into Beijing from the airport in the early hours of 1 June 1989, Marie found the atmosphere more tense than she had expected. Students had been occupying Tiananmen Square for several months, but the protests had been peaceful and the government had not moved against them. Now police and soldiers were prowling the almost empty streets. Bassam was on a two-way radio talking to the Palestinian Ambassador in Arabic, his tone ever more frantic. At the Palestinian Embassy a huge meal was served, washed down with wine, beer and spirits. Then came the bad news: the Chinese Foreign Ministry had asked Arafat to postpone his visit because of the unrest in Beijing. If Marie and Anthony wanted to interview the Chairman they would have to fly back to Tunis and accompany him to the Arab Summit in Casablanca. After two nights without sleep, three flights and the boozy dinner they could do nothing but laugh.

Through the windows of the Palestinian diplomatic vehicle, the cameraman filmed protestors throwing stones at the security forces. It was clear that the Chinese authorities were not going to tolerate the student demonstrators for much longer. Armed guards stopped their car at checkpoints and they held their breath, waiting for the moment when someone would ask why they were travelling on Palestinian documents, and not their own passports. The biggest news story in the world was unfolding around them, but Marie and Anthony were on a different mission. Delirious with exhaustion, they sped to the airport – only to find it surrounded by armed guards and closed to all but diplomats. There was only one answer: Marie, Anthony, the crew and the bodyguards crawled under a fence and sneaked into the terminal, where they bought tickets with cash. At the gate they caught sight of a BBC wildlife team that had been filming pandas and was now being deported. Anthony quickly handed over the film his team had shot so BBC News could air it and then he, Marie and their team took off again, soaring above Beijing just 48 hours before the tanks rolled into Tiananmen Square to quash the student protests.

At Frankfurt, Bassam once more insisted on carrying the kitchen knives he had bought for his wife and once more, to Marie and Anthony's amazement, he sailed through security. On the small plane from Frankfurt to Tunis the door to the cockpit was open so, as they came in to land, they heard the pilot say, 'Oh look! There's Arafat's plane on the runway!' Terrified of losing their quarry again, they persuaded the pilot to taxi across to block Arafat's aircraft from taking off. Bassam, Marie, Anthony and the crew disembarked and clambered on to Arafat's plane. By flying to China and back they had proved the seriousness of their intent – so Arafat gave them access denied to others. He took off his uniform, donned a tracksuit, and even let them film as he removed his keffiyeh – exposing a totally bald head – and settled down under his pink woolly comfort blanket for an on-board snooze. As he awoke, he slapped cologne on his stubble, ready for the obligatory kisses on both cheeks he always gave other Arab leaders.

Casablanca was a gathering of bogeymen: Saddam Hussein of Iraq, Hafez al-Assad of Syria, Muammar Gaddafi of Libya. Arafat asked Marie and Anthony if they were happy now – he knew that access to him had brought them close to leaders who usually shunned Western reporters. Their film did not, in the end, reveal much of Arafat's inner life – Marie sometimes wondered if he really had one – but they got closer than other Western journalists. For the final interview they were blindfolded before being taken to yet another Tunis safe house. Marie was nervous because she knew Arafat wouldn't like her line of questioning, but she had to ask: although he had distanced himself from more extreme Palestinian factions, what was his position on terrorist activities, such as the attack on Israeli athletes at the 1972 Munich Olympics?

'Did you know about the activities?' she asked. Arafat bridled.

'Is this an investigation?' he snapped. 'So it is clear what I am saying, you are speaking to the Chairman of the PLO, the President of the State of Palestine. Be careful of your investigation.' Anthony prodded Marie in the back to keep going. Out of the corner of his eye he could see a youthful guard cock his rifle.

'Did you give orders to stop these acts?' she pressed.

'What I mentioned is clear and obvious,' said Arafat, his ire rising. 'Please, please, this is enough.' And with that, the interview was over.

It took him several months to forgive her, but the encounter didn't spoil their relationship. He even gave her a double string of pale pink pearls fastened with a clasp. Her 'Arafat pearls' were her favourites and she wore them often.

* * * * *

Marie's star was rising. While politicians and readers who supported Israel didn't like Arafat being humanised, her editors loved the originality of her approach. 'She would see the leaders as men, individuals with emotions and quirks,' says Bob Tyrer, who held several editorial roles on the *Sunday Times* over the years. 'It was a strength of her reporting. She got inside them, showing that they weren't identikit monsters, but real people.' Despite her news agency training, at first her writing could be jumbled and at times almost incomprehensible. 'Marie was addicted to getting another quote and then she'd write in a terrible rush from her notebook in no order whatsoever,' Bob recalls. The joke in the newsroom was, 'Marie's copy's in – someone call Bletchley Park!' John Witherow, who was foreign editor for the early part of the 1990s, became a friend. When Marie was in London they would go for lunch together, or for a drink after work. He admired her glamour and charisma, but managing her wasn't easy. 'Marie worked by her own clock,' he says. 'A deadline for filing a story would be a cue for her to vanish.' Her excuses for filing late, or sometimes not at all, were varied. 'Arafat sent for me' was one. Or, 'I fell asleep.'

But Marie's scoops, including getting the first confirmation that Arafat was about to recognise the State of Israel and that the Americans had agreed to talks with the PLO, earned her high praise at the paper. Her editors realised that she had an extraordinary ability to persuade people to talk to her. They never saw her as a great stylist – it was the reporting that was exceptional. She was shortlisted for a major British press award, and both her piece in the *New York Times* and the TV documentary with Anthony Geffen gave her international exposure.

Professional success, however, could not compensate for personal suffering. Three months after she had seen him at her wedding, bad news came from Central America: David Blundy had been killed while covering the war in El Salvador. He and other journalists were at the location where six Jesuit priests had been murdered by death squads the previous night, when a single sniper's bullet hit him. 'One moment he was standing there, the next he was on the ground,' said a photographer who was with Blundy. No one else was injured. He was forty-four. Marie had seen less of David in recent years, but he was still her friend and mentor, her doppelgänger, her partner in crime from Morocco and Libya. One of his obituarists wrote that he was 'chronically reluctant to write about anything he hadn't seen for himself'. Marie was like that too. But he had put himself in the path of danger once too often and his luck had run out. No one could imagine David growing old but his death seemed so random, so pointless. He was the first of Marie's close friends to be killed.

The blow came when she was already feeling insecure and anxious. Patrick had cut short their honeymoon in Long Island to report from Beirut, but although disappointed, she was not upset: foreign correspondents have to change plans all the time and she was equally likely to miss holidays, birthdays and family events because of work. She returned to Jerusalem to prepare for their move to a new house on Balfour Street, on the Green Line, vowing to curb her wild ways and spend more time at home. She knew Patrick craved a stable domestic life so set out to provide it. For a few weeks she even cooked meals at home instead of always drinking at the Colony and eating out. But something in their relationship had changed. Patrick seemed less affectionate, somehow distant and withdrawn. When they'd first got together he had talked of having a baby, and now she was keen to try for one, but even though they were married, he was suddenly reluctant. She hoped for the best. Both of them were busy, travelling a lot, there was plenty of time for things to get better.

In May 1990, fed up with Jerusalem, Patrick persuaded his editors to let him cover the Middle East from Paris. It was as good a jumping off point as any and he would be nearer Central Europe which was stirring after the fall of the Berlin Wall the previous year. Marie was happy to return to the city she had loved in the mid-1980s, but soon after they moved, the blow fell. It was banal, as these things usually are – on returning from a trip she found a giveaway message on Patrick's answering machine. The affair with a French journalist that he had started a few months before he and Marie got married had not ended with the wedding. In fact it had intensified. Like hundreds of foreign correspondents before and since, Patrick had used reporting as a cover for infidelity. Curtailing their honeymoon had enabled him to see his girlfriend in Beirut where she was also on assignment. A purported visit to his sick father before Christmas had in fact been a trip to see her. Now that he and Marie were living in Paris, she was just up the road.

Marie felt sick. Patrick's elusiveness was not a trick of the light, but the truth. He had not just trodden on her dreams but crushed them. She confronted him and he wept, relieved that the burden of secrecy had been lifted. But the damage had been done. Overwhelmed with anger, she slashed his painting of *Leda and the Swan*, one of his favourites. She could not get over the betrayal. Again and again in her mind she ran through the events of the nine months they had been married. The trip back to Jerusalem from Romania he had routed through Paris. The unexplained long weekend in Geneva. His towering fury when he missed a plane that she now realised would have taken him to see his lover. 'Everything was false,' she wrote. 'Pictures of you at our wedding, looked happy, all false.' She started to drink more and to smoke incessantly, forty or more cigarettes a day.

Sometimes she ate nothing, at other times she gorged herself, as she had done in her early twenties. She spent hours on the phone to Katrina who was still living in New York. How could she not have seen it? Was it her fault? She felt ugly, unattractive – all the insecurities of adolescence returned. But she did not leave Patrick. She knew that somewhere in his mixed up, faithless, battered Catholic soul he still loved her. More to the point, she still loved him.

Salvation of a kind came from an unexpected quarter: Saddam Hussein. In August 1990, he sparked an international crisis that would absorb her energies for more than a year. After the decade-long war with Iran, Iraq owed billions of dollars to Saudi Arabia and to Iraq's southern neighbour, the tiny Gulf state of Kuwait. Neither government would write off the debt. Moreover, Kuwait was driving down the oil price not just by over-producing, but also – according to Saddam – by slant drilling under the border to steal Iraqi oil. Unrest was brewing as Iraqis grew poorer, and Saddam moved ruthlessly against anyone who crossed him. He ordered the execution of Farzad Bazoft, an Iranian journalist working for the *Observer* who had been arrested on trumped up charges of spying. Then he threatened to launch a chemical weapon against Israel and sent troops towards Kuwait, to which Iraq had a historical claim. Despite all this, no one really thought he would push further, least of all the US Ambassador to Baghdad, April Glaspie, who, after an inconclusive meeting with the Iraqi leader, in which she failed to explain the consequences should his forces invade its neighbour, went on her summer vacation back home. She was not the only one to misjudge events. Patrick flew to Kuwait but he and other reporters left on the advice of a British diplomat who likened the situation to 'a summer cloud on the horizon that will disappear'. As Patrick touched down in Paris on 2 August 1990, Iraqi tanks rumbled across the border.

Marie was in Libya when Iraq invaded Kuwait, so she immediately flew to Amman to get a visa for Baghdad. It usually took a while – visits to the embassy always involved lengthy waits at the guardpost, where a lowly official would take a journalist's passport. For some unexplained reason, when Iraqis say 'hello' they mean 'goodbye', adding to the general confusion. 'Come back in a week or two,' the official would say. 'Hello.' Marie, though, had a good contact in Nizar Hamdoun, Iraq's Deputy Foreign Minister. As always with Marie, she had devoted many nights to drinking with him and it paid off. She could usually get a visa when others were still at the guardpost trying to work out if they were coming or going.

It was through Nizar that she had got to know Baghdad, which had become her favourite city in the Middle East. An unlovely conglomeration of 1970s concrete structures, choked with traffic, fiendishly hot in the summer and prone to sandstorms that caked your hair and coated your teeth with grit, Baghdad's charms were not apparent to most foreigners. Nizar, however, introduced her to a bohemian restaurant called Al Gharib – The Stranger – where artists, musicians and intellectuals gathered. This was before Saddam banned alcohol, and empty Ruffino Chianti bottles in their wicker baskets were hung above the bar. Like a private house rather than a public space, the restaurant comprised rooms that led to other rooms, where people sat around on brocaded floor cushions in traditional *diwaniyah* style, talking, smoking cigarettes or *shisha* and drinking. Poets would declaim about love (translation was tricky: 'Her body like a snake, her body like a palm tree ...') and someone would always play the piano, violin or the traditional Arab lute, the oud. ('All our songs are sad,' one of Nizar's friends told her. 'Iraqis have a long history of being sad.') Often Marie was the only woman there. Dusk darkened to night and merged into the early hours; everyone got drunk and their tongues loosened as conversation inevitably turned to politics. Nizar might work for the government but regulars knew that he and a trusted friend like Marie would never betray them by repeating their conversation. She had learnt rudimentary Arabic by then but many middle-class Iraqis spoke English. Al Gharib revealed to Marie a side of Saddam Hussein's Iraq that foreign journalists, forced to stay in the Al Rashid Hotel and given government minders to watch their every move, rarely saw.

She had another good contact in Baghdad: the US Deputy Ambassador, Joe Wilson. Born into a Republican family, Joe had gone to university in California in 1968, rebelled against the Vietnam War and worked as a carpenter before joining the government. In short, he was not a typical diplomat, but as Ambassador Glaspie would not be returning from her holiday, he was in charge. Diplomats in Iraq struggled because the government restricted their movements, while journalists frequently found they couldn't file because they had no means of communication. Joe quickly realised that he and the journalists could help each other. He allowed US reporters – including Marie, whom he counted as American even though she was working for a British newspaper – to file on his international telephone line. Confined to official meetings, he found it useful to hear their accounts of the mood in the souk and on the streets. Marie and Joe got along famously. On a Friday she would often repair to his house. 'It was very stressful for her to meet deadlines,' he recalls. 'She'd come over and write at my place because the Al Rashid was so distracting with everybody there. She would spend an entire day wringing her hands and smoking cigarettes and then she would sit down and write a brilliant, thoughtful piece.' Marie introduced Joe to Lamis Andoni and to other knowledgeable journalists, including Chris Dickey of the *Washington Post* (who was an old friend of Katrina's) and Patrick Cockburn of *The Independent*. They became essential to his understanding of what was going on.

On 29 November 1990, the UN Security Council gave Saddam Hussein a deadline: get out of Kuwait by 15 January 1991 or face the consequences. President George H. W. Bush and his advisers believed that allowing Iraq to occupy Kuwait would give a green light to any dictator eyeing up his neighbour's territory. Moreover, the oil price, which had shot up, would stay high indefinitely. Saddam, however, had found favour with many Arabs by saying he would withdraw from Kuwait only if Israel ended the occupation of the West Bank and Gaza. The US was doing nothing to stop Israel from consolidating Jewish settlements on Palestinian land, many Arabs said, and, while they might not like Saddam's dictatorial ways, at least he was defending the Palestinians.

Across the desert in Saudi Arabia, Marie's husband was embedded with the US Marines as they and their allies, including the British, massed forces for a ground war. They would wait for nearly seven months.

Every few weeks Marie's visa would run out and she would be forced to return to Amman to go through the goodbye/hello routine again. On one occasion, as she waited at the airport for the plane back to Baghdad, she ran into Dominique Roch, a French-Palestinian journalist. Marie's suitcase was small, Dominique noted, but heavy, because it was full of books about Iraq and the wider Middle East. Soon Dominique realised that while Marie was plunging herself into the story, and enjoying Baghdad's end of days atmosphere as war approached, she was also deeply unhappy. 'All the diplomats were preparing to leave so we were helping them empty their fridges of champagne and delicacies,' she remembers. 'It was cocktail after cocktail. Marie would get drunk, then she would call Patrick from the American Embassy and scream and cry down the phone.'

Marie's *Sunday Times* stories were full of colour and insight. She wrote about the fanatical artist who insisted on having 10cc of his blood drawn so he could use it to paint a mural of Saddam Hussein, and the murmurings of discontent as Iraqis realised that war with America would bring them nothing but disaster. She felt concern about the people she met, from high government officials to drivers and shopkeepers, fearing that thousands of their sons who had been conscripted into the army might be killed if the war went ahead, not to mention civilians in Baghdad where US aerial bombardment was expected to be fierce. Everyone was concerned that Saddam might use chemical weapons, as he had in the war with Iran and against the Kurds. As the deadline agreed by the UN Security Council approached, the airwaves echoed with American government spokespeople and retired generals making threats against Saddam if he didn't withdraw. Marie went to see Joe Wilson. 'You know Saddam thinks you're bluffing because you're beating the war drum so loudly,' she said. 'If you want him to take this seriously, you guys ought to shut up.' Some would argue that she had crossed a line by providing advice to the US government. Joe thought she was simply trying to prevent a war she thought would be disastrous for her Iraqi friends. He also thought that she probably understood the psychology of the Iraqi government better than his bosses in Washington so he wrote a cable recommending that they cease the noise. For one weekend they did. Briefly it looked as if diplomacy might yet triumph. On 9 January, the Iraqi Foreign Minister, Tariq Aziz, flew to Geneva to meet the US Secretary of State, James Baker. It was too late. Seven hours of negotiation got nowhere: the Iraqis refused to withdraw from Kuwait and the Americans refused to lift the threat of attack.

Many news organisations pulled out their correspondents, some believing it was too dangerous for them to stay, others succumbing to pressure from patriotic lobbies saying journalists should not report from the 'enemy side'. Joe tried to convince Marie to leave with him. As embassy staff worked the shredder to ensure no documents fell into enemy hands, he paced up and down, rhythmically squeezing a squeaking yellow plastic duck from his bathroom, warning her that she would be turned into mincement – 'ground round in the ground' – if she stayed. She took no notice. The French Ambassador was the last diplomat to go, serving pâté and cheese washed down with champagne before clambering into his car just before midnight and making for the border. As he drove off, Marie dropped by the Palestine Hotel where the government had roped in a few morose Baghdad residents for a 'challenge the deadline' party at which everyone had to dance and wave Iraqi flags. A group of about forty journalists defied all warnings and remained in the Al Rashid Hotel. Several prominent broadcast journalists and their teams remained, and this became the first war to be shown live on TV. Three of Marie's close friends also stayed on – Patrick Cockburn, Lamis Adoni and Khalil Abed Rabbo, a former Palestinian fighter, now reporting for the French news agency, Agence France Presse.

Operation Desert Storm began in the early hours of 17 January 1991, and continued for 42 days and nights. The US and its allies dropped 88,500 tons of bombs on Iraq's military and civilian infrastructure in the most intensive air bombardment the world had ever seen. When anti-aircraft fire from the presidential palace heralded the first bombs at 2.30 a.m., Marie was on the streets.

17th January 1991. Fierce artillery fire was marked by plumes of bright tracer flares arching almost lazily across the sky, as rapid gunflashes peppered the cityscape, joined by occasional salvos of rockets and even pinpoints of futile machine-gun fire.

Back at the Al Rashid later that morning, she and the other journalists listened to Saddam Hussein's famous radio broadcast: 'The Mother of all Battles has begun! Victory is near!' Smoke poured out of a nearby building, filling their nostrils with an acrid smell, as Marie, Lamis and Khalil evaded the minders trying to confine them to the hotel. The bombing had been carefully targeted on military, government and communications facilities so they wandered round the largely undamaged centre of the city.

17th January 1991. Odd images of people on the street. Man in cheap gray suit, red and white keffiyeh, Kalashnikov in one hand, briefcase in the other. Drive past Defense Ministry, central section burning, flames through ancient arch.

Over the next few days, Marie and the others marvelled at the behaviour of cruise missiles.

Sunday Times, Baghdad, 27 January 1991
I thought it was going to hit the hotel, and I yelled out. But it turned right and skirted the building, as if following a street map, and hit the old parliament building about half a mile away, sending up a pall of white smoke. Another cruise [missile] landed even closer, disappearing with a deafening crash into breeze-block staff quarters next to the hotel. The hits burst into flames and shrapnel showered the lawn and swimming pool.

Saddam responded with far less accurate Scuds, lobbed randomly at Israel.

The *Sunday Times*, like most British newspapers, ran a line under Marie's copy saying it had been compiled under Iraqi censorship, but the controls in Baghdad were somewhat haphazard. In theory, a censor from the Ministry of Information would listen to reporters filing their copy over the satellite phone in the CNN or the BBC office, but it was a boring job, and the censors rarely listened very carefully. With propaganda echoing from all sides, Marie wanted to explain why so many Arabs looked on this war differently from Europeans and Americans, so she quoted Khalil: 'A year ago I would have told you I hated Saddam and his regime. But he has become a symbol for us. Saddam is the result of the humiliation of the war of 1967 and of all the humiliations we have suffered from the West ... it is a question of dignity. Saddam came along with his rockets and stood up to you.'

Air raid sirens, nightly bombardment, power cuts, eating by candle-light, drinking whiskey while watching the bombs fall, bathing in the swimming pool because there was no running water – all this fostered camaraderie and closeness amongst the journalists. Still agonising about her failing marriage, Marie nonetheless found distractions: after a brief dalliance with another journalist, she and Khalil became lovers. He fascinated her – an intellectual who had been a guerrilla fighter, a Muslim who drank neat vodka, a proud Palestinian who loved Western literature. Yet their romance was interrupted a few days after the start of the war, when the Iraqis forced most Western reporters to leave on a bus that drove them across the flat, rocky desert to Amman. There at least Marie could call Katrina, have a long bath, a good meal and a Bloody Mary, not to mention file her stories without the attentions of the Iraqi government censor. But the journey brought an unwelcome reminder of all she was trying to forget. Dozing in her seat, she over-heard a French woman in the row in front of hers chatting to a colleague about how '*charmant*' her British boyfriend was, and what a shame he was married. Marie found herself listening more closely. Surely, it couldn't be? But it was. Marie leant forward, tapped the woman on the shoulder and spoke in French. 'That's my husband you're talking about,' she said.

She called Patrick from Amman and they rowed on the phone. Over a tearful dinner with Chris Dickey of the *Washington Post*, she spilled out the details of her life, even telling him she had considered suicide.

'Over your father?' Chris asked.

'No, over Patrick,' she replied.

'What a waste,' he said. 'You're in a marriage that's going nowhere.'

She cried all the next night, and barricaded herself in her room in the morning, refusing to answer the door to Simon Townsley, a photographer sent from London to take her picture. Waiting for new visas, she and Patrick Cockburn went to the Crusader castle at Kerak, where Marie noticed a picture of Gertrude Bell, the diplomat who had travelled the region defying both the British and the Iraqi attitude towards women, and who had drawn 'the line in the sand' that defined the borders of modern day Iraq after the First World War. She too would be a female adventurer, Marie decided, dependent on no man.

A few days later she was back in Baghdad, the bombing routine by now. A handful of other journalists had been given visas, including Maggie O'Kane, a young Irish freelancer. 'Marie's room was the centre of all the action. It was kind of like being straight into the "in gang" at school,' Maggie recalls. 'She welcomed me with absolute generosity.' Having lived under the bombs, Marie was suddenly the experienced one, the person who could help younger reporters, a role she assumed with pleasure. Settling in for the long haul, Marie went to the *souk al ghazal*, the animal market, and bought a cage with two canaries – the male green with speckled wings, the female bright yellow, chirping happily. Khalil smiled and kissed her as she came in bearing the cages. 'You're crazy,' he said. She put them by the window and fed them bread and cheese. They seemed happier than in the souk, she thought, and she was beginning to think that, without Patrick, she could be happy too.

8th February 1991. The life of children and a house with light in France is a dream I leave behind, a dream that no longer has

anything to do with me. I go on ... I go back to myself as inde-
pendent, a brave woman going through the world alone ... [With
Patrick] it's all intellectual, there's no heart, no boldness. I have
that, emotion, passion ... perhaps at 40 I will be one of these bit-
ter childless women, but right now I rather like myself, sitting at
my typewriter in Khalil's sweater, eyes green, candlestick on
right side of my typewriter, two torches for light.

Khalil cooked for her in their hotel suite. They read each other's stories, told each other about their lives and made love as the bombs fell. It was irresistibly romantic. Marie worried that maybe she was going to fall in love with Khalil, who, she knew, was unlikely to settle down, and devoted to the Palestinian cause. Or maybe she was the problem? 'My dream is to be in a love that burns me to ashes but when I find one I run away,' she thought. She recognised herself as vulnerable, easy to hurt, but she wanted to be happy again. Watching the sky light up with another bombardment, she found words bubbling up from her childhood, words she hadn't said, or at least not meant, for as long as she could remember: 'O my God, I am heartily sorry for having offended Thee, and I detest all my sins, because of thy just punishment, but most of all because they offend Thee, my God, who art all good and deserving of all my love.'

* * * * *

Most Baghdad neighbourhoods had bomb shelters, built during the war with Iran, to which families retreated at night for protection from the air raids. The journalists, by contrast, slept in their beds in the Al Rashid – by mid-February Marie was often so exhausted she slept through the bombing, while if she felt anxious for any reason, she took Valium. Just before dawn on 13 February, American fighter-bombers dropped two one-tonne laser-guided bombs on to a bunker in the middle-class neighbourhood of Amiriyah. The journalists had no idea what had happened until mid-morning when grim-faced and angry minders arrived to take them to the site. What they saw was horrific:

the Amiriyah shelter had been packed full of women and children. The first bomb, according to eyewitnesses, had jammed the thick steel doors, preventing escape. The second one penetrated the hardened roof and exploded inside the windowless room.

Scores of bodies lay around the bunker; others remained inside where they had been incinerated. The shelter was still smouldering. Marie saw the body of a woman with charred breasts curled up as if she were still sleeping, a dead child wrapped in swaddling clothes, corpses so badly burnt it was impossible to say if they were men or women. No one knew at that point how many had died – the final death toll, worked out weeks later, was 408. As it was a Wednesday, Marie filed for the next day's edition of *The Times*.

The Times, Baghdad, 14 February 1991
One man, aged about 30, wearing an army uniform, simply leaned against a wall and wept. An older man lay prostrate on the pavement, beating his head on the concrete in uncontrollable grief … Inside the windowless, concrete shelter, down a long, dark, sloping corridor, ankle-deep in water and illuminated by torches and kerosene lamps, the scene was that of an inferno. Two rescue workers dived desperately inside a dark, smoky room. Again and again, they were driven back by the furnace-like heat, and kept tripping on blackened and water logged rubble. Finally, they hauled out the blackened but still intact corpse of a woman, dropped her and ducked back for air.

Marie interviewed a member of the Popular Army, a militia formed to defend Saddam Hussein's Ba'ath Party. 'My whole family is gone,' he told her. 'All the families round here spent the night in this shelter. We thought it would withstand a nuclear bomb.'

As images of the dead and dying filled TV screens across the world, the Pentagon suggested that the bunker had been a 'command and control centre' and the civilian deaths might have been 'staged'. The censors didn't even bother to listen to the journalists' copy that day, knowing they would report nothing but the horror they had witnessed. The incident renewed the row in Britain about whether reporters in Baghdad were part of Saddam's propaganda machine: the ire of right-wing members of Parliament and the tabloid media was aimed primarily at the BBC, which had broadcast pictures of the carnage, but Marie happened to be the only reporter for a British newspaper there at the time, so was also in the frame. Frustrated editors from papers whose staff had no visas huffed and puffed that reporting under Iraqi censorship was 'unpatriotic'. A few days later, Pentagon sources were admitting privately that the targeting had been based on out-of-date intelligence: during the Iran–Iraq War the bunker had indeed been a back up command centre and a shelter for the Iraqi leadership, but no one had checked whether its use had changed. An opinion piece in the *Sunday Times* defended Marie as one of a small band of 'skilled and undeniably brave reporters' in the Iraqi capital.

Marie was less concerned with snipers back home than with the darkening mood in Baghdad. Initially, Iraqis had welcomed foreign journalists who, as they saw it, had volunteered to share their suffering. Many Iraqis did not support Saddam's invasion of Kuwait, and, until then, the number of civilian casualties had been relatively small. But that morning it changed. A man shouted, 'I hope people lose their children in America and Britain so they feel like we do.' Marie saw hatred in people's eyes. A boy spat at the reporters.

Saddam Hussein disappeared from view for a few days, and people started whispering about a coup. Naji al-Hadithi, the Deputy Minister of Information, who Marie counted as an ally, yelled at her for 'passing messages' about the Iraqi leader's absence. She pointed out that she was just reporting what she observed, but she understood that if anyone close to Saddam accused foreign journalists of spying, al-Hadithi might pay with his life. The journalists in the Al Rashid Hotel were getting scratchy – adrenalin no longer compensated for exhaustion, petty jealousies surged, people got on one another's nerves, everyone was drinking and smoking too much. Their world had contracted; a reporter from Britain bringing newspaper clippings seemed like a visitor from another galaxy. 'Going further and further away from shore, sailing on the edge …' wrote Marie in her diary.

Realising that the war would end soon and with it her life with Khalil in Baghdad, Marie grew nostalgic in advance. War had rendered the mundane exotic.

21st February 1991. I know the merchants on Karadeh St. I know the store where they play backgammon and where we buy whiskey and Russian vodka and chocolate; the side street merchants with beautiful colors stacked on tables outside: green lettuces, small red tomatoes, bright red-and-white radishes, deep orange mandarins.

On 24 February, coalition ground forces moved into Kuwait and Iraq, meeting little resistance. Two days later Saddam Hussein announced Iraq's withdrawal from Kuwait, in a flowery speech that dressed up defeat as victory. Dense smog and rain enveloped Baghdad, and by mid-afternoon it was almost as dark as night. Iraqis celebrated by shooting wildly into the air; all they really wanted was the war to end.

Marie thought about her husband reporting with Allied troops – Humvees hurtling across the desert, tanks in formation, the dynamics of a conventional war stealing the headlines from the chaos of Baghdad under bombardment. 'Sure he's writing beautifully,' she thought. 'Imagine him, notebook in hand, baggy khakis, books I bought him.' The focus moved away from Baghdad, as US forces pursued retreating Iraqi soldiers north out of Kuwait, killing hundreds on what became known as the Highway of Death. Rebellions against the Iraqi leader erupted amongst the Shi'ite population in the south and the Kurds in the north. For journalists, it was a moment of danger and opportunity – its authority wavering, the Iraqi government could no longer control them, so Marie and Patrick Cockburn jumped in a taxi with a driver called Abed, whom they knew from the months at the Al Rashid, and headed south. There was no way of predicting what lay ahead – no mobile phones, no accounts from other reporters, no cars coming in the other direction to flag down. Approaching Basra, they could hear gunfire and see homes that had been destroyed in the uprising. Patrick thought it wise to turn back but Marie showed no fear at all. 'Come on, let's go on! Keep going!' she said, impatient with poor, trembling Abed, who was so terrified he had stopped the car to vomit. They reached Basra where a doctor at the hospital described how rebels had emerged from the marshes north of the city and shot several army officers. Someone had trashed the bar at the Sheraton – broken bottles of alcohol lay around and the hotel was partly burnt. They got their story and returned to Baghdad safe, more by luck than good judgement.

By now, most foreign journalists were desperate to leave, but Marie insisted on staying as long as she could. Displacement was more addictive than danger – she wanted to put off as long as possible deciding what to do about her marriage and where to live, and ignore the dull demands of filing her expenses and paying taxes. But reporting was also getting more interesting. The censors had given up and, furious about the waste of conscripts' lives in a futile war, Iraqis were speaking openly for the first time. 'I loved President Saddam,' one young woman told Marie. 'But now I have hate in my heart for him. How can I not? There were six men in our family. My brother-in-law was killed in Kuwait. My two brothers are missing. My third brother is a POW in Iran. Our country is destroyed. And for what?'

Knowing that if Saddam Hussein were overthrown, civil war would ensue, and power would most likely end up in the hands of factions supported by Iran, the Americans pulled back and allowed the government to reassert its authority. It promptly expelled all journalists. Marie, who was in the last group to leave, wrapped herself in an *abaya* Khalil had bought and slept for the ten-hour car ride through the desert to Jordan. For a few days, as they finished their stories, the two of them entertained the fantasy that she would move to Jordan, and they even looked at an apartment to share in Amman. But she knew in her heart that the spell had been broken. She would have to go back and face Patrick.

* * * * *

After the war, Marie and Patrick moved back to London but lived separately. She went to stay in Notting Hill with Olivia Stewart, who had been one of her bridesmaids. One evening as Marie sat in the armchair by the fireplace, smoking, Olivia asked why she had ever imagined that being married to Patrick would be different from living with him. 'I don't know – movies, literature ...' replied Marie. She plunged into work, rising at six every morning to work on a biography of Arafat, and read furiously, musing on whether the attitude toward women displayed by famous men she had previously admired might hold clues to her own situation:

> *14th October 1991. Reading Norman Mailer writing about Warren Beatty, writing about himself, writing about men ... I never before have been angered by their incredible belief that women want to trap men, all men want to do is be free and live their lives, when in fact men get into relationships, desperately, then say it's your fault I'm here.*

Although she usually went home at least once a year, either for Thanksgiving or Christmas, she couldn't face seeing her family now. Oyster Bay felt not like a refuge but a backdrop for humiliation, as scenes from her wedding reran in her mind and she tortured herself with the idea that it had all been fake. She didn't want to discuss her marriage with her mother. Her father's hovering ghost haunted her.

> *18th November 1991. Betrayed my father – married P in the dress in which he married my mother. I have let him down again. When I married I remember being so sad he could never meet P, now first time I'm glad; at least he didn't have to see what a cad I'd chosen to make a life with.*

She had to go back briefly, however, when her brother Michael broke his spine in a sledding accident and doctors feared that he might be paralysed. Slowly he recovered movement, but he became irascible, and their relationship more vexed and distant. Her family was no longer part of her daily life. She and Katrina still spent hours on the phone, both of them soaring in their careers while trying to recover from broken marriages. Still, looking round the room at a reception for Yale alumni at the US Ambassador's residence in London Marie felt out of place. 'Well fed Americans,' she noted. 'Feeling I can never go home; they grate on me. They are too open, too loud, too simple.' One of the few American friends she saw regularly was Katrina's cousin, Claire Enders, whom she had known at Yale, and who had moved to London a few years before her. In some ways Claire was like family, lending Marie money and telling her off for drinking too much. They were utterly unalike, but the bond was permanent.

One evening in early 1992 Marie got a call from the past: it was John Schley, who had loved her so desperately when she lived in New York. Having read her stories from Baghdad, he was full of awe. 'You're like a mystical character for me,' he said. It felt strange to hear him reminisce about seeing her at Trenton station and thinking she looked like Audrey Hepburn ('Can this be true?' she thought) and about her visits to his farm in New Jersey. She wondered how he could talk as if he knew her so well after all these years.

Marie and Patrick saw each other frequently – the flame trembled and guttered, but was never extinguished. Still, she needed to make her own life in London, so she bought a flat. 34 Pembridge Villas, on an elegant Victorian street near the Portobello Road, had lots of light, an open-plan kitchen and a sitting room. 'Panic, too much money but it feels like a house I desperately need. I can wander my rooms upstairs. Sat on stairs and felt like an adult,' she wrote. The next step was to make a new life without her husband. The problem was that she couldn't escape him, even when they weren't together. He disturbed her sleep. Most of her nightmares featured Patrick and his French girl-friend. In one, Marie sees the woman sitting at a table amongst their friends. Furious, she goes to hit her and realises with a thud that the scene is her own wedding. In another dream she and Patrick have a baby, and Marie finds the woman by the crib: 'Dragged her out by her hair, escaped Patrick, was going to throw her in the sea.' In another, she blames her mother for the demise of her marriage, and flashes back to imagined scenes from her childhood, including finding the severed head of a friend in a swimming pool. Occasionally she dreams of bombardment, but it's Oyster Bay not Baghdad that is under attack. 'They start smashing through the roof, it's clear they've targeted Patrick's house. I see stones smashing in. Everyone starts fleeing. I don't see P, he's abandoned me, my feeling is he doesn't want me with him. We're fleeing, we're all refugees.' In the dreams she often behaves violently – it was as if her rage could erupt only subconsciously.

Returning to Iraq, as she did several times that year, she would wake anxious and miserable and reach for her cigarettes. It would take two or more hours for her to force herself out of bed.

17th August 1992. Horrible disturbing anxiety dreams, can't remember them. Realization today: first I was bulimic, then I discovered smoking. Everyone, even Iraqis, comments on my chain smoking. 2 ½ packs a day, start when I wake up, before coffee. No desire to quit.

In September 1992, she flew with a group of reporters by helicopter to the marshes north of Basra, which Saddam had partially drained supposedly to make them more habitable, but in fact to control the Marsh Arab population. She remembered her first helicopter ride in Morocco with David Blundy, music blasting through the headphones. What a long time ago that was … Now, from above, the scattered sheep and clusters of mud huts amongst the crescent-shaped berms of tank emplacements looked like 'ancient writing aimed at the gods'. Huge crowds were organised to meet the journalists with chants of 'Down down Bush! We love Saddam!' As they drove across the dried out flatlands, guided by a tribal elder, Marie thought again of Gertrude Bell, who had spent time with the Marsh Arabs 75 years earlier, and who, unlucky in love, had devoted her life to travel. Iraqis always invoked

Bell as an example of foreign female courage. Eventually the reporter arrived at a series of sand dunes; the green of the marshes stretched for just a few miles beyond, reduced in size like an environmental museum. It was hot like a furnace, and silence fell; even the rent-a-mob gave up shouting their slogans.

On another trip she gave her minders the slip and drove north with an Iraqi friend to Mosul. They visited the historic Assyrian city of Nineveh and went on to Sinjar, home to the Yazidis who worship the Peacock Angel. The incense wafting from Chaldean churches, some dating back almost to the time of Christ, conjured Marie's Catholic childhood. One night she sat on the roof of an ancient monastery watching the city lights flickering twenty miles away. A full moon hung in the sky. Beyond the mountains to the north was Kurdish territory, still nominally part of Iraq but no longer under regime control. Children brought up beds for Marie and her friend to sleep on under the stars. Back in Baghdad, she spent her evenings at Al Gharib. Families invited her to their homes where they could talk more freely – she loved the Iraqis' hospitality, and their openness toward trusted foreigners, even more prized after the imposition of sanctions that turned so many against the West. The longer she stayed, the better she understood and loved Iraq and the clearer her sense of mission.

26th August 1992. What we as western journalists should do in Iraq, as anywhere else, is try to make it understandable. It is now a place of mystery and violence to most Americans. Always my family is worried when I say I'm here and doesn't believe me when I say Baghdad is one of my favourite cities in the world. But you are a difficult people to explain, people of extremes, capable of extreme toughness and extreme sentimentality.

She worked up a proposal for a book based not just on the war but on her broader experience and access to senior members of Saddam's regime, but her editors at the *Sunday Times* wanted news stories. This hanging out with Iraqi artists and intellectuals was all very well, but where was her copy? They were getting more frustrated with her inability to file on time, her refusal to turn up in the newsroom when in London, and her utter failure to do her expenses. Sometimes she lay on her hotel bed in Baghdad wondering what to do.

Undated, September 1992. Smoking in bed, warm confused thoughts. Longer I stay, longer I want to, deeper depression about how impossible to write anything about this place, more I want to live it. Dogs barking, dogs you never see in the day, Arabic music from next room. The less it seems possible to capture in words anything that makes any sense, the more I want to just quit and live out whatever it is that attracts me, obsesses me, makes everything I left behind which seemed so important fade. Not even desire to escape what I left behind, just to shed it.

* * * * *

Chapter 6

WAR, PEACE AND LOVE

Marie's access to Colonel Gaddafi was a huge boon to the *Sunday Times*. The Supreme Guide never forgot their first interview, and Marie could usually get an audience with him. Even after Reagan left office, Gaddafi was still widely regarded by the West as a terrorist because of his sponsorship of dissident Palestinian groups and his habit of sending death squads overseas to murder 'stray dogs', as he called his exiled opponents. He was big news in Britain because of his alleged involvement in the downing of Pan Am flight 103 over Lockerbie in 1988, in which 243 passengers and 16 crew were killed, and in the arming of the Irish Republican Army. With his outlandish costumes and wacky comments he was brilliant copy.

Nonetheless, Marie's relationship with Gaddafi made it no easier for her to get the Libyan bureaucracy to issue her a visa, so in 1992, shortly after the United Nations imposed sanctions on Libya for Gaddafi's failure to bring the Lockerbie suspects to justice, she mocked up a telex reading: 'You are invited to the Great Socialist People's Libyan Arab Jamahiriya', and bought a ticket to Tripoli. Smartly dressed in a Nicole Farhi suit, looking as if she were on a business trip, she was the only woman on the plane from Rome. After a brief altercation at the airport in which they tried to deport her to Malta, she managed to talk her way into the country. The Brother Leader, she said, was expecting her. It was the holiday of Eid so when they called

Gaddafi's office no one picked up the phone to deny it. She checked into a hotel. Days went by. Then weeks. More journalists turned up. Gaddafi, they were told, was suffering from tonsillitis so couldn't speak. Marie filled in the time seeing diplomats. 'How is Stringfellow's? How is George Best?' asked a Libyan contact, keen to show off his knowledge of London nightclubs and English football. Marie was used to batting away unwanted advances, but on this trip she got herself into a dangerous situation with a man who said he would talk openly about the regime but only in the privacy of his home. 'Closest I have come to being raped – physical fight, he turns incredibly strong,' she wrote in her diary. Luckily she was strong too.

As more journalists turned up, The Supreme Guide gave no guidance to his Ministry of Information officials, so they tried distraction, herding reporters on to buses. 'Only in Libya does the bus stop and ask a policeman for directions to the spontaneous demonstration,' noted Marie. They visited the General People's Committee for Social Work and, on May Day, the gathering to mark what Gaddafi had dubbed 'International Day of Cheating and Lying to the Workers'. All the functionaries wanted was for the problem to go away, so they drove the reporters out of town for a compulsory picnic at the Sabratha ruins and then staged a 'farewell dinner' involving lengthy declamations of Arabic poetry in the hope of boring their unwanted guests into surrender. All permissions were now cancelled, the functionaries said, and any reporter who left the hotel would be arrested. But the threats were not enforced and the growing band of journalists continued to wander round town. They did get one story: a plane carrying Arafat from Khartoum crashed in the Libyan desert in a sandstorm, and briefly it looked as if the Palestinian leader might have been killed. But he survived, apparently with only cuts and bruises. With her Palestinian contacts, Marie got more details than most.

The Sunday Times foreign editor, John Witherow, was frustrated. He wasn't getting a great deal from his correspondent in Tripoli. Marie chatted to him on the phone about the runaround reporters there were being given, and mentioned in passing the frustration of the government minder assigned to the BBC correspondent Kate Adie, the most famous British TV reporter of the time. Witherow pressed Marie to write an amusing piece about how Kate, in her desperation to get a story, was driving her minder to a nervous breakdown. Marie was reluctant – she thought the idea unsisterly and unprofessional. Moreover, Kate had received death threats. John told Marie she was in Libya for the *Sunday Times* and had no choice but to write what he commissioned. 'Feel dirty,' she wrote in her diary. 'John insists.' The day the report was published, Kate arrived to Marie's hotel room in tears. 'You're a mate,' she said. 'You've been used.' Editors denied that they ran anti-BBC stories at the behest of the *Sunday Times* proprietor, Rupert Murdoch, who was well known for his dislike of the corporation, but the suspicion lingered. Marie felt dreadful. She thought of leaving the paper. She couldn't be proud of such reporting. She resolved that it would be the last time she would acquiesce in such a thing, but it was the end of a friendship. Kate Adie never spoke to her again.

Eventually, nearly a month after she had arrived, following a theatrical press conference in a tent in Gaddafi's birthplace of Sirte, and endless entreaties and dinners with officials, Marie was summoned to the barracks at Bab al-Aziziyah in Tripoli and ushered into a huge reception room full of Louis XVI style furniture and hung with heavy curtains. The place, she noticed, was deserted apart from one servant bringing orange juice. Gaddafi appeared in a paisley shirt covered by a traditional Libyan robe known as a *jerd*, and a woollen blanket. It was hard to get him to say anything newsworthy as all he wanted to talk about was *The Green Book*, a collection of his sayings outlining his Third Universal Theory of government. (An aide had told Marie that Gaddafi came up with the idea while lying in a darkened room for weeks with a blanket over his head.) He kept turning the conversation back to her. 'How is your blood?' he asked, strangely. 'Do you remember when I asked you to put on Libyan dress?' Eventually she managed to squeeze out of him that he would not provide the British government with any information about his aid to the IRA. Nor would he hand over the Libyan men suspected of having downed Pan Am 103.

The morning after the interview a man arrived at Marie's hotel with a small package. It was a copy of *The Green Book*, inscribed, 'To Marie Kolvine, with best wishes, Muammar al-Qaddafi.'

For two decades Gaddafi was not just a fount of *Sunday Times* stories but also of anecdotes, some of which may have improved in the telling. Marie was a great raconteur. On that trip in 1992, she made a note in her diary after an interview: 'Margaret – if she loves me, wear something green,' adding, 'I love her. Do you have her private fax?' It seems Gaddafi was referring to Margaret Tutwiler, then State Department spokesperson. When Marie told the story afterwards, she said Gaddafi had requested Tutwiler's private number and told Marie to tell Tutwiler to wear green on TV to send him a signal that she reciprocated his love. In later years, he spoke to Marie in similar terms about Madeleine Albright, who became US Secretary of State in 1997. He certainly had a thing for powerful women, including Marie herself.

In another of her favourite anecdotes she would describe how, after an interview, she was woken by a knock on her hotel room door in the middle of the night, to find a tall European woman wearing a full nurse's uniform complete with hat and a short Libyan man who came up to his companion's hip. This, Marie was told, was Gaddafi's personal nurse, sent because the Supreme Leader had thought Marie was looking tired during an interview. 'I Bulgarian. I take blood?' the nurse said, pulling out an enormous hypodermic syringe. Marie knew she couldn't just say no to Gaddafi so she prevaricated, persuading the nurse it would be better to return to take her blood the following afternoon, when she was less tired. The next morning she went to reception to check out and leave the country, but the staff had been given strict instructions not to release her passport. 'Luckily,' she wrote many years later, in a story about her relationship with the Brother Leader, 'Arafat was in town again and was seeing Gaddafi. Members of Force 17, Arafat's elite bodyguard, had decided to have a coffee in the hotel while they waited for him. When they walked into the lobby they saw me in distress.' Knowing that 'Mary' was a favourite of their boss, they wrested her passport back from the receptionist, drove her to the airport and saw her safely on to a plane. 'The next time I went to Libya I was nervous,' Marie wrote. 'But Gaddafi started the interview by practically slapping his leg and laughing: "Remember the time I tried to take your blood?"'

Little of this detail came out in Marie's copy at the time. It was before the fashion for journalists being the heroes of their own stories (except in the bar), and she may have feared jeopardising future access. Neither did she manage to report in any depth on violations of human rights under Gaddafi, mainly because Libyans were too scared to talk. She knew that he played on foreigners' fascination with his outlandish clothing and appearance, and quickly saw through the myth of him as a desert Bedouin living in a tent, but she never investigated the political murders and disappearances of those who opposed him. The *Sunday Times*, like other newspapers, was more interested in Gaddafi's antics abroad than the arbitrary cruelty he meted out at home.

* * * * *

'Don't miss London. Life seems more intense abroad working. London scene falls away,' Marie had written in Tripoli, but when she was in Notting Hill that spring and summer, between trips, she threw herself into life without Patrick, moving into a new circle of friends. She went to Italy with the TV producer Jane Bonham Carter, often called JBC, on the first of many holidays at Bussento, south of Naples, in a house built by JBC's grandmother. It had frescoes, a courtyard complete with fountain and a verandah looking out over a lawn rolling down to the river. JBC was descended from a long line of Liberal Party politicians, including Herbert Henry Asquith, the Prime Minister at the start of the First World War. At Bussento they would be joining JBC's father Mark, a Liberal peer who was also a publisher and a patron of the arts. Marie felt nervous, as if on trial. At college she had been drawn to the Yale aristocracy, but this was the real thing. She loved talking with Mark but worried she couldn't keep up. 'You feel you should study a bit before lunch,' she wrote in her diary. 'You're likely to be quizzed for an informed independent opinion on anything from Yugoslavia to British press laws.' There was no need to worry – Mark found her conversation intriguing. Having fought in the Second World War and escaped from a POW camp in Italy when Mussolini fell, he relished discussing their differing experiences of conflict.

She also got to know Rosie Boycott, the founder of the feminist magazine *Spare Rib*, now editing *Esquire,* as well as the writer James Fox, the fashion designer Bella Freud and the journalist Helen Fielding who was soon to achieve fame as the author of the Bridget Jones books. Tchaik Chassay and Melissa North, her friends from the Groucho Club and 192, invited her to parties at the enormous Notting Hill flat they had bought from the painter David Hockney. Aristocrats, artists, film-makers, politicians and poets – the friends she made at this time were the kind of people who got written about in the papers, rather than reporters. Her closest London friend was Jane Wellesley, who ran a production company making drama and documentaries for British and American TV. As the daughter of Arthur Valerian Wellesley, the eighth Duke of Wellington, she was officially Lady Jane but rarely used her title. The two women were in many ways opposites – Marie passionate and public in her emotions, Jane very private – but they developed an intimacy that would last. Jane didn't replace Katrina, but she was to become equally important: a kindred spirit with a different sensibility, an unfailingly loyal friend.

Patrick was spending much of his time covering the war that had just started in Bosnia. He cried when she told him she finally wanted a divorce, but they both knew it was inevitable. She saw old friends including Charles Richards, one of the American Colony gang, who was returning to London as Middle East editor for the *Independent* after two years in Rome. He was married now, his wife Tina pregnant. Marie was envious of the security he had achieved. 'I feel so deeply sad to see how happy and proud he is,' she wrote in her diary. Weddings served as a reminder not of what she had lost, but what she bitterly felt she had never had. She and Mark Bonham Carter talked one night about the meaning of success. He said he was a failure, because he had aspired to but had never achieved political power. 'He has a family, though. A life,' Marie thought.

There was nothing for it but to plunge into the single life of dinners, parties, drinks and the occasional line of cocaine, and look for someone new. That summer Marie and her friends would gather after hours at the Globe, a cramped, sticky-hot underground West Indian dive that played reggae music, had a postage-stamp-sized dance floor and, Marie thought, a 'shabby Lower East Side feel'. One evening she took John Witherow. As they entered, a large man wielding a knife loomed over them on the stairs. Instinctively, John pushed Marie behind him to protect her as the man charged past. He never heard the end of it. 'Hey Joooohn,' Marie would say, drawing out his name in her New York accent. 'Remember that evening when you saved my life? You're so brave!' The Globe was open all night, so people would roll up after dinner. 'It reeked of dope – you could get stoned just walking through the door,' remembers the poet Alan Jenkins. 'You sat crushed next to each other on these incredibly uncomfortable benches like pews along wooden tables. The music was very loud and we had to shout.' Alan would turn up most evenings with another poet, Mick Imlah. More often than not they would find JBC and sometimes her father, Mark, as well as Jane Wellesley, Alex Shulman – who had just been appointed editor of *Vogue* – and Bella Freud's father, the painter Lucian Freud, with his young male lover and his dog. Alan had met Marie at a party at Groucho's some years earlier but they had never really talked. The night they met at the Globe they clicked.

Marie was apprehensive again. Alan was intensely intelligent, but understated – a poet who wrote not about international events but about love and loss and the everyday. She felt he came from another world.

15th June 1992 Dinner w/ Alan Jenkins. Nervous. He's far more intellectual than I, knows the poems and literature I wish I knew, late one night walking me home from the Globe quoted Auden, cadence no comparison to my paltry knowledge of Yeats.

They would sit in her flat until the early hours drinking Jack Daniel's, listening to music and analysing song lyrics like teenagers. They argued about Israel, where he had been to a poetry festival and from which he'd come back rather impressed; her stories of the intifada and the legal rights of the Palestinians convinced him he had been misled. He even loved sailing and knew about boats. They ate in a neighbourhood Italian restaurant where Marie would order *risotto nero*. 'You look like a printer's assistant,' said Alan, as she wiped the black squid ink stains from her fingers.

For several months, they worked together on a film script based on Marie's experiences in Iraq, fantasising that Jodie Foster would play the lead role of a young female journalist with a deep understanding of Iraqi culture (not unlike Marie), who has a combative affair with an assertive male reporter who spends his time getting embassy briefings rather than experiencing the real Iraq (not entirely unlike her view of Patrick). Nuclear war is coming and it turns out that Jodie's famous Vietnam War hero father (a version of Marie's own father, maybe?), from whom she is estranged, is to be in charge of American forces. The plot gets more fanciful as he turns up in a helicopter to make her leave before hostilities begin. She convinces him to turn back the bombers, but one still gets through, hitting the Al Rashid and killing a receptionist. (In real life, a US bomb did indeed hit the Rashid and kill a receptionist Marie knew.) Somewhat melodramatic, with a bizarre Hammer Horror twist involving the Yazidis as devil worshippers, the script is nonetheless revealing. Iraq is a backdrop for a psychological drama, in which the heroine – the only person who can see the truth – tries to prevent war by confronting male authority, first in the person of her journalist lover, and then of her father. It is about a woman being believed and taken seriously but, more than that, it is about men having to accept that they are wrong and she is right. Psychology apart, and after many a whiskey, Marie and Alan fantasised that the script would make their fortune. She sent it off to someone she had met who worked in Hollywood with a note reading, 'Send check, please' and that was the last they heard of it.

Sometimes she and Alan made love. Khalil had been a fleeting war romance, but Marie dared to wonder if this might be something more. She loved Alan's Englishness, his 'too large floppy raincoat, green shirt that's beautiful with his eyes', but she was not ready.

17th June 1992. Impossible to reconcile. About A, excitement that for first time since meeting P, I can feel that desire for some-one, to see them, be near them, just that feeling that isn't satis-fied unless they're with you. At same time, when I see P I fall back into old love.

As for Alan, he was still involved with another woman, and unable to respond with the unequivocal passion Marie craved. He would, though, become one of her closest friends, someone she would trust for the rest of her life.

Just as she and Katrina had prided themselves on giving the wild-est parties at Yale, Marie vowed to do the same in Notting Hill. 'Marie always gave really good parties,' recalls Alex Shulman. 'You never knew who would turn up – there would be gatecrashers, people got off with other people, got drunk, took drugs. The doorbell would still be going and people would still be piling in at 1.30 a.m. and the party would go on until dawn.' On occasion there was a fight, or at least the beginnings of one. A hard core, always including Marie, would keep drinking, dancing and talking until long after the others had left. 'Parties formed around her,' said one friend. She had an easy air of dan-ger, a potential for going 'too far' that excited those who were drawn to her. Occasionally a friend like Bassam abu Sharif would appear at one of her gatherings, thrilling London socialites unused to sipping whis-key with someone who had been blown up by an Israeli letter bomb.

Marie wrote in her diary: 'Want to put my life together, piece by piece, as if somehow I can make it whole again.' London friendships, especially with women, enabled her to do that. She and Jane Wellesley were always there for each other. Marie frequently called from abroad and they spoke every day when she was in London. Sometimes they went to the theatre or an exhibition, but often they just hung out together and talked. Jane was at the centre of a large circle of friends, giving Marie the secure base to return to that others might have got from family. The two laughed a lot and went shopping for clothes, gossiping about who was going out with whom one minute, and politics or books the next. Marie never saw her adventurous profession as more significant than the lives and work of the friends who sustained her.

'She gave you permission to be yourself,' says Alan Jenkins. 'What I absolutely loved immediately was this feeling that she liked you unconditionally – you had a sense that her affection would never be withdrawn. She was with you and behind you in some way. There was a sharpness, an immediate checking on to the wavelength. She made you feel you had something to give and she was always interested.'

* * * * *

Marie had been spending less time in Israel and the Occupied Territories, but in September 1993 the story shot back up the news agenda. After months of secret talks in Norway, Israel and the PLO had signed the Oslo Accords, marking the start of what became known as the Middle East peace process. The PLO had recognised Israel and renounced terrorism; now Israel would recognise the PLO and start to withdraw troops from Gaza and parts of the West Bank, making way for a Palestinian Authority. The complex details of Jewish settlements, the status of Jerusalem and what would happen to Palestinians who had been forced to flee their homes in 1948 and 1967 would be left until the end of the negotiations. 'It was,' wrote Marie, 'the Middle Eastern equivalent of the fall of the Berlin Wall.'

Marie had played a tiny role, introducing her Israeli friend, the military intelligence agent turned journalist Uzi Mahnaimi, to Bassam abu Sharif. A life at war had convinced both men that rapprochement was the only way forward, and Uzi's stories were amongst the first in the Hebrew press to show that Palestinians were not all terrorists, and that their cause should be considered. The two men got along so well that they even wrote a joint memoir, *The Best of Enemies*.

Marie had had an inkling that things were changing back in December 1992 when she interviewed the Israeli Prime Minister, Yitzhak Rabin, a gravel-voiced former soldier, who indicated that he thought Israel should stop demonising the PLO and do a deal. Rabin's awkward, military demeanour was the key to his credibility with Israelis who revered military men. 'He did not even say hello when I met him. He just nodded and sat down behind his desk,' Marie wrote in one story. They bonded over smoking. 'During television appearances he looks desperate to get off camera for a cigarette.'

Still, Rabin had a hard job convincing Israelis that they were not giving in to terrorism. 'I will not try to paint a rosy picture of the PLO,' he said to his Labour party after Oslo was announced. 'But you don't make peace with friends but with unpleasant enemies.' Fifty thousand right-wing Israelis responded by chanting 'Coward! Coward!' outside his office. Voices on the Palestinian side, including Marie's friend Lamis Andoni, dissented, seeing the accords as capitulation to Israel. But Arafat knew he had to come up with something to satisfy the youths who had started the intifada, and who were drawn to the radical Islamist movement Hamas – which the Israelis had seeded as a rival to the PLO. Increasingly frail after the plane crash in the Libyan desert, his hands and lower lip trembled – Arafat believed this was his only chance to regain at least some of the land the Palestinians had lost.

Marie flew to Washington for what became known as 'the handshake on the White House lawn'. Rabin and Arafat signed the deal in front of President Bill Clinton and the world's TV cameras, everyone acutely conscious of history being made. Marie's friend from Paris,

Judy Miller, was also reporting on the ceremony. She bounded up to Marie with the good news that she and her partner had decided to take advantage of the presence of so many friends in Washington DC to get married the following Sunday. It was an occasion when work trumped friendship. Arafat had invited Marie to accompany him on his plane back to Tunis. 'I said, this is important, Marie, I've waited a lot of time for this,' Judy recalls. 'But I just knew she would not be able to say no to Arafat. I was half amused, half hurt and utterly unsurprised.'

Teetotal Arafat, reported Marie, did not drink the champagne served on the Boeing 707 that took him back to Tunis. 'Maybe it is the most important event of my life,' he mused as he unzipped his black ankle boots, leant back in the red leather armchair and put on eye-shades. His bodyguards curled up on the floor next to him. On flying into Washington, they told Marie, they had been terrified that it was a trap and the American secret service would arrest them. 'We were very surprised,' one said. 'They were very nice with us.'

Back in Tunis everyone was queuing up to see the Palestinian leader: US TV networks who would previously have balked at inter-viewing a 'terrorist', European businessmen looking for deals with the new Palestinian Authority, exiled Palestinians angling for a sinecure back home. One of Arafat's main concerns was simply surviving – the Israelis might no longer be plotting to assassinate him but radical Arab leaders who opposed Oslo were. A distinguished London literary agent, Gillon Aitken, had taken on Marie with her proposal for an authorised biography of Arafat so she wanted to spend as much time as possible with the Palestinian leader, but he suddenly decided he was unhappy about something she had recently written and was refusing to meet her. In her anxiety she was smoking three packs a day. Arafat's aides were sympathetic – one even took Marie horse-riding as a distraction – but the 'old man', as they called him, was stubborn. It took Marie weeks to get back into his good books.

It was around this time that she got to know the Palestinian lead-er's wife. Arafat was fond of saying 'I am married to Palestine', but in

1990 he had secretly married Suha Tawil, a buxom, blonde Palestinian Christian half his age, usually described as his secretary and interpreter. When the marriage became public Marie was unsurprised – some months earlier, on a plane journey, she had noticed the two of them removing their shoes and playing footsie while the bodyguards slept. Marie's friendship with Bassam abu Sharif let her into many secrets. 'She was often with Bassam at his house,' recalls Suha. 'I was dating Yasser and Bassam knew but it was not yet public. One evening when I came, he and Marie put on an Arabic song which says, "The girl is blonde and I'm in love and I don't know what to do!" And everyone started to dance!'

When Arafat got married, those around him reacted 'with the jealousy of lovers', Marie observed. 'Their male world was disrupted: Arafat had actually publicly acknowledged a woman.' The mistrust was reciprocated. Arafat lived a spartan life, but Suha, who had grown up in a bourgeois Paris suburb, expected a degree of creature comfort as First Lady of the putative Palestinian state. 'She had married a president, and she liked the red carpet,' wrote Marie. 'She wanted a decent house, not a home that was a doss house for his extended entourage.' Marie reported that Arafat acquiesced when aides advised him that Suha should not go to Washington for the Oslo Accords ceremony, on the pretext that Palestinians dying in Gaza would be offended to see her in a Paris couture outfit, hobnobbing with the Clintons and the Rabins. Suha got her own back by donning 'a tasteful scarlet number decorated with jewelled buttons' and inviting a CNN correspondent to come and watch the ceremony *chez elle*. Her commentary was broadcast live from her house in Tunis.

With her husband travelling and his aides conspiring against her, Suha was often lonely so she welcomed Marie's company and the two became friends. Marie was always careful to dress modestly in the Arab world, but even her long gauzy linen shirt prompted Suha to remark wistfully that her husband wouldn't let her wear clothes like that – if she went to the office in a knee length skirt, the officials would fix their eyes on her knees, as if she were wearing something risqué.

Arafat might have been a hero to the Palestinian people and a mystery to the world beyond, but as far as Suha was concerned he was just like any husband, calling her Imelda Marcos because he thought she had too many shoes ('But I only have eight or ten pairs!'), and complaining when she took too long to get ready to go out. 'He's like a cranky old bachelor living with a bright young bird,' thought Marie. The pressures of being his wife sometimes got Suha down, but, 'fortunately we love each other. If I did not love him, nothing in this world would make me live this life.'

Suha could also help Marie. Late one night, Marie called from her room at the Tunis Hilton. A member of the PLO Central Committee was drunkenly banging on her door demanding that she open up. Suha recalls hearing him yelling, 'Mary! Mary! Let me in!' Suha told her to hang on. 'I said I would send my bodyguards – my army!' At first her chief bodyguard said he didn't dare, because the man at Marie's door was his senior in rank, but Suha insisted. 'I said, "Whether he's famous or not you have to hit him!" They went and took him to his house. I told Yasser what happened when he came back from his travels, and he took this man aside and said, "Mary is under my protection – if you dare to touch a hair on her head you will be in prison!"'

According to Suha, Arafat trusted Marie like no other journalist. 'She had his confidence,' she says. 'If he wanted to say something, he would tell her exclusively. We felt she was one of us and not an intruder.' Such access was invaluable for her book, for which she was taking assiduous notes, but some colleagues at the *Sunday Times* worried that she was too close to the Palestinians. She would push Arafat on key issues, asking repeatedly for example why the PLO Charter had not been amended to recognise the State of Israel, but she trod a fine line.

Marie spent New Year 1994 in Tunis, staying in one of Arafat's safe houses. Jane Wellesley and Mick Imlah joined her. Bassam and others would regularly drop by for a chat and a drink. They celebrated New Year's Eve with Arafat's entourage, enjoying dinner at the Pomme d'Or restaurant followed by dancing and singing late into the night at the

Tropicana discotheque. Mick sang 'The Bonnie Earl o' Moray' to great acclaim. Marie was in her element, drinking and talking with the hard men of the PLO, ushering in a year that might – just might – bring peace to the Middle East.

* * * * *

There were those on both sides trying to derail the peace process. Marie was in Cairo when Baruch Goldstein, a Jewish extremist, entered the Ibrahimi Mosque in the Cave of the Patriarchs in Hebron, and opened fire on Muslim worshippers, killing 29 and wounding 125. She and Chris Dickey jumped in a cab and drove for ten hours across the Sinai to the Israeli resort of Eilat, up through the West Bank to Jerusalem. The next day they joined Dominique Roch and headed for Hebron, where thousands of Palestinians were protesting not just about the massacre but also against the peace deal. It was another occasion when being a woman was an advantage. Dominique and Marie persuaded a Palestinian working with the Israeli military to get them in. 'He said, "Cover your heads and I'll say you're my cousins visiting from Australia and you want access to the shrine,"' remembers Dominique. Men were still cleaning the blood off the walls with water hoses as the two journalists entered to talk to the grief-stricken guardian of the mosque.

Rabin condemned Goldstein as a 'villainous Jew', and 'a degenerate murderer' but Palestinians wanted more decisive action against settlers than the Israeli leader was prepared to take. For a while it looked as if the peace process would be scuppered, but in the end neither side wanted to give up just yet. Despite everything, it was a time of hope. The early secret meetings to establish the Oslo Accords had been held at the American Colony, which was one of very few places where Jews and Arabs mixed and was now full of diplomats, UN types and journalists. Marie was in Jerusalem so often that the Colony's owner, Val Vester, now in her eighties, allocated her a room above the courtyard. Another regular at the Colony was the Reverend Dr Jerome Murphy-O'Connor, a biblical scholar with a white beard like an Old Testament prophet who was partial to Val's perfect gin-and-tonics, and known to all as Father Jerry. Every Sunday morning he would escort a group for a walk around Jerusalem, debunking the myths propagated by other biblical scholars and tourist guides. (He enjoyed pointing out that they were all going the wrong way round the Via Dolorosa.) Val and Father Jerry had been mentors and advisers to generations of journalists, listening to their problems, mediating in their arguments, or just picking them up when they were drunk.

Amongst the crowd at the Colony was Juan Carlos Gumucio, known to many as JC, a correspondent for the Spanish newspaper, *El País*. Marie knew him as a friend and something of a legend, as he had stayed in Beirut during the war while others left, surviving partly because his barrel-belly, wild black hair and thick beard made him look like a member of Hizbollah. With his deep voice and a ready laugh, he could have been mistaken for an opera singer. Con Coughlin, a correspondent for the *Telegraph*, remembers going to see him in his Beirut apartment towards the end of the Lebanon war. 'It had iron doors as protection from the bombing,' he recalls. 'JC had the windows open with a gale blowing in. Wagner was playing at full volume, and he was completely out of his skull.' In his book *From the Holy Mountain*, William Dalrymple recounts asking Juan Carlos if he was not terrified of being kidnapped and chained to a radiator. 'I've been married three times,' he responded. 'It's not so different.' The epithet 'larger than life' was often used – Juan Carlos had a huge appetite for drugs, drink and sex – but his warmth and humour endeared him even to those who might otherwise disapprove. Patrick Cockburn saw him as a Falstaffian figure: 'He had immense charm, energy and originality.' The American journalist Charlie Glass wrote, 'Every time Juan Carlos arrived at a big story – or a dinner party – it was an event, as if Godot had finally shown up.' With his swashbuckling attitude toward war and women, and seemingly effortless ability to write in three languages, he was often compared to Hemingway. One weekend back in London, Con invited him for lunch and asked whom else Juan Carlos would like him to see. 'Marie Colvin,' he replied without hesitation. Juan Carlos and Marie arranged to go to Gaza together. That was the beginning of it.

'I never saw her happy like this in her life,' says Alexandra Avakian, the photographer who had accompanied Marie on her early trips with Arafat. 'She was fully, deeply, madly in love. I think JC just lit her fire and their intimacy was something great. He unlocked something in her.' Dominique was surprised. 'We used to say JC should wear his helmet in the American Colony bar because he kept falling off his stool. He was always drunk.' When Dominique asked Marie what she saw in him, she replied, 'He's so loving and warm – I've never met someone so affectionate.' Patrick Cockburn was delighted that two of the people he liked best in the world had got together. Theirs was a passionate relationship, full of laughter and shared good times. Chris Dickey, who had known and liked Juan Carlos in Beirut, was pleased to see Marie happy again. 'The only thing was that I could see it was a co-dependent relationship because of alcohol,' he says.

A few months earlier, Marie had been in Connecticut, at Katrina's second wedding. Winter Mead, who worked in the theatre, seemed like a man who could make her friend happy. Maybe hers and Katrina's lives would mirror each other again. She called Katrina to tell her that she too had found someone. Katrina met Juan Carlos on a visit to London. 'He was an ebullient presence,' she remembers. 'His manners were somehow exaggerated – he would leap from his chair to pull your chair halfway across the table, but not in a fawning way. He had this enormous personal generosity about him.' Marie sent Katrina photographs of dinner parties at Juan Carlos's apartment and nights out on the town. 'They were living in this extraordinary bubble – there was this zany domesticity about the scene,' she recalls. Marie wrote little about the relationship in her diary – she was too busy being in love.

Val and Father Jerry looked on with a mixture of amusement and concern. They knew both Marie and Juan Carlos of old. Everyone could see what fun they were having, how Marie was shaking off the sorrow of her marriage to Patrick. But they were a volatile combination and Val worried that ending in tears would be the least of it.

*****

Arafat delayed his return to Gaza, supposedly because he was getting Arab leaders on board with the peace process; or, according to Marie, because he was anxious about the power and popularity of Hamas. The Islamist group had increased its terror attacks inside Israel, hoping to destroy the agreement. Knowing that she had spent years visiting the West Bank and Gaza while he was in exile, Arafat often sought Marie's opinion. She told him he had to go back immediately if he was to have credibility amongst the Palestinians, but it wasn't until July 1994 that he left Tunis to settle in Gaza. Marie was on the bus carrying his delegation over the border from Egypt when unsmiling men in civilian clothes and Ray-Bans, clearly Mossad agents and Israeli soldiers, boarded the bus in a blatant display of power. They shouted questions and roughly shoved aside the Palestinian officials. PLO fighters jumped to their feet and for a moment it looked as if there would be an altercation. 'Here we see how far peace has to go,' she noted.

The mood was subdued and only a few people gathered to cheer Arafat's high-speed motorcade as it sped along Gaza's potholed streets to the Palestine Hotel where he would establish his headquarters. The Israelis had blocked entry to Gazan labourers after clashes at the Erez Crossing. With no income, the workers were increasingly frustrated and angry. Hamas had pulled its fighters back from the streets, but that was a tactic, not a retreat – they were biding their time before mounting their challenge. Arafat knew that if he were unable to provide jobs and prosperity, Palestinians would see the peace process as surrender and the PLO as quislings, while Hamas pushed its potent message of defiance and religious certainty.

Suha Arafat was appalled by Gaza. For a start, her husband wanted to live in a small house that she did not regard as fitting for a

President – they compromised on a three-bedroomed villa. Then there was no decent hairdresser. After a few weeks she got someone to come to the house to tint her hair, which promptly turned orange with highlights of green. Marie was laughing so hard that Suha had to laugh too. Arafat had been saying she should put on the veil because Gaza was very conservative; now she thought she might just do that because her hair looked so awful. 'It was terrible! Mary told me to put tomato on it, and that worked because it became sort of blackish,' Suha recalls. In November Marie joined the Palestinian group flying to Oslo where Arafat, Rabin and the Israeli Foreign Minister, Shimon Peres, were to receive the Nobel Peace Prize. Suha was allowed to go this time. Arafat was in a jovial mood. Marie described how the pilot of the aircraft sent by the Swedes came on the intercom to say: 'Ladies and gentlemen, I am proud to be flying the President of Palestine ...' Arafat interrupted him, 'shouting from his seat like a schoolboy at the back of the bus: "There are no ladies here!" and giggling to the accompaniment of guffaws from around the plane.' Sitting on the armrest of her seat, Arafat told Marie that defeating those who opposed the accords was hard because so little of the money pledged by donors had actually arrived. 'We are starting from zero,' he said. 'We have an infrastructure that has been completely destroyed.'

Once they were in Oslo, any number of mishaps occurred. Peres's bodyguards thought he had been shot when he fell flat on his face while leaving prayers – in fact he had just tripped, but he needed stitches in his forehead. Arafat accidentally locked himself in his room and had to be rescued by a pair of Norwegian security officers. He looked nervous at the ceremony, Marie thought, dwarfed by the vast marble walls behind him. At dinner afterwards, Rabin said the Israelis and Palestinians didn't deserve the prize because they had not yet achieved peace. 'If we do not achieve a guarantee of security, we will continue to negotiate until we do,' he said. Suha remembers it as a happy occasion, a moment to reflect on enmities overcome. 'We had this nice atmosphere with the Israelis and everyone telling stories.' But back home, Jewish settlers continued building on Palestinian land, and Palestinian extremists were still attacking Israelis. Marie believed in the peace process, but she could see the pitfalls ahead.

Juan Carlos was also at the Nobel Peace Prize celebration. He and Marie agreed they would now tell their former partners of their plans. She had decided to move to Jerusalem to be with him, taking a leave of absence from the *Sunday Times* to finish her biography of Arafat. Juan Carlos's most recent ex-wife, Agneta Ramberg, a Swedish journalist he had met in Beirut, accepted the news calmly but Patrick was horrified. Juan Carlos, he said, was a pathologically unfaithful alcoholic who procured prostitutes and would chase other women the moment Marie was out of town. She didn't need her former husband's blessing, but she thought he could have made a little more effort to be happy for her.

Marie was tired. Throughout 1994 she had scarcely stopped working and travelling, oscillating between London, Jerusalem and wherever she was reporting. Some pages of her journals are full of 'to do' lists for her life in Notting Hill ('Call window cleaners; Rosie's dinner Wednesday') while others are covered with tiny, closely written notes detailing battles and encounters with warlords. She had spent three dangerous weeks on the front line in Yemen, as a southern militia fought a futile campaign against the north, and had gone to New York to chase down a dissident Saudi exposing a secret programme to acquire nuclear weapons. She had analysed Hafez al-Assad's policy on the peace process and lunched in Paris with the arms dealer Adnan Khashoggi. A holiday at Bussento in September with the Bonham Carters had come to an abrupt and terrible halt when Mark suffered a heart attack and died right in front of her and JBC. He was seventy-two. Marie had loved and admired Mark. He frequently took her to lunch at the House of Lords, where they sparred about the events of the day. It was shocking to see him die, and it inevitably made her think of her own father's premature death. The London clan gathered to comfort the family and to remember Mark who had been such a big figure in all of their lives. Marie was torn – she wanted to be with her friends, especially now, but she wanted to be with Juan Carlos in Jerusalem as well.

23rd August 1994. Finally after a long despair, a long blackness, I now live with that blackness at the edge but no longer every-thing for me.

Maybe the dream of a family she had once shared with Patrick could happen for her with this new love. He was seven years her senior and had a daughter from his first marriage, from whom he was estranged, and another with Agneta. Six-year-old Anna was being brought up by her mother in Stockholm. Worried about Juan Carlos's drinking, Agneta had not allowed the little girl to stay with him on her own since they had separated, but now, with Marie on the scene as a stabilising influence, she hoped that Anna could spend the school holidays with her father. Full of excitement, Anna went to Jerusalem for Christmas. Juan Carlos had told his daughter on the phone that Marie would love her 'like a mother'. Young as she was, Anna knew that wasn't quite right, because she already had a mother, but she soon felt secure that Marie loved her too. Just as she had with her younger sister Cat all those years before, Marie incorporated Anna into her life without making any changes. 'She was really cool. She took an interest in me and treated me like an adult,' remembers Anna. 'I would lie on the sofa in Jerusalem while my father and Marie were watching *The X Files* and *Men Behaving Badly* – things my mum would never let me watch.' They played dressing up games, Anna daubing her face with Marie's makeup and clomping around in her shoes. Neither Juan Carlos nor Marie asked Anna much about schoolwork, but if she wrote a poem or took a photograph they praised her talent and creativity. They went horse riding at a ranch overlooking the Sea of Galilee, even taking along Foozie, the stray cat they had adopted and whom Anna adored.

'When you had my father's attention it felt as if the sun was shin-ing on you,' says Anna. 'You felt that nobody would ever love you like that again.' Marie felt that too. She was intrigued by Juan Carlos's romantic Latin American background. His family saga read like something out of a Gabriel García Márquez novel, with a complex network of relatives back in Cochabamba, Bolivia, tin mines gained and lost, and a father who he said had abandoned him when he was small. At the age of fifteen Juan Carlos had run away to the Amazon, and later been exiled from Bolivia to Argentina and then Brazil because of his left-wing activism. He still had a picture of Che Guevara up in his room, and a bust of Lenin on a table. In Jerusalem he and his friends, the *Financial Times* correspondent Julian Ozanne and Youssef Ibrahim of the *New York Times,* would frequently go on a bender and come back drunk and high. On good days he was the most generous man imaginable but on bad, he was moody and aggressive. Sometimes he would take friends to an Israeli shooting range where he would let off steam, firing hundreds of rounds into alarmingly human-like targets. When pressed, Marie would say that Juan Carlos was 'wrestling with his demons'.

Some of her friends were worried. Dominique remembers Marie sobbing, saying Juan Carlos had pushed her against a wall on their way to the American Colony the previous evening. 'Promise me you won't marry him,' said Dominique. On a visit to Jerusalem, JBC saw him fly into a black mood at a restaurant and refuse to speak to Marie for two days. Val and Father Jerry told Marie that she and Juan Carlos were too alike for the relationship to work in the long term. Head inclined, eyes narrowed, drawing on her cigarette, Marie listened to their advice and ignored it. She and Juan Carlos were deep in their own myth: he was Hemingway, she was Martha Gellhorn. If she had considered how badly that relationship turned out, she might have hesitated but instead they decided now was the time to have a baby. In 1995, Marie became pregnant, but miscarried. She had little time for those who thought she should change her lifestyle if she wanted a child; after all, her own mother had drunk through pregnancy, she said. Rosemarie, though, had been twenty-two when she first conceived, while Marie was now nearly forty. More than that, several years earlier, she had been diagnosed with endometriosis, a condition that has no outright cure and frequently leads to infertility. To outsiders the very idea of Juan Carlos and Marie having a child seemed crazy. 'How can you, if you work and you are all the time travelling?' asked Suha, who was also planning a family. 'With all that stress, you can't have children.'

While Marie longed for the fulfilment and security she felt motherhood would bring, she didn't always understand what parenting required. Once when Anna was staying with them in Jerusalem, Juan Carlos got blind drunk at a party, and Marie – not entirely sober herself – stormed off home without him. No one at the party took responsibility, so Anna, then aged seven, had to help her father stagger to a taxi to get home. Still furious, and seemingly unaware of Anna's needs, Marie refused to speak to Juan Carlos for days. 'I had to try and patch up their relationship,' recalls Anna, who didn't tell her mother what was going on. 'I told my dad we should go shopping for something nice for Marie. First it was flowers and next it was a ring. I think they just forgot I was a kid.' She heard them arguing about everything, but mainly about Juan Carlos getting drunk, screaming 'Fuck you!' at each other until their rage had subsided, at which point it changed to 'I love you'. Each blamed the other, never getting to the root of why they rowed, nor managing to change the dynamic.

* * * * *

The peace process faltered on, each step forward matched by a setback: a terror attack, protests by the quarter million Jewish settlers or a detail everyone thought had been sorted out that one side or the other later rejected. Marie stood in the crowd waiting for Arafat in Jericho, everyone clapping, whistling and chanting 'Abu Amar! Abu Amar!' as his convoy roared up and soldiers lifted him up so the people could see their hero. Someone fired into the air and his bodyguards panicked, hustling him into a nearby building. Arafat was always in danger, even now – or maybe especially now – he was amongst his own people. 'We will continue to protect the peace of the brave,' he said, as he always did. Rabin didn't realise that he too was in danger from his own people. When his political rival, Benjamin Netanyahu, presided over rallies of virulent right-wing Israelis who not only opposed the peace process but called Rabin a Nazi and chanted for his death, no one took it literally – after all, a Jew would never kill another Jew. On 6 November 1995, Rabin addressed a huge peace rally in Tel Aviv. 'I was a military man for twenty-seven years. I waged war as long as there was no chance for peace,' he said to the 100,000-strong crowd. 'I believe there is now a chance for peace, a great chance, and we must make the most of it.' As he walked down the city hall steps to get into his car, a young religious scholar named Yigal Amir fired three deadly shots. Not wearing a bullet-proof vest, Rabin stood no chance.

Marie was having dinner at the American Colony when she got the news. Her friend Uzi Mahnaimi had been appointed *Sunday Times* Middle East correspondent while she was working on the Arafat book, but now Marie was pitched back into news reporting. She and her colleague Jon Swain co-wrote a long piece based partly on conversations with Yigal Amir's fellow students, who told them that not only was he a member of a far right-wing group but he had tried to murder Rabin before, shortly after being rejected by his girlfriend.

Sunday Times, Tel Aviv, 12th November 1995
Now he became outrageous, outspoken and dangerous. The extremist, angered and rejected, had tipped over into a potential assassin. 'I think that not only political views caused the murder, but also his feeling of disappointment in his personal life,' the friend said. 'Suddenly we heard him talking about the duty to kill Rabin.'

On the advice of Israeli security, Arafat did not join world leaders attending the Israeli leader's funeral, but he paid his respects privately to Rabin's widow, Leah. It was, Suha told Marie, a matter of great sorrow that he could not publicly mourn and salute the man with whom he had tried to forge peace.

Marie knew this was a moment of change. Shimon Peres, the Israeli Foreign Minister, pledged to continue the peace process, but it was doomed after Netanyahu was elected Prime Minister a few months later. The murder of Rabin had blown history off course. Marie had had enough of the Middle East – so much hope had been extinguished with those three bullets and now she saw extremists gaining ground on both sides. Moreover, she had failed to complete the biography: after countless hours with Arafat and endless interviews with his aides and with Suha, she had filled dozens of notebooks, but could not synthesise her reporting into prose. Once, when she had spent weeks without seeing Arafat, she had jokingly suggested calling the book *Waiting for the Chairman*; now her agent might have called it *Waiting for the Biography*. There was always something to do that didn't involve sitting down at a desk for long hours and forcing herself to write. When the *Sunday Times* offered her a position as a London-based foreign correspondent, covering crises and conflicts across the world, she was only too keen to accept. Anyway, she told herself, she might still finish the book in between reporting assignments.

Juan Carlos was ambivalent about living in London. Marie had her flat and her Notting Hill friends, but it was alien territory for him. She managed to persuade him to give it a go and when *El País* offered him the job of London correspondent, he agreed. The glory days of reporting the Middle East – the war in Lebanon, the intifada, the peace process – were over. It was time to move into a new era. They would try again to have a family. In the meantime, Marie did the paperwork and bought a crate for Billy Smith, the latest stray cat – a large, fluffy, at times belligerent tabby – so he could also move to London. As if on cue, her decree nisi from Patrick was issued. In 1996 she was free to remarry.

* * * * *

Marie laid out the plans for her wedding to Juan Carlos in an invitation letter to her Yale friend Bobby Shriver.

> *Thursday night: small dinner for the fun people (us) at 192, my neighborhood restaurant when I live in London.*
> *Friday night: Dinner chez Jane Wellesley. Very informal, about 40 family, good London friends, out-of-towners.*
> *Saturday: 9.30am (ouch!) wedding at Chelsea Town Hall, Kings Road. Short and sweet, if you're late you'll miss it.*
> *Directly from wedding: Champagne breakfast chez Claire Enders. A friend is bringing a kilo of caviar from Moscow so we will feast.*
> *8pm: Party . . . .*

Just as Cat and Rosemarie had ended up organising Marie's wedding to Patrick, this time it fell to Jane to make the practical arrangements. Seven years earlier Marie had gone for suburban tradition, all white lace and Laura Ashley, but this would be a fashionable, alternative London wedding. Marie wore a low-cut apple green mini-dress that Bella Freud had designed for her. The party was held at a film studio, a designer having custom-built a set featuring purple velvet sofas and exotic spirals of flowers. Rosemarie, Cat and Boo came over for the occasion. 'I had mixed feelings,' recalls Rosemarie. 'To tell you the truth I didn't think there was anything lasting there. I wasn't sure it was the best thing for her.' Still, it was a day of exuberance and delight, with much champagne consumed and everyone dancing the merengue late into the night. Charlie Glass remembers Marie and her mother dancing together in perfect formation as if they were the Rockettes. Little Anna loved it. She wore a blue dress patterned with tiny flowers that Marie had picked out for her at Fenwicks. For one day, the jigsaw of Marie's life was assembled into a colourful whole. Her Notting Hill circle mixed with Juan Carlos's Bolivian relatives and mutual friends from Jerusalem. The writer Mario Vargas Llosa, who was in some way related to Juan Carlos, came; as did Anna Blundy, David's daughter.

Katrina was there with her husband, Winter. Gerald Vitagliano, whom Marie had met on her very first day at Yale, flew in from New York. He was not sure about this new Marie. 'There was a frenziedness at this wedding party that didn't feel authentic to me,' he says. 'But Marie was a great partier and had many disguises.'

Juan Carlos had asked all three of his friends – Charlie Glass, Youssef Ibrahim and Julian Ozanne – to be the best man, so there was some confusion at the registry office. In the end they sat at the back and Anna handed over the rings, which she dropped, but no one minded because she was only eight and it added to the sweetness of the occasion. Julian made a speech at the party. One good thing about this match, he joked, was that neither bride nor groom needed to worry about ruining the other's reputation. He talked about the wild times they had all shared in Jerusalem, and everyone's wonderment at Juan Carlos's decision to marry for a fourth time, reporting Marie's response: for them both, she had said, it was a triumph of optimism over commitment.

The newly-weds flew to Naples to join JBC, Alex Shulman and a few other friends for a long weekend in Bussento. This may have been Marie's idea of bliss, but Juan Carlos was furious, making it clear that Marie's friends were not his choice of company for his honeymoon. He was a silent, glowering presence over dinner. 'It was obvious he didn't want to be there,' says Alex. 'Marie shouldn't have made him do it.' They were gone before breakfast. It set the tone for the months to come: Juan Carlos called her friends 'The Brady Bunch' after the American sitcom about a couple trying to accept each other's children from previous marriages. He was jealous of the men and thought the women were poisoning Marie against him. 'They think I'm a barbarian,' he would say. A few weeks later, the couple went to Bolivia to see his family. Marie had met some of the relatives at the wedding, and was excited to see the real life magical realism background that she had heard about, but it was not a successful trip. Juan Carlos's mother and sisters had expected them to spend their time having family lunches and dinners, but instead – wrapped up in each other – Juan Carlos and

Marie went out to drink and party on their own and he fell out irrevocably with his sister.

To the couple's delight, Marie became pregnant once more, but to their despair, again she miscarried. They were distraught. Marie felt that Juan Carlos blamed her for not being able to carry a pregnancy. He felt that she was blaming him for her unhappiness, even though he had given up his life in the Middle East and followed her to London. However tumultuous the relationship, Jerusalem had been somewhere they shared, but London – especially Notting Hill – was Marie's place, and Juan Carlos was not a man to accept living in his wife's territory, and on her terms. The dream of having a child was ebbing away: they were left with each other.

* * * * *

PART THREE

The World
Beyond

Chapter 7

WE'RE GONNA MAKE
YOU A STAR

John Witherow, elevated from foreign editor to editor of the *Sunday Times*, wrote to Marie to confirm her new job as senior writer on the foreign desk. 'Our intention is to promote you as the paper's star writer and scoop merchant. All you have to do is deliver!'

That was quite some pressure. Marie knew she had competition on her own paper as well as on rival Sundays. Jon Swain was famed as the only British reporter to have stayed in the Cambodian capital, Phnom Penh, when it fell to the Khmer Rouge in 1975, and had been portrayed by Julian Sands in the film, *The Killing Fields*. Several of her colleagues had achieved major scoops, or had impressive regional knowledge, and John Witherow would poach additional correspondents from rival newspapers if he needed them. In the years since the Cold War ended, conflicts had unfrozen across the former Soviet bloc, while instability swept the Middle East and Africa. It was an era of intervention, with Royal Air Force jets patrolling the skies over Iraq to enforce the no-fly zone, and Britain providing troops for the UN force in Bosnia. John regarded having the best foreign coverge as critical for the success of the paper.

Selling about 1.3 million copies a week, the *Sunday Times* outsold other broadsheets, and there was plenty of money around for foreign coverage. The main competition was the rather staid *Sunday Telegraph*, which employed excellent foreign reporters, but Rupert Murdoch also wanted the *Sunday Times* to entice readers away from the *Sunday Mail*, a brash tabloid. The proliferation of 24-hour TV news was a growing threat – a Sunday paper had to have something special to attract people who could now watch the news more or less as it happened. Headlines became snappier, graphics larger and more colourful, photos more prominently displayed. The copy had to match. Sometimes this led to genuine exclusives and original stories, but Marie also wrote a lot of sensational pieces about Saddam Hussein and his sons, based mostly on information from exiles and often jointly bylined with Uzi, who had Israeli intelligence sources. Some of the stories were true – Uday Hussein and his brother had, as reported, murdered their sisters' husbands. But some stories were rumour from dubious Iraqi contacts; over a period of months, Uday was gradually resurrected after Marie reported him possibly dead, then paralysed and eventually just impotent and depressed. Saddam Hussein himself was also reported impotent. It was not Marie's best journalism, and the Iraqis responded by denying her a visa.

John appointed a new foreign editor. Sean Ryan had little international experience, but he had run Focus, the section of the paper in which they displayed big stories, both domestic and foreign, and he had a talent for putting together what they called 'the package' – copy, graphics, photos, sidebars. Soon he realised that the stories Marie filed were often not as compelling as the experiences she recounted over the phone or when she returned from an assignment. 'I wanted her to put it all in,' he says. 'I felt that she could develop a distinctive style because of the force of her personality that would give us something to distinguish the newspaper from the rest.' Jon Swain was reluctant to personalise his reporting, but Marie was already using the first person. If she had exciting experiences but didn't put them in her copy, Sean would write them in himself from what she told him over the phone. The paper was now adding photo bylines, so readers got to see as well as read the star correspondents.

Sean was a hard taskmaster. Marie would often ring the assistants on the foreign desk to find out whether he was 'pink, red or puce'. No one wanted to be on the wrong end of his temper. If a story wasn't up to scratch he would swear and shout, knowing that he might get similar treatment from John Witherow. It was a harsh, competitive sink-or-swim atmosphere from the top down. No time was wasted on niceties. When Sean called a correspondent in the field, the first question was, 'What have you got for me?' As competition tightened, Sean and John saw winning awards as a way of promoting the brand, and the pressure increased. 'Newspaper of the Year' was displayed under the masthead and 'Journalist of the Year' attached to a byline. Conflict reporting had the edge over equally important but less exciting stories. If the personal experience of a war correspondent was incorporated into the story – especially if it was heart-stoppingly dangerous – awards judges, like readers, experienced a vicarious thrill. It was no longer just about getting a story no one else had, but also about showing how you had diced with death to get it. Some reporters were uneasy about the new direction, but not Marie. She liked the idea of being fêted as the boldest of the bold.

* * * * *

Anyway, it was good to get away from home. While Marie was making frequent trips back to the Middle East and expanding her horizons to Africa and Afghanistan, Juan Carlos was kicking around London, snorting mind-blowing quantities of coke and blaming her for his unhappiness. Trailing in her wake, he felt emasculated. After years of war reporting, he found covering the royal family and British politics tedious beyond measure. The only respite was the occasional foray to Belfast, where at least there were sporadic terror attacks.

Marie had miscalculated how difficult it would be to transplant the relationship. Their love had flourished in a time of conflict, where the nearness of death made them love life. In Jerusalem, living on expenses in rented accommodation, where the only thing that mattered was getting the story and having fun, they could put off dealing with the mundanity of everyday life, but in London it was harder to keep reality at bay. It didn't stop them from trying. They ignored the red reminders from the electricity company and British Gas that dropped through the letter box. Marie was always broke, because she spent money with no regard for her means. Anna, who rode the bus to school in Sweden, noticed that when she stayed with her father and Marie they took black cabs everywhere. They paid for her to have riding lessons in Hyde Park, one of the most expensive stables in the country. Some of their happiest times involved less expensive entertainment, such as making a fort out of sheets in the living room, evenings at Pizza Express and playing with the Jerusalem street cat, Billy Smith, who rejoined the household after being released from quarantine. But she hated it when her father and Marie were drunk or high. 'They became different people – amplified versions of themselves. I felt really treasured by both of them until they forgot I was there.'

Juan Carlos had always been jealous, but now he became possessed by the notion that Marie was having an affair with Alan Jenkins. (She wasn't.) One evening when the couple was having dinner at 192 Marie spotted Alan sitting at another table, so she went over to talk, getting on the same level by kneeling next to his seat rather than leaning over. It was too much for Juan Carlos who, wildly drunk, thundered over, roaring in cartoon macho style, 'My wife does not kneel in front of another man!' A few days later, at a party at Jane Wellesley's house, Juan Carlos challenged Alan to a fight. Not normally given to extravagant gestures, Alan nonetheless lumbered out into the street after him. Luckily, James Fox, ever the diplomat, came out, threw an arm around Juan Carlos's shoulders and gently guided him away, ably assisted by Helen Fielding. Everyone laughed – it was so absurd, so old-fashioned, so stereotypically Latin and very un-Notting-Hill. On another occasion, Marie went to see Jane after a row. Alan happened to be there too, so Marie regaled them with the latest absurdity, turning it into a funny story as she so often did. Suddenly she heard Juan Carlos calling her name. Had he come to drag her away? Eventually they realised that he was yelling at her down the phone. She had pocket-called him on her phone and he had heard every word she had said about him. What to do? They laughed uproariously and had another glass of wine.

After a while it ceased to be funny. Juan Carlos was spiralling out of control. He would go to a seedy pub on the Portobello Road, drink himself into a lather, go home and start an argument. 'You want your life to be one long round of dinner parties with the friends of Marie,' he snarled at her. 'Our marriage is second to that. I don't want to be Mr Colvin.' (When he accused Marie of putting her work above him, he was unwittingly echoing his hero, Hemingway, who cabled Martha Gellhorn when she was covering the Second World War with the message, 'Are you a war correspondent or wife in my bed?') Marie felt he was making her the target for all his rage at the world and himself. He would demand sex when she didn't feel like it and accuse her of denying him his right as her husband. When she feared that anger would lurch into violence, she turned to Charlie Glass, who was living round the corner. 'She would call me, upset and crying,' he says. 'She'd tell me to get him outta there, so I'd go round and take him over to my house.' On at least one occasion, she called the police, but she would also lash out herself from time to time. Another friend recalls Marie asking for a bed for the night because she didn't want to go home and face Juan Carlos after she had smashed some of his framed pictures, cutting him with flying shards of glass. On one of her visits, Anna noticed a photo of the two of them in happier times that one or the other had ripped into pieces.

16th April 1997. I told him, stay in the Middle East and play Ernest Hemingway. You've got a few years before you blow your head off with a shotgun ... Destroyed new growth of love, just green and new and growing in ashes of earlier fights. I had started again looking at him as he slept with overpowering love, affection, desire, heartbreaking. Now that is gone.

Marie and Agneta, Juan Carlos's former wife, conferred about his drinking. The two women got along well, although Agneta worried that Marie didn't provide the stability for Anna that she would have liked. One time Marie took Anna Rollerblading so Agneta could have a word with Juan Carlos, and for that week's holiday, to Anna's great joy, they drank only Coca-Cola. Marie arranged for Juan Carlos to go to the Priory, a rehab hospital famous for its celebrity clientele, but he checked himself out early. By September 1998, two years after their wedding, Marie was chronicling in her diary the demise of her second marriage. Juan Carlos said he was going to Hawaii for a conference but she didn't believe him. Normally they would speak on the phone most days, but in the two weeks he was away, he had rung just twice and left messages without giving her a number she could call, fuelling her suspicions that he was having an affair with a film star she knew he had recently met. When they finally spoke they yelled at each other.

'So you think I'm having an affair?' he screamed.

'Answer me – tell me why you didn't leave a number! You're a liar!'

'You have no right to call me that!'

'Yes I do!'

'If you call me a liar one more time I'll never speak to you again!'

'You're a liar.'

Unable to write the still unfinished Arafat biography, and not travelling that month, Marie lay on the sofa in the evenings with Billy Smith, reading detective novels or watching rubbish television until the early hours, wondering where her husband was and with whom.

9th September 1998. Have forgotten what it is to go to bed and sleep. If I go to bed before 3, lie awake for hours, mind spinning. Drink helps, fall asleep, but morning is lost. So lie in bed reading until the print finally blurs, morning lost again.

She and Juan Carlos were torturing each other, she wrote. Sometimes the psychological pain was so acute it was almost physical.

10th September 1998. Stab someone over and over, sometimes twist the knife to make an even larger hole, first few stab holes can be sewn up. More and more holes, blood pours out until none left in the body. Can keep pumping the heart but if there's no more blood inside, it's useless. And the pools of blood on the ground, gone from the body, are useless.

Sometimes she extracted humour from the melodrama – as she was already living a 'hermit existence' in what could be described as 'virtual Wiltshire', she could avoid a weekend in the countryside that her friends had told her would be beneficial.

11th September 1998. Had brainstorm – everyone thinks I'm in the country, so I DON'T HAVE TO GO! Country for more than 48 hours fills me with dread. Sheep, green, same people every day. The weather examination, the clothes … so here I am at 34 Pembridge. Another 4am night. Woke up to Billy Smith curled into duvet against my stomach.

She didn't reflect on the warnings friends had given, while the idea of compromise in a marriage horrified her. 'Want everything perfect, break up. Compromise, you keep your man. Puke,' she wrote. It made her think not just of her failed marriage to Patrick but also the first man who had left her. She remembered her father lying in his hospital bed, and the young woman she had been trying to think what to say to him as he faced death – 'the worst memory of my life'.

14th September 1998. All my anger and rage at Juan Carlos is rage at loss, the lost life we might have had, the joy and love that are gone … but nothing I can do or say will bring back what we lost.

The nightmares returned. One that she wrote down in detail starts as a normal worry-about-work dream, the kind that most journalists have: she has forgotten to interview Gaddafi as planned and is now stuck in the wrong place desperately trying to sort out trains and planes and ferries back to Tripoli. Then suddenly she's at a bus stop in London, surrounded by teenage boys including one with a knife. 'Get a life,' she tells him and wrests the knife out of his hands. As she argues, fearing that she will never escape, men arrive and start hitting her with more knives. A group of girls is looking on. She escapes by holding on to the bumper of a bus, and the cops show up. Everyone is screaming. Her mother appears, but is angry rather than sympathetic, saying Marie had been attacked only a month earlier, and implying that it's her own fault. Suddenly, the scene changes to a courtroom where Marie is lecturing the girls for not coming to her aid. The men and boys have gone unpunished. 'I really want hospital,' she wrote. 'Pulled up my trouser leg, one lady cop says they've razor-bladed you and I can see perfect strips of skin, pus, fat and some blood oozing out – and they've done it systematically so one lies flat and the other flaps off, but it's all cut away from flesh. My legs? They'll never be the same. "You'll have fat legs. It's not so bad, I've had fat legs all my life," says the lady cop.' As she yells in agony, her brother Michael appears and sets her feet on fire. 'Why?' she asks one of the boys milling around. 'So you couldn't grow up to control us,' he replies, and she wakes up, thinking she's in Libya. It was, she concluded, the 'worst nightmare of my life'.

Marie wrote down her dreams without interpretation, so it's impossible to know if she saw that the issues that had troubled her all her life came together in this nightmare. As a journalist, she frequently observed male violence, always aware that it could be turned on her. She felt that her mother never sympathised or understood when she took risks. In her personal life she had always challenged men, starting with her father and brothers, then lovers and husbands. In the dream, the damage to her legs didn't only threaten her ability to run away from danger, but also threw her femininity into doubt with the invocation of 'fat legs'. And what had she and Juan Carlos been arguing about if not who was in control? No wonder she postponed going to bed as long as possible, when sleep churned up such fear and anxiety.

In late autumn, Juan Carlos moved out of Pembridge Villas, first to stay with Tchaik and Melissa, then into a flat of his own. By then Marie was pretty sure that he was having an affair with a mutual friend, although he denied it. Overcome with rage, she made Katrina, who had come to London on a visit, accompany her as she broke into his new flat to look for evidence of the relationship. She took nothing and destroyed nothing, just walked around, as if being in the place that he was now sharing with another woman could calm her fury.

The London friends he so resented were her life support system. Having few boundaries, she told them everything, and most took her side without question. 'Tears on the phone to Jane who is so strong in her loyalty, pain goes away,' she wrote after a conversation with Jane Wellesley. She got some comfort from exchanging confidences with Alex Shulman, whose marriage was also breaking up. 'If you were her friend, you would always be in the right in her eyes,' recalls Alex. 'As for the other person, it was always – how *could* they?' Marie and Rosie Boycott went to the gym together. Working in glossy magazines, Rosie got lots of freebies from cosmetics companies. 'Like little girls we went through the bags, pulling out Chanel eye make-up and Guerlain pancake as we gossiped,' wrote Marie. Helen Fielding was another who understood and who could be relied on to make her laugh.

And then there was Alan Jenkins.

'I used to be fun,' she said to him.

'You still are, 'Rie,' he replied.

Having just bought a part share in a yacht, he persuaded her to join him on a navigation course at the London Corinthian Sailing Club at Hammersmith. It was a joke amongst her friends that Marie, the great traveller, couldn't read a map and knew nothing of London beyond Notting Hill. She seemed surprised to find the Thames flowing through west London, as if she had thought it started near Wapping in the east where the *Sunday Times* building was located. 'The sunlight was on the river as we walked down from the Tube,' remembers Alan.

'She was looking around and her spirit lifted. From then on she wanted to live there.' She immediately felt at home at the club, with its mahogany bar and pictures of boats, just like the Seawanhaka in Oyster Bay. It was hard work getting her mind round latitudes, longitudes, degrees and charts but she relished the distraction. Beforehand, they would have a drink at The Dove, a tiny pub dating back to the seventeenth century on an alleyway just a few yards from the water.

> *21st October 1998. Navigation class. Highlight of my life. Sitting at pub with A before class, our charts spread out on table, drinks and cigarettes, madly trying to plot courses, our homework … call out answers in class, afraid to be wrong. Glory of charts as artwork. Worry of English waters: 'submarine testing ground' or 'ammunition dumping ground.'*

She decided to sell Pembridge Villas, which was indelibly associated with the marriage. Jane was converting her loft in Kensington into a self-contained flat, so towards the end of the year Marie and Billy Smith moved into the eyrie, as she called it. It gave her time to look for another flat and work out how she would manage this new phase in her life.

* * * * *

Marie had never thought of herself as a great analyst, knowing that her strength was as an on-the-ground reporter. But in the late 1990s she found she knew about a phenomenon that was taking others by surprise: Islamist terrorism. When al-Qaeda bombed the US Embassies in Nairobi and Dar es Salaam, she understood the change in the nature of terrorism.

Sunday Times, London, 30th August 1998
For those of us covering the region, it did not seem all that different at first. When these groups started carrying the Koran

as an intellectual accessory, rather than the Arabic translation of the collected works of Karl Marx that was so fashionable in the 1970s, this new development seemed to make some sense – the Middle East was never going to go Marxist. The extent to which the change had been underestimated only dawned on us gradually.

She wrote about the rise of Hamas, which used its radical Islamist message to eclipse the PLO. Across the Middle East she met young people who, disillusioned with the old, corrupt, secular leadership, were turning to Islam as an alternative; it could make interviewing Arabs somewhat laborious, she noted wryly.

Sunday Times, London, 30th August 1998
Before the advent of Islamic extremists, events before 1948 – the year of the partition of mandatory Palestine – were rarely discussed. But since the rise of the fundamentalists, such conversations inevitably begin with the golden age of Islamic domination during the 14th century. So I find that the whole process takes rather longer.

In Afghanistan she sought an interview with Mullah Omar, the leader of the Taliban, who was hosting al-Qaeda and Osama bin Laden. It was one of the few occasions when being a woman proved to be a disadvantage. A personal reply to her request, hand-written on pink paper, read (in translation): 'I am extremely busy and I only receive visits from those who are very important and highly responsible. As women in our society do not have very important responsibilities, up to now the necessity of receiving any woman is not felt.' She learnt that under the system of 'Pashtunwali', the code by which ethnic Pashtuns lived, a guest has honoured status. As the Taliban were Pashtuns, she realised that bin Laden would never be expelled from Afghanistan and that this would not be the last that would be heard of him.

In the meantime, a new conflict was brewing in the Balkans, and – having largely missed out on Bosnia – Marie decided to make this her story. Yugoslavia's new borders had left unsolved the problem of Kosovo, which remained a province of Serbia with a restive ethnic Albanian majority. Serbian rule was brutally enforced; as a result a guerrilla group, the Kosovo Liberation Army, had started to fight for independence. When the KLA attacked Serbian police posts and other targets, Serbian forces razed Albanian villages in brutal reprisals. Criticised for being late to the war in Bosnia, at the cost of many lives, President Bill Clinton didn't want to repeat the mistake, but President Slobodan Milošević was ruthless in his determination that Serbia would not relinquish Kosovo: by mid 1998 the stage was set for another conflict pitting Western forces against the Serbians and Marie was on the scene.

The conflict reached a turning point in January of the following year, when Serbian forces marched forty-five Kosovar Albanian farmers to a forest at Račak and shot them. It was an atrocity too far, and NATO determined to intervene – but only by air because Western governments thought voters wouldn't tolerate their troops coming home in body bags. At the end of March 1999, after a failed peace conference, NATO started to bomb. Fearing worse reprisals, some 800,000 Kosovars – three quarters of the population – moved en masse by foot and on tractors into Macedonia, where NATO forces were gathering, and to Albania, where the KLA had its reinforcements. Kosovo was cut off.

Marie headed for Kukës, a small town in Albania near the Kosovo border, where refugees mingled with KLA fighters, Western spies and US special forces. Like most journalists, she had one aim: to find a friendly KLA commander and be the first into Kosovo with the rebels. She climbed the aptly named Accursed Mountains to report on KLA fighters, including a group of women, who had been recruited not just from the refugees but also from Kosovars living in exile in Europe.

Sunday Times, Kukës, 11th April 1999

Lying on the mountainside with a .50 calibre rifle pointed ahead, Giylsime Rama blows the auburn fringe off her forehead and pulls the trigger. A delighted smile breaks her look of intense concentration. It is the first time this new recruit to the Kosovo Liberation Army has fired a gun. There are new soldiers from Germany, France, Switzerland, Spain and Croatia. One young Kosovar arrived from Germany in what looked like a dinner jacket; he had enlisted and been picked up at the restaurant where he had been waiting at tables. There had been no time to change.

Even Marie, with her lack of interest in weaponry, could see that this bunch didn't have a clue. When an instructor demonstrated an AK47, 'the young recruits put their fingers in their ears. They clapped excitedly when he fired, beaming like schoolchildren.'

The following week she walked fifteen miles through the mountains, led by a local teenager with a grenade in his pocket for protection. At Padesh, a few hundred yards from the border, she found a more effective group of rebels who had been fighting inside Kosovo for a year. In her story, she wrote that what she had seen after a few hours on the Kosovo side contrasted with NATO video releases showing 'clinical' airstrikes from 30,000 feet.

Sunday Times, Padesh, 18th April 1999

KLA soldiers crouched in a cold, wet bunker with a big yellow dog for comfort; a weary line of soldiers slogged up a muddy slope towards the fearful moment when they would go 'over the top'; two exhausted soldiers embraced as one returned from an attack and waved his helmet in the air at the pure joy of survival. There were hours of cold and waiting and boredom, punctuated by moments of terror. I cannot imagine there is much to compare with the terror of an incoming shell. I was sharing a cigarette with a KLA commander just under the lip of a shelf of rock overlooking the plains of Kosovo when it came ... we sought cover.

A few minutes later, a KLA soldier intercepting Serbian military communications realised that their location was about to be attacked so they ran, the rolling thunder of artillery echoing around them. At the whistle of another incoming shell, a soldier pushed Marie down into a muddy stream before they retreated from the border area as fast as they could. 'I escaped the shelling of that valley unscathed but during my three days on the front dozens of KLA soldiers suffered appalling wounds and 10 died,' she wrote.

Going further into Kosovo with the rebels would be even more dangerous. Several journalists decided it was not worth the risk, including the photographer Simon Townsley, with whom Marie was travelling, who had already been robbed at gunpoint in an Albanian hospital. 'It's too early in the war to be wounded,' he said, before lending Marie his flak jacket and teaching her how to use a pressure bandage. Sean told her there was no need to file that week – Jon Swain had flown to Croatia, taken a boat to Montenegro and trekked overnight through the mountains to become the first journalist into Kosovo from that side. His story of a Kosovar girl whose arm had been shredded by a Serbian mortar, and who had endured amputation without anaesthetic, brought home to readers the desperate situation of civilians. Marie was determined to find as good a story.

After much late night cognac drinking, she persuaded the KLA unit she had met at Padesh to take her over the border. Optimistically named Delta Force, the unit was led by a fighter called Gashi who Marie thought had 'an air of competence'. Amongst the others were a bespectacled medical student called Doc, a Christian nicknamed 'Angel', 53-year-old Dine, and Nasim Haradinaj, who told Marie that he believed in 'peace, pigeons and democracy'. (He meant doves, she realised.) A couple of weeks earlier, the KLA had driven Serbian forces from a barracks, which lay in a gully at Košare some six miles beyond the border. That was where they would establish their headquarters, and open a supply route from Albania to units deep inside Kosovo. They set off in the middle of the night, walking single file along a track to avoid the minefields on either side. Marie wrote up the experience in her diary.

23rd April 1999. Terrifying walk in night down slope from camp, log over a stream. Dine hands me butt of his rifle as I almost slip in. Walk through compound of stone homes. Deserted. Roofs crashed in by mortars. Lights of Djackovica about 1 km away. Can't tell what's happening there. Camp in a gully. Camouflage sheets up over branches. Stack of sleeping bags but they are damp with rain all day. Guards go out with heavy sniper rifles. Sleep is cold – pile wet sleeping bags on top but sleeping in a flak jacket is like being an upended turtle with a detached shell – have to sleep on back and keep sliding down. Bursts of automatic fire and shots during night, one sustained about 2am impossible tell where coming from.

The shots were Serbian snipers in the woods all around. The compound she mentions had been destroyed first by Serbians driving out the Albanian peasants who had lived there, and then again by the KLA driving out the Serbians. Living conditions at Košare were rudimentary with no electricity, Gashi having vetoed any use of the generator because of the noise.

Sunday Times, Košare, 25th April 1999
It is a barracks with no comfort. The windows have been blown out by shellfire. Off-duty soldiers cook on wood-burning stoves, heating up big pots of stew from tins left behind by the Serbs ... Coffee, cigarettes and sometimes bread arrive by donkey from Albania. Soldiers cluster round to greet them. Days are spent cleaning out the barracks. A sodden pile of detritus from Serbs is in the courtyard – fatigues, sweaters, playing cards, empty soft-drinks bottles and letters. Soldiers amuse themselves by looking through photographs of Serbs in uniforms with their girlfriends.

The *Sunday Times* wrote in the 'standfirst', the introductory paragraph, 'Marie Colvin, the first reporter to enter Kosovo from Albania, is with a KLA unit fighting to open supply lines. She braved sniper fire and shelling to send this report.'

Whether she really was the first is open to contention – teams from CNN and the BBC had been over the border briefly during the initial fighting over Košare. But Marie stayed longer and went in deeper, spending five days inside Kosovo. Patrols probing Serbian positions invariably came under fire, so accompanying them was terrifying. Fighters in forward positions were calling in the coordinates of Serbian positions to NATO liaison officers in Kukës, who would relay the information to Brussels, but the rebels were frustrated at what they saw as the slow pace of the air campaign. They couldn't understand why NATO didn't bomb the three Serbian artillery and tank emplacements that blocked their way. Jet fighters roared overhead, but the bombing of Belgrade they heard about on the radio seemed far removed from their desperate, low-tech guerrilla struggle in the mountains.

At night, when the boom of artillery kept them awake, the fighters would tell Marie their stories: families in Pristina or Zurich, dreams of being an architect or going back to college, jobs and girlfriends left behind. Some had fled Kosovo because of discrimination against Albanians, while others had had relatives killed in Serbian attacks. One man had by chance found his long lost sister in the mountains and taken her and her exhausted children to a refugee camp in Albania. 'He told us this story every night in the barracks, as if by telling it he would somehow understand how that miracle could happen,' Marie wrote in a reflective piece for the *Times Literary Supplement* a few months later. She was the only foreigner and the only woman in the group, but the bonding experience of being together under fire dissolved such differences. 'Perhaps in all barracks in a war there is a camaraderie that – intensified by the ever-present possibility of sudden death – thrives on deep and immediate intimacy, that removes the need for formalities, and that, once established, is only broken by death,' she wrote.

As the KLA consolidated its hold on the border area, more journalists found the route in. 'Kosare now so secure it's a journalist theme park,' Marie snorted. She had reported her first stories during the gloriously anarchic and usually short golden period before a guerrilla army appoints media managers to restrict journalists' access. On her way back up the mountain she found that three photographers she knew had been confined to a bunkhouse room as the KLA argued about what to do with them. She convinced Dine, her KLA escort, that they were good guys. 'Let us release the prisoners,' he said. Her old friend from her UPI days, Jonathan Landay, was also on his way in. They had dinner on the border. Still full of intense enthusiasm, he was 'jumping up and down in his seat' about the lack of coordination he observed between NATO and its Kosovar allies. Marie just wondered why the US wasn't helping the KLA directly. Having been captured and held by the rebels a few months earlier, Jonathan was less wide-eyed about them, but Marie had been convinced that their cause was just. That didn't mean she was going to accept a 'tall, blue-eyed Prussian uberman type' who called himself 'Press Officer of Operations Group 3' censoring her copy. She refused to alter the numbers of dead and injured for the simple reason that his figures were untrue. Uberman also wanted to stop her from going back in with Delta Force to another camp. 'We want you to be secure and in peace,' he said. Marie stamped her feet and shouted, 'I don't want to be in peace!' which at least made him smile.

Buoyed by the sense of being utterly alive that journalists experience in war zones – 'a larger version of pinching yourself to make sure you can feel' – she headed back to Kukës to restock batteries, film and other supplies, and to wash her clothes, get some more cash and consider her next move. She called Jane to check that everything was all right at home and that someone was taking care of Billy Smith. A new batch of journalists had arrived, many of them young freelancers, ready to head up to the border and get their piece of Kosovo action. One evening Marie was in the only bar in town, at a table stacked with beer bottles, regaling the newcomers with her stories from inside Kosovo when a dark-haired figure pushed his way through the crowd to the table where she was sitting. She paused and looked up. It was her ex-husband, Patrick.

* * * * *

In the time that Marie and Juan Carlos had been together, Patrick had seen very little of her, but gossip had a way of filtering out and he knew she had been having a hard time. When he heard that the marriage had collapsed, he worried. 'I knew she'd do something extreme to compensate, that would be her therapy,' he says. 'I felt an overwhelming urge to stop her doing anything too crazy.' Assigned to Albania by the *Daily Telegraph*, he resolved to persuade her not to cross into Kosovo. At the guesthouse where most journalists were staying they told him he was too late – she'd been into Kosovo and was already back, and in the bar. 'She was holding court with these admiring young men hanging on her every word,' he recalled later. 'Her eyes were shining and the story was punctuated by that delicious earthy chuckle of hers.'

Marie gave a different story of the encounter. At the journalists' guesthouse, she told friends, she saw familiar clothes amongst the belongings dumped in a collective dorm, but couldn't work out whom they belonged to. At first she thought that Juan Carlos had pursued her to Albania. Should she hide? Then it occurred to her that they might belong to Patrick. Current or former husband? She braced herself for a meeting but had no idea with which. When it turned out to be Patrick, she was delighted. They talked all night. Troubled by lingering guilt, he felt the need to make amends for the way he had treated her, and both were carried away by the romance of finding each other again in a war zone. They knew it was like a scene from a B movie, but that just made them laugh. It felt right.

At the end of May, in one of the worst mistakes of the air war, NATO jets bombed the Košare barracks, killing seven KLA fighters and injuring twenty-five. Inexplicably, the site had remained on the target list, even though it had been seized from the Serbians by the KLA six weeks earlier and visited by dozens of journalists. Marie, who was back in London for a short break, thought about the young men she had met who had convinced her that they were fighting for freedom.

Times Literary Supplement, 4th June 1999

I'm not sure how any of these young men feel now that the planes we saw flying overhead every day and that were supposed to destroy the artillery and tanks between them and their villages and families have instead bombed their barracks. I'm not sure whether they are still alive. I think anyone who met them would think it hypocritical for a NATO spokesman to get up on television every day and talk about the success of hundreds of warplane sorties, and for diplomats to brief journalists that NATO is doing all it can to defeat Milošević, and not to help the only people who are fighting his troops and paramilitaries every day and are willing to die doing it. There was no talk in the Košare Barracks about zero tolerance for returning body bags. They saw too many.

Spring blossomed into summer, and the war turned against the Serbians. NATO airstrikes weakened the Serbian military inside Kosovo, and wore down President Milošević in Belgrade. On 3 June he accepted an international peace plan; nine days later columns of NATO troops moved in from Macedonia to impose order and provide aid. More than half a million Kosovar Albanians decided to go home. Roads were choked with NATO tanks and troop carriers, alongside tractors laden with returning Kosovar families, some cheering and waving at the troops they saw as saviours. Blood-red poppies bloomed in the fields around blackened, burnt villages. Marie had already written about a massacre in the village of Meja, interviewing more than a hundred refugees who had lost relatives or witnessed the Serbian attack. Now she visited the area around Djakovica, gathering evidence like a forensic investigator, filling her notebooks with names, ages, dates and eyewitness accounts. Meticulously, she reported atrocities carried out by Serbian paramilitaries, carefully correlating accounts and visiting burnt villages.

Sunday Times, Djakovica, 20th June 1999

The human body, when burnt, is reduced to an almost child-like size. It is a horrible piece of knowledge that comes with reporting from Kosovo. In house after house, village after village, I have seen those bodies, so small that it seems they must be those of children, yet they are not.

As the ethnic Albanians re-established themselves in their ruined towns and villages, the few Serbs who had remained became the target of revenge attacks. Marie reported on the murder of Godsa Draza, a 78-year-old Serb grandmother who had stayed to tend the animals after her sons and their families had fled.

Sunday Times, Pristina, 15th August 1999

Her two withered feet were sticking up out of a pile of hay that had been dumped on the rubbish tip at the bottom of her garden. Some time on Tuesday night, Draza had been shot in her bed, shot again at the back door of her house, dragged down the garden and hidden. None of her neighbours admitted hearing or seeing anything unusual.

The cycle of ethnic hatred had turned. Serbs had called NATO the 'KLA airforce' but now they relied on NATO troops to protect them against Albanian vigilantes.

Marie never practised partisan journalism, the kind that adopts a cause and reports only the facts that advance it. Having no ideology, she never flinched from reporting stories that cast a bad light on people for whom she had sympathy. She was simply drawn to the underdog. In an interview with the Australian journalist Denise Leith three years later, she reflected on the question of objectivity in war reporting. 'When you're physically uncovering graves in Kosovo, I don't think there are two sides to the story,' she said. 'To me there is a right and a wrong, a morality, and if I don't report that, I don't see the reason for being there.' She felt that journalism, especially the early reporting of atrocities in 1998, had made a difference, pulling NATO in to defend the Kosovar Albanians, and that was good. The revenge killings appalled her but didn't change her view of the Kosovar cause. Patrick, by contrast, described Kosovo as 'a blighted land of blighted people' – like many journalists who have been through several wars he didn't see good guys and bad guys but history and politics. He believed that you had to pull back and see the geostrategic context, while Marie had Martha Gellhorn's derision for 'the big picture'. For her, context mattered, but the experience of individuals in war, whether fighters or victims, was the essence of the story.

The editors at the *Sunday Times* were delighted with Marie's stories, which they thought had more urgency than similar accounts of atrocities in rival newspapers. Sean Ryan took her out for lunch when she got back. 'She had a sense of mission and a zeal, an almost evangelical air about her when she talked about Kosovo,' he says. 'I realised that she had this passion that set her apart from anybody else I knew.'

Alan Jenkins felt that Kosovo had affected Marie more than previous stories. 'When I asked her, she would just say it was awful,' he recalls. 'There were no anecdotes about soldiers or officers, no funny stories.' She could not unsee what she had seen, and he feared she was losing her ability to distance herself from horror.

* * * * *

By early September 1999 Marie was on to a new story. East Timor had long been known as a dangerous place for journalists. Back in 1975, Indonesian soldiers, who were invading the territory at the end of Portuguese colonial rule, had killed five journalists working for Australian television. It was no accident: they wanted to ensure there were no witnesses to their brutal campaign to seize control of East Timor against the will of its people. In the two decades that followed, up to one-third of the Timorese population was killed or died of hunger and disease, and their plight became a *cause célèbre* amongst human rights activists. Britain and the US saw the Indonesian dictator, Suharto, as a stable force in the region and East Timor was largely ignored until 1998 when Suharto stepped down and a new Indonesian government agreed that the UN should organise a ballot on independence for the territory. Polling day was 30 August 1999.

It was clear that the Timorese would vote for independence, but not that Indonesia would cede control without a fight. Others on the paper predicted mayhem and thought it too dangerous, but Marie was determined to go. Violence surged in the run-up to the poll. Wild-haired militiamen terrorised Timorese civilians and on one occasion used swords, machetes and iron bars to attack a car full of journalists while Indonesian police looked on. In April, some two hundred Timorese civilians were killed in the priest's house next to the Catholic church in Liquiçá. Blood ran down the walls after the militia shot through the roof to murder terrified people hiding under the eaves. The massacre had a horrible resonance for the UN mission overseeing the referendum, reminding them of the genocide in Rwanda in 1994, when tens of thousands were slaughtered in churches where they had taken refuge, while UN peacekeepers failed to come to their rescue.

Polling day was emotional: music blared from the churches, everyone dressed in their best and more than 98 per cent voted, some queuing for hours in the hot sun. Even before the result was announced, militia attacked pro-independence supporters outside the compound of the United Nations Mission in East Timor, UNAMET, in the East Timorese capital, Dili. A hotel where journalists were staying was ransacked and a BBC correspondent was nearly killed when militiamen kicked his head and hit him with a rifle butt. After that, most editors pulled out their correspondents. The Indonesian strategy was clear: whatever the outcome of the referendum, the government planned to use the militias to intimidate and threaten all foreigners – journalists, aid workers, election observers and the UN – until they left.

Marie and Maggie O'Kane, whom she knew from Baghdad and who was now writing for the *Guardian*, were on the last plane into Dili. They checked into the Hotel Turismo. 'Where is everybody?' Marie asked two Dutch journalists, Minka Nijhuis, who wrote for a Dutch newspaper, and Irena Cristalis, who was filing for the BBC. Both had been to East Timor several times and knew the story well. They explained that only a couple of dozen journalists remained. 'But the story's only just beginning,' said Marie. She took a room with a balcony from which she could see the Red Cross compound, where a thousand terrified Timorese who had taken refuge were being attacked. A soldier pointed his assault rifle at a woman, while other women were kicked or hit with rifle butts. Militiamen roamed the courtyard, shouting and firing in the air. The Red Cross workers were powerless. After about half an hour some soldiers and militiamen drove the aid workers to the airport while others looted the refugees' possessions. They separated out the women and children before marching the men away, as the police again looked on passively. Soldiers and militia were banging on the doors of the journalists' rooms at the Turismo. No one answered, but it was clear they couldn't stay. The Australian Ambassador came to the rescue, loading the journalists into diplomatic vehicles. There was no time to collect their belongings. 'What do you want, your life or your clothes?' he yelled at a reporter who tried to get a bag. Marie managed to grab her computer and satellite phone. The journalists were driven to the UNAMET compound, two miles away.

They were not the only ones taking refuge there; chased by militia, desperate Timorese men and women had scaled the walls, braving razor wire coiled on top – several threw their babies over and at least fifty people were treated for gashes. The next day more refugees arrived, including an organised column of 800 led by an elfin nun called Sister Esmeralda. Holding her bible, she had walked up to a unit of Indonesian army and militia who, she said, had made a corridor like the Red Sea parting for Moses. UNAMET was located in the Teachers' College, surrounded by hills and with a swamp in front and a single road out. It was indefensible and the mission was unarmed. UN security officers felt naked – how could they protect themselves, let alone the refugees? But some thought it was better that way, because even the Indonesian military might hesitate before attacking unarmed foreigners.

Inside the compound pandemonium reigned. Several local UN staff from outlying areas had been murdered, so the rest, including their families, had arrived along with the internationals. UN officials knew they couldn't abandon local staff as they had in Rwanda but they were short of food, and fuel for the water pump was running low. More than 2,000 terrified people were cooking over small fires, sleeping on the ground and using the increasingly insanitary toilets. The head of the UN mission, Ian Martin, was holed up in his office talking on the phone to the Indonesian Defence Minister, the UN Secretary General and world leaders, trying to find a way to pressure the Indonesians into stopping the violence, which they were clearly orchestrating. For the UN Public Information Officer, Brian Kelly, the arrival of twenty-six journalists was a mixed blessing. 'I more than welcomed the presence of Marie because she was a genuine professional,' he recalls. 'But a lot of the "journalists" in that batch were single issue activists using journalistic reasons for gaining access in Timor. They were demanding and excited and very difficult to handle.'

They were also highly critical of the UN, which they felt had been unprepared for the chaos following the referendum and was not doing enough to save the people of East Timor. Some UN staff, desperate to leave before they were slaughtered along with everyone else, saw Marie as a troublemaker too because she would say loudly that if they left, the refugees would be massacred, and the UN would have blood on its hands. No activist, Marie nonetheless saw a clear choice between right and wrong in East Timor.

Two days after Marie reached the compound, Indonesian soldiers allowed militiamen to ambush a UN convey they were supposedly escorting on a mission to retrieve supplies from the port. Every night gunfire sounded just outside the compound. One evening Marie and Brian were chatting outside when a bullet, probably a stray, swished through a tree and hit a UN car about 10 metres away.

'Heavy leaves here,' said Brian laconically. The press officers were receiving constant calls from media across the globe on a satellite phone left by the Australian Broadcasting Corporation. Brian asked the reporters to take some of the calls. 'They could talk emotionally and dramatise it more than was permissible to a UN spokesman,' he explains. 'It drew more attention to what was going on and indirectly kept up the pressure on the UN as well as the Indonesians.'

Eight thousand miles away in London, Sean grew used to hearing Marie's voice on BBC Radio 4. He heard her say that militiamen were about to break into the compound. 'I thought they were coming in, and everyone was going to be slaughtered, and Marie wouldn't stand a chance,' he recalls. 'By the time I managed to speak to her myself the militia had pulled back, and the immediate danger seemed to have passed.' He didn't mind her broadcasting, but he suggested that she send him a 500-word file every day so they could compile a piece for Sunday even if communications had gone down by then. She sent nothing.

With supplies alarmingly low, and unable to guarantee the security of UN staff, Ian Martin recommended to the UN Secretary General that they evacuate. After days of negotiation, he had an agreement from the Indonesians that local Timorese UN staff could go too, and from the government in Canberra that they would be allowed to enter Australia. A whisper went through the refugees in the compound: the UN is going to abandon us. Thinking it would be safer than staying in the compound, which would undoubtedly be overrun the moment the UN left, some slipped away into the hills where a guerrilla force was gathering. Gunfire erupted as they escaped and some were shot dead. Marie walked through the compound giving the children yellow tennis balls left by a departing Australian delegation. Everyone was filthy and exhausted, but Marie, Minka and Irena were feeling a bit better because they had broken open a suitcase left by Portuguese election observers and looted clean clothes and snack bars.

Marie and Irena decided to slip out of the compound early to see what was going on and try to retrieve some belongings from the Hotel

Turismo. So as not to look like journalists, they took nothing with them, not even notebooks or cameras. A militiaman with a machete ran a finger across his throat to warn them what might happen if they didn't turn back, but at that moment a soldier pulled up in a truck and in surprisingly good English invited them to his office, a small dilapidated building with an old sofa and chairs round a wooden coffee table. Lieutenant Dendi Suryadi turned out to be, in Marie's words, 'articulate and professional'. He served them noodles and omelette – the first hot meal they had eaten for days – and talked of his desire to go to the US military academy at West Point. They asked him to drive them through Dili to the Turismo.

Sunday Times, Dili, 12th September 1999
It was an apocalyptic vision. Hundreds of militia roamed the streets, some walking, some riding up to three on a motorcycle with one carrying looted goods, the second an assault rifle, the third driving. It was a frenzy of looting. The post office was still burning, but most of the other buildings were burnt-out skeletons. The lieutenant drove grimly. Gunfire sounded nearby. There were no civilians or cars on the streets. It was as if the barbarians had taken over. One motorcycle passed us, the militiaman on the back waving his pistol at us and smiling maniacally, showing no fear of the army vehicle or its occupants.

At the Turismo things got even more surreal – the militia had looted her La Perla bra and silk knickers but had left her flak jacket. Lieutenant Suryadi insisted on driving them on what Irena called a sightseeing tour of the war zone. 'We came to win the hearts and minds of the people,' he said. 'I think we failed.' They watched militiamen torch a building. 'Look carefully,' said Lieutenant Suryadi. 'It's important that you remember this.' By pure chance, the two journalists had come across an Indonesian officer who wanted journalists to see the terror his comrades were inflicting on the Timorese.

Back in the compound, Ian Martin gave a press conference, announcing that the UN staff, international and national, would evacuate. Any journalists who stayed would have to leave the compound. Marie suggested to Irena and Minka that they grab some food and set themselves up in a small house nearby. For protection they would borrow a sporadically vicious black-and-tan dog which belonged to one of the refugees. As they walked to the gates for a recce, a couple of militiamen came by on a motorbike, grenades in hands. The UN guards shooed the three of them back to the compound. That was the end of that idea. It would not be possible to stay elsewhere.

Refugees were crying and praying, singing hymns and reading the Bible. Marie allowed some to use her satellite phone to call their relatives overseas or in West Timor. Many wept, convinced this would be their last communication before they were killed. Sister Esmeralda shouted at the UN staff: 'Now you leave us to die like dogs. We want to die like people!' She called her Mother Superior in Rome on Marie's satphone. 'In twelve hours we will all be killed,' she said. The atmosphere was febrile. UN staff huddled, dismayed at the turn of events. They had come to East Timor to protect the people, and now they were abandoning them. A group of reporters went to see Ian Martin to protest about the plan to evacuate, while a petition circulated for UN staff to sign if they wanted to stay on an individual basis. 'Well, there goes a hot bath,' thought Brian Kelly, as he got out his pen. The evacuation was delayed by 24 hours.

Most of the journalists, including Maggie O'Kane, had already left. Everyone was hungry, tired and on edge, talking endlessly about the risks of staying – would they starve or be killed? Marie shrugged. 'Forget it, I'm not leaving. This is the biggest story in the world,' she said to Irena and Minka. 'She was very focused,' says Irena. Marie called Jane to talk over her decision, but there was no doubt. 'She was determined to stay,' recalls Jane. Marie knew it could be a fateful choice. 'She called me to say goodbye as she was likely to be killed,' remembers Cat. Later Marie explained her thinking. 'I just couldn't leave. We'd been living with these people for four or five days, sleeping next to them, getting rice from them,' Marie told Denise Leith. 'In a way it was a hard decision, because you had to think, I could die here. But equally I just didn't feel I could live with myself if I left. It was morally wrong, the idea that we would walk out, say goodbye and all those people knew they were going to be killed. It was not a decision I could have made the other way.'

* * * * *

The next day, reporters for mainstream media left with the bulk of international UN staff and the local employees. Eighty international staff, including Brian Kelly and Ian Martin, remained on a voluntary basis, knowing their gesture might at best be futile, and at worst suicidal. They were human shields. As the last truck trundled away, Marie called Sean. He would have liked a say in her decision but it soon became apparent that it was a fait accompli. He asked who amongst the journalists had remained, and she explained it was just Irena, Minka and herself.

'Where are the men?' asked Sean.

'They've gone,' replied Marie, and, without missing a beat added, 'I guess they don't make men like they used to.' It was a great line, oft repeated afterwards.

In fact two journalists (men, incidentally) had gone into the hills with the guerrillas, and at least one activist who saw himself as a journalist even if no one else did remained in the compound. But the three women were the only professional reporters broadcasting across the world from the UN compound, as militiamen prowled the perimeter, threatening to attack.

It was Friday. By Saturday morning, Sean had received no copy from Marie. 'She was still merrily popping up on Japanese TV and CNN, and not writing a word,' he recalls. So much had happened in one week, that she was struggling to get it all in. Also, she had broken her glasses, which were now attached to her ears with a rubber band. When she finally filed on Saturday afternoon, the copy was chaotic, like her early stories. 'Marie's written in code!' said John Witherow. There was less than an hour to decrypt and rewrite before the final deadline. In Marie's defence, it has to be said that the situation was changing almost minute by minute – even as she was filing, the Indonesian defence minister was in Dili with a delegation from the UN Security Council. But weekly journalism was not her priority at this point. Her aim was to save the people in the compound, and she knew that hour-by-hour live broadcasting would have far more impact than a chronicle of events to be read at leisure on Sunday.

News of the pitiful state of the refugees and the bravery of the journalists and UN staff who had remained influenced public opinion and put huge pressure on world leaders who, in turn, pressured the Indonesian government. The *Sunday Times* ran a thundering editorial saying Marie's 'account of the hell inside Dili ... confronts the world's leaders with searing evidence of the scale of the calamity that has overwhelmed East Timor'. It placed Marie, Irena and Minka in 'the honoured tradition' of great female journalists of the past: Clare Hollingworth who reported the German invasion of Poland in 1939, the *Sunday Times* Second World War correspondent Virginia Cowles and, of course, Martha Gellhorn. Marie's report, the editorial said, 'exposes the huff and puff of the world's leaders over East Timor for what it is – a disgrace.' The Americans had only just suspended arms sales to Indonesia; Britain had a long record of 'nuzzling up to Indonesia's rulers'. Australia was worse. The UN came in for criticism, as did the International Monetary Fund and the World Bank. The *Sunday Times* called for an international force to come to the aid of the people of East Timor, as it had in Kosovo.

That Saturday, Dili remained calm – proof that the Indonesians could turn the militia on and off like a tap. Visiting Security Council envoys were horrified by the deteriorating conditions in the compound. Under mounting international pressure, the next day the Indonesians agreed that all the refugees sheltering with the UN could leave for Darwin with the rest of the UN staff, and plans would be put in place for an international force, led by the Australians, to restore order to

East Timor. The siege was over. Marie left a few days later with the refugees. As the trucks prepared to pull away in the darkness just before dawn, a refugee had a heart attack. 'We just left the body lying there,' recalled Marie in her interview with Denise Leith. 'We couldn't take a body into Australia and there was nothing more we could do for him. Someone said a little prayer over him.' The drive to the airstrip was terrifying. 'Every house and building was burning – it was like driving through hell. We didn't know if the militia would come or not.' Few of the refugees had ever been on a plane before. An elderly Timorese woman clung on to her so tightly during the flight that when they disembarked in Darwin, Marie realised that her ribcage was bruised.

* * * * *

Maggie O'Kane of the *Guardian* met her at the airport. 'It was such an extraordinary thing that Marie had done,' she recalls. 'She got off the plane in this slightly forlorn manner, completely strung out.' They went to a fish restaurant for a long, relaxing lunch washed down by white wine in the Darwin sun. 'She was incredibly self-effacing about it, as she always was,' Maggie says. 'Kind of playing it down. But I felt like I was in the presence of something really special.'

After a few days of sleep and food, Marie returned to Dili with the Australian-led force. Scores more journalists were arriving, including Patrick. He and Marie moved back into the Turismo. Marie was on a high, the heroine of the hour credited with saving the refugees. A few militiamen were still prowling the ruined streets, but others had fled to West Timor, fearing that their neighbours would take revenge. Many had been local men and boys, paid by the Indonesians to terrorise and loot. In a suburb of Dili Marie saw graffiti reading 'Please forgive me' sprayed on the street. The danger for journalists was not over: Sander Thoenes, a Dutch freelance writing for the *Financial Times*, was killed in an ambush. Jon Swain, who had driven in from West Timor, was also attacked, while his interpreter, Anacleto Da Silva, was abducted and never found.

After another week, Marie and Patrick stopped off in Singapore on the way home, staying at the Raffles Hotel for a night. It was a good place to wind down and relax. 'She calmed down quite quickly,' he recalls.

The impact of the three reporters remaining in the UN compound in Dili has been disputed ever since. 'What journalists did was hugely important in terms of the whole international climate and that contributed to the pressure on Indonesia, but I don't believe it was a significant element in the UN's decision making,' says Ian Martin. Marie, however, was convinced that their presence had shamed the UN into staying. 'I felt proud that my reporting contributed to the reversal of the UN's decision to pull out,' she wrote in a later piece. 'I embarrassed the decision-makers and that felt good because it saved lives. It is rare to see such a direct result in journalism.'

* * * * *

Chapter 8

LEAP BEFORE YOU LOOK

Marie was much celebrated on her return from East Timor. The *Daily Express* (admittedly edited by her friend Rosie Boycott) ran a story about her under the headline, 'As the UN prepared to flee East Timor, one woman refused to go. Her courage saved 1500 lives'. The issue of being brave while female drew attention to Marie's work, but she found it irritating that people kept asking her what it was like to be 'a woman war correspondent'. In a *Sunday Times* piece entitled 'Courage knows no gender', she quoted Martha Gellhorn who said, 'Feminists nark me. I think they've done a terrible disservice to women, branding us as "women's writers." Nobody says men writers; before, we were all simply writers.' The image of the glamorous female correspondent, fluttering her mascara-heavy eyelashes was far from the mark – Marie hadn't looked very glamorous trudging through the mud in Kosovo, or sleeping rough in the UN compound in Dili.

Sunday Times, London, 10th October 1999
I don't have to dab Chanel under my ears or play dumb for it to be easier for me to get through a checkpoint manned by surly militiamen with automatic weapons. They do react differently to me because of my sex. They feel less threatened by a woman, however crazed they are.

But she pointed out that men had their own advantages. 'Male reporters can play on the boys' club mentality, swapping dirty jokes with soldiers, or discussing the merits of different weapons.' Although more women were covering conflict than when she had set out on her career, Marie wrote, war reporting was still dominated by men, so female war correspondents were probably more driven because it was harder to succeed. 'Maybe we feel the need to test ourselves more, to see how much we can take and survive.' While she didn't think women were more sensitive than men, nor that what she saw as a moral choice to stay in East Timor had anything to do with gender, she thought that women were more likely to spend time with victims, coaxing the story out gently, rather than rushing on to the next thing. 'From experience I know men think differently from women, but since I've never been able to figure out their behaviour in other walks of life, I find it just as impossible to explain why they think differently in wars,' she wrote.

Two extreme assignments in one year would have been enough for most people but Marie was on a roll. As the autumn of 1999 wore on, she turned her attention to an even more brutal conflict. While she had been absorbed by East Timor, Vladimir Putin had become Russian Prime Minister in August. One of his first moves was to restore federal control over Chechnya, a former Soviet territory that had declared independence at the end of the Cold War, and which Russia had fought between 1994 and 1996. Putin saw the withdrawal of Russian troops at the end of that conflict as a humiliation. Chechnya, which was run by warlords, some Islamist, some simply criminal, was a source of instability in the region. In October 1999, after a Chechen militant incursion into the neighbouring Russian republic of Dagestan, Putin sent Russian troops back in.

Reporters who had covered the previous Chechen War knew that Russian artillery would pound the Chechen capital, Grozny, until the rubble bounced. Chechen gangs would kidnap Russian conscripts, journalists and anyone else they could find. There would be terror attacks in Moscow. And, worse than anything, the Russian airforce would relentlessly bombard Chechen villages and towns. Neither side would show any mercy; civilians would flee and die and no one would do a thing to stop the killing. Most journalists went to the Russian republics of Ingushetia or Dagestan to interview refugees who had fled across the border, and sometimes briefly cross into Chechnya with Russian troops. Marie was one of very few journalists considering going in with the Chechens.

Patrick begged her not to go. At last their relationship was working. 'Being a good Catholic I thought my sins would be wiped away, absolved,' he says. 'I was tremendously grateful to be given a second chance, all my bad doings would be gone ... she seemed to be up for it as well.' Always more pious than Marie, Patrick saw falling in love again as a kind of miracle. Marie saw it more like coming home. They alternated weekends between London and Paris where he was living and were talking about Marie undergoing IVF so they could start a family, even though she was now forty-three. She listened to Patrick but the lure of the story was irresistible. It was midwinter, when temperatures in the Chechen mountains fall well below freezing, so on Jane's insistence she went to Harrods and bought the warmest – and possibly the most expensive – jacket she could find, properly waterproof and lined with fur.

At the airport, she ran into Maggie O'Kane and a *Guardian* photographer, Sean Smith. They had been in touch with the same Chechen exiles in Amsterdam who had arranged for a contact to pick up both teams when they landed in the Georgian capital, Tbilisi. From there, they would be taken over the border to meet Aslan Maskhadov, the President of the self-declared Chechen Republic. Maggie looked up to Marie, so she was shocked to see her getting drunk on the plane, and ending up in no fit state to talk to the conservative Muslim Chechens who met them at the carousel as they picked up their luggage. A young Russian photographer, Dmitri 'Dima' Beliakov, who had been hired to translate for Marie as well as take pictures, was alarmed to see the state she was in. He quickly realised that he was in a difficult position, as the Chechens were even more suspicious of a young Russian man of military age than a drunken American woman with a cigarette dangling from her lips. It was not an auspicious start. Marie didn't write about the incident in her diary – maybe she had been anxious, and alcohol helped calm her nerves, or maybe she had been worrying about her decision to ignore Patrick's entreaties. Maybe she had an inkling of just how perilous this assignment would be.

The next day, Chechen rebels accompanied by Georgian police drove them to an airforce base from where they were taken by helicopter to the border. They crossed by foot under the light of the moon. 'The first night we were holed up in this tiny wooden hut full of freezing refugees,' recalls Maggie. 'We moved out to sleep in the car to make way for women and kids who were walking out of Chechnya.' It was Saturday so Marie filed a short piece. On Sunday the commander designated by the Chechen leadership failed to show up. Monday passed. Everyone was getting agitated and impatient. 'The next day suddenly this random commander tips up at the hut. We've no idea who he is and who sent him,' says Maggie. 'But Marie is completely gung ho and they're going with him.' It seemed like a risky thing to do, but Marie wasn't prepared to wait. She and Dima drove off, leaving Maggie and Sean behind.

Commander Hossein Isabaev was a massive, bearded hulk of a man, notorious for kidnappings, feuds and all the other venal activities practised by Chechen warlords. In deference to a *fatwa* issued by a more senior rebel leader ordering that journalists be protected, he assured Marie and Dima they would be safe with him. Travelling by night to avoid being spotted by Russian bombers, they drove through the mountains towards Grozny, passing fighters in jeeps making for the battle and convoys of refugees driving Russian-made Ladas heading the other way. Isabaev told Marie and Dima not to stray – they were his guests, and he would have to fight any warlord who kidnapped them, which would distract him from fighting the Russians. Most Chechen units were made up of clansmen of the commander, who was responsible for food, weapons and ammunition as well as building bomb shelters on the front line. Dima saw them all as bandits – it didn't help that they baited him with jibes like, 'Wanna know how many Russians I've beheaded?' – but Marie was more sympathetic. She thought they were fighting a brutal enemy for a good cause, like the rebels she had met in Kosovo.

By day the fighters would sleep in makeshift stone and timber shelters, warmed by a wood stove. On one occasion they stayed in a rough dwelling of flat mountain stone with a raised platform where between five and twenty fighters could sleep, while Isabaev's wife – known as the deputy commander – cooked and made tea.

Undated, December 1999. A woollen hat dries on a grenade launcher. In the corner a Kalashnikov hangs from a hook with a handwritten roster for two-hour watches … Lunch is sheep, plum conserves, bread cooked by wife, flat and chewy, tea and water from mountain stream, pickles, sugar always on table. Dirt floor, foot stools for seats. Beds built on wood log frame. Sword. Old hunting rifle in metal scabbard. Collection of weapons against wall. Hunting rifles, kalashnikov, shoulder grenade launcher. Men spread sheepskin on beds and stand facing Mecca to pray while scantily clad singers on TV. Everything public – men brush hair, one mirror on wall, sleep while others sit and drink tea and play cards.

Marie lay down on a bed and pulled out two uncomfortable lumpy things from under the sheepskin: hand grenades. Placing them carefully to one side, she turned over and slept, annoying the fighters and embarrassing Dima by snoring like a train.

While Maggie and Sean were taken to see Maskhadov as planned, Marie and Dima ended up meeting the fundamentalist leader, Ibn al-Khattab, a Saudi veteran of the war against the Russian occupation of Afghanistan, and an associate of Osama bin Laden. With his shoulder-length black ringlets carefully oiled, and wearing a tall fur hat and freshly laundered fatigues, al-Khattab paced up and down the courtyard, holding hands with another commander in the Arab style. Marie thought he moved like a catwalk model. His right hand was encased in a black glove to hide the loss of two fingers to a grenade, while the fingernails on his left hand were manicured. He talked of how the fighters had no fear of death because Allah was with them. The fighters, Marie thought, were somewhat sceptical, not just because they liked a drink, but because, unlike him, they were spending terrifying days and nights under heavy bombardment in the mud and ice. They referred to Khattab and his followers as Wahhabis, puritanical Saudi Muslims, whereas their cause was nationalism, rooted in their pride in being Chechen.

The refugees had horrific stories of villages being relentlessly shelled by Russian artillery and then bombed from the air. The children, they said, had started to go deaf from the noise of explosions. The refugees were used to the tough life of a peasant, but this was something else: a woman in a red velour dress, her head covered by a kerchief, told Marie that when the barrage started she ran into the yard to pull her cow into the basement, only for a missile to hit her house a few seconds later and eviscerate her husband and five children. She was travelling with her brother who was bleeding from a shrapnel wound in the foot. 'I want the world to feel ashamed for what is happening,' she told Marie. 'The world is safe and is doing nothing while we are being slaughtered.' Marie's notebooks are filled with similar stories. At the few hospitals that were still functioning, she found dozens of injured civilians, some targeted from the air as they were trying to escape along the road the Russians had designated as a 'safe corridor'. Looking down from the mountain over a landscape of white roofs, dirt roads and barnyards of cows and chickens, she realised she had a similar perspective to that of the Russian pilots, and wondered how they could drop their bombs on such an obviously civilian scene.

All day long they could hear the jet fighters overhead and the thunder of artillery. At night, fires started by missiles flared from the mountain ridges like a flickering crest on a dragon's back. One night as Marie and Dima, accompanied by a handful of fighters, were approaching the front line south of Grozny, a missile struck a few yards away, making a huge crater that swallowed the other vehicle in their convoy. Luckily no one was hurt, but the next morning, now reduced to one car, they came under attack again. Their vehicle was blasted by shrapnel, its windows blown out. Everyone leapt out and took refuge in a snow-covered field, staying deadly still for fear of being seen from the sky if they moved. It was freezing cold; bracken and beech trees, their winter branches bare, provided minimal cover. Planes came back every 15 minutes, sometimes dropping their payload just a few metres away. Smoke rose from explosions on a ridge just across the road. The pilots, Marie thought, knew there were people in the field and so were trying to scare them into making a run for it. 'Don't look up, your face is like a shining white spot!' she snapped at the terrified Dima, who had not been through anything like this before. In one of the intervals between bombing runs, she used the satellite phone to call Sean Ryan in London to tell him she was trapped and thought she was going to die. 'There was nothing I could do,' he recalls. 'It was awful.' As the temperature fell, one of the Chechens wanted to build a fire, even though that would undoubtedly draw the pilots' attention. 'I would rather die warm than live cold,' he said, accusing Marie of cowardice when she objected. A spy plane flew over to assess the damage. The Chechens got out their hunting knives and cut rough lumps of bread which they ate with sweetened condensed milk. In between the bombing, the scene was strangely pastoral. 'Sound of stream,' Marie noted later. 'Birds flee in quicksilver little flocks.'

> *Sunday Times*, Chechnya, 19th December 1999
> I spent 12 hours yesterday pinned down in a field by a road south of Grozny. The planes, evil machines with the sun glinting off their sleek silver bodies, circled again and again. They trailed thunder, dropping bombs that whined as loudly as high-speed trains as they fell ... It takes no imagination to understand the fear of civilians who have to endure this day after day and who must decide whether to flee and face a day's drive on the open road, or take their chances in a basement.

It was time to turn back. Dima's photos were exceptional and Marie had filed an evocative piece for that Sunday. Moreover, it was only five days to Christmas and Patrick was expecting her in Paris, before she went to Jane's house in Scotland for the millennium New Year. That evening brought bad news: Russian paratroopers had seized Melkhist, an ancient centre known as the Dead City, on the only road back to Georgia. Any vehicles that passed would be shot at. The two alternative routes, via Dagestan or Ingushetia, were blocked by fighting or constantly being attacked from the air. They were trapped. There was only one other option: trek across the Caucasus Ridge. 'They'll drown in the snow,' said one fighter.

The *Guardian* team, who had also been pinned down under fire, had just got out to Georgia before the road was cut. Back in London, Sean consulted security advisers but no one could come up with a better plan. He rang Patrick, who was beside himself with anger. In his view the *Sunday Times* should never have sent Marie to Chechnya, or let her go, depending on how you looked at it. It was insanely dangerous and irresponsible, he said. Even if the road was being bombed it seemed to him a better option than walking through the mountains. He didn't see how she would make it. As far as he was concerned, Marie's editors were effectively sending her to her death. He shouted at Sean and hung up.

Marie told Sean she would try to touch base once a day. As long as they were in a vehicle, she could charge the satellite phone, but once they were on foot, the battery would run low pretty quickly. The journey might take four or five days. There was no chance of making it home for Christmas; the only issue was survival.

It was Tuesday, 21 December. They put their trust in Magomet, a small, wiry Chechen in jeans and lightweight climbing boots who had lived in the mountains all his life and would be their guide. All day long the bombers attacked, setting the mountainsides ablaze, so they waited until after sunset to leave. One of the fighters said he knew a Georgian general who would send a helicopter to rescue them for $2,000 if they reached the border, so he made a call before they set off.

The first hour was exhausting. Marie's back was in agony, as she walked in her flak jacket carrying a pack containing her computer and the satellite phone. 'Can I do this?' she thought, in a moment of uncharacteristic doubt. Dima was using his camera stand as a walking stick. They reached two ancient moonlit gravestones. Fire from a bomb was spreading towards them across a field but Magomet insisted on waiting for his friend, a tough bear of a man who turned up wearing full combat gear and carrying a Kalashnikov. His dream, he said, was to join the French Foreign Legion, but in the meantime he would protect them from smugglers and kidnappers. Marie was already too worn out to worry. Frightened of being attacked from the air again, or freezing in the snow, she knew the only thing to do was keep moving.

She struggled to breathe, regretting every cigarette she had ever smoked – especially those in the last few terrifying days, when she had shared the fighters' cheap Russian tobacco. Every now and then Magomet would check to see that she was 'normal'. 'Normal,' she reflected, meant something different to a Chechen. At some point along the path they were joined by three more young men, who carried Marie's pack and Dima's camera equipment. Marie scooped up snow to quench her thirst. By the time they reached a roofless hunters' lodge where they could snatch a little sleep, they had been walking for six hours, but Magomet let them rest for only a couple of hours before they moved on again. Dima was walking slowly, so as she waited for him to catch up, Marie would stop for a few minutes and take catnaps, lying in long grass. 'If they left me here I could just die in my sleep,' she thought.

They walked under the light of the moon towards a mountain lined with veins of snow, which seemed less beautiful when Marie realised that one of the veins was the path they would have to climb. Dima sat down, saying he could go no further. Marie knew that despair was even more dangerous than the cold. 'Get up! Keep moving!' she urged. He lost his temper. 'Shut up, you cunt!' he shouted. The word echoed round the mountains. Marie knelt in front of him. 'Don't you ever call me that again,' she snapped. 'If you want to die, fine, just stay here.' Dima was feeling sorry for himself. 'Just leave me,' he said. 'Someone will find my body.' Magomet quietly persuaded him to try again. They climbed the gorge, sleeping and walking, walking and sleeping, knowing bombers could return at any minute, the silence between Marie and Dima as frosty as the landscape.

The next morning their way was blocked by a waterfall, frozen in silvery motion, thirty feet across without footholds, with a drop of several hundred feet if you slipped. Two Russian jet fighters flew overhead, reminding them that they were nowhere near safety yet, and giving them a shot of adrenaline that made them speed up. Dima slipped and fell on his back – Marie was less worried about him than the satellite phone which he had in his backpack, and which, when tested, no longer worked. Climbing up yet another river bed, Marie stepped through thin ice up to her hip. Not for the first or last time, she silently thanked Jane for making her buy the expensive jacket that ensured that at least part of her was warm. They had been walking for 24 hours.

By now the young men had disappeared. 'Town boys,' said Magomet, derisively. They were wannabe weapons smugglers but had decided the route was too hard, he explained. Suddenly, a young man named Murad who said he was going to Georgia to buy a weapon appeared. 'The next twelve hours passed in a daze, one foot in front of the other, up and over another mountain,' Marie later wrote. 'The air was so thin that I could not fill my lungs, and the wind was so strong that several times I was almost blown off the mountainside.' Just before dawn they reached a snow-covered field amid the peaks. Dima was so weak by then that Magomet placed him on a plank of wood he found and hauled him across on it. The Georgian border was marked by a small pile of stones, but as they approached, two shots rang out. They dived into the snow and another two shots sounded. 'It seems unfair that we're going to die here, yards from the border,' Marie thought. Magomet began shouting in Chechen and the shots stopped. They crossed the border. They never established the source of the gunfire.

Marie had been dreaming of coffee and a bed but they couldn't find the border village, just a shepherd's hut, so they built a fire and settled in for the night. 'Be careful, don't burn the house down,' said Magomet as he set off to look for a village that might have radio communication. They needed to find out if the Georgian general one of the fighters had called before they set off, was sending a helicopter. Dima decided he had better apologise to Marie so they shook hands. She got out her notebook. Every now and then, while pausing on the mountains, she had scribbled notes but now she was thinking on paper how to survive.

24th December 1999. How bad is situation: we can survive cold and environment in <u>house</u>. Don't think we would have lasted otherwise.

<u>Water</u> plenty – snow and river 3–4 km away. Probably not worth walk – calories used.

<u>Food</u>: problem. Down to bread ends. If that sawdust stuff is flour, mix with water and cook? Desperate enough, bucket of onions and garlic, moldy.

Murad has pistol – animals?

Small things: Murad found bag of nails, were able to fix plastic sheets.

Look for red berries.

Mistake to let fire go out – cold seeps in.

Things they never tell you: constant battle to keep fire going.

Murad fixed the head of an axe that they found lying around, so was able to chop logs rather than use a tree trunk for the fire. They cooked up the flour and water they had found into a kind of tasteless porridge – Murad said the dish even had a name: *kasha*. The mouldy onions and garlic made it almost palatable. As the full moon rose over the mountain, Marie looked at the stars and realised that it was Christmas Eve. There was some symbolism, she thought, in spending it in a shepherd's hut.

24th December 1999. Should be in Paris cooking Christmas dinner. Snow storm closes in midday, obscuring the mountains

*in a haze, starting on the small gentle white flakes then cloud of
white. Dima thinks of writing a letter to his wife. I'm not worried we won't survive just how long we have to be here and the
worry I will cause those who care. Does make me think who
cares – Mom if she knows will have a terrible Xmas, Patrick will
be worried and furious; I can't tell what he will feel – I think he
does love me but it's a love where he wants his own life and me
to fit into it, hard to describe even to myself, because he doesn't
want me around all the time, more knowing I'm there and the
comfort of time together. Jane I miss – will I even make it for
New Years?*

The following day she turned on the satellite phone and to her amazement the battery light flickered, so she dialled Sean in London.

* * * * *

The Ryan children had been looking forward to Christmas but Sean
told them that celebrations would have to be postponed because Dad-
dy was working. Nothing had been heard of Marie and Dima in the
four days, since they set off across the mountains. 'At about 4 p.m. on
Christmas Day my phone was on charge in the bedroom upstairs, and
when I went to get it, I noticed there was a voicemail,' he remembers.
'It was Marie saying "Sean, I've reached the Georgian border. Just
want to let you know I'm OK, and I hope you have a great Christmas."'

White knights to the rescue, Jon Swain and Patrick were heading
to Tbilisi. Sean told them the good news as they changed planes in
Geneva. Then he called Jane, who was spending Christmas at her parents' house at Stratfield Saye. Her father, the Duke of Wellington, was
fond of Marie, frequently taking her for lunch at the Cavalry and
Guards Club on Piccadilly, where she loved to hear his stories of fighting in Syria and Iraq in the Second World War. 'We were in a terrible
state,' recalls Jane. 'We thought she was dead.' For a few hours, everyone was just relieved to hear that Marie was alive. 'Christmas was

uncancelled, presents were opened, and champagne uncorked,' says Sean. Then he realised that the problem wasn't really solved. 'We still had no contact with Marie. All I knew was that she had arrived at the border, but I didn't know how she was going to get to safety.'

The Colvin family was gathered in Oyster Bay for Christmas, worried out of their minds. Because Marie was American, Cat thought that the US government should be doing something to help. 'It was the first time I worked the phones to the State Department,' she recalls. 'I was up all night, making calls, receiving calls, trying to find her.' An old Yale friend who was now Director of Press Relations at the State Department spoke to the US Embassy in Tbilisi, but days went by and they heard nothing. Marie's mother had learnt to steel herself to believe that no news was good news. 'Sometimes I'd not hear from her for weeks when she was in one of those places,' Rosemarie remembers. 'But 1999 was very tough.'

* * * * *

In the evening, Magomet returned to the shepherd's hut with a Georgian soldier bearing noodles, tea and sweets. With no news of any helicopter, they would have to look for a village the next day. Marie felt like crying. 'Tired of this great adventure now,' she thought. But they had no choice, so at dawn they walked down the river valley to Giveri, a collection of dark stone houses, deserted for the winter. They went from house to house, looting flour, a tin of peas and a jar of apricot jam, eventually finding a house with a stove. A storm was building and they realised that no helicopter could land there, so Marie fried up the last of the flour to make flatbread and the next day they set off again.

The dawn was clear and cold, but the storm had left another foot of snow. A few miles downriver they found Bartanz and Elizabetha Kacunkubev, an elderly couple who were too poor to leave their village for the winter. 'They took us into their tiny stone house, where a portrait of Stalin looked down from the wall, and gave us fried potatoes, preserved cabbage and a shot of vodka each,' wrote Marie later.

'Bartanz then drew a map, showing us how to get to another village, Omala, which he said had a radio.'

It was 29 December. Walking through the woods, heading for the next village, they heard a sound which was not branches creaking, nor snow melting, but a whirr, growing louder all the time – rotor blades! They rushed into a clearing and Dima unfolded his photographic light reflector, holding it up to the sun to attract the pilot's attention. They waved madly. As the helicopter dipped its nose to land in a field below they scrambled down to meet it. Georgian soldiers were clustered round a tall figure in a baseball cap with a white beard and a blue snow jacket who Marie thought looked like Hemingway. The bearded man held out his hand. 'Jack Hariman, American Embassy. Are we glad to find you …'

The Georgians said they would have to search Magomet and Murad for weapons, so Marie deftly hid their pistols in her backpack before they all climbed on board. At the airforce base in Tbilisi, she quietly tipped the firearms into the boot of a car the Chechen rebels had sent to meet them. After Marie was debriefed – it must have been very useful for her Hemingway lookalike to get a first-hand account of the war in Chechnya – an embassy car took Marie and Dima to the hotel where Patrick and Jon were waiting. It turned out that the Georgian general who the Chechen fighters had contacted had been reassuring Sean, Dima's wife and anyone else who called that everything was in hand but had done nothing until the embassy – alerted first by calls from Cat in the US, and then the arrival of Jon and Patrick – twisted his arm. Since the State Department has no record of a Jack Hariman, the man who rescued them was probably the CIA station chief using a pseudonym – Patrick remembers an office in the embassy full of charts and maps that came in handy when trying to pinpoint exactly where Marie and Dima might be.

Marie was nervous about seeing Patrick. She knew he would be angry that she had ignored his entreaties and persisted in such a reckless trip. Instead of greeting him with the delight he might have expected, she pulled back when he went to hug her. It was easier to deal with those who she knew would simply be delighted to hear her voice, so she called Cat and turned the whole thing into a funny story: 'You won't believe what I had for Christmas lunch,' she said. 'Mouldy wild garlic!' Then she, Patrick, Dima and Jon drank vodka and ate caviar in the hotel bar. Dima was relieved, emotional and slightly surprised to be alive.

'You are like my older sister – you are a second mother to me now!' he cried.

'Yeah, you needed one,' replied Marie drily.

Her mind was less on the row she had had with him and more on the one with Patrick that she knew was coming. It started as soon as they closed the door to their hotel room. As they had missed spending Christmas together, Patrick had hoped that Marie would join his family in Paris for a long-planned New Year celebration. After all, it was the beginning of a new century. He was hurt and angry when she decided to stick to her original plan of spending it with the Wellesleys and various friends at Jane's farmhouse in South Ayrshire, so they flew to different destinations. Somewhere between Tbilisi and Glasgow, British Airways managed to lose her luggage, so she turned up at the door in the indestructible Harrods jacket. It had survived the trek and kept her warm. In fact, she told Jane, it had probably saved her life.

* * * * *

Marie was now famous. Other reporters dodged bullets and took risks, but to escape bombardment by climbing the Caucasus mountains in midwinter, risking freezing to death, was unprecedented. The fact that Marie was a woman just added to her allure. In a long piece for the *American Journalism Review*, Professor Sherry Ricchiardi used her as the ultimate exemplar of a new British 'passionate style of reporting'. Other British reporters also put themselves in the story but Marie, she suggested, had taken 'the personal touch in war reporting to new heights'. This was in contrast to the buttoned up style of the *New York Times* and the *Washington Post*, where the reporter, still never using the first person, was always a dispassionate observer.

Marie had found her voice and her method – it was all about making readers care. 'The people I meet and my reactions to them – that is part of the story,' she is quoted as saying. 'It's quite often stronger to write "I saw this."' Marie also talked about her attempt to break down barriers between herself and the people she was reporting on. 'If you go in bare and eat what they eat, drink what they drink, sleep where they sleep, there is less separation,' she said. More traditional journalists, including Patrick, believed in maintaining a certain distance, observing suffering without allowing it to colour their analysis, but plunging in and identifying with the people she saw as victims was the defining characteristic of Marie's reporting from Kosovo, East Timor and Chechnya. She was not alone in this – after all, Martha Gellhorn had been a passionate advocate of the Republican cause in the Spanish Civil War and of the Allies in the Second World War – but Marie courted more danger than Gellhorn ever did. 'Risk-taking has become as much a part of her reporting agenda as developing inside sources and delivering scoops,' wrote Ricchiardi. 'Her storytelling goes beyond survivors who have made it to refugee camps. Instead, she opts to record the misery of those still trapped. That means gaining access to places that have been declared off-limits by one side or other in a conflict. It is here that she becomes vulnerable.'

Vulnerable indeed, not just because such reporting put her in danger, but because she and her editors let it define her. Sean is quoted as saying, 'She takes risks to get to the truth, and I salute her for that, no matter how many sleepless nights she gives me.' Yet Patrick was not the only one who was uneasy about danger becoming the brand the *Sunday Times* was developing for Marie. The two Janes – Wellesley and Bonham Carter – collared Sean at a party to warn him that the paper was putting Marie's life at risk. He knew that she had survived Chechnya only by luck and endurance, but the truth was that while he and John Witherow might fret about it from time to time, Marie's risk-taking was getting them the best stories. Even Rupert Murdoch who took Marie and Sean for lunch, listened, rapt, to stories of her adventures.

* * * * *

After working relentlessly in 1999, Marie took several holidays in the year 2000. In February, she and Katrina met in Paris. Katrina was now editor-in-chief of the tech magazine, *Wired*, succeeding, like Marie, as a woman in a male-dominated sector of journalism. It was a high-powered job, with monthly trips to New York from San Francisco where she and Winter now lived. She was not only responsible for a publication that had started small and independent and now had a growing circulation and was increasingly commercial, but was also bringing up twins, who were now toddlers. Both women needed a break. Marie took another vacation in March, when she and Jane went to Vietnam. In Hanoi, they visited the Ho Chi Minh Mausoleum and the 'Hanoi Hilton', the prison where American POWs were held during the war Marie had protested against as a teenager in Oyster Bay, but much of the time they relaxed, travelling in the Mekong Delta and lying on the beach. 'We set the guide the challenge of not seeing one single other tourist, so we went *off piste* and ended up in a little village having the best meal ever for about £1,' recalls Jane. A holiday with Patrick in Italy in August was less successful. In her appointments diary Marie notes, simply, without elaboration: 'Drive to San Remo – big fight.' A week in Barcelona with Katrina for the wedding of mutual friends later that month was far more peaceful: 'Joan Miró museum, eat at tapas bar, Las Ramblas, sleep late,' she noted. Sometimes a holiday with a trusted friend was a more relaxing option than being with Patrick.

The same year Marie turned her attention to Africa, reporting from Zimbabwe and Ethiopia. In May, British forces had intervened in the West African state of Sierra Leone after rebels took hostage UN military observers and threatened the capital, Freetown. She reported on the West Side Boys, a gang of drug-crazed warriors who had captured eleven British soldiers, starting her piece with a filmic image:

Sunday Times, Freetown, 3rd September 2000
It is hard to talk to Junior Savage. He has sewn the front half
of a rat's pelt to the baseball cap that is pulled down low over
his forehead, so the beady eyes of the dead rodent stare at you
as a human voice talks from somewhere below. The tail and
another bit of the pelt hang off the back of the cap – every once
in a while he turns it around and then you look into the dead,
flat eyes of a young West Side Boy.

In another piece she told the story of the hostage rescue from the perspective of the SAS soldiers who carried it out. Although her stories
were brilliantly observed and written, she was frustrated because
other British journalists were covering the same ground. From Marie's
perspective, 1999 had been a triumph because she had distinguished
herself from the pack. She was on the lookout for a story that no one
else was covering – or would dare to.

In 2000 she received three awards: Journalist of the Year from
the Foreign Press Association; the British Press Awards Foreign
Reporter of the Year for her reporting from Chechnya (Jon Swain
had scooped it the previous year for Kosovo); and the Courage
in Journalism Award from the International Women's Media
Foundation in the US, with a ceremony in New York and a reception
in Los Angeles. Cat and Katrina were in the New York audience.
'Marie looked very chic in this amazing suit, beautiful boots and
her hair like a halo,' remembers Katrina. 'But when she got up on
stage, one side of her glasses was missing and she had to do the
whole thing holding it like a lorgnette!' They laughed about it for
ages after. Mike Wallace, a senior reporter for CBS, read the citation. 'Colvin's stories are vivid because there's no distance between
her and those she covers,' he said. 'Marie is brave but it's bravery
with a purpose. She covers stories from the point of view of those
least able to capture media attention … For most of us one war,
perhaps two, in a lifetime would be enough. But for Marie Colvin
covering war is a lifestyle.' Marie responded with words that would

become a mantra. 'Getting at the truth is why we all entered journalism,' she said. 'We have to bear witness. We can make a difference.'

The LA reception was a starry affair hosted by the actress Maria Shriver, the sister of Marie's old Yale friend Bobby, who also went along. Someone told Marie that she didn't have to buy a dress because a designer would lend her one, so she found herself in the Armani VIP lounge sipping champagne and trying on frocks. At the reception she shook hands with the film star Warren Beatty, who suggested that her life story should be made into a movie starring his wife, the actress Annette Bening. What a strange life it was: one day tramping through the snow and mud of the Caucasus mountains under Russian bombardment, the next dressing up in a designer suit and hobnobbing with film stars. Which was more real?

She went on to Oyster Bay to celebrate Thanksgiving and her sister Boo's 40th birthday. After finishing her undergraduate degree at Harvard, Boo had married, moved to Atlanta and devoted her life to motherhood. While Marie was still close to Cat, she hadn't spent much time with her other sister and the two felt they had little in common. That evening, they talked in a way they rarely did, reflecting on the diverging paths of their lives.

'You've got this amazing international award, but I've just got three kids and I've not done anything,' said Boo, who did not regret the choices she had made but could see how extraordinary her sister's life had become.

'I could never do what you do and you could never do what I do,' replied Marie, who found Boo's choices equally hard to fathom. 'Maybe that's the way it's supposed to be.'

Marie thought about how her life had diverged from those of her other siblings and her closest friends in the US. Cat, now a corporate lawyer, had got married and started a family. Katrina was a high-flying editor and a mother. Now aged forty-four, Marie reflected in her diary about what it meant to grow older.

Undated, 2000. Middle age has inevitable disappointments. A time of reckoning. Love is only thing with redeeming capacity. You're still not out of the theoretical stage – always something over the horizon.

The Juan Carlos era was definitively over. The rage they had felt towards each other had calmed and Marie had even been to his 50th birthday party at Tchaik and Melissa's just before she went to Chechnya, but in 2000 he lost his job with *El País* and returned to Bolivia. She knew he was broke, and still addicted to cocaine and alcohol, but there was nothing she could do about it – he was out of her life. She remained in touch with his daughter Anna, who was living in Sweden with her mother, Agneta, but they saw each other only occasionally, and Marie wasn't good at keeping promises about birthday treats and visits. She and Juan Carlos were separated, not divorced, but she often told people that she and Patrick had remarried. It made for a good, romantic story and Marie, so scrupulous about her journalism, was not above exaggerating for effect when telling stories about herself. Anyway, that's how it felt. They were living together in a flat Marie had recently bought in Bassett Road, Notting Hill. 'To all intents and purposes we *were* remarried,' says Patrick. 'There was no hesitation, no fuzzy areas, we were committed to each other, both faithful to each other.'

At New Year 2001, a year on from her Caucasus mountain adventure, the couple went on holiday to the Maldives and made a list of resolutions. Patrick was thinking of leaving daily journalism and becoming a full time writer – he had already written a couple of successful books of military history. Marie's list read:

1. *Get pregnant*
2. *Win awards*
3. *Inherit fortune from eccentric billionaire philanthropist*
4. *Go sailing etc.*

Alas, the first aim would prove as difficult to achieve as the third. Having a child was an attempt to recreate the late 1980s when the couple had envisaged a life together with children running around a country house in France. But despite seeing IVF specialists in Paris and London Marie never became pregnant again. Patrick was bitterly disappointed, but Marie accepted the inevitable. 'She always loved kids, but was very philosophical about the fact that she had led a life that made it very difficult to have them herself,' says Katrina. 'She was an older woman and the window was closing. She didn't say she wished she had led her life differently.'

The rhythm of her life gave Marie comfort and security, with female friends as her primary source of support and love. At the beginning of 2001, she went to the World Economic Forum in Davos, where Katrina was giving a presentation on digital media before coming to London to stay for a week. She had separated from Winter, and was bringing up the twins, Gabriella and Lucia, on her own. 'I don't think our friendship ever really changed,' reflects Katrina. 'We had this tremendous understanding of each other and could speak in shorthand. When I got into some kind of romantic scrape she could see it very clearly even from a distance. We just trusted each other.' As their forties hurtled by, Marie shared confidences with her Notting Hill friends, some divorcing and remarrying, others struggling with motherhood and career, most still battling to be taken seriously without losing the femininity by which they defined themselves. She and Jane would go out for dinner just the two of them or with Alex, JBC, Rosie and Helen, or they'd have lunch with Jane's parents in the country – normal activities that didn't involve being brave or making life-and-death decisions. Her diaries are full of appointments – lunches, dinners, weekends away – and people's birthdays. She was generous with gifts, many bought while travelling: a rug, a scarf, a piece of pottery, something in colours she knew her friends would appreciate. Every time she returned from a trip she would get her hair cut and dyed, and have a pedicure, manicure and facial. It was part of her ritual as she moved back and forth between her two worlds. She liked to look good, especially now that she was getting older. Her nail varnish would chip the next day but that was just how it went. Her mother and Cat sometimes came to stay, and she would take them to the theatre and restaurants, letting them glimpse her London life, which was so much easier for them to understand than the war zones she inhabited. She loved London, but when months went by and she hadn't had a story she could really get her teeth into, she grew restless.

* * * * *

Where should she go next? Everyone told her it was too dangerous to return to Chechnya. Back in Israel, the second intifada had started – there were multiple Palestinian suicide bombs, and huge Israeli incursions into Palestinian territory – but returning to the Middle East was like going back in time. Just as Marie was casting around, a PLO contact who liaised with 'liberation movements' across the world offered to link her up with the Liberation Tigers of Tamil Eelam or LTTE, popularly known as the Tamil Tigers, a militant organisation that had been fighting a war of secession from Sri Lanka since the 1980s. The Tamils in Sri Lanka suffered discrimination as the government favoured the Sinhalese majority, but the Tigers could by no means be thought of as good guys. Not only did they recruit child soldiers, but the elite Black Tigers developed the art of suicide bombing – it was a female Tiger suicide bomber who had assassinated the former Indian Prime Minister, Rajiv Gandhi, back in 1991. Six years had passed since a foreign journalist had crossed into territory controlled by the Tigers; it had become a forgotten conflict. The situation of the Tamil people was grim. The Tigers would not let them leave, and the government was using food as a weapon of war, trying to starve them into submission. Aid workers spoke of an unreported crisis of mass hunger and deprivation in the Vanni, an area of 2,000 square miles under Tiger control, where more than half the population had been displaced by war.

Much of the Tigers' financial support came from the Tamil diaspora in London. In early 2001, Marie met three well-connected contacts in a west London restaurant. 'We came up with the idea of her going to the Vanni and meeting the boys,' says one who still doesn't want his name to be used. 'It was a very tough time to go in – there was heavy fighting.' They negotiated for her to interview the Tiger leader, Vellupillai Prabhakaran. Personally responsible for several assassinations, he demanded that fighters share his fanatical devotion to the Tamil cause, including carrying a cyanide capsule to swallow if they were captured. Marie's interest was piqued by the mystery surrounding him, and the fact that he hadn't spoken to a foreign journalist in eight years.

She convinced Sean and John that she would get exclusive access. 'It sounded like a cracking story, and classic Marie,' Sean remembers thinking. Aid workers still managed to cross into Tamil territory so, after making a few enquiries, Marie and her editors thought it safe enough. 'Her argument was that nobody had done this because nobody cared,' recalls Sean. Patrick, as usual, had a different perspective. He thought that if Marie interviewed Prabhakaran, he would just spout propaganda and the story wasn't worth the risk. 'Again, one knew it wasn't going to be fine. I'd come to expect some bad ending,' he says. But he also knew there was no deterring Marie, and he had given up shouting at Sean and John.

Marie flew to the Sri Lankan capital, Colombo, where she went for a background briefing with Steve Holgate, the Public Information Officer at the American Embassy. 'We spoke for about an hour, and I felt this was someone I could trust,' he recollects. 'I walked her to her hotel. She had told me she was going back to London.' He had no idea that in fact she intended to sneak into Tiger territory. Marie took a bus to Vavuniya, the northernmost town controlled by the government, where she met up with Tiger sympathisers who had army passes and could get through checkpoints. If asked where she was going, she was told to say 'Kanthaudaiyarpuvarsankulam'. 'Fortunately,' she wrote, 'no one asked.' She slept on the concrete floor of a school near Mannar, on the west coast. Her diary details the journey across the front line.

6th April 2001. Morning wake pre-dawn gray. Wash face and hands well. I'm with fanatical non smokers. Sneak to pee. Standing in field of peacocks, how beautiful, remember conversation about landmines and head back over field. We walk to concrete ruin of sweet shop. Army was here until 97. No ppl. This was Muslim land – they went south and can't come back. Remnants of dirt trenches.

As dawn rose, columns of grey clouds drifted across the pink and orange sky, and ten Tamil Tiger fighters arrived, armed with grenades and automatic weapons, wearing flip-flops and bright sarongs, which they later changed for shorts.

6th April 2001. Leave in wagon pulled by tractor. Through open roads – if this is cleared area, doesn't bode well for government. Go through ruins of cashew plantation, destroyed in fighting and now overgrown, abandoned Buddhist temple. Open field, jungle now too thick for tractor, eat lunch of 'piku' carefully wrapped in plastic and then newspaper like little presents. 10:30 am – this is your only meal. I think they're joking – they're not.

They continued on foot. After the track petered out, the thick foliage closed overhead to form a claustrophobic green tunnel. Cascades of white butterflies glimmered in shafts of light filtering through the canopy. Scouts went ahead to check for Sri Lankan soldiers, while Marie and the others followed in single file at ten yard intervals, so if someone stepped on a landmine, the person following would not be blown up too. She was told that if a wild boar attacked, she should shimmy up a tree.

6th April 2001. We seem to be on a schedule, although not clear what it is. 2pm come to a wide open field and wait to 3:30, scouts go first, crouched and running, we then proceed, separated, single file ... Searing heat, humidity such that swing bare arm

makes feeling that there is fur on your arm. Drink soft drinks
Fanta + coke, don't like but not sure of water and this is not the
place to get an attack of dysentery.

They walked all day, until just before sunset when they waded chest-high through a river, holding their belongings above their heads. By 9 p.m. they had reached territory controlled by the Tigers. 'The sense of relief was overwhelming,' wrote Marie, but they still had to walk further, now by moonlight. Despite exhaustion she could see the funny side when she sat on a mound and suddenly felt dozens of tiny bites.

6th April 2001. I sit in ants – how do you pull your pants down
w/ male recon unit? Decide to endure.

At the side of the road, waiting for a vehicle, she fell asleep. A sudden crack of what she assumed was gunfire woke her, but her companions explained it was just an elephant snapping branches.

Marie's escorts were village boys and some girls who had joined the cause. The female Tigers told her that they knew they would be raped if captured by the Sri Lankan army (this was undoubtedly true), so they would rather commit suicide. Some had Christian rosary beads around their necks with their cyanide capsule as a pendant. One showed Marie that she had screwed hers into the top of a pen. 'Where do they get all this cyanide from?' Marie wondered. The recruits were unpaid, and fervently loyal to Prabhakaran. 'We cannot compare our leader to any other leader in history,' said one. 'His military tactics and strategies and his ideas make him unique.' The Sri Lankan government wanted to kill him, so his obsession with security was not unwarranted, but Marie's London contacts had not nailed down the interview quite as securely as she had been led to believe. 'During the visit they suspected Marie was an agent because she was close to the Americans,' says the contact. 'There was some confusion amongst the leadership about whether they should meet her.'

Marie spent several days at a hideout with the Tigers' political leaders, Seevaratnam Pulidevan and S.P. Thamilselvan. They said little of interest except that they thought there should be a political solution to the Tamil question. 'Federation, confederation, northeast council, autonomous region, we can accept any of these solutions as long as we are guaranteed our equal rights, our dignity and justice,' said Thamilselvan. This message, she was told, came directly from Prabhakaran, but if she didn't hear it from the man himself, it had less significance. Marie was getting frustrated. 'Now fed up,' she wrote in her diary. Despite his assurances that everything was going to work out, she suspected that Thamilselvan could not deliver Prabhakaran after all. 'Constant smile that does not go to the eyes,' she noted. Even the peacocks were getting on her nerves, sounding as they did 'like deranged cats meowing over loud speakers.'

Although she was deep in the zone controlled by the Tigers, the government retained some institutions in the cities. Interviewing a teacher, she learnt that he was still paid by the government even though the Ministry of the Interior had him on a 'wanted' list. There was no mains electricity, no telephone service, no fuel for cars, water pumps or lighting. People travelled by bicycle. Marie's Tiger escorts took her to Kilinochchi, which had been bombarded by government forces five years earlier and where she saw children going to school amongst the ruins, and hospitals chronically short of surgical supplies. International aid agencies, which were banned by the government from distributing food, said 40 per cent of children in the area were malnourished, but the siege was porous – food did still get in and people cultivated crops. Marie saw hardship and hunger, but it was endemic misery rather than the kind of starvation she had reported on in Ethiopia the previous year.

After nearly two weeks in Tamil Tiger territory, she had filed one story and the chances of seeing Prabhakaran seemed to be receding, so she decided to cut her losses. The Tigers said she should leave the way she had arrived, but she began to understand that the return journey would be more dangerous, because the Sri Lankan Army had increased its patrols, on the lookout for Tigers infiltrating government territory. Using her satphone, she called the US Embassy press officer Steve Holgate, but she didn't have his mobile number and he was out of the office. 'My secretary said Marie had called but didn't leave a message,' he says. 'It turns out that when she called me she was in the north and realised getting into Tamil Tiger country was one thing, but wanted advice on getting out. Within the cities there were places that the government was operating. I would have told her to turn herself in to the police.' Marie never got that advice – and who knows if she would have followed it if she had? She might not have wanted to risk being interrogated about how she had got in or on the whereabouts of the senior Tigers with whom she had been staying. In the past, journalists who had sneaked into Tiger territory had walked out along the road, to be arrested, questioned and sometimes deported, but nothing worse. Marie, however, appears to have been convinced by the Tigers that her situation was different and that the only way out was to go by night back through the jungle.

For three days she tried to cross the lines but was forced to turn back. 'This involved walking thirty miles a night through jungle and knee-deep water and mud of marsh and rice paddies – only to end up sleeping on the same straw mat, on the same dirt floor, in the same mud hut,' she wrote in a later article. 'Even the bugs were starting to look familiar.' On the Sunday night, just fifty yards from the front line the man leading the group made 'a somersaulting motion with his hands' – the sign to walk back. They could not slip past the military post. 'My mistake,' he said. 'Military alert. Too dangerous.' They walked back again, and Marie spent another night on the floor near the Catholic church at Madhu where 10,000 displaced people were living in tents and huts. At dawn, she collapsed into sleep. 'Monday night was supposed to be third time lucky,' she wrote later. 'As the sun slipped below the horizon, I sat with my guides under a banyan tree, looking out over a silvery lake, waiting for dark in a rare moment of peace and beauty.'

The group included civilians and Tigers. One old man carried a string shopping bag with two bottles of Pepsi. The leader of the group was armed with an old rifle, which he said was to protect them from wild boar and elephants. They were heading for his family house which lay just inside government-controlled territory where the Tamils would turn back and Marie would take the bus. She smoked a last cigarette – for the seven-mile walk they were about to take there would be no smoking, talking or even coughing. They trekked along jungle trails, and through thickets of thorn trees. From the edge of a lake, through which they waded waist-deep, they could see the lights of an army post. At around 8 p.m., they crept through dark scrub and waited in a marsh while a scout went ahead. Mosquitoes whined and bit but they couldn't slap them off for fear of making a noise. Marie took off her shoes to walk more quietly. At a signal from the leader, they followed him to the road and climbed through barbed wire on both sides. Marie would remember for the rest of her life what happened next:

Sunday Times, Sri Lanka, 22nd April 1999
We were running through the last dark field for the line of jungle ahead when the silence was broken by the thunder of automatic weapons fire about 100 yards to the right.

I dived down and began crawling, belly on the ground, for some cover. For a few minutes, someone was crawling on top of me – protection or panic, I don't know. Then I was alone, behind weeds.

A tree was 10 yards away, but it seemed too far. The shooting went on and on. Flashes and light came from an army post nobody had seen.

The shooting stopped and dark and quiet descended. There had not been a sound from my side. I could not tell where anyone was. The only sound was the occasional bellow of a cow which had been hit.

I had a few mad moments of thinking it was over, I had survived. But I knew this was not true. We had been spotted. The army would think this was a Tamil Tiger patrol and would come after us. They would be scared and trigger-happy ... I was lying in a field with a decision to make: run for it, lie still or shout.

I lay there for half an hour under the penetrating glare of the flares. I turned my face to the earth when one came drifting down directly above me, worried that my white skin would reveal my hiding place.

Bursts of gunfire began across the road about half a mile away. The search and destroy patrols had come out. I heard soldiers on the road, talking and laughing. One fired a burst from an automatic weapon that scythed down the weeds in front of me and left me covered in green shoots.

If I didn't yell now, they would stumble on me and shoot. I began to shout.

'Journalist! Journalist! American! USA!'

A soldier sighted on the sound and fired.

As blood poured from her eye and mouth, Marie thought she was going to die – the pain was acute, the noise deafening, the sense of defeat overwhelming. She started to shout 'Doctor! Doctor!' and eventually a voice screamed in English: 'Stand up, stand up!' This was an occasion when being a woman was no help, because the Tigers often sent female suicide bombers into government territory. Eventually the soldiers seemed to understand that she was a foreigner. The next few minutes were agony.

'Take off your jacket,' came the voice. I dropped my blue jacket and stood straight up, hands in the air. Blood poured down my face so I could not see much. Someone yelled, 'Walk to the road.' I stumbled forward.

Every time I fell, feeling faint, they would shout hysterically, afraid that I was pulling some trick, and I would struggle up again. I made it up the incline to the road and was shoved to the ground, flat on my back and kicked by shouting soldiers. A bright light shone in my face. I could not see any of my captors.

I am not sure how long I lay there on my back. I was searched for weapons, then told to walk at gunpoint, prodded by the weapons.

At first Marie thought they were going to shoot her, but eventually she convinced them she was a journalist, and they put her in a truck. As they bounced along potholed roads, a kinder soul kept saying in English, 'We are taking you for medical treatment, you are going to be okay.' Marie was struggling to breathe, her lungs bruised by the shock of the grenade that hit her. At the military hospital in Vavuniya they removed shrapnel from her head, shoulders and chest, and she realised that she could no longer see with her left eye. They put her in another truck and drove for an hour to the Victory Army Hospital in Anuradhapura, where her eye was X-rayed: there was shrapnel inside. 'You are going to lose your eye anyway. I can operate now,' said the army surgeon but she begged him to wait and call the US Embassy.

* * * * *

Steve Holgate was woken at 5 a.m. by a call from the marine on duty at the embassy: the Sri Lankan army was trying to get hold of him because an American journalist had been hurt. Although Marie hadn't told Steve she was going north, he figured out pretty quickly who it must be. When he got through to an officer at the Victory Army Hospital he realised that, although she was badly injured, she would survive because he could hear her hollering, 'Give me the phone! I want to talk to Steve Holgate!' Eventually she was flown by helicopter to a hospital in Colombo where she was laid out on a stretcher against a wall in a crowded emergency room, surrounded by hostile soldiers. 'Miraculously, Holgate showed up minutes later, clipboard in hand, and simply told the soldiers he was taking me into the custody of the American Embassy,' Marie later wrote. 'It was like the moment in a classic Wild West movie when the quiet guy faces down the armed and dangerous gang. I was safe.'

Sean was on holiday in Ireland, so his deputy, Peter Conradi, called the *Times* South Asia correspondent, Stephen Farrell, who happened to be in southern India. He jumped on the next plane to Colombo and rushed straight to the hospital. 'She had a green hospital mask loosely around her face and neck, and her damaged eye was covered with a bloodstained bandage,' he recalls. The immediate danger had been a collapsed lung and shrapnel in her chest. Although Marie was still struggling to breathe, her condition was now stable. The damage to her eye was not life threatening, but there was still shrapnel inside. Steve could see that painkillers had not dampened her fear. 'She was worried about several things – will I be blind in that eye? Will I be arrested? And what do I say to my family?' Stephen knew Marie of old and understood that she would also be worrying that this would be the end of her career. She told him the story, speaking unnaturally fast, a sign of shock. Mobile phones were not allowed in the hospital, so he went outside to call Patrick. 'I put the phone in my pocket and strolled back, sat on the bed and slipped it under the covers. She pretended to be asleep and then started talking to him.'

The Sri Lankan government insisted that the Tamils who had accompanied Marie were armed Tigers who had shot at the soldiers, and that she had been caught in crossfire. After she recovered, they planned to arrest her. The US Ambassador, who had visited her in the hospital, dealt with that. 'He spoke to them and said, you can do what you want, but do you want to arrest a badly wounded woman who can put her story on the front page?' recalls Steve Holgate. Marie was well enough to be amused by the contrast between the American and British response to her situation. The British High Commission, she told Stephen Farrell, had sent a diplomat in a Laura Ashley skirt, carrying a parasol, who told her there was nothing they could do: after all, Marie had gone to the north illegally. 'Marie said she had never been more grateful to be an American,' he remembers.

By now the news of Marie's injury had got out, and was being reported across the world. In amongst the worry and the logistics,

Sean, who had just returned from holiday, had neglected one of the most important things: to tell Rosemarie. She rang him at 4 a.m. A journalist had called her asking for her reaction and she had no idea what had happened. She was distraught. Others began the practical work of finding an eye surgeon. Both Cat and Katrina went to work, and even Rupert Murdoch got involved, determined that Marie should be treated by the best. In the end, all roads led to Dr Stanley Chang, a pioneer of revolutionary ophthalmic surgical techniques who practised at New York Presbyterian Hospital.

When Marie's condition had stabilised further, she and Jon Swain, who had flown to Colombo, took a flight to London, where they were met by Patrick, who accompanied Marie on to New York. Cat and Rosemarie were at the airport, shocked to see Marie, pale and anxious, swathed in bandages across her body and her eye. After quick greetings, her immediate concern was that her computer had been lost in the attack and so she had nothing on which to write her story. Rosemarie was furious – couldn't the *Sunday Times* leave her alone just this once? 'Mom, this is my deadline, you should know that by now,' said Marie. Her mother's anxiety was already getting on her nerves. Using her brother Billy's computer, she wrote the story of the attack and her survival. 'I am not going to hang up my flak jacket as a result of this incident,' she wrote.

Sunday Times, Sri Lanka, 22nd April 2001
Why do I cover wars? I have been asked this often in the past week. It is a difficult question to answer. I did not set out to be a war correspondent. It has always seemed to me that what I write about is humanity *in extremis*, pushed to the unendurable, and that it is important to tell people what really happens in wars – declared and undeclared.

On the phone to Sean after filing she said that she was desperate for a cigarette and a vodka martini. He added the line to the end of her story as the payoff. It became part of her legend. Marie and her editors had invented a myth for her, an identity that they promoted even when she was gravely injured. She had to play a part, albeit one she had helped create. 'Normal?' Magomet her guide in Chechnya had asked her when she thought she would perish in the freezing mountain pass. 'Normal.' It sounded reassuring. But what would 'normal' mean now?

After examining her, Dr Chang said he would operate in a few days' time, when she was rested and he had a slot open. She had hoped that he would be able to extract the shrapnel in such a way as to allow her to retain some peripheral vision, but he said there was no chance. He would, however, try to save the eyeball itself. That made her cry, the first time she had wept since she was shot. 'I think it was because it only hit me then that my life would never be the same,' she wrote later. It hadn't occurred to her that she might end up with no eye at all. Despite shrapnel wounds all over her body, she resisted Rosemarie and Patrick's entreaties that she wait for the operation in Oyster Bay. 'Marie didn't want to be trapped at Mom's house,' Cat recalls. 'I negotiated between them. Mom was really uncomfortable with anyone other than her taking care of Marie.' Marie felt not just that Rosemarie wanted to infantilise her, but that this was her mother's opportunity to say 'I told you so', to tell her that she had to stop being a war correspondent and do something else. Patrick also thought that staying in Oyster Bay made sense, so that her siblings could see her easily and she could be looked after, but she was obdurate. 'That was Marie,' he says. 'I asked her why and she couldn't tell me.'

The only person who understood was Katrina, who came to New York and booked a room for the two of them at the St Regis. She knew that Marie didn't want to be fussed over and needed to put her mother's distress to one side if she had to make decisions about the surgery. They returned to the hospital, where a young surgeon talked to them at length, explaining that he would be carrying out the surgery as Dr Chang was now too busy. Marie was at the end of her tether, tearful and unable to argue. Katrina took the young doctor aside and explained as calmly as she could that Marie would not be doing the surgery with him. They would wait until Dr Chang was free. In the week that followed, Katrina dressed Marie's seeping wounds, winding and unwinding the bloodied bandages. 'There was still a risk of infection,' she remembers. 'There was a lot of pain and blood. She had trouble breathing and we plumped up the pillows so she could sleep at an angle.'

Marie felt a need to rid herself of the last possession that reminded her of the fateful trip, so they dumped her black leather Furla bag, still full of the dirt of Sri Lanka, into a New York City trash can. 'It was liberating, a shedding of something dark and poisonous,' Marie wrote. She had almost no clothes with her, so they went shopping, but as she entered Lord and Taylor she couldn't cope with the people coming at her from her blind side. 'She was very panicky and shaky,' Katrina recalls. Nonetheless she insisted on going out for dinner at a fancy French restaurant, and refused to obey the doctor's orders to stop smoking and drinking. One evening they heard a knock at the door of their hotel room, and a waiter came in wheeling a trolley bearing a huge glistening silver chalice full of ice and every kind of vodka imaginable. The card said it was a gift from her friends from East Timor. Her Dutch journalist friend Minka Nijhuis had read the last line of her story, and had arranged for the biggest and best vodka martini imaginable. Marie and Katrina laughed uproariously, even though it hurt Marie's chest. Her mother would have fussed and told her she mustn't drink, but Katrina just poured the cocktails. They reminisced about the old days at Yale, gossiped about their friends and remembered happier times. Katrina made her feel she was still the same Rie – they were the girls who held the best parties, who were 'going for the gusto', determined to make a success of their lives. Thinking about the past felt a lot better than trying to imagine the future.

Marie went into surgery not knowing how she would emerge. The 6mm piece of shrapnel lodged along the optic nerve had caused haemorrhaging, and blood had pooled behind the retina. On advice, she chose a local anaesthetic for the five and a half hour operation to remove the blood clots and inject silicone oil into the eyeball to keep the retina in place. As they scraped away in her eye she could hear the surgeons talking.

'That lens has to go,' said one. Dr Chang leant over.

'How are you doing in there?' he enquired.

'Stop the whale music,' she croaked.

The supposedly soothing sound they were playing in the operating theatre was driving her nuts. Despite the anaesthetic, the sense of pulling in the eye was unbearable. The good news was that Dr Chang saved the eyeball; the bad news was that he couldn't remove the shrapnel. It would stay there indefinitely.

For the next week Marie would have to lie on her front to keep the oil and retina in place. Waves of nausea and pain engulfed her. She feared going blind in the other eye, a reaction known as 'sympathetic ophthalmia'. Patrick was back in New York from London and initally they stayed in a serviced apartment near the hospital, where he nursed her as best he could. The first time she looked at her eye in the mirror was a shock: 'It was swollen to the size of a peach, bright red, with a thin line – like that little indentation that peaches have across their middles – the only evidence that the two lids had ever opened or would ever open again.' She agreed to go back to Oyster Bay for the rest of her recovery time. Friends sent books, flowers and tapes to keep her amused. Tamils from across the world sent greetings and thanks – she was their heroine now.

* * * * *

Chapter 9

THE FACE IN THE MIRROR

If you put a hand over one eye and start walking you can understand the importance of depth perception – objects aren't where you think they are. Back home in London, Marie found that she could no longer take for granted everyday actions such as unlocking a door or turning on the oven, and she could see nothing coming up on her left-hand side. Reading took huge effort. Over time she learnt to compensate, until she could light a cigarette or pour a glass of wine without setting the curtains on fire or ruining the tablecloth. She couldn't drive, but then she had always hated driving and didn't have a car. After the swelling went down, she looked fine without the patch – her eye was sightless, although still there, still green – but Dr Chang had told her to keep it covered to guard against infection. The patch would have to become part of her identity. It wasn't so bad. People on the street stared, but when she met the Prince of Wales at a reception, he declared the patch 'very fetching' and several friends gave her patches studded with rhinestones or sequins for parties. She liked the way children asked why she was dressed as a pirate, much to their parents' discomfort. (Her niece, Cat's daughter Justine, remembers making an eyepatch for herself so she could look like her adored aunt.) There is no introspection in Marie's surviving notebooks, but the draft of a story Alex Shulman commissioned for *Vogue* on how Marie would dress from now on was, she wrote in the covering note, 'a bit like a private psychotherapy session'.

Vogue, Unpublished, 2001

When I looked in the mirror I saw a different person. It's unsettling to be in your fifth decade and suddenly be changed utterly, on the outside at least. I've always liked my eyes, in fact thought they were one of my best features. And now I only had one, and a large black eye patch over the other. Worse, without the patch, when I looked at my left eye nothing looked back … I'd lived a life where I stayed one step ahead of my nightmares. Now something had happened to me that was irrevocable.

She worried that people might think her vain but, then again, she couldn't stop caring how she looked just because in Chechnya or Kosovo worse things had happened to other people. Anyway, it wasn't simply vanity. If she went out in an old cardigan, patch over her eye, hair like a rat's nest, people gave her a wide berth on the street. She needed to find a way of presenting herself that matched her sense of who she now was – not a different person but one who had been indelibly marked by her life experience. That meant overturning both the expectations of others, and the image she previously had of herself. Alex maintained that when they first met, back in the 1980s, Marie was wearing camouflage, which Marie strenuously denied, as she had always avoided clothes that suggested a macho war correspondent image. It was a joke between them, but Marie thought Alex must have invented the memory in line with what she had expected. In the field, Marie wore something utilitarian on the outside, fancy and feminine underneath. After her La Perla underwear was looted from the hotel in East Timor, she had claimed replacement costs on expenses. The (male) accountants rejected her claim, on the grounds that underwear couldn't possibly cost so much. 'Marie's does,' responded the (female) foreign desk manager. Again, it had become part of her legend. After seeing pictures of her in the hospital in Sri Lanka, an editor asked her to write an article about her 'lucky red bra'. The bra was originally cream, she pointed out drily – it was red only because it was drenched in her blood. Before going on holiday to Spain that summer she remembered shopping after other homecomings.

> *Vogue*, Unpublished, 2001
> I indulged myself by coming home after weeks spent in the Chechen Mountains without bathing to mine The Cross Shop for a dress that said frivolous, slinging on some kitten heels, and heading out to a fun evening looking like a girl ... Packing for Spain, as I tried on the lacy edged cardigans, the flimsy silk Tracy Boyd sundress, the clothes of other summers, I realised that nothing in my wardrobe worked. The black eye-patch somehow unbalanced and dominated everything. I looked like I was in someone else's clothes.

The fashion solution was not so hard, especially with the help of her friend, Bella Freud. Marie wrote she needed a 'sleeker, more structured wardrobe', clothes that were 'more architectural in cut than the lacy or flowing styles' she had previously favoured. But now she had to internalise the changes that were so apparent on the outside.

> The patch had become part of me in a way, something that would make a clear division between life before and after, which is how I felt ... I think the process of rethinking my wardrobe in some way mirrored rethinking my life and was just as effective (fingers crossed) as the psychiatric counselling some advised. After surviving the trauma, I found there were dark places that were too difficult to go for a while. It was easier to think about the surface until the nightmares become just memories.

Again, she was lauded for her bravery. The Foreign Secretary, Robin Cook, wrote her a letter saying, 'You have long stood out from the pack as an outstanding reporter ... I hope you will soon be fully fit and back at work.' But the nightmares would not go away. One of her allies on the *Sunday Times* was Caroline Mansfield, the foreign desk manager, who in the past had often gone round to Marie's house to trawl through her expense receipts while Marie lay on the sofa drinking coffee. She had seen Marie falling over drunk and in despair over both Patrick and Juan Carlos. But she had never seen her shaking and crying as she did after she returned from Sri Lanka. 'She was so fragile, and not just physically,' Caroline says. 'I remember sitting by her bedside and holding her hand. She was in a bad state.'

Caroline had made arrangements for reporters to contact a clinic for counselling if they had been through a traumatic experience, but at the *Sunday Times* there was still a stigma attached to 'not coping', and Marie said she couldn't see the point of sitting down with a psychotherapist who had no idea what it was like to be in a war zone. 'It's got nothing to do with my father or my childhood. My childhood was quite happy,' she told the Australian writer Denise Leith. 'It's got to do with an extremely traumatic event which I know about. I know why I'm feeling this way and I'd rather just get through it.' She had been forced to accept the fragility of her body, but was not ready to acknowledge the fragility of her mind.

A few months after her injury, she met someone who understood only too well the psychological impact of seeing too much. The war photographer Don McCullin, who had taken haunting pictures in Biafra, Vietnam, Cambodia and other war-torn places, had just brought out a new book. Interviewing him, Marie could see instantly that he was 'as much a victim of the decades of war he recorded on film as the victims whose misery is pictured'. Like her, he saw a virtue in laying himself open to injury, in narrowing the difference between himself and his subjects. But what haunted him were not his own injuries – which were several – but guilt for walking away after taking pictures, for surviving.

Sunday Times, London, 2nd September 2001

For those of us who cover wars, he is our conscience, the one who has earned the right to express doubts about the profession of war correspondent, while at the same time the example we all aspire to … Talking to him, I hear the dark voice I try to suppress: am I merely a voyeur, taking advantage of people *in extremis*? Did anything I wrote or photographed matter? He knows it's not all misery for us. There's the adrenalin rush of life-and-death situations. There are the boring details of life you can leave behind. Face up to everything, McCullin says. I have.

It is an honest assessment of the lure of the life she had chosen, as well as of the doubts she had in more anguished moments. But while McCullin had retreated to Somerset to take landscape photographs and heal his damaged soul, Marie had not found her equivalent.

Patrick grew exasperated by her refusal to rest and reassess her options. She even rowed with Katrina, who thought she should demand more money from the *Sunday Times* which was paying compensation according to an actuarial scale. 'Hey,' said Marie, 'I should have lost an arm, then I would have gotten more!' Katrina felt that the company should be paying her indefinitely. 'You have to tell them you need a fully comprehensive insurance package that means they'll take care of you for the rest of your life no matter what issues come up,' she said. She worried that Marie might yet lose the sight in her good eye, as Dr Chang had warned, but Marie feared that her employers would pension her off if she asked for money for life. She and Katrina argued so much about it that their old Yale friend Dave Humphreville had to intervene. Marie was obdurate – Katrina could think whatever she liked, but she would soldier on.

Permanently tired, she needed to sleep in the day, but then her mind transported her back to Sri Lanka and the recurrent nightmare about the moment before she was shot. It was, she thought, her brain trying to find a different outcome, going back over events again and again hoping that this time she would get up unharmed and with her sight intact. She needed a way of keeping those thoughts at bay, as well as the terrifying images from other conflicts that drifted into her sleeping mind, so she drank, not just wine in the evenings, but vodka, often in the morning, just to help her get through the day. Sometimes, when Patrick was away, she would ask Alan Jenkins to stay the night, not for sex, but because she hated to be alone. 'She became skeletally thin, restless, anxious and trembly,' he says. 'She was deeply troubled. I remember one night she started sweating because of the terrible nightmare.'

Patrick suggested she accompany him to mass on Sundays, hoping religion might help her as it helped him. In Sri Lanka, she had worn a Miraculous Medal, a Catholic charm believed to be imbued with spiritual properties, and in more superstitious moments she thought it might have saved her life. But, unlike Patrick, whose Catholicism was genetic and undisturbed by questioning, she didn't have the right kind of faith to return to the Church in any organised way. 'I have a very deep belief in there being a spiritual being, something beyond this world, but it's challenged and threatened constantly, because the question is, if there is a God, how could he let these things happen?' she said in an interview. 'You see such extremes, you have to believe in God, but equally that old God, all powerful, all good God, seems to be a total contradiction.'

In July, Jane celebrated her 50th birthday at Apsley House, the first Duke of Wellington's townhouse on Hyde Park Corner. Marie put on her cocktail dress and chatted until late with Jane's father. In September, Jane was going to La Torre, an estate near Granada awarded to her ancestor in gratitude for helping Spain in the Peninsular Wars. The whole gang went: Marie and Patrick, Mick Imlah, JBC, Alex Shulman, Helen Fielding and several others. Early in the afternoon of 11 September, they were sitting outside on the terrace when the agent who oversaw the estate came running up, very agitated, asking if they had heard the news. Something had happened in New York, he said, something terrible. They rushed in to the sole TV, a small black-and-white set in the staff living room, and watched a plane fly into the second tower of the World Trade Center. 'It's bin Laden,' said Marie.

She and Patrick started making calls immediately, speaking to people they knew in the Arab world, trying to firm up what they were pretty sure was true. There was no question of rushing to the scene because Marie was not well enough, and US airspace would be closed for days. She wrote a story about the nature of suicide bombing, struggling to make sense of the enormity of what had happened. 'It was strange and disturbing to be in this idyllic place,' recalls Jane, 'but I don't think she was champing at the bit to get on a plane.' By the time Marie got back to London, when it became clear that the US would attack Afghanistan where bin Laden was still being sheltered by the Taliban, she was. 'It drove her nuts,' says Sean. 'She thought that, as an American, with knowledge of the Middle East and Islamist terrorism, she should be the one leading our coverage. But she was fragile and delicate. She knew that it would take her a while to recover.' For the next few weeks, she mined her previous experience in Afghanistan, Chechnya and the Arab world to write background pieces. How frustrating it was to watch from London.

* * * * *

Marie did not want to rest on her laurels, but the recognition she received did help her through this period. A reader wrote a letter praising her 'wonderful humanity' and her identification with 'people who through no fault of their own have the least to hope for in the world'. He added a personal note. 'Your work has a special resonance to me because my mother was a combat photographer in WWII.' It was Antony Penrose, the son of Lee Miller. After his mother's death, he had devoted his life to preserving her archive. He told Marie that his mother had been present at the liberation of four concentration camps, including Buchenwald and Dachau. 'Her concerns and her writing had much in common with yours ... after the war she suffered terribly from depression, and although she never spoke of the cause, I learnt from her letters it had much to do with believing nothing had changed. She felt that no-one had a care for the sacrifice and suffering that had taken place.' It was a remarkable, sensitive letter which Marie kept always.

At the Woman of the Year lunch in London in October 2001, she was thrilled to meet the solo yachtswoman, Ellen MacArthur, who was also receiving an honour. 'She's done the only thing I ever really wanted to do – sail round the world,' said Marie in her acceptance speech. But she also wanted to be in Afghanistan where US and British forces were trying to root out bin Laden and overthrow the Taliban. There had never been a greater need for frontline reporting, she said, yet no Western journalists were behind Taliban lines. She was wrestling with the same problem as Lee Miller: the question not of how dangerous it was to get the story but of how to maintain a sense of outrage in the face of apathy or the blind acceptance of government propaganda.

'The real difficulty is having enough faith in humanity to believe that someone will care,' she said.

* * * * *

In 2002, Marie's stepdaughter, Anna, now aged thirteen, was to move to London with her mother, Agneta, who was starting a new job as UK correspondent for Swedish radio. Anna was looking forward to spending time with Marie, whom she had seen only a few times since the split with Juan Carlos. In late February mother and daughter were in London to visit Anna's new school and to check out the flat where they would be living. One morning during their stay Anna woke to find her mother in tears.

'Papi's dead,' sobbed Agneta. Anna asked what had happened – after all, Juan Carlos was only fifty-two. There was no way for her mother to cushion the blow.

'He took his own life,' she said. He had shot himself.

Agneta had already called Marie, who was in the hotel lobby, waiting to take them to her flat. At this moment of crisis, Anna's mother knew Marie could provide some of the comfort her daughter needed. The phone in Bassett Road rang constantly, people were arriving with flowers and everyone was crying. Marie's former colleagues from Jerusalem, Con Coughlin and Patrick Cockburn, both good friends of Juan Carlos, turned up and they mourned together. Dominique, who was on assignment in Jerusalem, staying at the Colony, remembers getting a call from Marie who said, 'Darling, sit on your bed, I have something to tell you.' She started sobbing as Marie told her the news. 'It was his demons,' said Marie. There were phone calls to Bolivia where relatives said things like, 'At least he's at peace now.' Anna and her mother stayed with Marie for a week.

It had been four years since Marie and Juan Carlos had separated, two since he'd returned to Bolivia. Sinking deeper into addiction, he had failed to make a new life at home and had sold most of his valuable possessions. Although he had never been diagnosed with bipolar disorder, his moods had always been erratic, as Marie had learnt in the years they lived together. He was prone to despair and extravagant gestures. That week, the landlord had told him that he and his girlfriend had to leave their apartment, but they had no money to rent another place. Reportedly, the last thing he said to her was 'I'm going to catch some rays', before climbing on to the roof terrace and shooting himself in the heart. He left no note.

Marie was shocked, but not entirely surprised. They had not been in touch very often since he returned to Bolivia, but she knew he was in a bad way and had always worried that he might shoot himself, like Hemingway. She scribbled on an undated piece of paper what might have been notes from a telephone conversation or her own thoughts:

Favourite rifle, it was his baby. This is pain – I want to feel this. He didn't want to rewind his life. Didn't want to start again ... nothing else to live for, finished what he came to do.

Always respected him – I loved him so much. The way he saw
life. That great person back in my mind. … Always said he
loved guns …

She wanted to remember Juan Carlos as he had been when they met – a great, funny bear of a man, with his unruly black hair and huge beard, engulfing her in his warmth and wit. Her photos showed them fooling around, dancing, laughing, playing with Anna. She had no love for the man he had become, only for the man he had ceased to be. If she had regrets, it was that she could not save him from himself. The obituaries harked back to his glory days in Beirut and Jerusalem. Charlie Glass wrote, 'Winning his friendship was like acquiring a brother. Although his loyalty was legendary, he nonetheless hurled contempt at colleagues who committed either of what he regarded as the two cardinal sins of journalism: bragging about being in danger and writing clichés about war … He made his friends laugh in countries where humour came hard – the humour Mark Twain said came from "a deep well of sorrow".'

Marie and Con organised a memorial service at St Bride's, followed by a reception at the Groucho Club. The choir sang 'He Who Would Valiant Be' and 'Forever Young'. Anna had written a short piece but sobs overcame her when she tried to read it, so the vicar quietly took the paper from her trembling hands and read it for her.

Juan Carlos's brother Mauricio read out Pablo Neruda's poem 'The Danger', which seemed to have been written expressly for Juan Carlos.

Maybe others will live out their lives with
no more than an occasional spill on the ice.

I live with this horror; when I tumble,
I go down into blood.

* * * * *

250

Neither injury nor grief would stop Marie from working, and the year after she lost her eye, she was back in the West Bank, reporting a stand-off between Israeli forces and the Palestinians. Not everyone at the *Sunday Times* was happy about her deployment. Sean and John had tried to get her to work on the desk, but she refused to show up in the newsroom. It was no secret that she drank too much – she always had done – but now the problem was acute, and there was no hiding it. Other correspondents worried that her judgement was flawed and she was being exploited for the sake of competition – her photo byline, complete with eyepatch, had become not just her trademark but the paper's, as if risk-taking were in itself evidence of good reporting. Before the trip, she had dinner with Uzi. 'Marie, you know, after the injury they owe you a lot,' he said. 'You can do whatever you want. Why not go here and there, but not to war zones? Be a columnist.' But she didn't trust Uzi, whom she saw as a competitor on the paper, and she still wasn't confident about her ability to analyse, a requirement for columnists. Anyway, she said, she didn't drink when she was in the field. It was galling to see others tell a story where she knew all the characters and the history. So Sean and John agreed. After all, it was true – she did know the story best. And they didn't know what else to do with her.

The Middle East peace process that Marie had followed so closely eight years earlier was in its slow, agonising death throes. Palestinian groups had carried out a string of terror attacks on civilians within Israel. Prime Minister Ariel Sharon responded by sending the Israeli military to reoccupy Palestinian land and destroy the institutions of the putative Palestinian state. Marie reported on a particularly egregious terror attack during Passover in Netanya, a coastal town in central Israel, in which thirty Israelis were killed and 140 injured by a Hamas suicide bomber. The Israelis held Arafat responsible for failing to stop the terrorists if not sponsoring them, and had surrounded the Muqata, his administrative headquarters in Ramallah, rendering him a prisoner. They had banned reporters from the town, so when a US negotiator was going to see Arafat, Marie and others who needed to cover the story had to find a back road. They were waiting outside the compound when Israeli soldiers roared up in a jeep and started firing. Marie's first thought was for herself: 'This cannot be happening again.'

Sunday Times, Ramallah, 7th April 2002
Soldiers stood up through openings in the roofs. They gave no warning before they lobbed grenades at us. By the time the second exploded I realised they were stun grenades and contained no shrapnel. As I raced for the armoured car in which I had arrived, more followed. Two hit a CNN TV crew on the feet. An ABC cameraman was struck on the calf ... A group of us were on a banal mission, awaiting the arrival of an American envoy, when we were fired on. One can only imagine what happens to Palestinian civilians without the protection of a foreign passport, away from the gaze of international cameras.

Later in the year, she had lunch inside the Muqata with Arafat, who had by then been under effective house arrest for eight months. Shocked that someone had injured his Mary, he grasped her by both shoulders and kissed her eyepatch seventeen times, until one of his aides growled, 'Enough, Abu Amar.' Marie was equally shocked to see the damage that time and relentless pressure had wrought in him, finding the man she had known for a decade and a half 'diminished, suddenly old and frail. There were non-sequiturs and long gaps in conversation. He would start to answer a question, then look into space for 4 minutes or so before continuing. His hands were pale after so long without sun.' She called Suha, who was in Paris with their daughter, Zahwa, to give her an update. A few weeks later, when she saw him again, Arafat seemed to have recovered his strength. The prospect of death had invigorated him, she thought. 'One of the greatest problems with Arafat was that he really was ready to die,' she reflected later. 'That was when he was happiest.'

Marie was back into her stride, slipping inside the besieged Palestinian camp in Jenin, while Israeli forces prowled the perimeter.

The Israelis had lost thirteen soldiers in a battle; the Palestinians said that Israeli troops had massacred civilians. Marie found a family to stay with inside the camp. Preparing for an Israeli attack, she wrote on the back of her notebook: 'I'M IN A HOUSE IN JENIN. IF THIS IS FOUND, THERE ARE NO FIGHTERS OR GUNS HERE – JUST FAMILIES. MANY WOMEN AND CHILDREN. MARIE COLVIN.'

Marie's investigation was scrupulous, aided by Uzi's reporting from the Israeli side. When rescue workers pulled out human remains of what Palestinians said was a small child, Marie consulted a doctor. 'This person has been reduced; I think in a fire,' the doctor said. 'See that bone?' He poked at a large, adult thigh bone. It was a lesson Marie remembered from Kosovo: she knew too much about what happens to the human body in war. Her conclusion – which she said would not satisfy propagandists from either side – was that there had been no deliberate massacre, but that the Israelis had often shot without establishing whether a target was civilian or not. Her own experience a few days after the battle backed up her assessment.

Sunday Times, Jenin, 21st April 2002
Late in the day, when all was quiet, I was walking past the Jenin Hospital. Nearby, women and children were slowly making their way back to temporary lodgings after a day trying to find their homes and relatives. An armoured personnel carrier pulled up at the end of the street behind us. The Palestinians took no notice – until the soldier in the turret opened fire straight down the street with his machinegun. I dived for shelter. Children cried in terror ... Then the soldier waved his hand in anger, yelling, 'Go, go'. I think he just wanted everyone off the streets.

After the APC lurched off, Marie tried to walk away, but the women ran after her, hoping the letters 'TV' on her body armour would protect them and their children. By the time they reached the place where she was staying, Marie was shaking. The women begged her to walk with them to their homes, but, hearing another burst of gunfire and the grinding of another APC manoeuvring nearby, she just couldn't do it. Fear had finally caught up with her.

Fortunately for the families, Marie's guide and interpreter, Imad Abu Zahra, a burly 34-year-old local Palestinian journalist also wearing a flak jacket marked 'TV', agreed to accompany them. He later told her it had taken five hours and they had been shot at twice. Imad was one reason – Marie would have said the main reason – her reporting from Jenin was so good. 'Indefatigable in his desire to discover what had happened,' as she put it, he was also infuriating because he stopped to talk to everyone as they walked through the camp. 'It took an unnervingly long time to get anywhere.' But of course, she knew perfectly well that his popularity was the key to her uncovering what had really happened. Affiliated with no political faction, he was an independent journalist, a rare thing in the Palestinian territories. She worried about his safety. When she told him he had to be more careful, he said, 'I'm from Jenin. I'm a journalist. I have the right to walk on my streets. Don't worry ...'

Three months after the siege of Jenin, Imad was killed by the Israelis. A gunner on an Israeli tank shot him in the leg as he was photographing an armoured vehicle that had run into an electricity pole. The Palestinian Red Crescent, the equivalent of the Red Cross, said he bled to death because Israeli soldiers halted the ambulance that was trying to reach him. Marie thought how brave Imad had been, escorting the women and children when she had been too scared. 'He knew he was taking too many chances,' she wrote. It was not just an individual tragedy but a sign that reporting in the Middle East had become much more dangerous than when Marie was there in the 1990s. It would only get worse.

* * * * *

Patrick wanted to buy a house in Wimbledon, where he grew up, but that was too suburban for Marie so they settled on Hammersmith. 1 Weltje Road was perfect – just ten yards from the Thames, between

The Dove and the Corinthian Sailing Club, and a walk along the river from the Tube. She had started sailing again, and it was her aim to spend more time on the water. She found it soothing, therapeutic. The house was a beautiful Victorian terrace, its side to the river, with bay windows and high ceilings and a small garden at the back. She loved its proportions, the space she had never had before, and the potential for decorating it with the paintings and other beautiful things she had bought around the world. She and Patrick still fought, but were committed to one another. Life was stably unstable. At work, by contrast, she felt less secure. Although able to function with one eye, she had lost confidence and become more anxious. John had recruited two more foreign correspondents: Christina Lamb, an award-winning reporter poached from the *Sunday Telegraph* who had written books on Zambia and Afghanistan, and Hala Jaber, a brave Lebanese journalist with excellent contacts whom Marie knew from Beirut. The fact that they were both women shouldn't have made a difference but it did. Marie worried about being upstaged. The three of them, plus Jon Swain, were seen as 'the A Team' – the ones who did the dangerous reporting. Other correspondents had long muttered that Sean and John were obsessed with stories that showcased courage – or recklessness – and won awards, nothing else. The issue was about to get more pointed, because the US and Britain were readying for war.

Twelve years on from the Gulf War, which Marie had covered from Baghdad, Saddam Hussein was once again on the minds of Western leaders. Iraq had been under sanctions since the war, its belligerent leader seemingly contained, no-fly zones preventing him from attacking by air the Kurds in the north or the Shi'ites in the south of Iraq who had risen against him in 1991. Every few years there was a flurry of diplomatic and military activity, usually when the US thought that the Iraqis were rebuilding their stockpiles of chemical, biological and nuclear weapons. Now, in the wake of 9/11, the US President, George W. Bush, elected in 2000, and his ally, the British Prime Minister, Tony Blair, were preparing to attack Iraq again. The Americans were trying to link Saddam to bin Laden, and were claiming that the Iraqi leader had failed to declare all his weapons of mass destruction to UN inspectors. By the end of 2002, it was clear that nothing short of regime change was going to satisfy the US.

Marie couldn't do as she had in 1991 and hunker down in the Iraqi capital, because she was denied a visa, so she went to see the man the Americans favoured as Iraq's next leader, Ahmed Chalabi, the head of the opposition Iraqi National Congress. He and his fighters planned to base themselves in the Kurdish north of Iraq, which had been effectively independent since the end of the war in 1991, and which one could enter by land from Turkey without a visa. The plan was to sweep down into Baghdad in triumph when the US gave the signal. Chalabi agreed that Marie could come with him.

As British and American forces gathered in Kuwait, Marie consulted an old soldier who knew something about fighting in Iraq: the Duke of Wellington, Jane's father, now aged eighty-seven, who had commanded a mounted brigade fighting to capture Baghdad in the Second World War. His concern, he told her, was that the next battle for Baghdad would be fought with little clarity about its aim, nor proper planning for the aftermath. 'I have an awful suspicion that the role of the British will be to occupy and pacify the country,' he said. It was a prescient remark, and Marie understood from her own experience the sensitivity Iraqis would have about being occupied. But, like many journalists who had spent years interviewing people who had escaped Saddam's prisons, or relatives of those who had been tortured and killed, she supported the war. She understood the perils of regime change, but was swayed by the Iraqis she knew who craved a future without dictatorship.

At the last minute, the Turkish government decided not to allow any movement across its border, so Marie flew to Damascus and spent days battling the Syrian authorities for permission to enter Iraqi Kurdistan across that border instead. Chalabi had told her that his Free Iraqi Forces, made up of semi-trained exiles, would be an essential part of the battle for Baghdad. She had expected them to be like the KLA in Kosovo, but they turned out to be a motley crew. They were also the focus of a turf war in Washington. The CIA and the State Department had concluded that the intelligence Chalabi was providing was at best exaggerated, and at worst fabricated, so they did everything they could to block the Pentagon from backing him. At the last minute, the Pentagon assigned as Chalabi's liaison Colonel Ted Seel, a Vietnam War veteran then attached to the US Embassy in Cairo. He and Marie got on famously, which was good, because nothing else was going according to plan.

The northern front turned out not to be a front at all because, in the wake of the Turkish decision, the invasion was launched entirely from Kuwait in the south. On 21 March, when the US mounted its 'shock and awe' bombing of Baghdad, Chalabi and Marie had to watch on TV two hundred miles away from the action. Two weeks later, they were still in front of the screen drinking tea and watching US forces taking over Baghdad airport. Marie had missed the war, which was reported by Jon Swain and Hala Jaber in Baghdad and Christina Lamb with the invading forces in the south. After much bickering in Washington, the Pentagon finally sent planes to transfer Chalabi and his army of exiles to a disused base in the desert near Nasiriyah in the south. 'It was a total disaster,' recalls Colonel Seel. 'We were put in buildings that had been bombed out in the first Gulf War with no supplies at all. There was a fledgling US support element nearby, so we were able to get water but no containers to put it in.' It was becoming clear that the US military had been given instructions to sequester Chalabi's forces as far from the action as possible.

At this point a sandstorm blew up, filling Marie's computer and satellite phone with tiny particles, so she couldn't file. (She was hopeless with technology, frequently erasing stories by accident and needing help to file from her computer, but on this occasion it really wasn't her fault.) Eventually, Chalabi's nephew, Salem, acquired enough vehicles to take the leadership and some bodyguards to Baghdad. 'I had a brand new Hilux twin cab so I led the convoy because US forces had been told anyone driving a Toyota Land Cruiser was the enemy,' remembers Ted Seel. 'We lost one vehicle because it went to look for diesel and the guy got apprehended by US forces and didn't return for the better part of a week.' Unfortunately for Chalabi and his acolytes, it was the first day of *Ashura*, the festival where Shi'ite Muslims mourn the killing in AD 680 of Hussein, Prophet Mohammed's grandson and the founder of their sect. Under Saddam, only a few had been allowed to take part in the ritual, so now, free at last, millions of Iraqi Shi'ites packed the streets of the holy cities of Karbala and Najaf. 'We got held up in a sea of humanity,' remembers Colonel Seel.

Eventually the exiles made it to Baghdad, where Chalabi took over the Hunting Club, a compound previously favoured by Saddam's son Uday. Marie had a first-hand glimpse of American confusion when two US tanks burst through the gates.

'We have orders to secure this compound,' yelled one of the soldiers.

'For us or from us?' asked one of Chalabi's men.

'Don't know, sir!' replied the American.

Apart from great colour scenes like that, Marie's reporting at this point was not her best. She continued to believe that Chalabi would be Iraq's next leader long after it should have been obvious he would not. Later, her old friend Jonathan Landay did a major investigation, concluding that Chalabi and the Iraqi National Congress had fooled not only Marie but many other journalists, including Judy Miller, who ended up entangled in a controversy about her reporting in the run-up to the war. Essentially, Chalabi lied to US intelligence and to journalists in order to drum up support for the overthrow of Saddam Hussein. His team fabricated evidence that Saddam retained weapons of mass destruction when in fact he had destroyed them. The previous year, Marie had written a long piece based on a videotaped interview with a supposed defector that turned out to be false, but when Jonathan called to ask her about it she was defensive. 'I believe they acted in good faith,' she said. 'Over seven years, I would not say there was a story I was fooled on.'

Why did Marie not see through Chalabi? Maybe because he was a source of what seemed like good stories, and as with all plausible fabricators, not everything he said was untrue. But maybe her sympathy for the underdog had blinded her. 'Marie was one of the best war correspondents and she had a gigantic heart for people who were suffering,' says Jonathan. 'That's a problem when you start identifying with the people that you're covering to the extent that she did ... It's a motivator, it makes you go out and get the story, bring the suffering and tragedy to the world. But you become susceptible to the Iraqi opposition and its story. I think that's why she fell into this – because it all made sense to her.'

Still, as looters rampaged through Baghdad and the Americans struggled to maintain control, staying at the Hunting Club had its benefits. Marie had full access to the archive of the Iraqi army which Chalabi's men had seized from the private homes where it had been hidden. She was also there when a man turned up to confess to a crime that had remained unsolved since she was in Baghdad during the war twelve years earlier. Six hundred Kuwaitis had gone missing in that conflict. After their disappearance the Kuwaiti government had offered a $1 million reward for information that might reveal their fate. The man, whom she called Feras in her story to protect his identity, said he had been a member of the Iraqi secret police, and that the Kuwaiti citizens had been brought to the compound where he worked. Wearing the traditional Arab dishdashas, eyes blindfolded and hands tied behind their backs, they were prodded on to a firing range in two horseshoe-shaped groups. Senior military officials, including a half-brother of Saddam Hussein, gave the order to fire. Feras said he had been the driver of one of the trucks that took the bodies to a secret police base near Fallujah. Three trenches were dug and the bodies thrown in. It was an extraordinary story. 'But how were we to believe a man like Feras, who was expressing interest in a reward, in the new Iraq where people are so desperate for money?' pondered Marie. Then she had an idea – in the journalistic golden moment of anarchy after the invasion, you could do anything. So she hired a mechanical digger with operator. As they headed for the base where Feras had said the bodies were buried, she told him she would believe his story only if he could point out the graves.

Sunday Times, near Fallujah, 18th May 2003
The first object to come out of the ground was a blue and white trainer. Delicate brown foot bones could be seen

inside ... As the arm of the mechanical digger carved out one bucketful after another from the desert, ever more gruesome evidence followed that Saddam Hussein had executed 600 Kuwaiti prisoners of war who have been missing since 1991 ... After three more scoops, the digger's jaws were dangling dishdashas, rotten yet intact, and some had bones inside them ... then a skull tumbled down, and another, and more leg bones. The putrid smell of death filled the air even though the bodies had spent 12 years in ground pounded by heat.

At this point, Marie asked the digger driver to stop disturbing the dead – she had enough evidence.

She investigated other mass graves, accompanied by a film crew making a documentary about five female journalists covering Iraq. The producer of *Bearing Witness*, Marijana Wotton, had tracked down Marie at the Hunting Club after months of sending emails that were never acknowledged. Marie was a natural on screen, seemingly oblivious to the camera, giving a glimpse of her life on the road that friends at home had never seen. In jeans and a lime green long sleeve T-shirt, hair tinted lighter than before to disguise the grey, her face dominated by the eyepatch, she interviews a man as he tries to identify his missing friend from bones covered in shreds of clothing. People fill bags with bones while women in chadors crouch on the ground crying. When given information that isn't specific enough, Marie is kind but firm. 'Tell him I'm very sorry and I know it's difficult but could he just tell us a little bit about his friend,' she says to the interpreter. 'I don't want to say there are hundreds of people here, I want to tell the stories of each person. These are not numbers.' When the interpreter starts to panic, saying that someone wants to arrest or possibly kill the film crew, she is calm and humorous but determined.

'Okay, where's our useless guide?' she asks, trying to get everyone into the car. 'He wants to kill us? Let's not just sit here, let's get organised and go. *Yalla!*' And then, like an exasperated schoolteacher herding recalcitrant students, she adds, 'You getting excited makes everything worse.'

She is frank about her feelings. 'I probably do get too involved and I have nightmares but I think that it still matters,' she says in an interview segment. 'When it stops mattering to me then I'll stop doing it.' Filmed with other correspondents at the Hunting Club, where she's sleeping on the floor of a room where no one ever turns out the lights, she laughs, explaining that one advantage of being blind in one eye is that when she sleeps on her right hand side it's automatically dark. As they drink vodka round a campfire, a young male reporter points out that the 'tough war correspondent' is wearing pink socks. Marie chuckles. 'We have to have a bit of femininity, don't we?' she says.

After six weeks in Iraq she returned to London, the film crew in tow. Her mother came to visit with three of her nieces, and Marie took them shopping, buying them clothes she couldn't afford but knew they would love. The film shows her talking about losing her eye while the girls, all aged seventeen, listen rapt – their aunt's life is beyond their imagination.

Marie and Marijana Wotton became friends. Throughout 2003 and the first part of 2004, they went back and forth to Iraq, usually staying at Al Hamra, a small, family-run hotel where journalists, aid workers and other foreigners lodged. One night, still unable to understand technology, Marie racked up a $20,000 bill by inadvertently leaving on the satellite phone after filing a story. It was a wild time. 'We had a bottle of vodka one evening,' recalls Marijana. 'The entire journalistic community descended on our little room and then spread out to the pool. Everyone ended up skinny dipping, Marie leading the charge.'

Marie often let a young aid worker stay in her room. Marla Ruzicka, known as 'Bubbles' because of her curly blonde hair and effervescent personality, was doing what Marie in some ways longed to do – saving individual lives. Understanding that the US military would not admit legal liability when they injured or killed people by accident, Marla thought there must nonetheless be a way to help those families, so she founded the Campaign for Innocent Victims in Conflict, or CIVIC, extracting money from US officials by calling it charity, rather than compensation. After helping hundreds of Afghans a few years earlier, she was now doing the same in Iraq. US generals in Baghdad and members of congress in Washington found it hard to say no when she knocked on their door asking for funds. Journalists were always coming to her with cases requiring assistance – a little girl who needed epilepsy medicine after US Marines accidentally shot her in the head or a family whose breadwinner had become 'collateral damage'. Marla's energy was boundless, but there was something vulnerable about her. As the months wore on, she looked more drawn and tired. The needs of the Iraqi people were endless, and she found it hard to accept the limits of her ability to solve their problems. She would leave Marie notes saying how much she loved and respected her. Marie wanted to protect Marla from the harsh world in which she operated. In the young woman's inability to distance herself from the suffering she saw around her, maybe she could hear an echo of herself.

The victory that President George W. Bush had announced on 1 May 2003 was turning sour. In August, a massive bomb destroyed the UN headquarters in Baghdad. Marie had been inside two days earlier, interviewing Sérgio Vieira de Mello, the diplomat heading the UN mission in Iraq, who was killed in the blast. Less than a week later she was in the holy Shi'ite city of Najaf just after the revered cleric Mohammed Baqir al-Hakim was murdered by a car bomb. Dressed in a full length *abaya*, head covered, she was talking to people outside a mosque when someone glimpsed her shoes and realised that she was not an Iraqi. 'A man I was talking to began shouting "Kill Americans! Kill Americans!" and pumped the air with his fist,' she wrote. 'The crowd around me joined in. Someone led me away, walking slowly, so as not to arouse any predators, and I reached the safety of a small hotel.'

Iraq was getting increasingly dangerous for journalists but there was one story Marie could not miss: in December 2003, Marie was at a pre-Christmas party in London when Saddam Hussein was discovered hiding in a hole in Tikrit. Within hours she was on a plane to Amman. Her colleague Matthew Campbell, who joined her to share the eight-hour drive across the desert to Baghdad, was amused to notice that she was still wearing her cocktail dress and high heels. She wrapped herself in a blanket and slept for the entire drive, waking only as they entered the Iraqi capital.

* * * * *

It had been an intense year. When back in London, Marie had been working on a TV documentary about her heroine, Martha Gellhorn, which was broadcast on the BBC. 'The way Martha Gellhorn thought and wrote about war coloured my thinking and career,' Marie says near the beginning of the film. 'When I pack my bags, among the necessities is a well-thumbed copy of Martha's book *The Face of War*.' Martha and she reported as they did, Marie said, because brutal images of war 'are the strongest argument against war'. She does not draw attention to other similarities, although any friend watching would have seen them. Marie notes that Martha's private life was 'messy and volcanic', and mentions not only Gellhorn's tumultuous marriage to Hemingway, but other troubled liaisons. Martha's father – 'a man of principle' – thought she was 'unfocussed' when, aged twenty, she railed against injustice without knowing how she would 'carry out her crusade on behalf of those without a voice in society', and the two clashed when she had an affair with a Frenchman of whom he disapproved. Martha, who was twenty-seven when her father died, was haunted by a feeling that she had somehow failed him.

Martha, like Marie, had strong convictions, dismissing 'all that objectivity shit'. The two journalists would have clashed on the issue of the Palestinians, but Marie would have understood why Martha was so strongly pro-Israeli. The day she reported from Dachau, Martha said, 'a darkness entered my spirit'. The feeling never quite left her. Many years later, she wrote to a friend, 'It is as if I walked into Dachau and there fell over a cliff and suffered a lifelong concussion ... I have never again felt that lovely, easy, lively hope in life which I knew before.'

At least one of Marie's colleagues was experiencing something akin to that despair. After the US invasion, Jon Swain had returned from Iraq exhausted. Years earlier, in his memoir about Cambodia, he had written, 'One can be romantic as well as cynical about war. There can be a magic attraction about tragedy; there can be exhilaration as well as exhaustion. When death is close, every object, every feeling, is golden. Camaraderie is stronger, love is deeper.' Now, overwhelmed by thirty years of reporting violence and cruelty, he could no longer see the romance, only the pain and frustration. On medical advice, he had taken time off and negotiated a deal whereby he would in future balance reporting conflict with more life-enhancing subjects. Another colleague, Christina Lamb, had had a near miss during the war in Iraq, driving along a road half an hour before a British TV team was killed in exactly the same spot; she had determined to take fewer risks in the future.

Marie said she was fine but the warning signs were there. Her stepdaughter, Anna, would call needing advice or just a listening ear, but Marie could not provide it – she was too trammelled by her own stuff. As Anna struggled to deal with her father's violent death, she found herself on the phone to a stepmother going on at length about her own problems. If she wasn't on a story, Marie could scarcely muster the energy to get out of bed. She feared she couldn't sustain her relationship with Patrick.

8th August 2003. Figured out if we together, can't see me like this. Debt, procrastination, fear. Can I get out of it? Don't know because don't know why I'm in it. Always had a façade – never ever really me. Learned late I love you. You are there – I'm not. I want to be but I can't poison us any longer by being the person I am now. Paralyzed. I will change. If I can't I need to let you go. Cliché. If I can't I can probably muddle along. You deserve more. I see your handsome face and I cry ... I am not honest. About the time I waste, not about love. I do nothing mostly. It's like I'm waiting, or more procrastinating, putting everything off. Drink until I sleep, relief I have not had to appear as Marie.

THE FACE IN THE MIRROR

Sometimes she tried to pull herself together by telling herself how she should feel.

16th October 2003. Supposed to be:
1. *Reliable*
2. *Respectable – conventional, drinking consistent, emotional pitch undramatic*
3. *be more realistic – always think everything is possible when sometimes it's not*

In March 2004, Marie accompanied Sean and John to a News Corp conference in Cancún where she was on a panel about war reporting. They went to a club where waiters descended from the ceiling on elastic bands, squirting vodka shots into people's mouths. Marie drank so much at the reception that Sean had to pull her away from Rupert Murdoch before she embarrassed herself by slurring her words and repeating herself. Before the conference ended, news broke that the spiritual leader of Hamas, Sheikh Yassin, had been killed by the Israelis. Her editors asked if she would leave the conference early and go to Gaza. As they dropped her off at the airport, several News Corp executives asked if Marie was fit to travel. John and Sean thought she was fine – she'd just been a little drunk the night before like everyone else, they said.

But she wasn't fine. She was drifting out of reach. Sometimes she would refuse to answer her phone when Sean called, or would say she was away when he knew perfectly well she was at home. The foreign desk manager, Caroline, would be despatched to Weltje Road to coax her out. On one occasion, Patrick was away and neither Sean nor Jane had heard from Marie in days. Everyone was getting worried so Caroline knocked at the door. A weak voice croaked:

'Who is it?'

'It's me, Caroline. Come on! Open the door, come on!'

Marie opened the door. 'She looked like an old woman, sort of hunched and shaky,' recalls Caroline. 'I just put my arms round her and hugged her. And that went on for quite some time with neither of us speaking, just hugging. She was in a really dark place.'

Marijana was editing the documentary *Bearing Witness* in New York. 'Marie would call me at all hours of the day and night,' she remembers. 'She wanted to talk; maybe she needed praise. We'd giggle – often she had been drinking a lot. She would repeat herself over and over again on the phone. I just listened.' Whatever Marie came up with, Marijana absorbed it like blotting paper. Other friends encouraged Marie to stop drinking, to eat more, to seek professional help but it was easier for Marie just to ring Marijana and try to laugh about it all. Panic attacks would hit her when she least expected, and she felt a growing sense of unreality. Even Katrina couldn't reach her. Marie would be distant on the phone, unwilling to talk, often drunk and making little sense, hanging up and disappearing for months at a time. Katrina offered to visit, but Marie resisted. 'I'm okay,' she said. 'Maybe I'll come and see you, I should take a trip.' But she never did. 'She had been halfway round the world and I always knew where she was, and here she was in London, not going anywhere, and I couldn't find her,' recalls Katrina. Marie was like a wounded animal who had gone to ground, to a dark hole where even her closest friends couldn't reach her.

Bob Tyrer, then the *Sunday Times* executive editor, came round for dinner at Marie and Patrick's house, and suggested that she stop going to the frontline, and remain in London as a columnist. They talked about how she loved sailing and how in her UPI days she had once interviewed Jacques Cousteau. 'Right, let's stop everything, we have enough money, let's give up now and you go and spend a year studying marine biology at the Cousteau Institute in Monaco,' said Patrick. Initially Marie was enthusiastic, but she never took it up, slipping instead back into paralysis. 'She was immobilised,' says Patrick. 'She would just sit at home.'

Cat called multiple times on the house phone, finally yelling into the answering machine demanding that her sister pick up. 'She said she couldn't get out of bed. She had thrown her cellphone in the river,' says Cat. 'She was suicidal and needed help.' Cat decided not to tell Rosemarie – it would have been too much for her to handle. Sean, who, with several foreign correspondents now showing signs of distress, was rapidly reading up on the psychological impact of war reporting, told her that the paper had an arrangement with The Priory, the rehab hospital that her late husband Juan Carlos had briefly attended. 'I'm not going anywhere near the fucking Priory,' she said. 'That's for people who had a nervous breakdown because they missed the Prada sale.' She had told Denise Leith eighteen months earlier, 'I don't get numb … To write passionately, to get across the emotion of what you're feeling, you can't block yourself off … I've never become desensitised. It hits me every single time.' But now she felt nothing. It was like cutting herself but failing to draw blood. A friend who had been treated for depression recommended a psychiatrist on Harley Street and Marie made an appointment. He diagnosed Post Traumatic Stress Disorder (PTSD).

She drafted a letter to John Witherow.

Dear John,

I'm sending you this because it's difficult to talk about.

I need to take some time off to deal with a problem that has become too much to handle, both in work and personal terms.

Basically, I've been having anxiety attacks that result in a sort of paralysing depression. I know this sounds weird given that I seem fine when you see me, but the person I've gone to see says this is just keeping your head above water and can't go on.

I am dealing with it but any pressure just sends me back down so I avoid things. This is pretty hard to confess; as you know, I'm a 'just get on with it' kind of person, but it has taken over and I don't think I'm doing a very good job as a result.

I appreciate if you can keep this as confidential as you can. I felt I had to tell you.

Marie

The psychiatrist recommended she be admitted to a hospital to rest, recuperate and learn some techniques for controlling anxiety. In May 2004, Jane took her to the Princess Grace Hospital where she checked into a small, plain room and, much to the consternation of the staff, immediately forced open the window so she could smoke out of it. It was a relief finally to accept that she was burnt out and broken down, and needed help. One of the therapists she saw had experience with military veterans, but the soldiers he treated hadn't seen as much combat as Marie. The doctors put her on medication that calmed her down and helped even out her mood. Then she started a programme of eye movement desensitisation and reprocessing (EMDR). Marie had not been wrong when she said that her nightmare about the attack in Sri Lanka was her brain's way of trying to come up with an alternative outcome. She always failed, of course – nothing could bring back the sight in her eye. Now a psychotherapist enabled her to relive the experience in a way that helped her brain process the trauma. The idea of EMDR is that as you visualise a traumatic event that haunts you, the therapist gives you 'bilateral stimulation' – either moving a finger from side to side which you follow with quick eye movements, or tapping a part of the body or making a repetitive tone or noise. After each set of stimulation, you let your mind go blank and then see what thought, image or memory comes to mind. Marie learnt to reprogram her mind – from then on, if she felt stressed or panicky, she would tap her fingers into her palm as a way of calming herself down. She also underwent Cognitive Behavioural Therapy (CBT), which helped her replace negative thoughts with positive ideas and find ways to short-circuit the cycle of anxiety and panic that had paralysed her. She would never forget being under attack, nor the mass graves and wounded children she had seen, but she was learning to desensitise the memories so she could cope and carry on.

Marie was keen to see friends who had suffered similarly and would understand. Jon Swain dropped by. 'She thought the treatment was fantastic,' he says. He told her, 'Thank God you're here – don't rush out.' Anthony Loyd, a war correspondent for *The Times* who had written a book about his use of heroin while reporting the conflict in Bosnia, also visited. The two had shared many a drink in west London or on the road. 'I knew she had a vulnerable side but I was quite shocked,' he recalls. 'She was very depressed and listless – she wanted to talk but was really struggling to explain how she felt.' He understood how hard it was for her to acknowledge weakness. 'She was used to being Marie Colvin, known for her bravery and single-mindedness. Now she had to face this and she had no escape.'

Gradually she put on weight and the black cloud lifted. It was glorious just to sleep. Patrick was sceptical. He thought Marie's problems were less to do with what she had been through in war zones, and more to do with her drinking. Although she was routinely advised to cut back on alcohol consumption, she was not treated for alcoholism. After a few weeks at the Princess Grace, she felt well enough to go home. It was as if her settings had been rebooted. Patrick had visited her daily, but he didn't pick her up when she was discharged; it was not, he thought, as if she had suffered a broken leg or something that prevented her from getting home. She took a taxi back, and never forgave him.

Having acknowledged her PTSD, Marie no longer saw any need to keep it private. She became an advocate for treatment. 'I needed to take time to get whole again, centred again,' she said in an interview for *Bearing Witness* filmed shortly after her discharge. 'Foreign correspondents, we are like a little travelling family, supportive in a way, but nobody's supposed to be afraid – if you've been in the most terrifying situations you don't talk about it. Our support system is you go to the bar and have a drink and make some black jokes. And I realised I got into too black a place for that to be enough support, and I needed to talk to professionals. I needed someone who wasn't a friend and wasn't a colleague and I think I needed to say I'm vulnerable.'

She took six months off work, emerging only to write a piece about Yasser Arafat, who, after falling ill in circumstances that are still disputed, was flown to Paris. As he lay dying, Marie was in daily touch with Suha. It was more than a story. 'She gave me encouragement and strength every time she called,' says Suha. Arafat died on 11 November 2004. Marie wrote a long obituary, invoking the man as well as the politician, with characteristic affectionate detail. She recalled how he loved his baby daughter, Zahwa, named after his mother, but played with her as if she were 'an exotic marmoset, unrelated to his own species'. Interviewing him, she reflected, had been all but impossible.

> *Sunday Times*, 14th November 2004
> I found myself unexpectedly sympathising with Madeleine Albright, the American secretary of state, when I sat in on his end of a telephone conversation with her. She was trying to persuade him to stand down Palestinian demonstrations against a new Jewish settlement. He said he couldn't stop the violence until the Israeli bulldozers stopped. Albright said: 'Let's not get into a discussion of which came first, the chicken or the egg.' To which Arafat's cryptic reply was: 'But not to forget, in the end there is the hen and there is the egg.' There was a silence on her side – boy, did I understand ...

Right up to the end, she noted, he wore his uniform.

> He had utter faith in himself as the personification of the nation he had conjured up; and he would go anywhere, do anything, say anything to further this cause. He also had no compunction about using violence both against Hamas and the Israelis. He privately said he opposed suicide bombings but his failure to stop them was part of his greater failure. He had created the Palestinian nation but ultimately could not control the forces he unleashed. Nor did he have the vision to turn his creation into a state. Those uniforms spoke volumes: he would not give up being a guerrilla leader to become the statesman the Palestinians so badly need.

It's clear from the piece that she knew him far better than the academics and other journalists who would turn his obituaries into books, but she never finished the biography of him she had so exhaustively researched.

In September, Cat had come to visit with her six-year-old daughter, Justine. For a few days, Marie plunged into horse riding, trips to Pizza Express and above all shopping, buying expensive clothes the little girl loved but would soon outgrow. But the relief was temporary and, although she continued to see her therapists, the path back to health was littered with obstacles. One of the hardest moments came when she thought she was almost better: in April 2005 Marla Ruzicka and her Iraqi co-worker, Faiz Ali Salim, were killed by a suicide bombing on the road to Baghdad airport. Marla's was a futile, random death, and Marie felt it acutely because her friend was so young, and her motivation so pure. Friends held a memorial event for her in Marijana's apartment in Brooklyn. Marie, in her customary black cocktail dress, wine glass in hand, got up to speak. Marla, she said, was 'the girl with the broken wing'. It was a phrase that resonated, not just because it was so apt for the young woman who had tried so hard to mend the world, but because Marie too was struggling to stay aloft.

She and Marijana went on to the premiere of *Bearing Witness* at the Full Frame Documentary Film Festival in Durham, North Carolina and the Tribeca Film Festival in New York. Although four other female war correspondents were also featured in the film, Marie was the most compelling on screen, her charisma shining out. It wasn't a performance – it was her. Cat accompanied her to both festivals, basking in her sister's fame. Their mother attended the screening in New York, never quite understanding how her eldest had strayed so far, ending up in such a different world but proud of her daughter's achievements and the recognition she had garnered.

Antidepressants were making Marie feel cloudy and put on weight, as well as interfering with her ability to write. She stopped taking them. Her moods would swing, but she felt she was coping. She and

Katrina were back in touch, but the relationship with Patrick was fatally wounded. They fought all the time. She didn't confide in him, so he couldn't help. They went away on a last weekend, fanning the embers enough to feel the glow of the passion they had once had, but it was too late. They agreed to part. In May 2005 he moved into a flat in Bayswater, and they argued about money and the ownership of the house in Weltje Road for the next two years.

* * * * *

With her friend Jane Wellesley on the eve of Marie's wedding to Juan Carlos Gumucio, June 1996

Marie and Juan Carlos at their wedding in London

Marie and Juan Carlos dancing together, 1995

Marie with her step-daughter Anna Gumucio
in Hyde Park, London, 1997

December 1999. A guide helps Marie escape the war in Chechnya by
crossing the frozen Caucasus Mountains

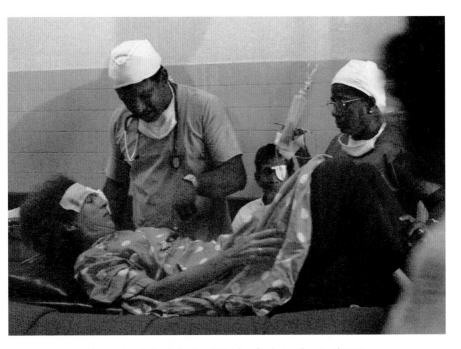

Marie in hospital in Colombo, Sri Lanka after being shot, April 2001.
The injuries she sustained would result in the loss of sight in her left eye

'I think of landmines & try to stay in footprints but not much use in tall grass.' A page from Marie's notebook before she was shot in Sri Lanka

leave on tractor - in wagon pulled by
tractor. Through open roads - if this is cleared
area, doesn't bode well for govt. *we'll* go
through ruins of cashew plantation,
destroyed in fighting + now overgrown, *area*
abandoned buddhist temple. open field,
jungle now too thick for tractor, can't launch
of "piku" carefully wrapped in plastic +
then newspaper like little presents. cigan flu!
is your only meal. I think they're joking -they're
not. Walking at first lovely - tunnel of.
eucalyptus + other trees shade sun,
cascades of white butterflies in shafts of
light, well worn path although narrow.
lots of signs of wild boar and tell we
climb a tree if one comes. we seem to be
on a schedule, although not clear what it
is. 2 pm come to a wide open field and
wait to 3:30, scouts go first, crouched +
running, we then proceed, separated, single
file. I think of land mines + try to stay in
footprints but not much use in tall
grass

Tim Lambon, Marie and Lindsey Hilsum in Jenin, West Bank just after
an Israeli siege, April 2002

Interviewing villagers resisting Al Qaeda in Diyala Province, Iraq in December 2007

Marie with Richard Flaye on his boat *Quadrille* off the coast
of Turkey shortly after their relationship began, 2006

Marie with her younger sister Cat, Thanksgiving 2010

November 2010. Giving the address at the St Bride's annual service,
to commemorate journalists killed while on assignment

In Tahrir Square, Cairo during the Arab Spring uprising, February 2011,
which would topple the Egyptian President Hosni Mubarak

In Misrata, April 2011, during the revolution in Libya

February 2012. In 'the widows' basement' in Baba Amr, Homs, Syria

Taking notes in a bombed-out building in Baba Amr. This was the
last photo taken of Marie before she was killed

PART FOUR

London

Chapter 10

ALL AT SEA

Undated, July 2005. Heave – puke – heave – puke.

The notes in Marie's diary might not suggest she was having fun, but she was. In 2005 she started sailing properly again. Not just pootling about on boats, but ocean racing, possibly the only form of the sport dangerous and exciting enough to distract her from war reporting. It was the less fortunate members of the crew doing the heaving and puking – she never got seasick.

Undated, July 2005. I make sandwiches – got so bad skipper said we need to eat – who's not seasick – everyone points to me – not the best at sailing, but inordinately proud can do <u>something</u>.

The first adventure was joining the crew of *Innovation*, a 13-tonne racing yacht, for the Middle Sea Race in the Strait of Messina, between Sicily and the boot of Italy. All was well until they hit a whirlpool and started spinning backwards in a series of 360 degree turns. If they started the engine they would be disqualified from the race, so they spun until the whirlpool spat them out into the path of an oncoming ferry, which rapidly had to change course. The next day, a force nine gale blew up. Sailing gave Marie something different to write about for the *Sunday Times*.

Sunday Times, Strait of Messina, 24th July 2005
Watching a storm in the early hours from the safety of one's home
is a world away from experiencing the same on a sailing boat.
First there is the noise: the crash of the sea, both beloved and
malevolent; the harsh, relentless slapping of the shredded sail;
the whipping cracks of halyards and lines; deafening thunder;
shouts of people trying to make themselves heard. Then there is
the cold, and flashes of lightning that seem to strike the vessel.

The sixteen-person crew, she wrote, felt like family as they endured
this life-threatening experience together. 'It's a mad way to stay sane,'
she told the film-makers Hugh Hudson and Carine Adler, who were
working up a film script about her life. 'It's the purity of what you're
facing – the waves and 16-mile-per-hour winds. You're cold and
trapped – you cannot get off. You've got to sail that boat and there's no
way out unless you can keep her afloat.' Her competitive instincts
were fully engaged. 'A hundred and nine boats started and only twenty-
five of us finished,' she said excitedly. 'A lot capsized, a couple broke up
on the coast of Sicily and quite a few others just chickened out. I didn't
chicken out. We won our class. We did not stop!'

She read Wordsworth, Blake and Coleridge and pondered a little
on how much she loved the sea compared to the countryside, which
bored her. The fear she felt at sea, she thought, was quite different
from the fear she had felt in Chechnya.

*Undated, July 2005. Maybe only terror brings nature to life. Sea
does that to me – racing and testing myself against her – longing
to be free ... I need awe and terror. Not fear [like when] trapped
in mountains in dark – but terror of a child that is really pure
pleasure – personal fear must be part of that, need to feel alive.*

After the Middle Sea Race, she went for a more relaxed week of sailing. Her old friend, Charles Richards, who had been part of the

American Colony crowd in Jerusalem in the late 1980s, had introduced her to Richard Flaye, a friend of his from Oxford. Richard was a businessman and venture capitalist, but his greatest love was sailing and he needed a crew for his yacht, which was moored off Sicily. Sundowners on deck and a luxury berth were more Richard's style than ocean racing. He was tall and muscular, a skilled and confident skipper. Marie found him attractive, but he made it clear that he was a 'hedonist'. That seemed to mean that, apart from his partner, he always had several other lovers or girlfriends, whatever you wished to call them. Marie didn't mind – she was on the rebound from Patrick, and not ready for anything serious. Sex and sailing were good enough. It was all part of her recovery.

In August she took part in the Fastnet Race, watching dolphins playing around the bow of the boat in the Irish Sea. Everyone laughed when the peace of the ocean was marred by exactly what Marie had been escaping.

Sunday Times, Cowes, 14th August 2005
The joy of sailing is that limitless expanse of water converging
at the horizon into the sky, the purity of aloneness with the
sea. On this particular race, that was interrupted by explosions
– inexplicably the Irish navy was conducting a firing exercise
at the same time as one of the world's biggest sailing races
passed through its waters.

She didn't mind being cold and wet, or sleeping in three-hour shifts, as it was liberating to be totally engaged with others in this joint exercise. 'Your brain doesn't turn off but it's involved in absolutely elemental things,' she told Hugh and Carine. 'It's physical danger, mental and physical challenge. I wouldn't want to be on shore having someone throwing cold buckets of water over me, why would you do that? If you're on a boat it's the same sensation but your whole mental and physical sense is different.'

* * * * *

The *Sunday Times* had agreed that Marie should ease herself back into work, starting with less dangerous assignments. After Cowes Week, a series of regattas off the coast near the Isle of Wight, she went to Israel to report on the evacuation of Jewish settlers from Gaza. Prime Minister Ariel Sharon had decided that instead of negotiating a deal with the Palestinians, he would simply uproot the settlements, while maintaining control of Gaza's borders, airspace and coastline. Marie was on good form. A few weeks earlier, she, Dominique and a young Israeli journalist named Aviram Zeno had started their preparations for the story by roaring down the highway between Jerusalem and Jaffa singing Tina Turner songs along to a CD. 'Simply the BEST!' belted out Marie before embarking on an even more exuberant rendition of 'What's Love Got To Do With It?' The Israeli Defense Forces had said Gaza would be a 'closed military area' during the operation to remove the settlers, so she wanted to explore the option of renting a sailing boat to get to Gaza. Purely for research purposes, she and Aviram went sailing while Dominique waited onshore, knowing perfectly well that the idea would come to naught because the Israelis would shoot at any unidentified boat coming ashore. (Marie often thought chartering a sailing boat was the best way to get to a story. It never was, apart from an occasion when she rented a dhow to get to Yemen.)

In the end, the three of them, like dozens of other journalists, stayed with the settlers so they would be at the heart of the action when the soldiers came in. The Israeli government wanted it to look as if dismantling settlements in Gaza were a huge concession to the Palestinians, despite the fact that the Jews had no historical claim in Gaza and the settlers would be rehoused nearby inside Israel or in the West Bank. Nonetheless, the settlers could be relied on to refuse to leave until dragged screaming from their houses, making it look as if the operation were much more of what the Israelis liked to call 'a painful sacrifice' than it really was. No one knew how long it would take, because the settlers said they would resist the soldiers, and the soldiers said they would not use force. On Marie's instructions, Aviram had prepared for a siege, buying torches and tents. Dominique teased Marie that she was behaving as if they were members of the French resistance in World War II. 'It was as if we were going with rebels in the *maquis*,' she says. They stayed in Neve Dekalim with the Jashi family, hardcore settlers who told Marie that they would rather die than leave their home in Gaza.

The night before the soldiers were due to remove them, Adiel, one of the Jashi sons, and his friends went on a 'resistance operation' to short out the settlement electricity with the aim of preventing the soldiers' entry. Marie and her colleages went along.

Sunday Times, Neve Dekalim, 21st August 2005
Our raid swiftly turned to farce. First, Adiel shouted abuse at a passing army patrol – not the best move for undercover saboteurs – and broke down in tears. The 'commando' team retired to the Jashi family's verandah to make him tea and soothe his nerves. Then it turned out nobody had brought any tools, obliging the boys to disperse to their parents' homes to find some. It was 3am, after another break for tea and hugs, when our group finally reached the electricity box. They poured their parents' barbecue accelerant onto newspaper, stuffed it into the box and lit a match. The paper flared and fizzled out and that was it.

Marie's story cut through the propaganda, pointing out that the army could have removed the settlers in 24 hours had it wanted to: the operation, which went ahead over a number of days, was largely theatre.

* * * * *

That year she reported from Tehran and Cairo – again, neither particularly dangerous places. It seemed she was heeding advice and avoiding conflict for a while. In the last days of summer, she flew to Martha's Vineyard. The holiday was courtesy of John Schley, the older man whom she had met at the Harvard-Yale game at the end of her university years, and who used to take her out for fancy dinners when she was a poor freelance in New York. After spotting an article about her and other female war correspondents in *Vanity Fair*, he had got back in touch. They had lunch at a Lebanese restaurant in London a couple of weeks after Patrick moved out, followed, some time later, by a typical chaotic Marie day when they were supposed to go to the races but she had lost her phone. They looked for it in the fridge where instead they found beer, which they drank while they continued to search until they gave up, arriving after the races were over. They had spent the night at a friend's house on the South Downs and slept together for the first time. Afterwards, John thought of little else. 'I was smitten but she never called,' he says. The years had done nothing to diminish his awkward demeanour. He was nearly seventy now, slow of speech and pedantic in manner, and it was hard to figure out what interested him, apart from Marie. Never married, he had stumbled through life, working in real estate for a while, then breeding horses, but never having to worry too much because of his inheritance, which included a beachfront property in one of the most sought after and expensive island resorts in America. The extent of Marie's cynicism is subject to conjecture, but this much is clear: he was in love, and she wanted a holiday on Martha's Vineyard.

Having expected a romantic getaway for two, John was surprised when Cat, Cat's three children and Marijana showed up on the ferry the day after he and Marie arrived. 'I was just happy she was coming, so she could get away with murder,' he says. Most mornings, Marie would take a blanket and a radio tuned to a country music station and go down to the beach. She told Marijana that in the old days war veterans were advised to go to the ocean for the positive ions. 'She wrapped herself up in the blanket and lay on the beach and pretty much slept all day,' Marijana remembers. John's black-and-white cocker spaniel, Karina, would keep her company. Sometimes they all had lunch in town, or visited an art gallery; John bought her a painting of rocks and seagulls. One afternoon Marie chased the children round the house until they were in a frenzy. 'Then she locked herself in the bathroom,' recalls Cat's eldest, Justine, who was then aged seven. 'We were going crazy banging on the door, trying to pick the lock but she had climbed out of the window and was drinking wine with Mom outside.' It was classic Marie – now aged fifty, still lithe and athletic, she had played the same trick on friends' children in London, convincing them she could teleport herself.

Lying on the beach, Marie contemplated the whitecaps and the luminescent greys and blues on the horizon. Her relationship with Patrick was over, so what now? She couldn't give all of herself like that again, she thought. She was tired of being Marie for the entertainment of others.

Undated, September 2005. Sound of waves rolling, crashing – alone and happy – not happy. I can't be there all the time with fireworks that make them look out of themselves and smile. I can always see how to make people happy – so I do it and then it takes so much time and energy I let them down. Nobody wins except maybe they have had a moment when they see the world differently.

A psychiatrist might have said that it was Marie who needed to feel she was bringing fizz and spontaneity into people's lives. Her real struggle was with herself – her fear of being alone, and a sense that her public persona as a brave war correspondent was out of kilter with the insecurity she felt inside. Her editors asked too much of her, she thought, and she rarely requested a pay rise, so suspected she was underpaid. She was always broke. Somewhere inside she must have known that John Schley was not the answer to the questions that plagued her, but she was struggling to find a way forward. One day she said to Marijana, 'I'm going to marry John – what do you think?' Marijana thought John and Marie were, to put it politely, an unlikely couple. 'If he makes you happy,' she said. She didn't feel she could give advice. 'Marie was the boss of him. Whatever she wanted she could get.

She controlled the situation.' But Marie was not entirely in control of her own life. That holiday she talked a lot about the past, about her days at Yale, as if trying to recapture something that had eluded her. Maybe she felt John could help her find something that she had lost.

Marie said to him, 'You can't have twelve months of me – I don't want to give it. All I can offer is some of me.' Something, he thought, was better than nothing. A few months later, when she was back in London, he stopped at a strip mall off the New Jersey Turnpike and bought an engagement ring. 'It wasn't Tiffany's on Fifth Avenue,' he admits. The Lebanese jeweller convinced him that not only had he heard of the famous journalist Marie Colvin, but also that yellow diamonds keep their value better than clear ones. John called Marie, who – once she had got over her horror that the ring had been bought in somewhere as suburban as Whitehouse, New Jersey – declared herself thrilled. She was struggling with back pain, caused by fused vertebrae and exacerbated by years of bouncing around rutted roads in four-wheel-drive vehicles. The discomfort was preventing her from getting out of bed and she was going to have to have an operation, so a week or so later she called him – could he fly over? Eager to oblige – not to mention formally propose marriage – John jumped on a plane. A pale shadow of doubt crept across his mind. 'We had only spent two weeks together after twenty-seven years of hardly seeing each other.'

When he called from Heathrow, she urged him to hop into a cab because she was in pain and needed help. He shouldn't worry about food because she had a chicken leg in the fridge. John did as bidden. The house was unlocked. He walked in only to find, to his surprise, a man in black leather motorcycle trousers lounging on the sofa, eating what looked suspiciously like chicken. It did not escape his notice that the man was taller and slimmer than he and acted 'as if he owned the place'. It was Richard Flaye, the man with the sailing boat moored off Sicily. Marie limped out of the kitchen. John looked back and forth between them. 'I think that's my chicken leg,' he said.

* * * * *

John decided not to present the ring that night, after Richard left. Marie had more pressing things on her mind: she had invited a dozen people for Thanksgiving dinner the next evening, but was going to be in hospital for her back operation. There was nothing else to do: John would have to host the dinner. It was already half prepared, she said, and her friends would heat everything up when they arrived. Rosie Boycott remembers it as one of the most bizarre evenings she ever spent at Marie's house. Everyone arrived late and a bit tiddly and for a long time no one could work out how to turn on the oven. When the turkey finally came out it was still bleeding. Then there was John, utterly bemused, whom Marie had mentioned purely as a purveyor of holidays on Martha's Vineyard for all her friends. 'She'd constructed an entire world of possibility around this man that really didn't include him,' Rosie recalls. John looked at Marie's friends' ring fingers. He was a rich man, but he couldn't help but notice the size of the rocks. 'They're ten times bigger than my little ring,' he thought. Unsure what to say, he decided to break the ice by asking, brightly, 'Would you like to see my ring?' He passed the box around. It was indeed quite a small stone with an unusual brownish-yellow glint. Everyone exclaimed how beautiful it was. 'I think they must have thought I was a cheapskate,' says John. In fact, they couldn't understand what Marie was thinking of, marrying a man who seemed to have no suitable attributes other than an attractive holiday home. But then, you could never tell what Marie was going to do next.

John visited Marie in the hospital. He had watched with intent the scene in *Bearing Witness* where she showed how she wore her wedding rings from both Patrick and Juan Carlos on the ring finger of her right hand, as a warning to herself never to remarry. In the hospital, he observed that she had taken off her rings. Another man might have thought it was probably because of the operation, but he took it as a sign. He proposed. She said yes. 'She just loved the ring,' says John.

Marie told him that after they were married, he would be allowed to live a 20-minute walk away and could visit two nights a week. 'That was better than her original idea, which was that I should live in Italy and she'd drop by on her way to and from war zones,' he recalls. 'I said, "Why I can't I be closer, say, France?" She said "Okay, you can stay in France". A month went by, and I said, "Why don't we live in the same country?" She said, "You could live near the Isle of Wight where I go sailing, I'd come on weekends."' As she was always pleading poverty, he gave her an American Express card, on which she spent freely. While they were living on opposite sides of the Atlantic, still unmarried, he took her to a fancy hotel in Anguilla at the end of the year. 'I'd go to meet her at the bar and she'd be sitting at the table with other people,' he recalls. 'I said "What the hell are you doing?" He would finally lie to them: 'Look we're here on our honeymoon. Could you leave us alone?'

Before Marie returned to London, they went to see her family in Oyster Bay where John asked Rosemarie if he could marry her daughter, as if they were in their twenties. 'I think that's a really bad idea,' said Rosemarie. 'My daughter is unmarriageable. You're not going to have a house with a picket fence, John.' They held an engagement party at 21, a conventional upscale New York restaurant in Midtown. A friend of John's made a toast and he got up to respond, launching into the story of how his grandparents, who had once owned the 21 Club, had sold it to a speakeasy. John thought himself a great storyteller – better than Marie, he sometimes said – but his stories tended to be long and winding, with much hesitation, many detours and no punchline. Eventually, Marie got unsteadily to her feet. 'I can't take it any longer,' she said. She walked over to another table and promptly collapsed under it. Her friend Judy Miller shudders at the memory. 'She was so drunk she couldn't get through the evening,' she recalls. The following day Judy went to see Marie at her hotel.

'Marie, this should not happen,' she said, firmly. 'You can't marry John.'

'But I could have a normal life, go sailing, do the things I love,' protested Marie.

'Oh c'mon, Marie,' said Judy. 'If you'd wanted that you would have done it years ago.'

Why was Marie so unkind to John? He was not a bad man, just unsuitable. Her yen for the picket fence life was a whisper from her upbringing that she could not quiet. It was as if she were rummaging around in her past to come up with something, or someone, to answer the questions that wouldn't go away. Why couldn't she be happy in a relationship? Why did she always seek out danger? Was being with the wrong man worse than being with no man? Her friends could see that, whatever the question, John Schley was not the answer.

* * * * *

Undated, 2005. Surviving a gunshot – you can feel insubstantial and unreal and still get a headache.

Some sensations were hard to explain to other people. Everyone said how brilliantly she had adapted to life with one eye, and it was true. She had determined that it would not stop her working and – apart from the six months she had spent dealing with PTSD – it had not. But she was scattier than ever, always losing her keys and turning up late because she couldn't remember where she was going, or had got lost, or had decided to take the Tube and half-slipped down the gap between the platform and the train. She would bump against a wall and the pictures would fall off – minor dramas and misfortunes plagued her. Most of the time, people laughed it off. 'Typical Marie,' they would say.

She would invite people for dinner, prepare some elaborate dish and then forget to turn on the oven so they'd end up eating at midnight when everyone was sloshed. Sometimes John would call from the US and she found it comforting to be on the phone for an hour or more, saying very little. At other times he annoyed her, calling five times to check she was okay when she was out at a party with the Janes. Just because they were engaged, he seemed to think he had the right to know where she was at all times, and have a say in what she was doing. When she was working in Pakistan, he drove her crazy by constantly calling, bugging her about whether it was safe, when she was concentrating on an undercover story about child trafficking.

She had a big row with the paper over not accounting for money she had spent on the company credit card. Meanwhile, a letter from the managing editor noted that Sean and her friends had expressed concern about her 'use of alcohol', but that her therapist had reassured them that 'any problem related to drink to quell panic attacks is now over'. Being out there, that was what made her feel real, the only thing that countered the sense of insubstantiality that sometimes washed over her, and her fear that one day she would wake up again and not be able to do her job, just as she had when first diagnosed with PTSD.

Foreign desk pressure remained intense. Sean would scan the *Sunday Mail* or the *Telegraph* to highlight stories he thought his foreign team had missed. Everyone grumbled that he shouted at them, complaining that he didn't understand the difficulty and danger of their work because he had never been a foreign correspondent himself. It started to get to Marie in a way it never had before. Dominique remembers her shouting down the phone to Sean when they were in the coffee shop near the Erez Crossing between Gaza and Israel. 'She started crying and said she was feeling insecure about her job,' she recollects. Furious about her refusal to do her expenses, on one occasion Sean had sworn at her and slammed the phone down. She was used to a newsroom where there was a lot of swearing and shouting, but this was too much. Determined to stand up not just for herself but also for younger female staff, who were frequently reduced to tears, she drafted a letter of complaint, but in the end she decided not to send it but to talk to Sean instead. She didn't hate him, despite his temper and the way he demanded the impossible from reporters, and she accepted his apology. John Witherow, who she knew put pressure on Sean, was a friend. All she wanted was to be allowed to get out and do the stories that mattered to her, preferably without being yelled at.

On the whole, she reported as well as ever, and her editors therefore believed that she had recovered. Fellow journalists on the road saw her out there beating the competition. She visited her family infrequently, which meant that Cat had only fleeting glimpses of her anxiety. And then there was John, still calling several times a week from the US, waiting for her to name the day. She floated between the spheres of her life, like a sailing boat in a gusting wind, tacking to one side or the other, at times steering with purpose, at others, drifting, trying to avoid the whirlpool.

John was expecting them to marry on Martha's Vineyard in the summer of 2006, but, in a burst of clarity like the sun through clouds, Marie realised she couldn't do it. She suggested – not entirely helpfully – that he find someone else to marry. 'That's when I considered the engagement finished,' he says. Smarting from rejection, he told her he wanted his ring back. It symbolised how cavalier she had been with his feelings. They spoke on the phone from time to time, including when she was in Lebanon, reporting on the war that had broken out between Hizbollah and Israel. 'I could hear the firing of weapons in the background,' he recalls. 'She said she was in a destroyed building near the border and Israeli commandos might be about to attack so she had better get off the line.'

'Marie,' said John. 'I've decided not to ask for the ring back. I can picture you in the rubble with your hand sticking out with the ring on.'

'I don't wear rings in war zones in case someone cuts my finger off,' she replied.

'I never thought of that,' he said.

Iran had increased its training and weapons supply to Hizbollah, which was now a far more effective force than when Marie had covered Lebanon back in the 1980s. This war had started after Hizbollah killed three Israeli soldiers and abducted two others in a border skirmish. Israel responded by attacking not just Hizbollah targets, but also national infrastructure in Beirut, including the airport, and later launched a ground invasion into southern Lebanon. More than a thousand Lebanese were killed, mostly civilians. Hizbollah escalated the conflict by firing rockets into northern Israeli cities, killing more than forty Israeli civilians. Uzi Mahnaimi was reporting from Israel and Hala Jaber from Beirut, so Marie went to the port city of Tyre, south of the Lebanese capital, which had been blockaded by the Israelis. Braver or more foolhardy journalists, depending on your perspective, were venturing south of Tyre toward the Israeli border.

Marie found herself uncharacteristically nervous, spooked by the roar of missiles overhead and the whine of drones. She called Richard Flaye, whom she had been seeing more often as her relationship with John faded. She knew he was still with his partner and that there might be other women, but she was disappointed when he seemed guarded and didn't really want to talk.

> *16th July 2006. OK my love – just wanted to talk but unsettling when you have to be cold/formal. Don't worry – I know it's part of the deal but going to border, Israel may invade w/ land forces. I really need my wits about me, so don't want the memory of you having to watch your words ... hard for me to ask for reassurance ... don't forget me and keep sending me messages cuz it makes me feel connected 2 you. That sound. Every minute out of hotel living on nerves.*

In the margin of her journal she wrote: 'I know no right or even desire to make demands.' On the next page she was screwing her courage to the sticking place: 'Fear a good spur to getting feel of story and people.'

Marie went to Qana, where she saw bodies in the rubble of a destroyed house, and on to Tibnine, just a few miles north of the villages that the Israelis were besieging. Terrified refugees were sheltering in the hospital and sometimes it was hard to hear what people were saying over the sound of explosions as bombs landed nearby. Her story focused on Abir Feras, a young woman who had given birth three hours before fleeing her village.

Sunday Times, Tibnine, 30th July 2006
First she took the intravenous drip out of her arm. Then she wrapped the newborn in a blanket as her husband Mohammed

gathered their three other young children together. With the scream of Israeli jets overhead, they began the nine-mile trek from Bint Jbeil, a southern Lebanese village besieged by the Israeli army ... Feras carried her baby for four hours until she reached the fragile safety of the hospital as more jets roared down in dives, terrifying everyone inside, and surveillance drones swarmed overhead like angry wasps.

Terrified, Marie was still able to muster self-control in the most desperate of circumstances. Her report gave no hint of her own fear. Other stories she wrote included an analysis of the battle and the political implications. Anxiety did not seem to affect her work, but other journalists noticed that she was drinking more in the hotel at night and seemed emotionally drained. Her old friend, Jim Muir of the BBC, thought she was painfully thin, and wondered if she had relapsed into PTSD.

On her return to London, Richard also noticed that she seemed frail. He had seen her grappling with sails and masts, so knew how strong she had been. 'She went to that war healthy,' he recalls. 'I don't know why she was affected by it more than previous wars but she stopped eating while she was there. She came back emaciated and had lost a large portion of her muscle. That wiry strength had gone, and she never got it back.' He has no recollection of being distant on a phone call, but he thinks that his apparent coldness might have been because he was on a boat with his children, who didn't yet know about the relationship.

He was not the only one to notice a change in Marie. Maryam d'Abo, a former Bond girl turned film-maker, had met Marie during the making of Bearing Witness. They would spend long evenings in the oak-panelled bar of the Frontline Club in Paddington or at La Famiglia on the King's Road, sometimes joined by Maryam's husband, Hugh Hudson, the film director who was working on a script about Marie. Marie called Maryam '007'; Maryam called her 'M'. Hugh was 'Hornet', after the classic 1950s Hudson Hornet car. 'When she came back from Lebanon she told me she suddenly felt fragile,' remembers Maryam.

'These huge missiles going overhead made her feel very tiny. She was shaky and teary. She had come to an age where she didn't have the physical endurance and courage she used to have. She was very open. She poured her heart out.' The nightmares were back, and when she got drunk she would cry. 'She would open up about her fear.'

Marie was easy to love and hard to help. Jane was always there for her, keeping a key for when she lost hers or locked herself out, checking on her if she went silent for a few days, trying to get her to eat, not just drink in the evenings. Rosie, who had recovered from alcoholism a few years earlier, recommended a twelve-step programme, but Marie reacted to advice on drinking as she did advice on relationships – she listened, brow furrowed, head to one side, and then ignored it.

Sometimes drinking brought clarity. In October 2006, the Russian journalist Anna Politkovskaya was murdered in Moscow. She had exposed atrocities committed by Russian troops in Chechnya, and many suspected that the FSB, the Russian secret service, had a hand in her killing. A week later, the Frontline Club was packed with journalists and human rights activists, come to hear a panel discuss Anna's career and the implications of her death. The panel had diverted into a more general discussion of democracy in Russia, when Marie arrived, late and somewhat the worse for wear. She leant against the back wall, her thin frame encased in a black leather jacket over a white vest, eyepatch dominating her face, her hair escaping from the pins that held it back so it stuck out like tufts of feathers on a bedraggled bird. 'I want to ask a question, right now tonight,' she bellowed, her words slurred but determined. 'Who killed Anna? That's the best thing we can do. I've covered Chechnya, I care about it, I had a car shot out from under me by the Russians. I don't want to hear this about democracy. Who killed Anna? That's what we can do as journalists ... I don't want to hear all this stuff about principles. *Who killed Anna?*'

It was an electric moment. Marie had cut to the chase, posing the only question that mattered at that moment. A slim man rose from the middle of the audience. 'I'm a former KGB agent. I know who killed

Anna,' he said. He turned around and addressed Marie directly. 'Come and see me afterwards.' She got his card and they talked that night, but she never had the chance to follow up. He was the dissident ex-spy Alexander Litvinenko. Ten days later he lay dying in a London hospital, a victim of poisoning from polonium, slipped into his tea by two Russian agents.

* * * * *

When Patrick told Marie he was marrying an aid worker and that his fiancée was pregnant, she struggled to be happy for him. She longed for such stability in her own life. By then, Richard had left his partner, and although she knew he was still seeing other women on a casual basis, her relationship with him was becoming central to her. Looking for a new place to live, he noticed that a house just a three minute walk from hers, overlooking the Thames, was on the market. Would she mind his buying a place so close? She was fine with it. His modern house with the better view was 'river gloat', and hers, whose side flanked the Thames, was 'river glimpse'.

At the end of 2006 they went on holiday to Cuba together. She kicked off her shoes and they danced in a nightclub, whereupon the shoes were stolen and she walked barefoot and happy down the hill back to the place where they were staying. They talked about their lives – his so different from hers, as he'd been brought up the son of a British District Commissioner in a remote part of Uganda, followed by boarding school and Oxford. He didn't share her love of literature and art, but his view that pleasure should come before work appealed, and if she was honest, she liked the fact that he was rich and could take her on sailing holidays anywhere in the world. They came back a couple, more or less.

Her Jerusalem street cat, Billy Smith, didn't like Richard, clawing and hissing when he was in the house. Prone to terrorising other neighbourhood cats, he frequently refused to come home, especially if Richard was around. Some of her friends were also uneasy. There was something about Richard that bothered them, that they couldn't put their finger on. Marie told Alan, 'You wouldn't like him, he's a businessman and very rich, not your type.' She was right. But when he went over for lunch on the day of the Oxford and Cambridge boat race, which went straight past Richard's balcony, Alan saw Marie 'playing the happy hostess', and wondered if he was wrong to be so suspicious. Some friends who went sailing with them disliked the way Richard bossed Marie around and she replied, obediently, 'Aye aye, Captain!' but others thought she probably found it relaxing to let someone else take charge. JBC and her partner, Tim Razzall, joined the couple sailing along the coast of Turkey. 'This is a man who doesn't want to change Marie,' thought JBC. That was the point, really. Patrick and Juan Carlos had both, in their own ways, wanted to tame Marie but Richard seemed quite happy with her as she was.

'I think everyone, at least I always have, longs for some order, structure in life. Allows you to savor the chaos all about you,' Marie had written in her diary many years earlier, soon after leaving Yale. Finally she was able to achieve that. She and Richard developed a routine of spending nights at his house. 'We would always sleep and have breakfast together,' he recalls. When Marie was not travelling, she had to go to the *Sunday Times* only once a week, so would spend the rest of the day working from her own house before returning to Richard's. 'We would reconvene about 7 or 7.30. She would cook, which she loved, and we would open a bottle of wine, which we would consume between the two of us,' he says. Dominique Roch remembers coming to stay and being shocked at how domesticated Marie had become. 'She cooked for two or three hours, reading the recipe! I was amazed,' she recalls. Marie laughed at her old friend. 'It's not rocket science, Dominique,' she said, but her friend wasn't really commenting on Marie's culinary skills – she meant that never before had she seen Marie making so much effort to please a man.

When he stroked her, Richard would sometimes feel tiny sharp objects – pieces of shrapnel working their way out through Marie's skin. It was as if her body were trying to expel the painful memories and feelings she had absorbed in two decades of war reporting. He tried to inject more order into her life, making a checklist of the things she needed to take on a trip, so she wouldn't forget phone chargers or her sleeping bag or her press accreditation letter as she so often did. She agreed a deal where she worked seven months of the year for the *Sunday Times*, with five months for other projects, so he designed a business plan with headings such as, 'Develop the MC brand', 'Widen my media platform', 'Distinctive Competences' and 'More Time Off'. There was even a grid of Opportunities, Threats, Strengths and Weaknesses ('Indisciplined networking' in the last category was possibly managementspeak for failing to get contact numbers because she was drunk).

She, in turn, made his new house into a home, not with furnishings but by her warmth of personality. Growing up, his three children had seen little of their father. Now they were young adults. When the youngest, Ella, had first met Marie, she was an impressionable seventeen-year-old. After a sailing holiday *en famille*, everyone drinking wine on deck late into the night and talking global politics, Ella was captivated. Marie helped the teenager with her university applications and Richard's younger son, Toby, with his Master's in Architecture. Her friends came for parties and dinners at Richard's house. 'She filled it with music, life, warmth, people,' says Ella. 'My dad is slightly introverted, but with Marie the house always had noise, and things going on.'

Richard never tried to stop Marie from going to dangerous places, although he did suggest she limit herself to one risky endeavour per assignment. She spent much of 2007 back in Iraq, sometimes embedded with US troops, sometimes operating unprotected. The country had become anarchic, with foreigners and Iraqis at risk of kidnappings. In December, she went to Basra as British forces prepared to leave. 'The British were putting a spin on their achievements in southern Iraq and it was a story everyone would report from the ceremony at an airfield,' Sean recalls. 'We thought, what about the real story? We both had noticed stories on the wires about summary killings and a breakdown of the law and order that the British claimed to have restored.' Marie stayed in Basra with a family she knew, moving around covered in an *abaya*. The police commander Major-General Jalil Khalaf showed her horrific photos of forty-eight women who had been murdered in the previous six months.

Sunday Times, Basra, 16th December 2007
All the women fell foul of the unwritten rules of the new Basra – they dressed wrongly. They left home to work, or perhaps they were merely rumoured to have a boyfriend … One woman found in a red dress had a 9mm bullet wound in her left hand, three in her right hand, three in her right upper arm, and three in her back. Two of the women were beheaded, one with a saw.

While other reporters were safely in the British airbase watching the lowering of the Union flag in the presence of the Foreign Secretary, Marie was inside the lawless city, observing Major-General Khalaf struggling to get checkpoints erected around town to catch the kidnappers of a young Christian woman. Having survived seven assassination attempts himself, Khalaf insisted on providing four trucks of soldiers to escort her and even gave her his personal Koran 'for extra safety'. She interviewed the leader of one of the main militia, who revealed that Iran was moving into the space the British were vacating. It was a brilliant story, combining affecting personal detail with incontrovertible evidence with which she could challenge the commanding officer of British forces in the province. Major-General Graham Binns, who was forced to temper the triumphalist narrative the British government was trying to promote. 'I was more of an idealist when I arrived and perhaps too ambitious,' he told Marie. 'I didn't think it would end this way.'

'Last week Marie Colvin became the first unembedded western journalist from a British newspaper to visit Basra for nearly two years,' read the standfirst to her piece. 'The city is extremely dangerous for those not under the protection of the security forces, with foreigners seen as kidnap targets.' Her editors were 'praising courage rather than celebrating risk', says Sean, but it was a fine line. The story from Basra exposed official lies and told vividly how the city had descended into violence. In other words, it was worth it, as it always would be until something went wrong.

* * * * *

Every year it became harder for Marie to explain her life to her family. It was so far beyond their experience. When she saw them she felt like a visitor dropping in from another planet – she could communicate with Cat, but none of her other siblings. Unable to drive, when she visited Oyster Bay, she felt trapped in her mother's house. Rosemarie's world was shrinking as she grew older, and Marie had no patience for small town gossip, the palaver of making lunch and dinner and endless chit-chat about the price of groceries. Cat found it difficult to deal with Marie's hostility to their mother. Rosemarie still followed the news, but her life was focussed on her family and on Oyster Bay as it had always been. It was Marie had who had moved away and changed.

What Marie enjoyed most was spending time with her nephews and nieces. With no children of her own, she didn't have to play the grown-up – a role in which she had so manifestly failed with Anna. Justine, Cat's eldest, remembers periodic phone calls. 'She would ask what I was wearing, what I was doing in school. It was kinda weird because we didn't see her that often, but she felt special and made me feel special.' There was the occasional eccentricity, like the time Marie asked Justine if she was playing 'babies' mass grave' with her Barbie dolls, but the kids loved their aunt. Justine's younger brother Chris must have been about eight when he wrote an essay about what had happened when they had a meal after ice skating at Rockefeller Center in Midtown Manhattan:

> I got coke and my Aunt got alcohol. I ordered a cheeseburger. After that the rest of my family came in. When the food came, I opened up my cheeseburger to put the ketchup on. Then I saw it! It was a giant red TOMATO. I said 'Aunt Marie, I told them, no

*tomatoes.' She said 'That's OK, let me have it. And then it hap-
pened ... She opened THE BUN. She took the red tomato and she
tossed it across the restaurant SPLAT! It landed on the counter.
Mommy exclaimed, 'Marie, I can't believe you did that.' Aunt
Marie said, 'What? he doesn't like tomatoes.'*

This was the kind of bad behaviour that horrified adults and delighted children, which was, of course, the point.

That Christmas, Marie flew from Iraq to Atlanta to spend the holiday with her family at Boo's place. She found Boo's 'big suburban non-smoking house with swimming pool' as stifling as Oyster Bay. Watching one of the children drive his radio-controlled truck into Boo's marble table, which promptly cracked, she decided she had no desire to accompany her nephews and nieces to Disney World after Christmas, much to her mother's disappointment. Nor did she feel ready to talk about Richard. Instead, she emailed Katrina to grumble about her family and share with her the good news about her promising romance. 'I have a great beau Richard although early days,' she wrote. 'He is a publisher/venture capitalist so has no side. He is bald but very handsome and has a 62-foot sail boat. If you want to sail in august/september/october off turkey coast, we'd love it. He calls my racing "head banging." His idea of sailing is his double cabins and cocktails at sunset when he puts into port.'

Back in London, she and Richard bought a battered old wooden fishing vessel with a diesel tractor engine to sail up and down the Thames. Her name was *Trade Winds* but Marie called her the *African Queen*. That was the best thing about living by the river – she could put on her wetsuit and putter up and down on a Sunday or invite her friends to join her. Helen Fielding recalls Marie inviting her to take the boat up to Parliament one Monday night. 'We could grab a buoy and start a barbecue, and clock how long it takes for MI5 to send a speedboat.' They did exactly that, cooking sausages on board outside the House of Commons, and waiting for the security service which never showed up, before steering unsteadily back, mooring the boat and teetering ashore across the mud left by the falling tide, handbags akimbo.

That was the fun side of life, but Marie was increasingly worried about the signs of ageing. Decades of smoking had discoloured her teeth, and she was in danger of losing them, so she borrowed money from her old friend Claire Enders and from Richard to have implants. Richard's continuing interest in other women added to her insecurities about getting older. A couple of bottles of wine would only heighten her anxieties. One evening when Marijana was staying, Marie invited friends for dinner at Weltje Road. Marijana went to bed early and, in what he describes as 'a drunken flirt', Richard followed her. Marijana says she was trying to get rid of him when Marie burst through the door and, seeing Richard sitting on the bed, threw a full glass of red wine at Marijana. It hit the wall above her head, spraying her with shards of glass, wine running down in rivulets, soaking the pillow.

Marie had told Richard that if they were going to be a real couple, he would have to be faithful. She wasn't worried about the odd one-night stand – she might indulge in one herself on the road in Kabul or Baghdad – but she couldn't bear the idea that she was one of several parallel relationships. She was suspicious that Richard was supporting other women; she wasn't sure exactly who or where, but something was going on. What made it worse was that he refused to talk about it – or about anything, really. 'Don't think he agonises,' she wrote in her diary. She wondered if she was just not brave enough to accept that Richard wanted a different arrangement. Maybe she should adapt. 'Problem? We've gotten too domestic when the me he fell for was the image of the opposite.'

They began to quarrel more, mainly about his infidelities, and she was unconvinced by his argument that being involved with multiple women meant that none was a threat and she had no rival for his affections. After agreeing to a trial separation she found she couldn't let go, calling him to scream down the phone when she found out that he had hooked up with an American woman in Paris. Eventually, not wanting to lose her, he agreed to change his lifestyle. 'Early on it was by tacit agreement, and later on, there was an assumption it was over,' says Richard. No more infidelities. They were real partners now.

* * * * *

From time to time Marie spoke at events on the continuing war in Sri Lanka. Some said she was a stooge of the Tamil Tigers, but she saw herself as an advocate for Tamil civilians, and they saw her as a living symbol of the risks a journalist would take to tell their story. It made no difference. By early 2009, the Sri Lankan government was on the brink of crushing the Tigers with no regard for the suffering of civilians. In January, government forces seized Kilinochchi, the Tigers' de facto capital, where eight years earlier Marie had reported on the schools and hospitals struggling to provide services amongst the ruins. The government announced 'no-fire zones' for the 300,000 civilians in the area, and then shelled them nonetheless. Marie had remained in intermittent contact with Seevaratnam Pulidevan and Balasingham Nadesan, the Tigers' political leadership. Now they were desperate. 'We call for a ceasefire, loudly and clearly,' Nadesan said to her by satellite phone. 'Continuous denial of humanitarian access to the civilian population, and non-stop artillery and aerial attacks, are creating an unbearable situation.' Marie spoke to Rohan Chandra Nehru, one of the few Tamil MPs in the Sri Lankan parliament, who was trying to negotiate the Tigers' surrender. Unsure how to proceed, and worried for his own safety as well as that of the besieged Tamil civilians, he was relieved when Marie phoned him. 'She had a beautiful laugh,' he recalls. 'She always said "Bloody hell!" She guided me, giving me words of encouragement.' Marie suggested that he call the US and German Embassies in Colombo and try to involve them in overseeing a surrender. 'I trusted her 200 per cent,' he says.

By April, some 15,000 Tigers and maybe 100,000 civilians were trapped on a bloody stretch of beach. Civilians dug shallow trenches in the sand, in which they hid from artillery barrages launched from both land and sea. The government said civilians were being held as human shields by the Tigers. That was partly true, but any civilians who made it across the front line were rounded up and interned in camps where torture was routine. Aid agencies, like journalists and diplomats, were barred from the entire area. The Sri Lankan government knew that scrutiny would interfere with their strategy for outright victory, because outsiders would call for negotiation. Secrecy was integral to its plan. When the British and French Foreign Secretaries flew to Colombo to discuss a ceasefire, the government ignored them. By mid-May the area where the Tigers and civilians were corralled had shrunk to about the size of Hyde Park. Several thousand bodies lay unburied – the stench of death hung over the living. Velupillai Prabhakaran, the Tigers' previously implacable leader, knew he had a choice: the cyanide pill or surrender.

On the evening of 17 May, Balasingham Nadesan called Chandra Nehru MP to say they were ready to surrender, but they needed an assurance that they would not be killed. Chandra Nehru called Basil Rajapaksa, the President's brother and adviser, to tell him that the remaining Tiger cadres and civilians wanted to give themselves up. Half an hour later, Rajapaksa told Chandra Nehru that the President had agreed. Nadesan managed to patch a call to Marie through South Africa. 'We are ready to lay down our arms if the Americans or British can guarantee our safety,' he said. 'There will be a tragedy if no one helps us.' He also wanted an assurance that the Sri Lankan government would agree to a political process that would guarantee the rights of the Tamil minority. Marie could hear the sound of heavy shelling in the background. The Tigers wanted security for fifty leaders and 1,000 lower-level cadres. Knowing that two divisions of the Sri Lankan army were making their way towards the beach in a pincer movement, they feared they would be slaughtered. More calls went back and forth – the shelling was so intense that Chandra Nehru could scarcely hear what Nadesan was saying. By the early hours, the Tigers had abandoned all political demands. Basil Rajapaksa called Chandra Nehru and they agreed that the Tigers would carry a white flag as they surrendered unconditionally. Marie called Vijay Nambiar, the UN envoy, who was less than pleased to be woken in the middle of the night. He told her that the Sri Lankan president had guaranteed that those who gave themeselves up would be safe, so he saw no need to go and oversee the surrender. Incredulous, she tried to persuade him that the presence of a neutral observer was essential, but he shrugged her off. Later, many questioned his impartiality, not least because his brother was a paid consultant to the Sri Lankan military.

It was just after dawn. Nadesan was on the phone to Chandra Nehru.

'We are ready,' he said. 'I'm going to walk out and hoist the white flag.' Chandra Nehru said, 'Hoist it high, brother – they need to see it. I will see you in the evening.'

The line went dead as the Tigers' senior leadership and their families emerged, white flag aloft. Few witnesses survived, but all indications are that the group surrendering was mown down, women and children too. Those who were not killed instantly were shot later. For a while, the government claimed that they were killed in crossfire, but in the end it didn't bother to make its story credible. It had won. That was all.

Marie had crossed a line. 'I am in a difficult position as a journalist reporting this story,' she wrote in something of an understatement in her copy that Sunday. 'Her main preoccupation early in the week was that she was going to save them,' recalls Sean. 'She had got close to their cause and made a personal sacrifice and that was making her very intense and emotional.' Journalists are not negotiators, but she had felt a moral responsibility to urge the UN to observe the Tigers' surrender. 'This was not the chaos of battle. It was a negotiated surrender. Promises were made and they were broken,' she said later to a journalist investigating what had happened.

Chandra Nehru feared for his life. 'If you stay, something will happen to you,' Marie told him. 'You must leave the country for a while.' She spoke to officials at the American Embassy in Colombo, who took him to the airport in a bulletproof car, ensuring that he got on a plane to Singapore, where they booked him into a hotel far beyond his means. When his credit card was declined, he called Marie, who sent him enough money to tide him over until the Americans paid. When the British refused to grant him a visa, she called people she knew at the Foreign Office, who intervened. After two months he was able to travel to Britain and claim asylum. 'We spoke on the phone but she was always very busy,' he says. 'We never met.'

The Rajapaksa regime prevailed because it allowed no witnesses to its ruthless actions. The Sri Lankan counterinsurgency strategy, as it became known, was studied in war colleges and defence ministries across the world. Its tenets were clear: to bring a swift end to an insurgency the military must be allowed to do whatever it wants, with no regard for civilian life or international law, in utter secrecy, and in defiance of international opinion. The victorious government can then impose a political solution. This doctrine was not dissimilar to the Russian strategy in Chechnya. If Western journalists were barred, there was less pressure from Western governments – anyway, the US was fading as a superpower and Sri Lanka looked to China for economic and political support. Grisly videos came to light showing Sri Lankan soldiers raping Tamil women and torturing and murdering Tamil men. It was the soldiers themselves who had filmed this with their mobile phones – these were trophy videos, but they provided evidence of the atrocities government forces had committed. The best journalism was being carried out not by on-the-ground reporters like Marie, but by people far away piecing together video they had found online or which had been shared amongst those who thought brutality fun. In the years to come, the new counterinsurgency doctrine developed in Sri Lanka and alternative forms of journalism used there would affect Marie more than she could imagine.

* * * * *

In August 2009, Marie and Jane Wellesley were commissioned by Condé Nast Traveller to write a jointly bylined piece about driving from Rome to Florence in a BMW. Travel writing was a departure for Marie – it would be fun to do something different. Jane was mourning her friend, Mick Imlah, who had died in January after agonising months with motor neurone disease. Marie – who was also fond of Mick – had flown back from Gaza for his funeral in Oxford and the burial near Jane's house in South Ayrshire. Jane had supported Marie through dark times, and Marie had in turn helped Jane in her grief. Both of them needed a holiday. They had been away together many times, but had somewhat differing travelling styles. 'An intrepid war correspondent, she can seem impervious to comforts,' wrote Jane. 'I am more likely to demand a different room, or cross-question a waiter about whether the orange juice is freshly squeezed.' They stayed in a Palladian villa near Assisi, fresh lilies in their rooms, waiters serving white wine and olives as they looked out over the Tuscan hills from the terrace. The infinity pool revealed another difference: Marie wore her underwear because she had forgotten to pack half her bikini. She would throw a few things into a bag at the last minute, while Jane always packed days in advance to make sure she had thought of everything. Jane was driving, leaving Marie – who could neither read a map nor operate the satnav – in charge of navigation, which was a cause of some tension, as was Jane's insistence that they spend a mere 15 minutes at the Prada outlet because they were late. To cap it all, they very nearly missed the plane home. But the four-day break brought home how important female friendship was to Marie. When they got over the bickering, they laughed uproariously as they drove in circles trying to find their hotel, listening to the imperious voice of the satnav ordering them to 'Perform a legal U turn.' There was another argument on their return when Marie not only failed to produce her copy on time, but – in an outrageous fib – pretended she had. Of course, in the end, Jane forgave Marie as she always did.

The palazzos of Umbria seemed a long way from Baghdad as she emailed Jane a few months later:

I thought you would like to hear my latest experience – the most disgusting of my life! I am staying at the Guardian house, which you would think was civilised.

I was brushing my teeth when I heard a disturbance in the toilet. I turned to see this oily, scaley THING whipping above the bowl! I thought it was a snake! No it was the tail of a live RAT that had come up through the pipe into the toilet bowl.

I shrieked, various guys came running and said 'oh my God it's huge' (no kidding). I flushed, and spent the night with a 2.5kg weight on top of the (closed) seat. I poured some petrol down yesterday morning. But what if I had been SITTING DOWN?

The rat in the toilet ranked alongside Colonel Gaddafi and the Bulgarian nurse, Arafat's cornflakes and a dozen other tales that she would recount at the Corinthian Yacht Club where she had a new audience of craggy old sailors who loved this traveller from a world of adventure they could only imagine.

Marie was spending more time in Afghanistan, frequently reporting on US troops' doomed attempts both to turn the Afghan National Army into an efficient fighting force, and to grapple with the drug addiction and corruption that characterised the Afghan police. She captured some of the humour of the culture clash in a piece focusing on a hapless local police chief trying to answer questions from his American mentors, and some of the tragedy interviewing a US army medic who had seen five of his comrades killed in front of him. 'Tuitele's platoon is one of the hardest hit of any unit deployed in Afghanistan,' she wrote. 'Tears start running down the young medic's face at the memory of what happened. He keeps speaking, just wiping away the rivulets from brown eyes that reflect his anguish.'

In 2010, her reporting from Afghanistan won her a second British Press Awards Reporter Journalist of the Year, but the accolade that made her proudest was the Martha Gellhorn Prize, awarded annually for 'the kind of reporting that distinguished Gellhorn: in her own words, "the view from the ground".' Accepting the prize, Marie said: 'She reported just the way I think is important: put on your boots and get out on the ground where people are.' The chair of the judging panel said Marie had been honoured partly for 'cutting through official drivel' and partly in recognition of her bravery across the world from East Timor to Sri Lanka. 'For years, few took notice of the Tamils and conveyed their suffering and tragedy to the outside world. Marie Colvin did tirelessly and almost paid with her life. Martha Gellhorn would have recognised her as a kindred spirit.' That meant a lot.

Richard accompanied her to the awards ceremonies, sharing in her pride and basking in the reflected glory. She was planning to take him to Oyster Bay to introduce him to her family. It would be a short visit – just enough time for him to meet everyone, have a couple of dinners and see the place where she had grown up and the bay where she had first fallen in love with sailing. Despite their problems, she felt that she and Richard had achieved some stability and that she was balancing her life, reducing the frequency of risky assignments. She began to spend more time at home, and with the help of an interior designer, wallpapered the staircase with dark stripes and redid the kitchen. She even planted her small garden, so that whenever she came home from a trip something would be in bloom.

The nightmares had receded, and on the whole she slept well, but one late August night she lay in bed next to Richard at his house, unable to sleep. Something was troubling her, some flicker of doubt, some fear she had suppressed. In the early hours she padded upstairs to his study where she found, next to his computer, a small file containing his passwords. She wrote them down. At home the next morning, she turned on her laptop and keyed in the series of letters and digits she had copied, which included the word 'bimbo'. She opened his email.

What she found was worse than she could ever have imagined. Dozens of emails to five or six women, evidence that he was conducting multiple relationships in several different countries. He had been having sex regularly with at least one woman in London, not just when Marie was away, but when she was around and they were spending nights together. It seemed to her that some of the women were barely educated, while at least one appeared to regard Richard as a partner. There were graphic descriptions of sex acts, and plans for assignations in the months to come. Nothing was hidden now; she could see it all. How foolish she had been to think he would change his ways. Of course he had lied. That's who he was. Yet she had believed him. Everything about their relationship was a lie. The life she had led for the last four years, the stability she thought she was enjoying, the love, the trust – it was all a chimera. All her memories were fake, nothing had been as she thought. She worked through the emails with journalistic rigour to establish exactly when, where and with whom.

Then she let the waves of grief, fury and despair engulf her.

* * * * *

Chapter 11

A RECKLESS TIDE

Marie was not private in her grief. She called Jane, Rosie, Alex and other friends sobbing so uncontrollably they could barely catch her words. When they converged on Weltje Road she showed them the emails. Not everyone wanted to read in sordid detail exactly who had done what to whom and when, but Marie was relentless, as if by making others read the evidence, she would have no choice but to accept it herself. 'She was crying, and banging away on the computer, and she kept muddling it up, and having to reconnect it, get back to Richard's emails,' recollects Rosie. 'Tears were falling down her cheeks, and she was just in a terrible state. It was harrowing.' On one level, she must have known – otherwise why had she felt the need to look at the emails in the first place? Yet she was in shock. She had not prepared herself for betrayal on so grand a scale.

She called Richard's daughter, Ella, who was on holiday in Morocco. 'The women, the women, so many women, and one of them can't even read,' she said, weeping. In the weeks that followed, she would stumble up to the 24-hour petrol station at the top of the road in the early hours to get another bottle of vodka. She knew she should stop drinking, and she researched an alcohol rehabilitation centre in Arizona, but it was too expensive and she never followed up. In the past she had given up alcohol for Lent, or when on assignment, but it was hard to stop in this moment of crisis. Ella would drink with her, sometimes almost until dawn, Marie seemingly unconcerned that she was spilling emotional and sexual details to the daughter of the man she was railing against. On the phone to Cat, she talked through it all again and again. She went to parties and told everyone what Richard had done. It was as if she were walking around London with her skin peeled off.

Just as when she had discovered Patrick's infidelity all those years ago, small strange incidents suddenly made sense. There was the occasion when she and Richard had gone to stay with JBC's sister, Virginia, and her husband Charles at their house in Devon, and Richard had ignored texts Virginia was sending about the route while he was driving. Now she understood – he hadn't wanted to hand the phone to Marie, because she would have seen that he had been texting back and forth with other women earlier in the day. Sometimes she was analytical, thinking through how she had got herself into such a desperate, vulnerable position.

August 2010. Undated. I was blinded by your looks and the sex and so tried to ignore what my brain was telling me – that there was a lack of intellectual content and that you were lying. So I drank more and read less and my world telescoped down to yours – sex, looks and money.

She realised with a shudder that she had better go for an HIV test. 'Sometimes pain so great it's stupefying', she wrote. She thought about him: 'Brilliant heartless cynical leading to your own destruction'. Then about herself: 'Sentimentality and self pity and gnawing sense of waste'. Her memories of sundowners on deck, and the cosy evenings at home playing happy families, were all contaminated.

August 2010. Undated. On top of the pain it is the humiliation. You knew who you were with for our years together and knew you were loved. I have to face I was not loved. I do not know who I was with. I was laughed at behind my back and humiliated ... How could you have so little regard for me? Exhibitions I wanted to go to, just do the things couples do, Portobello or bicycle upriver to a pub lunch – you spent the day with A., a fuck and lunch, I suppose. I was lonely but thought I'd seem clingy to insist.

She cancelled the holiday in Oyster Bay, which would have been over Richard's birthday. 'It was to be a bonfire on the beach at Oyster Bay Cove last night … to start your birthday, sail this morning and barbecue on Centre Island beach today', she wrote in a fractured letter that she never sent.

Jane invited Marie to spend a few days at her house in South Ayrshire, to walk on the beach collecting cowrie shells as they always did and sit by the fire talking. Marie's pain overwhelmed all else. 'She was in a terrible state,' recalls Jane. 'I would find an empty bottle of wine under her bed in the morning.' Marie was inconsolable. 'It was as if her whole basis, her relationship with herself, who she was, what she believed in, her trust in herself and her judgement – all those things were gone,' says Jane. In her teens, when she discovered the poetry of Yeats, Marie had carefully typed out 'When You Are Old' and stuck it on a piece of card, dreaming of how such a love might feel.

> *How many loved your moments of glad grace,*
> *And loved your beauty with love false or true,*
> *But one man loved the pilgrim soul in you,*
> *And loved the sorrows of your changing face.*

She wondered how she could ever have thought that Richard might love her like that.

Marie flew to California to stay with Katrina who recalls her being 'in complete meltdown', going over and over what had happened. Sometimes she vented about the other women, sometimes about the expensive Balenciaga leather motorcycle jacket Richard had promised to buy her, only to substitute it for a cheaper version, as if she wouldn't notice. (It hung unworn in her house in Weltje Road, a constant rebuke and reminder of his disregard.) She wept and despaired, but Katrina noticed that she was, nonetheless, still speaking to Richard every day.

Richard talks now about what happened with a detachment that jars with the rage and grief revealed in Marie's diary and the accounts of her friends. 'I was being a chancer, thinking I could have my cake and eat it,' he says. 'I was continuing with my way of life. It was terribly hurtful and I bitterly regret the pain I caused her.' He says he understood why she was angry, but not why it ruined the memory of their lives together. 'I think she really loved me and I loved her. It was a terrible betrayal.' He still hoped that she might get over her anger, but he knew that the fact she had told all her friends the details of his transgressions made that much less likely. So he carried on with his 'hedonistic' ways.

* * * * *

What a relief it was to return to Afghanistan in October, to get back to her other life. The day she arrived in Kandahar, the Taliban assassinated several government officials, shooting dead a tribal leader and leaving his twelve-year-old son fighting for his life. Marie's notes on the story are interspersed with small bursts of pain over Richard, like stab wounds: 'I cannot stop thinking who you are with', 'Banality – sordid'. 'Readers' wives – low brow'. She was also trying to buck herself up, to reach into her dwindling reserves of hope and come up with meaning.

> Undated, October 2010. Use my skills as a writer to help those who can't find justice anywhere else. I cannot and will not stop trying ... Acting despite fear – it matters. Show world what cannot see first hand. No death wish. I have too much to live for.

Like all good war correspondents, Marie was not fearless but had learnt to manage her fear. The photographer João Silva, whom she had known for many years, was in Afghanistan at the same time and over coffee they talked frankly about how every time they took a step while on patrol with the US military, they were steeling themselves for an explosion. Two days later, on a routine foot patrol through a village with US soldiers, João stepped on a landmine. Both his legs had to be amputated below the knee, and he endured several operations to repair damage to his stomach.

In an address she gave at St Bride's, on Fleet Street, on her return, Marie talked about what had happened to João.

St Bride's, 12th November 2010
The expectation of that blast is the stuff of nightmares. We always have to ask ourselves whether the level of risk is worth the story. What is bravery, and what is bravado?

It was a hard question to answer. The address was part of the annual service to commemorate journalists and support staff who had lost their lives in the course of the year. Marie herself standing at the front of the church, thin in her short black jersey dress, glasses over her patch and her one good eye, embodied the risk. It became the signature speech that defined her philosophy of reporting.

Covering a war means going to places torn by chaos, destruction, and death, and trying to bear witness. It means trying to find the truth in a sandstorm of propaganda when armies, tribes or terrorists clash. And yes, it means taking risks, not just for yourself but often for the people who work closely with you. Despite all the videos you see from the Ministry of Defence or the Pentagon, and all the sanitised language describing smart bombs and pinpoint strikes, the scene on the ground has remained remarkably the same for hundreds of years. Craters. Burned houses. Mutilated bodies. Women weeping for children and husbands. Men for their wives, mothers children ... Our mission is to report these horrors of war with accuracy and without prejudice.

She made the case for the on-the-ground reporting she believed in, following in the tradition of Martha Gellhorn, Lee Miller, John Hersey, and the man credited as the first war correspondent of the modern era, William Howard Russell of *The Times*, who was sent to cover the Crimean War in the 1850s.

> In an age of 24/7 rolling news, blogs and Twitter, we are on constant call wherever we are. But war reporting is still essentially the same – someone has to go there and see what is happening. You can't get that information without going to places where people are being shot at, and others are shooting at you. The real difficulty is having enough faith in humanity to believe that enough people, be they government, military or the man on the street, will care when your file reaches the printed page, the website or the TV screen. We do have that faith because we believe we do make a difference.

In her darker moments, she questioned herself. The story of how she lost her eye had briefly catapulted Sri Lanka to the top of the news agenda, but it had fallen soon after and Tamil civilians had later perished and suffered in far greater numbers. Chechnya was the same. In East Timor she could claim that her actions and her reporting had alerted the world and put pressure on those with power. The story of the young woman shot by the Amal sniper in the Palestinian camp in Beirut had also had an impact. Yet Marie's was a true faith and she believed it utterly. She still had her American seriousness of purpose, her heart proudly visible on her sleeve, uncorrupted by British cynicism. She was the champion of bearing witness so that even if no one stopped the wars, they could never say they had not known what was happening.

For many in the congregation that evening hers was a rallying cry. Journalism was getting more dangerous, because every warlord or two-bit commander watched satellite TV and knew the value of propaganda. With the internet, they could easily read reports, so they knew if a journalist was talking to their enemies, or investigating the atrocities they had committed. It wasn't like the old days when it took the Iraqi Ministry of Information weeks to work out what Marie had written and get belatedly annoyed about it. Kidnapping was becoming widespread. Gone were the days when being a journalist was a form of protection; now it made you a target. And the currency was getting cheaper. Marie's personalised style of reporting had been fresh and different back in the late '80s. Now lesser reporters saw a return to the war zone as their opportunity for a nostalgic first-person piece about how it had changed, or not, since the last week-long trip. Marie was used to writing three or four thousand word stories spread across two broadsheet pages, but the *Sunday Times*, like other papers, was cutting foreign coverage and beefing up sections that attracted more advertising. People could get foreign news for free online, and after a decade of wars involving British troops, editors thought the public had had enough. Marie, then, was speaking for the tribe, the stubborn and curious who refuse to accept official information and have to see for themselves, and who felt under pressure as never before.

Many of you here must have asked yourselves, or be asking yourselves now, is it worth the cost in lives, heartbreak, loss? Can we really make a difference? I faced that question when I was injured. In fact one paper ran a headline saying, 'Has Marie Colvin Gone Too Far This Time?' My answer then, and now, was that it is worth it.

* * * * *

Two weeks later she flew to New York, on her way to spend Thanksgiving with her family at Boo's house in Atlanta. Irritated that Cat couldn't get off work to meet her in the city, she called John Schley, and they had dinner in a small, quiet oyster bar in SoHo. When John declined Marie's invitation to Boo's house for the holiday, as he was going to Martha's Vineyard, Marie grew angry and jabbed at his eye with a fish knife. The manager approached. 'You'll have to leave if you don't stop,' she said. 'You're frightening the other customers.' Marie calmed down. After dinner John drove her to her hotel. He could have sworn that as she walked away from the car he heard her say, 'John, I love you.'

Although they were travelling to Atlanta on different airlines, Marie ran into Cat and her children at the airport. Marie was at her most disorganised – she had neither Boo's address nor any idea how she would get from the airport to the house. 'She was mad at me because she didn't know where she was going,' Cat recalls. 'I ripped a page out of a book and gave her Boo's address. We had a meal together at the airport. She was in bad shape.' Marie could talk of nothing but Afghanistan and João, but she had remembered to buy Cat's children presents, which she gave them there and then. Her flight landed first, but instead of waiting for Cat at Arrivals as they had agreed, she called Boo's house and asked her brother Michael to pick her up. When he told her to take a cab, she yelled at him that she'd go to a hotel instead. 'She's probably been drinking on the plane,' thought Cat, who found her at the airport trying to book a hotel, and had to cajole her into going to Boo's.

The family divided along the usual lines. Cat, Billy and Rosemarie wanted to hear about Marie's exploits and read her St Bride's speech, while Boo was busy dealing with kids and cooking, and Michael made a big play of his indifference. Like all arguments in families, it started with something small and childish. Michael mixed himself a cranberry vodka. Marie drank it. He shouted at her, and 'she completely lost it,' remembers Cat. 'She started crying and saying "They're fucking assholes, all of them."' Rosemarie was crying too – it was Thanksgiving and her children were yelling at one another, on the verge of coming to blows. 'She's crazy, she's wrecking the holiday,' said Michael. Boo, realising that Marie had just come from Afghanistan where her friend had been injured, was more sympathetic. 'I thought, we don't usually see her just coming from a war zone, normally we see her after she's had a chance to process it,' she says. 'Also it was the first time she seemed to want us to be aware of her career. But we were caught up in raising our children. We weren't used to her wanting to be part of the conversation.'

Cat followed Marie upstairs to her room. They lay on the bed and slept alongside each other as they had done as children, when Marie used to tell Cat stories about Amazon queens and give her 'postage stamp' kisses to send her to her dreams. When they woke, Cat suggested that Marie needed to acknowledge her siblings' lives, but Marie didn't want to hear it. Absorbed in grief about the wreckage of her own life, she couldn't deal with what seemed to her their petty troubles. More worryingly, she was making no sense, insisting that she hadn't been in New York at all, and had not met Cat at the airport. Not only had she lost her memory of it, but she was furious with Cat for contradicting her. 'I had become the enemy,' realised Cat. They cried and made up before leaving, but Cat was disturbed to see the change in her sister. There were many conversations in the months that followed, but Cat never stopped worrying.

* * * * *

Marie was dreading the end of the year. First there was Christmas. The previous year she had been with Richard and his children, and they had done it in style, with decorations, carol-singing, a champagne breakfast and beautifully wrapped presents. (She always gave generous gifts to Richard's children.) Then they had gone skiing. Before the breakup, they had talked of sailing in the Caribbean this year. Instead she ended up spending the first part of the holiday in Norfolk, at the country house of Vaughan Smith, the founder of the Frontline Club, and his Kosovan wife, Pranvera, who were hosting the WikiLeaks founder, Julian Assange, who was on bail, charged not with stealing official secrets as one might have expected, but with rape. The case was later dropped. She and Assange had long conversations about freedom of speech and the ethics of releasing classified information, all of which, to her disgust, the *Sunday Times* edited out of her copy.

From Norfolk she went to see Jane Wellesley and her father, who were mourning Jane's mother, who had recently died. She went on to JBC and Tim in Wiltshire for Christmas Day. 'She was in a terrible way,' says JBC. 'Very vulnerable. Thin skinned.' They invited her to spend New Year's Eve on the Hebridean island of Colonsay where they had taken over a hotel with a group of friends. On arrival, she embarked on a lengthy conversation with a local man at the bar, quizzing him about his unusual pastime of 'tractor sailing'. It took a while for her to realise that his accent belied a less thrilling job: tractor *selling*. Everyone hooted with laughter at that. Marie spent a lot of time alone in her room, from which her friends would extract her to go on long walks in the unseasonably warm weather.

The next hurdle was her 55th birthday. At first she felt she didn't have the heart for a big party, but her friends persuaded her that she should. She started to make lists. Invitees covered five pages of an A4 notebook. Then there was the 'Need to Do' list: nails, eyebrows, hair, and practical decisions to be made on the music and where guests would put their coats. Journalists, poets, politicians, artists, novelists and the odd film star as well as a few gatecrashers whom no one knew gathered at Weltje Road. The cocktails were lethal, and the dancing and drinking continued into the early hours. Marie's entire London life was gathered – apart from Richard, of course. She seemed happy, in a little black dress as usual, slightly brittle maybe, but only if you knew what she had been going through. Three days later, on the Saturday, she wrote a diary entry as if it were a letter to a stranger.

15th January 2011. I can take pretty much anything since I have been shot and lost my eye and I think, well, I can always step off the Hammersmith Bridge. I've gone up there and looked at it and I could get over that green iron thing before anyone could stop me ... I didn't want to be alone on my birthday so I invited 100 people round to my house ... everyone had a great time and the house was full and now I am sitting in the chair looking

out of my window at the Thames and I am so so so sad. I am
crying and my father said Colvins don't cry. I'm writing this
because I grieve so deeply … stomach pain. I miss him so much …

It was the sordid nature of Richard's betrayal that tormented her, the
idea that screwing multiple women, some of a different class or colour,
was exotic.

You're dragging me back to the banality of the suburbs, where
fucking someone different is considered 'oh so breaking the
boundaries' … I escaped at 16. Four years … his choices were the
banality of the bourgeois life I thought I left behind in Oyster
Bay.

Two days later, she picked herself up, packed her bag and flew to
Tunis.

* * * * *

When Mohamed Bouazizi set himself on fire in the Tunisian town of
Sidi Bouzid just before Christmas 2010, no one knew it would trigger
revolution across the region. His despair echoed that of countless
youths Marie had met over the years in Gaza, Cairo, Tripoli and elsewhere. Forced to leave school in his late teens to earn money for his
mother and younger siblings, he was a street vendor, one of millions of
young men in the Middle East and North Africa who had dreamt of a
university education, and now found themselves on the bottom rung
of society. Humiliation overwhelmed him the day a municipal officer
confiscated his small barrow of vegetables for 'not having a licence'.
What she meant was, for not paying a bribe, because Tunisia was corrupt from the bottom to the top. Zine al-Abidine Ben Ali had ruled for
more than two decades, plundering the country's wealth. Bouazizi's
funeral turned into a protest, awakening an entire generation of Arab
youth.

By the time Marie got to Tunis on 17 January, the Ben Ali family had fled the country. She investigated the greed of Leila Trabelsi, the First Lady, who had demanded that the Tunisian central bank hand over one and a half tonnes of gold before she left. An interim government took control, and the protests eased, but what became known as the Arab Spring was under way. From Tunis, Marie flew to Cairo, where youths had occupied Tahrir Square in an attempt to overthrow the corrupt, sclerotic regime of Hosni Mubarak.

For a quarter of a century Marie had witnessed coups, wars and terrorism but now frustrated young people were trying to bring change by peaceful revolution. Islamists had been the only effective opposition to corrupt and dictatorial governments, but suddenly people were asking if there might be another way. Marie felt that her whole career had been building up to the Arab Spring. This was *her* story, and she revelled in the moment of optimism. She would go out into Tahrir Square and call her friends around the world so they could hear the chants of the crowd, and get a flavour of the atmosphere. Later, when repression was renewed, journalists who sympathised with the protestors were criticised for getting carried away and not predicting doom. Marie was well aware of the perils in Egypt. 'There appear to be three possible outcomes,' she wrote. 'A transition to democracy; a new dictatorship, perhaps led by a general around whom the old guard would coalesce; or an Islamic state.' But only a cynic could have failed to be moved by the idealistic young people who thronged Tahrir Square in those early days.

She watched the swelling crowds from the balcony of her hotel room, and then stood in the square as protestors ran past, eyes and noses streaming from the effect of tear gas fired by the police. She told the story of a young man who tried to save the life of a woman who had been struck on the head by a tear gas canister, and who died in his arms. 'I feel the injustice in my country. We feel humiliated every day,' he told her. Realising how big this story was, Marie's editors decided to send two more correspondents to Egypt: Uzi Mahnaimi, who had contacts with Egyptian intelligence, and Matthew Campbell who was to interview Alaa Al-Aswany, one of the country's most famous novelists. Like most correspondents, Marie would rather have had the story to herself. She was especially annoyed about the arrival of Uzi. They had grown apart over the years, partly because she mistrusted his stories, many of which were based on Israeli intelligence sources, and partly because she saw him as a rival. Although she had nearly run out of cash, she was less than grateful when he brought her the money she had requested.

'What are you doing here? This is my story!' she snapped as he arrived at her hotel just before midnight.

'Marie, it's a big enough story for all of us,' he replied.

On the Monday afternoon, when they could relax as their paper didn't come out again for another week, Uzi went up to her room. 'She was sitting on the balcony watching the crowd,' he says. 'I looked down and saw those little bottles of vodka from the minibar on the balcony. She was drunk.' He asked about her plans, and was alarmed when she said she was going to Imbaba, a dense labyrinth of dirt alleyways, home to more than a million poor Egyptians, out towards the Pyramids. 'I wouldn't have gone there before the revolution and I certainly wouldn't go there now,' he said. 'It's too dangerous.' Marie said she would be with an Egyptian journalist whom she trusted. She looked out over the crowd. According to Uzi, she said, 'Listen. I would rather jump off the balcony than not get my story.' In her diary she wrote, simply, 'Uzi confrontation'.

Uzi told Sean that he thought Marie was behaving in an irrational manner and was headed for a nervous breakdown. Sean asked Matthew to go and check on her. 'I didn't see bottles on the balcony,' says Matthew. 'She seemed a bit detached, but not drunk. A bit spacey.' He emailed Sean to say Marie seemed to be okay. Sean told Uzi that, although he had thought Marie sounded rough a few days earlier, she was better the last time he spoke to her and that Matthew thought she was all right. He assured Uzi that he would keep a close eye on her.

A few days later Marie and Madiha Qassem, the journalist who was acting as her interpreter, set off to interview the grieving family of

Mohamed Salah, a young protestor who had been shot by the police. They parked the car and walked through the winding alleyways of Imbaba to a ramshackle old building. While they were in the apartment, a mob gathered below. Word had passed round the neighbourhood that a foreigner was there, and state TV had been broadcasting that foreigners were agitators and Israeli spies. Family members took Marie and Madiha's press cards to show the crowd but it made no difference. Marie crept down the narrow, unlit stairway and peeped outside.

Sunday Times, Cairo, 6th February 2011
About 100 men had gathered, shoving each other, shouting that I was a spy, or maybe worked for the hated Al-Jazeera television station. Some had knives shoved in the waists of their trousers. The men of the family formed a circle around Madiha and me to protect us and try to get us out of the alley. It was a terrifying moment. In a mob, there is no individual responsibility and these people were working themselves into a frenzy. The men shouted and cursed. The few women in the crowd spat in anger.

The two took cover in a shop in the same building. Marie called the *Sunday Times* foreign desk, while Madiha talked calmly to a series of young men. There was no question of calling the police, because they no longer had any power. As the anger of the crowd waxed and waned the two women made a break for it, managing to get to the car, which had been brought closer. The crowd pounded on the vehicle. Eventually, they reached a checkpoint where luckily the commander was calm and articulate. He shooed everyone away. 'Go to your hotel,' he said to Marie and Madiha. 'It is very dangerous on the streets now.'

Marie was not the only reporter to face the mob in Egypt in those days. A few days later, on the night Mubarak stepped down, a female TV reporter, Lara Logan of CBS News, was sexually assaulted by a crowd of frenzied men in Tahrir Square. In the uncertain weeks that followed, female journalists and activists were frequently set upon, and suspicion grew that much of the violence was orchestrated by the state, as a way of deterring protestors and journalists alike. Sean thought Marie sounded tired and anxious on the phone. He worried that he could detect the telltale signs of PTSD recurring. 'She was taking a long time to respond to messages. She was not forming sentences fully, and sometimes spoke very fast and then struggled to find the words.' He suggested that she come home but she wanted to stay on to see the story out as she always did.

When she finally left, the story was moving so fast she had to turn round within a week, allowing scarcely any time in London for her usual rituals of dinner with the Janes and other pleasures that helped her balance her life. The next domino was a country she knew well, where she never dreamt she would see change in her lifetime: Libya.

Gaddafi had been in power for forty-two years. Although Marie had listened to him ramble on for hours about how he wasn't a president but a 'guide', and how it was 'the people' who governed Libya, she knew that he held absolute power. The only question was which of his spoilt playboy sons would seize the crown after his death. The Great Socialist People's Libyan Arab Jamahiriya was really a Mafia state, which enabled the Gaddafi children to live the life of princelings, while the health service crumbled and anyone who could afford it sent their children abroad to school. The Gaddafi family never dreamt that the Libyan people would rebel against them, as Egyptians had against Mubarak, but the uprising in Egypt spread over the border, erupting first in the eastern cities of Tobruk and Benghazi, where Gaddafi was widely hated. His loyalists were quickly ousted, and soldiers either shed their uniforms or fled. A revolutionary council of lawyers and civil society activists was installed, but their control didn't extend far along the coastal road towards the capital where Gaddafi still held power.

The *Sunday Times* executive editor, Bob Tyrer, commissioned a long historical piece on Gaddafi, but Marie was focused on the news. 'Tyrer wants profile,' she wrote in her diary. 'I ignore.' As she flew into Tripoli, demonstrators were surging on to the streets in defiance of the bullets that had met previous protests. 'Once blood is spilt, there is no going back,' a demonstrator told her. Secret police had arrested scores of young people. Government minders tried to prevent journalists from talking to the protestors but the situation had spun out of their control: Libyans had lost their fear.

Ever since Marie had first interviewed the Brother Leader a quarter of a century earlier, he had felt they had a bond, and in recent years she had got to know his second son, Seif. Father and son sometimes called her, even though she had been to Libya less frequently in recent years. So, if anyone could get an interview with Gaddafi, Marie could. She worked the phones. After a few days, a message came back: Gaddafi would see her, but he also wanted to be on TV. Marie agreed to bring along correspondents from CNN and the BBC. That was not good for her, because the interview was scheduled for a Monday, which meant that everything Gaddafi said would have been broadcast long before her story was published, but history wasn't going to wait for a Sunday newspaper deadline. This was very different from interviews of previous years, when she had been ushered alone into the bunker at the Bab al-Aziziyah barracks.

Sunday Times, Tripoli, 6th March 2011
Gaddafi's message that he was determined to fight on began with his choice of venue for our interview. We met in a fish restaurant with floor-to-ceiling windows that looked out over the sparkling blue water of the Tripoli harbour. It was chosen to put paid to rumours that he had fled Libya, and to show that he had no fears about travelling anywhere in his capital ... He arrived dressed in a brown turban and a flowing ankle-length robe in a white BMW and walked up the steps to the restaurant.

When she asked if he might leave the country, he laughed. 'Does anybody leave his own homeland?' he said. 'Why should I leave Libya?' Marie thought he was coherent, although it was always hard to tell what he believed and what was bluster. 'My people, they love me,' he said. 'They love me, all.' To Gaddafi, democracy was a sign of weakness. 'Today's presidents who say I should go, I say to you that you will serve out your terms and then you will retire,' he told Marie. 'But I will still be leader of the revolution.' She emailed Helen Fielding: 'Seriously, what a hoot! World leaders never say anything interesting in interviews anyway. At least he understands theatre.'

Marie's long association with the Gaddafis did not temper her enthusiasm for the Arab Spring. 'It is a new era in the Middle East,' she said in a live internet text chat from Tripoli with *Sunday Times* readers. 'These rebellions are not about power, they are about individual rights in the face of political repression, corruption and hopelessness. They are the first demonstrations I have seen in years in the Middle East where not one American or Israeli flag has been burned. They are about the desires of people in their own countries.' She had known that in Egypt the desires of the people would most likely be crushed by 'the deep state' – the power at the heart of the military and the bureaucracy. Libya had the opposite problem – there was no state at all. 'The most likely immediate aftermath here is chaos,' she said. 'There is no parliament, no political parties, no NGOs, no civil society structure at all.'

Marie was keen to keep reporting, but the *Sunday Times* decided she needed a break and replaced her with Miles Amoore, the Kabul correspondent, a young reporter to whom she was something of a mentor. The *Sunday Times* had trained Marie and several other senior correspondents in TRiM, trauma risk management, which involved listening to other reporters when they had been through difficult situations. Miles had talked to Marie on several occasions. 'She was fantastic,' he says. 'Very understanding and sensitive and extremely helpful. She gave me lots of advice.' Now, though, exhausted and tearful, it was Marie asking for reassurance from Miles. 'What's Sean saying about me? Why have they sent you?' she kept asking.

She didn't have to worry: Libya would provide enough stories for everyone. The rebels in the east were losing ground and Gaddafi had threatened to send his forces into Benghazi to kill everyone 'like rats'. At the end of March, a UN resolution was passed giving NATO a mandate to intervene to stop the slaughter of the city's residents. The next day French warplanes bombed a column of government armour on the outskirts of the city. They didn't stop there. Continued NATO bombing changed the course of the war, as the rebels now effectively had an airforce. Marie was on holiday, sailing, but it was time to return to Libya. Gaddafi's forces were besieging the port city of Misrata, which lay between Benghazi and Tripoli. Here, revolutionary brigades were surrounded by government forces on the three sides and the sea on the fourth. It was the most dangerous but, at this point, the most significant battleground of the Libyan revolution.

* * * * *

The only way into Misrata was by sea from Benghazi, a 24-hour-long voyage along the Mediterranean coast. Marie flew to Cairo, drove overland to Benghazi and looked for a boat. For this adventure she had a companion: the photographer Paul Conroy. Marie was notorious for having little patience with photographers if she felt they were slowing her down or getting in the way. Sometimes, if she wanted to get rid of one without having to explain herself to either the desk or the photographer, she would arrange to meet for breakfast at 8 a.m. and leave an hour earlier. But in Paul she recognised a fellow maverick spirit. They had met in Syria in 2003, when both were trying to get into Iraqi Kurdistan for the war in Iraq. While other journalists spent endless hours listlessly waiting for a Syrian permit to cross the border, Paul had lashed together a boat from truck tyres, rope and wood on which to cross the narrow river that divided the two countries. Unfortunately, the night he and his companions tried this trick, they ran into a patrol, whereupon they were arrested and spent several days at the pleasure of the Syrian authorities. Amused and rather impressed, Marie had nicknamed him 'the boatman'. A Liverpudlian with a strong accent and a rumbunctious sense of humour, Paul had an appetite for alcohol and that cigarettes matched hers (although she had been trying for several months to give up both). In a former life he had been in the Paras, so his knowledge of military matters was very useful. The fact that he was an excellent photographer was lower on Marie's list of priorities, but it helped.

They managed to talk their way on board a ship commissioned by the International Organization for Migration to take supplies into Misrata and bring out refugees. Planning on spending only a few days, they took little with them – satellite phone, laptop, cameras, a change of clothing, flak jackets and helmets. Marie's legendary immunity from seasickness stood her in good stead on the voyage. As the ferry chugged into Misrata port on a cold, overcast morning in late April, they could see plumes of black smoke rising over the city and hear the rumble of artillery. The rusting steel bow doors had scarcely been lowered before hundreds of people rushed inside to unload the cargo of food, fuel and medicine. Stocks in Misrata were alarmingly low; there was desperation in the air. Marie and Paul had just found a rebel fighter with a vehicle to take them into town when a round of Grad missiles screeched overhead and landed about half a mile away. Gaddafi's forces were attacking the port. Their car careened along potholed streets littered with shell casings, past buildings blackened and gouged by artillery shells and dimpled by small arms fire. Marie wanted to go straight to the hospital. A white tent had been erected in the car park to serve as a trauma unit, and emergency staff were running in all directions as ambulances tore up, sirens blaring, disgorging wounded fighters and civilians. As they talked to the hospital administrator, a photographer covering the conflict rushed up, eyes red with tears, with terrible news to relate: a few hours earlier, while Marie and Paul were on the boat, two photojournalists had been killed while taking pictures on the frontline.

Tim Hetherington and Chris Hondros were well known members of the tribe. Marie had met them both in previous conflict zones. Tim had come to prominence recently for his film *Restrepo*, a fly-on-the-wall documentary about US soldiers in Afghanistan. Chris had been photographing wars since the late '90s, and had taken pictures at Ground Zero after 9/11. Paul, who had learnt battlefield first aid in the military, went to see if the photographers really were dead or whether there was anything he could do, but Tim had already bled out and Chris had died of a massive brain injury. A mortar round had impacted just where the two were taking pictures on Tripoli Street, the front line between the part of Misrata still controlled by Gaddafi's forces and the area taken by the rebels. Two other photographers had also been injured. It was a sign of how random and dangerous the battle for Misrata had become, with ill disciplined, lightly armed rebels firing wildly at forces equipped with artillery and heavy weapons. A rumour spread round town – Gaddafi's forces were wearing gas masks. Maybe they had chemical weapons, maybe Gaddafi had never given up his stockpile. It wasn't true, but it panicked Misrata residents and the few journalists in town, most of whom opted to leave on the ship with their wounded comrades and the bodies of Tim and Chris. Marie and Paul decided to stay. They had only just arrived, and Marie was determined to tell the stories of the people living under siege. It was like East Timor: civilians were under threat and she felt it was not only her job but her responsibility to be there, to bear witness.

They found a place to stay, and started to look for stories. 'People say that Marie lived for the front, but she didn't,' says Paul. 'She was really anxious.' She fell quiet when they drove towards the more dangerous parts of town. That was why she and Paul trusted each other – they laughed and joked but each knew the other understood danger. 'I respected her because she could overcome her fear,' he says. 'You wouldn't want to be with someone who wasn't scared.' He did, however, worry about her lack of tactical awareness. 'She would walk along the top of a berm silhouetted with her pen and notebook.' Marie and Paul were frequently in the hands of fighters who thought that all reporters wanted to see action, and it was hard for her to explain that while photographers and camera operators are looking for 'bang bang', she wanted stories about civilians. The problem was that in Misrata, the front line was right in the middle of town, and moved several times a day, so you could be interviewing a family somewhere relatively safe and then suddenly, without warning, be in the thick of it.

Marie had always scoffed at boy reporters who liked to identify weapons, but if she was to understand the battle for Misrata, she needed to know what was killing people, and the distance that projectiles could travel. Paul was shooting moving pictures as well as stills, and Marie began to do video reports for the *Sunday Times* website. In one, the pair drive west towards Dafniya, from where Gaddafi's forces are attacking. 'We're not really sure what's up the road,' says Marie. A volley of gunfire erupts and in the next shot we see her, eyepatch squeezed up against her helmet, lying against a sand dune for cover. 'We were just sniped,' she says, matter-of-factly. 'There are mortars coming in and going out ... We're basically in the middle of a firefight.' It was the first time readers had seen Marie in a battle, as they would a TV reporter. Although many print journalists struggle to speak fluently on camera, especially under fire, Marie had no problems. As gunfire exploded around her, she was clear, articulate and, above all, calm.

Sunday Times, Misrata, 24th April 2011
Yesterday, as they retook the fruit and vegetable market that had been held by Gaddafi's men for a month, I sheltered behind a charred tank that had been hit so many times that sunlight shone through the holes ... When I finally entered the market, every shop had been shelled or shot up. Inside, the furniture and stalls were smashed. Some of the stalls were still burning ... At the market's entrance, I had to wade through a carpet of brass bullet casings about 4in deep. Unexploded cluster bomblets littered the street.

The memory of Tim and Chris was always with her, especially when the rebels secured the spot where the two had been killed. She emailed Katrina, who had known Tim. 'A shiver of mortality,' she wrote. 'The forecourt of the car repair shop still bears the mark of the mortar shell that killed them, and a starburst of chips in the concrete where the metal flew out as shrapnel.' Paul knew when Marie was under stress: she massaged her temples with her fingers and spoke in rapid bursts. But she managed to subdue the terror that had afflicted her in Lebanon five years earlier when she had worried that she might be losing her nerve. She could still endure life under fire, in extreme hardship, and for far longer than most journalists because she was so motivated. 'She'd get furious when she saw large-calibre weapons being fired at houses with children in,' says Paul. 'That would get her temper up. She'd be driven by the fact that these weapons were being used against kids.' The hospital was particularly horrific. 'To start a heart doctors cut open the side of the chest and reached in halfway up their bloodied forearm and pumped the heart with a bare hand,' she wrote. 'Few survived. It was more like the Spanish Civil War than a modern war of smart bombs and drones.'

The David and Goliath aspect of the battle for Misrata enthralled Marie – it seemed impossible that the untrained, lightly armed rebels could push back Gaddafi's army but house by house, street by street they were doing just that. NATO bombardment was weakening government forces but in Misrata street fighting was crucial. Marie couldn't help but admire the rebels' bravery. 'She was terrific – on top form,' recalls Sean, who spoke to her every day. 'It was obvious that she was exhilarated by what she was seeing. In terms of mental health, I had no concerns.' She was taking better care of herself too. It was hard to get alcohol in Misrata and she resisted the temptation to smoke. 'I'm smoking for two,' Paul would say, as she asked him to blow his smoke in her direction because she missed it so much. She emailed Hugh 'Hornet' Hudson:

I am now like a character in a modern remake of Stalingrad. The city is in its second month of a siege. I pause in my race to the shelling at the front and veer over to the roadside when I spot someone selling onions from a wooden table on the verge.

I have a low-tech early warning system. I am staying on the floor of a hospital room, and there is always commotion outside. But when I hear a chorus of 'allahu akbars' (God is great) shouted from the doctors, medics and rebels in the parking lot I know a body or a severely injured person has arrived and I head down. There is always a story at the end of a rocket [...].

On the positive side, this is like a health reservation without the counselling. No booze, no bread. Off to the front in my Toyota pickup. Handful of dried dates, can of tuna.

Being back on an absorbing story had distracted Marie from her misery over Richard. She emailed Jane in May:

A quick note to say hi from Misrata ... Gaddafi is just standing back and lobbing in huge rockets. Heartbreaking the flow of wounded and dying every hour. Send some news from home. Missing you. Otherwise all well ... Gaddafi's folk have mined the port, so not sure there is a way out even if I wanted to leave. Extraordinary story and leaving means deserting these people to a terrible fate.

Every Friday, Sean thought it might be time for her to leave but she always came up with a new angle – the diary of a Gaddafi commander that a rebel had found and given to Paul, the plight of women who had been raped, a university professor who had organised his students into a brigade. She and Paul ended up staying nearly two months. In Misrata, all her contradictions came together: she could survive seven weeks in a war zone without alcohol even though, by many measures, she was an alcoholic. She had suffered PTSD because of her conflict experiences, yet she was in her element in a place where death was a constant danger. Personal pain could blind her to the needs of others, yet she thought of her friends in London while under extreme stress and when communication was difficult. She identified too closely with those she saw as victims of war, and yet her reporting was calibrated and contextualised.

Marie made a point of regularly visiting the bombed out building where the penniless freelance journalists were staying in Misrata.

'The other staff correspondents didn't do that,' says Ruth Sherlock, a young British reporter stringing for multiple outlets. Marie swapped information and gave advice if they asked. In Ruth and the others she saw her younger self, making her name in Libya twenty-five years earlier. By the second week of June, Misrata was firmly in rebel hands, and the focus of the story had moved back to Tripoli where the regime was tottering. Gaddafi had disappeared from public view. After consulting with Sean, Marie asked Ruth to write for the *Sunday Times* when she left. 'I was so grateful to her for giving me that chance,' says Ruth.

On leaving, Marie wrote an email to Katrina.

I am sitting in the gloaming on the stern of a Turkish boat in Misrata harbor, looking out over an ugly seascape of cranes and broken concrete and blasted buildings from months of bombing. I am finally homeward bound.[…] It will be strange coming out of this world that, however mad, has a simplicity to it of sand and courage and bombs and sleep and canned tuna and a few shirts, washed out in a bowl when the dust threatens to take over.

* * * * *

Marie had a secret she was keeping from her friends: all through the Arab Spring she had stayed in touch with Richard. They would meet from time to time in the brief interludes between trips. The contrast with her journalistic triumph in Misrata is painful to read. Some days in her diary she made small sad notes. 'R dinner – cook at home cry a little.' 'Friday. Was to see R – cancel. We decide not to speak, he feels accountable.' 'Talk to Richard. Fight, he has not bothered to call.' She is trying to make an accommodation with his perfidy, to find a way to live with herself without letting him go. Sometimes she notes down the names of other women he is still seeing. She knows what is going on.

One day in early summer she called him. He was cycling along the Thames. 'I have to tell you how much I miss you,' he said. 'To tell you the truth, I feel lost without you.' She thought about it. Her fury had subsided, and she missed him too. He promised that this time it would be different – he would give up his hedonistic lifestyle and be faithful to her. Nothing in her diaries gives away whether she believed him or not. Eventually she told Jane, who asked if she was sure she was going back into the relationship with her eyes open. Yes, she said, she was.

She and Richard were planning a sailing trip together in August, but when Gaddafi fell from power, she abandoned the holiday and rushed back to Tripoli. Jubilant revolutionaries were posing for selfies on the statue of a fist grasping a jet bomber that he had erected in commemoration of the 1986 Reagan bombing. Marie finally wrote the profile Bob Tyrer had commissioned in February, reprising her many encounters with Gaddafi, including all the costumes she had seen him wear, from the red silk pyjamas to the uniforms with more medals than a Latin American generalissimo. The piece was titled 'Mad Dog and Me'.

Sunday Times, Tripoli, 28th August 2011
Beneath the ludicrous military caps his eyes were dark. They never revealed any emotion other than a canniness, as if a reptile within was always plotting. For his own people he was, in their words, 'the leader'. He preferred 'supreme guide' and fancied himself as their mentor, patriarch and uncle. It was the people, though, who felt the vicious side of his character, and where the lack of pity in those eyes mattered most. He was feared and hated. He would stop at nothing to maintain power.

Libyans and foreign journalists alike wanted to get into the Gaddafi family's luxurious residences. Never one to be deterred by physical obstacles, Marie scaled a wall to enter a massive compound that had been occupied by Gaddafi's son Mutassim. Men from the victorious brigades had prised open the bomb-proof door to his bunker so she descended three flights of stairs and wandered around a vast warren of corridors, finding endless rooms including a fully equipped operating theatre. It was strange to think that she had unknowingly trodden on top of this secret underground world every time she had visited Libya.

She joined a ramshackle convoy of rebels searching for the run-away Brother Leader in the southern desert. As they entered the town of Sukna, his loyalists attacked their convoy.

Sunday Times, Jufra, 25th September 2011
Another rocket propelled grenade hit the side of the road and my car skewed to a halt. One of the convoy's commanders thrust a Beretta pistol at me from the front seat and shouted: 'Take this. If they overrun us, can you use it?' I nodded and jumped out, running doubled-over to avoid bullets, and threw myself down behind a sand dune. Then I decided it was too low and crawled to a rock. I had a pistol, a notebook and a pen.

Fortunately she was not called upon to use the pistol as she was undoubtedly more skilled with the pen. Not that the rebels were much better – they scared off the enemy this time, but on entering the town of Jufra they fired randomly into the air in excitement. A falling bullet struck Marie on the shoulder 'stinging like a bee'. Her story showed the at times farcical nature of the Libyan revolution, in which over-excited young men hurtled around the country, high on the sniff of freedom, intent on revenge rather than reconstruction. She got a tour of the luxurious homes Gaddafi had built in the desert but the dictator himself was nowhere to be seen.

* * * * *

In October, Marie had an appointment with the past. Gerry Weaver, the man she had yearned for so deeply at Yale and when she had first lived in New York, was visiting London. Since leaving Washington nearly twenty-six years earlier, she had seen him just once for a quick lunch. In the early 1990s, while working as Chief of Staff to a Democratic congressman, Gerry had been imprisoned for distributing cocaine. Marie had written to him in jail, but they didn't meet again until 2010, shortly before she split up with Richard. When he said he was thinking of writing a literary novel based on his prison experiences she encouraged him, but she was ambivalent about having him back in her life. She told the foreign desk that if Gerry rang they shouldn't tell him where she was. She would nonetheless call him herself from time to time, including from Egypt where she described how she had escaped from the mob. 'She told me the story in a dispassionate way, how she had run down the alley. All without emotion,' he recalls. Marie had called a lot of people from Egypt (including John Schley), partly because she was so thrilled about the Arab Spring, and partly because she was lonely and needy. Gerry was flattered that she had let him into her world. Back in their early days, he had treated her casually, but now the power had shifted. He was fascinated. 'Lots of times I had no idea what she was really thinking or feeling. Maybe she didn't really know,' he says.

They spent the day he was in London at her house, going through his novel. He stayed the night. Gerry wondered if it might be a new beginning, if history might repeat itself, only with a different outcome. Then the call came: Gaddafi had been killed. 'I cooked her breakfast and helped her pack,' he says. 'I went with her in the car to the airport. She said no man had ever done that for her before.' As she kissed him goodbye at Heathrow, he believed there would be more encounters to come.

Marie's mind soon turned to the story, and getting back to Misrata where Gaddafi's body was on show at a refrigeration plant. Rebel fighters had found him in Sirte, the futuristic city he had built near his birthplace, where Marie had interviewed him years earlier. Chaotic, blurred trophy video shows fighters dragging him from a storm drain where he was hiding, kicking and punching him, sodomising him with a metal rod and shooting him in the head and chest. Marie teamed up with Paul Conroy again, and together they found the one-storey building where Gaddafi had spent his last days. Much to Marie and Paul's amusement, the *Sunday Times* requested a photo of the unmarked grave in the desert where Gaddafi had just been buried. Resisting the temptation to send a picture of a random expanse of sand, preferably with camels, they asked their contacts where the grave was. Its location had been kept secret to prevent it becoming a place of pilgrimage, but the commander who had buried the Supreme Guide told Marie that she had been at the very spot some months earlier. The Commander had taken her there. It was 50 kilometres south. Didn't she remember the hill? And the trees? She and Paul spent five days searching, their driver growing ever more anxious about bandits and Gaddafi loyalists hiding behind trees. In the end they gave up. Marie might have learnt a little about weaponry but she still had no sense of direction and no geographic recall. Paul took a picture of her scouring the desert, while Gaddafi lay undiscovered and undisturbed, they knew not where.

So many eras were over. Arafat was dead. Now Gaddafi was dead. Regimes that had been stable Marie's entire journalistic life had crumbled. Journalism itself was changing. 'Sometimes I feel like the only reporter in the Youtube world,' she said after watching another piece of wobbly video posted online, purportedly showing an important event that had happened without any journalist present as an eyewitness. Marie invited Ruth Sherlock to share her room in Tripoli, and advised her on what stories to pursue as the war for control in Libya fragmented. She always tried to help young reporters who wanted to be on the ground. Just as Martha Gellhorn and John Hersey had handed the torch on to Marie's generation, she would eventually pass it on to the next – she would show them how to hold it, but she wasn't ready to surrender the flame quite yet.

* * * * *

By November the news from the Arab world had calmed a little, so Marie and Richard went back to their old routine. The months in Libya had been so exhilarating, she hadn't thought too much about her personal troubles, and – although there had been the odd bottle of Jack Daniel's in someone's hotel room – she had scarcely been drinking. Now, though, it was hard to keep the blues at bay. Ella noticed that the glass of water by the cooker at breakfast time was in fact vodka. Marie barely ate. She talked a lot about the past, with a nostalgia Ella had never heard before. 'She used to cling on to stories and repeat them multiple times, even on the same night, sometimes with different endings each time.' Some stories were about occasions when Ella was present, so she knew that Marie was exaggerating or forgetting or just making things up. As Marie's renewed relationship with Richard was only semi-public, the house was quiet apart from the strains of Patsy Cline or Lucinda Williams that Marie played. 'The sociable dinners that she and Dad used to have were a thing of the past,' Ella says. 'They spent a lot of time just the two of them. And with me because I was there.'

Marie's friends found it hard to understand her choice. Alan thought she might have shed her romantic delusions and become more pragmatic. 'She was back with Richard but on different terms,' he says. 'The veil had fallen from her eyes and she saw him clearly. She felt more in control; she was nobody's victim.' Others were not so sure. She showed little sign of being happy with Richard. After a November afternoon sailing along the Thames in the *African Queen* together, she noted: 'w/R in afternoon. Crack up a bit. Cry on pontoon.'

She would go for weeks without seeing her friends and then call, saying, 'I went into my little black rabbit hole.' She told Maryam that she was having nightmares again, mostly about powerlessness, of not being able to do anything. She kept repeating the story of how Tim and Chris had been killed. 'Her eye would twitch and she would rub her hand against her forehead as if she was trying to massage her brain,' recalls Maryam. She talked about growing old. 'She didn't like the fragility,' she adds. 'Her memory would get confused – booze doesn't help. She had a dread about her long term ability to do the job.' She cheered herself up by making plans. Why not sail the Atlantic? With her old talent for roping others into her adventures, she persuaded John Witherow that he'd like to come too. The idea of reversing roles tickled her: he might be her editor, but not on a sailing boat. 'I'll be skipper,' she said. 'That means you have to do what I say. No arguments. This is serious.' John said they would need a song as they cruised along. That was easy. 'Bridge Over Troubled Water,' she said. 'I want to be the silver girl who sails on.'

At Christmas she joined Richard, Ella and Toby sailing in the Caribbean. In port, Marie grew grouchy. 'She couldn't bear the lack of movement,' says Ella. They had a row because Marie was determined to have lobster for Christmas lunch, even though the island had run out and they would have to take a dinghy to another island and pay an extortionate price. 'She seemed on edge, emotionally unhinged,' says Richard. Over and again she went through the death of Tim and Chris, once retelling it in grisly detail in front of a teenage girl and her parents who she and Richard had only just met. Marie drank so much she could no longer cook, but she didn't seem to care if a meal was inedible. Some short notes in her diary are practical and seemingly happy – 'Hurray! We swim, find lobsters, dive off rock' – but the most frequent word is 'exhausted'. 'Weird half dreams – R doesn't listen,' she writes, and on Christmas Eve: 'Decorate boat, who cares.' She also noted in her diary that on Christmas Day she discovered that Richard had texted one of the other women in his life: 'Fester then explode at night.' She called Gerry three times over the trip, but he didn't know if she meant it when she said she loved him. He knew she was with Richard. 'Lots of times she would just say things. She was pulled in different directions,' Gerry says.

According to Ella, the only time Marie seemed at peace that Christmas was the night a huge storm blew up while the two of them were on watch. The wind howled as twelve-foot waves broke across the deck, ripping the mainsail in half and flooding the bilge pump so the engine couldn't work. The rope that kept the foresail in place unwound, leaving it flapping; they were tossed on the waves with no means of propulsion. Ella and Toby went into the cockpit while Marie and Richard climbed up on to the foredeck, wrapped their legs round the forestay and re-wound the rope. 'It took about an hour and a half,' recalls Richard. 'There were constant waves over us, but she was in her element. I just wanted to get the bloody thing fixed, but for Marie it was an adventure. She was absolutely brilliant.'

As they sailed into the storm, the boat terrifyingly small and vulnerable in the violent swell of the sea, Ella realised that in that moment Marie wasn't just calm, she was happy. The happiest she had been in a long time.

* * * * *

Chapter 12

BABA AMR

On 8 April 2011, while Marie was absorbed by the drama in Libya, a group of Syrians had taken to the streets of Baba Amr, a neighbourhood in Syria's third largest city, Homs. Protests against the regime of President Bashar al-Assad had been building across the country for more than a month, after teenagers in the town of Daraa sprayed graffiti reading, 'It's your turn, Dr Bashar al-Assad.' The Syrian President had no trouble reading the writing on the wall: if his security forces didn't crush dissent right now, he would be deposed like Mubarak, or worse. The teenagers were arrested, beaten with cables, hung by their wrists from the ceiling and forced into tyres which were rolled down a prison corridor, slamming into a concrete wall.

The Baba Amr demonstration was met with bullets. The first person to die was a construction worker named Naif al-Omar. 'He was shot in front of my eyes,' says Wa'el al-Omar, his cousin. 'We were shouting in Arabic "*Salmia! Salmia!*" which means "Peacefully!", but they opened fire with live ammunition. Naif was the first link in a chain.' Funerals turned into protests and more were killed. Members of the *mukhabarat*, the secret police, went from house to house detaining scores of young men and women, who were imprisoned and tortured. 'People started to arm themselves to stop regime forces from reaching the demonstrations,' says Wa'el. By late July, the uprising was morphing into civil war across the country. A group of military defectors formed a rebel group called the Free Syrian Army, or FSA. In Homs, Christians and the President's Alawite sect had always lived peacefully with Sunnis but mostly in separate neighbourhoods. Now the Sunnis, who were in the majority, had turned against Assad, while the minorities began to fear a Sunni backlash if Assad was toppled. The city fractured into a jigsaw of rival districts, with military checkpoints guarding exits and entrances. The people of Baba Amr, who were mainly Sunni, became more militant. In autumn 2011, fighters armed with Kalashnikovs and rocket propelled grenades took over the neighbourhood, whereupon government forces imposed a siege.

All over Syria young people were chronicling the protests and the brutal response with their smartphones and small cameras, and uploading video to the internet. A group of young men had founded the Baba Amr Media Centre, located in an apartment down a narrow alleyway. In December 2011 they acquired a portable satellite transmitter so they could send video and make Skype calls to international media without going through the public internet service provider. They were not members of the FSA but it was a fine distinction: every family in the neighbourhood had sons who were fighting and others who were unarmed activists. 'The relation with the FSA is family and organic – you cannot deny or escape it,' says Wa'el, who, on finishing his compulsory military service, had become a pacifist. 'I didn't carry weapons and I totally disagree with it, but I had to work with them, because they were the guys who would carry the medical supplies and the injured people.'

President Assad made no distinction at all. To him, 'armed gangs' and 'terrorists', sponsored by foreign powers and supported by 'media groups', were all the enemy. Controlling information was as important as retaking territory. 'They want us to surrender through waging on us a virtual war using the media and the internet,' he said in a speech to the Syrian parliament.

* * * * *

Marie called Sean from her Caribbean sailing holiday. John Witherow was keen that she should pursue a story in Saudi Arabia but she was determined to go to Syria. Once back in London she applied for a visa. Having reported from Damascus several times in the past, she was sure that she would be able to duck and dive and get a story despite government restrictions. In the meantime, she interviewed human rights workers by phone, quoting one in her notebook: 'I have not seen torture at this scale ever.' She made notes on the type of torture practised: prolonged beatings, the use of cattle prods, electric wires on sexual organs, and the 'flying carpet' in which a person is shackled hand and foot and hung upside down for hours.

She also noted that detainees were shifted from prisons when monitors from the Arab League visited. Under international pressure, the Syrian government had allowed the monitors to deploy in late 2011, but used bureaucracy and spurious concerns about safety to frustrate their mission. Arab solidarity, the regime hoped, would prevent the monitors from saying anything too negative. They had not reckoned on the Algerian human rights activist Anwar Malek. To the anger of the Syrian authorities, he and other monitors insisted on crossing the front line to visit the Baba Amr Media Centre. 'I saw no arms, no FSA personnel,' recalls Malek. 'They were activists, like journalists. They had the internet and many cameras. That was all.' The centre had hosted several foreign correspondents, mainly from Arab TV channels, who had sneaked across the Lebanese border without visas. Over dinner in early January, the Deputy Defence Minister, Assef Shawkat – who happened to be the President's brother-in-law – told Malek that if it weren't for the foreign journalists with their cameras bringing the world's attention to the siege, he could destroy Baba Amr immediately. 'In reality, they are not journalists. They are agents of the Israeli and American intelligence services who are trying to infiltrate Syria,' he said. 'Each journalist who enters into Baba Amr without state authorisation – for us these are terrorists. They are targets for our military services and our security services.' Soldiers and police manning checkpoints around Homs were told to arrest activists who spoke to the foreign media, and a reward was offered for anyone who captured a foreign journalist who had entered the country illegally.

Marie grew impatient. It was taking the Syrian Embassy too long to issue her visa, and she was afraid she would miss the story. A few weeks previously her colleagues Miles Amoore and Paul Conroy had been smuggled over the border from Lebanon, but had pulled back because of the danger. Paul was willing to try again. Other journalists had managed to report briefly from inside Baba Amr. It was full scale war now with the Fourth Division of the Republican Guard, commanded by the President's brother, Maher al-Assad, the most effective force of the Syrian military, launching artillery into the neighbourhood where 28,000 civilians were trapped. 'We knew that Assad or his commanders would stop at nothing to put the rebels down,' says Sean. 'And that if they won in Homs then there would be repercussions across the country. But if the rebels succeeded in Homs that could be the beginning of the end for the regime.'

Marie saw her friends as she prepared to leave. Some had withdrawn a little because she could be difficult company – when she drank too much she would repeat herself, and she was evasive about her renewed relationship with Richard. One evening she turned up several hours late for dinner with Rosie Boycott, staggering and making no sense. Furious when challenged, she repeated angrily: 'I'm not drunk, I'm not drunk.' Yet a week or so later, at a party for the *Sunday Times Magazine*, she scarcely drank at all and was on good form, raring to be off to Syria. She and Jane went for a plate of pasta and discussed another film someone wanted to make about Marie's life. The night before she left, she stayed over with Richard and went home in the morning to get organised. She sat with Ella, talking about how hard it was to find the right man, impressing upon her that love matters more than anything. After packing she came down to the kitchen, pulled a bottle of champagne from the fridge and went back to Richard's for lunch. She and Paul were leaving on the early evening flight for Beirut.

* * * * *

Lebanon hadn't seen so many foreign correspondents since the civil war in the early 1980s. It had become the place to base yourself to interview refugees fleeing Syria, wait for a visa or link up with the FSA and get smuggled across the border. Someone decided to revive the Foreign Correspondents' Club for one night only and Marie and Paul met old friends in a hotel bar. The buzz was all about the dangers and possibilities of crossing the border. Who dared go? Who had been and lived to tell the tale? Could you trust the smugglers or the FSA? Marie went for dinner with three old friends, including Jim Muir of the BBC, whom she had met on her first visit to Beirut twenty-five years earlier. He teased her when she got lost between her hotel and his flat, all of 100 metres away; having only one eye, he said, must be making her walk in circles. She laughed, dismissing his concerns when he tried to dissuade her from crossing the border. 'They're doing terrible things,' she said. 'We have to be there.' He lent her a pair of large, ill-fitting Y-front long johns to keep her warm, because it was snowing in Homs.

Jim's colleague Paul Wood had made the perilous trip into Baba Amr a week earlier, pulling out when the artillery bombardments intensified. 'I assumed the rebels had days, maybe hours there – they'd nothing to fight back with,' he says. 'I thought that when this place is sealed off government forces will go house to house kicking the doors, and then we'll be arrested and disappear for ever into the Syrian prison system.' Everything Wood was hearing from his contacts suggested that the situation was worsening as Syrian troops closed in. 'I have taken some stupid risks in my time, but this is the stupidest risk I ever took,' he told Marie. 'I know that you probably won't listen to any of us, but you really shouldn't go.'

'Well, I'm going anyway,' she said. Paul Wood wondered if she had fully taken on board how dangerous it was. Marie had a similar conversation with a Sky News correspondent who had also left Baba Amr rapidly. She was not dismissive of the danger – how could she be when they had described it so graphically? But, although she was nervous, she thought it was worth it.

Paul Conroy understood the danger too: a Lebanese intelligence source had told Miles that Syrian forces had orders to execute Western journalists they found around Homs and throw them on to the battle-field claiming they had been killed in crossfire. How seriously should they take that? It was hard to tell. Those were the kind of threats that were put out to scare off journalists. On the other hand, it might be true. Paul was in touch with Leena Saidi, an experienced TV producer and fixer who had made the arrangements for him and Miles to cross the border the previous month. Now she introduced Marie and Paul to a smuggler, who they met in the not-so-covert rendezvous of a Starbucks. He agreed to take them across.

They prepared for a long wait in Beirut while arrangements were made. To while away the time, Marie had brought the draft of Gerry's novel which he had asked her to critique, but within a couple of days Leena told her and Paul to pack only the essentials, put body armour on under their clothes and be ready to leave. Marie stuffed a bag with the manuscript and a few other possessions to leave in Beirut and emailed Katrina in California.

I am now in Beirut, negotiating with smugglers to get me across the border. After six weeks in Libya, under shelling and that low level of anxiety every day brings, I had said I'll do a bit less of the hot spots, but what is happening in Syria, especially Homs, is criminal, so I am once again, knapsack on back with my satellite phone and computer, clambering across a dark border.

Jim Muir worried that she was making a mistake. 'There was something of the anxious little girl about her as she set off,' he wrote later. 'She took only a small knapsack containing her satellite computer, some granola bars and a jar of instant coffee she said she couldn't live without.'

* * * * *

Major General Rafiq Shahadah, the head of the Homs Military-Security Committee, was getting frustrated. The Baba Amr Media Centre was one of the most active in the country and he was receiving regular reports from contacts in Lebanon about foreign journalists being smuggled over the border and staying with the local media activists. According to sworn testimony by a defector, code-named 'Ulysses' to protect his identity, General Shahadah instructed the Computer and Signals Section of Military Intelligence Branch 261 to intercept and eavesdrop on satellite transmissions from Baba Amr. They installed a listening device in a vehicle that circled the neighbourhood, but it could never pinpoint the exact location of the satellite phones. General Shahadah turned to a former drug smuggler, Khaled al-Fares, who had connections with Maher al-Assad. He was tasked with developing a network of informers who could provide on-the-ground intelligence to back up that supplied by the Signals Section. In Syria, there were several reasons a citizen might work secretly for the regime. Many families had members who were in prison, so information might be exchanged for the offer of a cousin's release, or news of a sister or brother. Some people would tell you a lot if you threatened them or their relative with prison, and everyone was getting poorer so inducements were hard to resist. General Shahadah knew there would be a way to get someone in Baba Amr to talk.

* * * * *

On Monday, 13 February, a dark blue Mercedes saloon collected Marie and Paul from the hotel, but unexpectedly dropped them on the outskirts of Beirut, where they were picked up by a rickety minibus with brass trinkets all over the dashboard. 'Syria?' asked the driver. They nodded. 'He put two fingers to his temple in the shape of a gun and mimed someone being shot in the head,' wrote Paul in his memoir *Under the Wire*. Near Baalbek in the Bekaa Valley, they swapped into a light blue pickup and bumped down a dirt track towards the border. Marie was quiet. She didn't like not knowing exactly who was driving or how they would get into Syria, but they had entrusted themselves to Leena's contacts so they had to go with it. At the border they were dropped at a house where Miles and Paul had stayed before so that, at least, was reassuring. Some of the men greeted Paul like an old friend. The headman, Kalashnikov at his side, lay on the floor watching a TV broadcasting endless amateur footage from inside Syria: tanks firing, civilians screaming, jagged broken walls that used to be people's homes. Amongst the fighters and other men hanging around was a French journalist, Jean-Pierre Perrin, known as J-P, a large, balding man who Paul and Marie reckoned must have been at least sixty-five. Someone muttered something in Arabic. Paul asked a young man who spoke some English to translate. 'He says things must be serious in Syria: first they send young journalists but now they send us a woman, a pensioner and an idiot who wants to go back.'

As dusk fell, the headman indicated that they should be ready to move. Paul thought Marie looked like a stocky commando with her black quilted Prada jacket pulled over her body armour, tight black jeans and a black rucksack. The border area was mined, so they trod carefully in the footsteps of three armed rebels leading the way along a track skirting the fields. Occasional bursts of machine-gun fire from Syrian border patrols pierced the night. They felt like hunted animals. As they tramped through heavy mud, a man appeared out of the dark and guided them between two derelict buildings and into a deserted village. A rebel appeared on a motorbike and gestured for Marie to get on the back, so she sped off. A few minutes later a vehicle appeared for the others, and they reunited at a safe house in territory controlled by the FSA.

Marie and Paul hugged. They had made it. They were in Syria. As always in the Middle East, someone appeared with glasses of hot, sweet tea. It was good to stop and regain their breath but soon a minivan turned up to take them along muddy tracks to the next staging post. Paul noticed that the rebels seemed well organised and professional, always in touch with a control centre by radio, and taking up defensive positions if the vehicle stopped for any reason. Having defected from the Syrian army, they had proper training, unlike the excitable gunmen he and Marie had met in Misrata. They spent the rest of the night sleeping on mattresses at a farmhouse full of armed men. In the morning Marie persuaded a rebel general to take them to al-Buwaydah, which was only about ten miles from Homs. Travelling by daylight now, they drove through villages of nondescript concrete buildings, down lanes lined with cypresses and poplars, past orchards of bare-branched apricot and apple trees. It would have seemed bucolic if the shelling hadn't been so alarmingly close.

At the next safe house they made the acquaintance of Wa'el, the young man whose cousin had been the first person killed in Baba Amr. Before the war he had worked as an English tutor. A tall, dark-haired young man, he was not only a pacifist but also a vegetarian – almost unheard of for a Syrian. He watched Marie standing in the room handing out business cards to the rebel commanders, telling them how important it was that she get in and tell the story of Baba Amr. 'I explained that she might be one of the main targets of the regime, but she wasn't listening,' he recalls. 'She was only focused on human suffering, on children dying. I thought I could work with this person because she has no ideology, she's just concerned with human beings.' He agreed to accompany her and Paul to Baba Amr as an interpreter, but refused to accept any money. 'I would be privileged to be part of this team,' he said.

The worst part of the journey was yet to come. They slept another night, Marie in a house of women, Paul, J-P and Wa'el in a room of rebels. Another day passed. Marie was impatient, but there was nothing they could do to speed things up. A commander arrived with good news – they could get into Homs via the 'special way'. They knew what that meant because other journalists had warned them: a three-kilometre-long storm drain. To get there they would have to drive through territory still under the control of Assad's forces, then walk across open fields with trenches dug on either side. They set off that night. It was pitch black – difficult for anyone, almost impossible with only one eye. Paul caught sight of Marie several metres away, heading in the wrong direction.

'Where the fuck are you off to – Damascus?' he whispered, as he pulled her back on track. She was embarrassed.

'I can't see a fucking thing,' she said. 'I keep moving in circles.' He took her by the hand. 'The comfort of another person's hand in yours at such a moment is a wonderful feeling. It gives hope when it is most needed,' he later wrote.

The next obstacle was a wall they had to scale. 'Unfortunately, Marie got stuck on top. Her body armour snagged and she began to spin in a circle like a turtle stuck on its back, unable to move', Paul remembers. Marie chuckled. A quick push and she was over. Even as they negotiated boulders, trenches and another wall, machine-gun fire and the rumble of artillery in the background, she never flagged. Sailing and running had kept Marie fit, but she was fifty-six, a former smoker, and weighed down by eight kilos of body armour and several more kilos of equipment in her knapsack. Determination and the fear of being caught kept her going. 'I knew how demanding this journey would be mentally and physically,' says Wa'el who was twenty-five years younger. 'She was just made of iron – so hard and resilient.'

They arrived at a muddy hole, the entrance to the storm drain through which the FSA brought out the wounded and took in food and other supplies, including weapons. A deep breath and they were lowered into a dark, dank, claustrophobic tunnel. Filthy water sloshed over their shoes and if they stood upright, they cracked their heads on the concrete. J-P said he couldn't do it, but there was no way back now. Marie's voice trembled as she tried to make light of their situation. 'Don't worry, I've got the fear too,' Paul replied. They started to walk, bent over, muscles tightening, the way ahead lit by faint torches. Their breath came in short bursts as the oxygen thinned out and the atmosphere grew hotter. After a while they heard a giant rumble coming towards them and the fetid air filled with fumes: a motorcycle was approaching. J-P had collapsed, gasping for breath. As the motorbike manoeuvred round in a small space built into the tunnel, he tried to say that Marie should get on the back, but it was clear he needed the bike more, so he sped off, leaving the others to follow. They tramped on. It seemed to take for ever. Eventually the air began to smell better and they could hear the sound of raised voices. 'That old saying about light at the end of the tunnel is nonsense,' joked Paul. 'At the end of the tunnel there is a bunch of arguing Arabs.'

As they were hauled out, Paul and Marie laughed – they couldn't believe they'd made it to Homs. Their situation was so absurd, so extreme, so surreal, there was no other response. But they hadn't yet reached Baba Amr. They still had to avoid checkpoints as well as schools, hospitals and factories occupied by government forces. They climbed into a pickup truck that, to their horror, sped along with its headlights on, the rebels in the back shouting 'Allahu Akbar!' Inevitably the Syrian army opened fire. Once everyone calmed down they were transferred to a small car, which was also shot at, as they sped through the empty streets.

Marie looked out at the rubble, broken glass and wrecked cars, buildings with gaping holes from tank shells fringing the route, some with twisted steel rods sticking out like skeletons. This was Baba Amr. It reminded her of Grozny, in Chechnya. Eventually they arrived at a building that was relatively undamaged – the third storey had been destroyed but the lower floors remained more or less intact. They climbed the stairs and opened a wooden door into a large room, where by the light of a single tungsten bulb, they could see fifteen or so young men wearing headphones sitting on mattresses on the floor, wrapped in blankets, tapping at laptops or shouting into microphones. The air was thick with cigarette smoke. Chipped coffee cups and cigarette butts stubbed out in saucers lay on a low table. A tangle of cables snaked around the floor. After more than 48 treacherous hours on the road, they had arrived at the Baba Amr Media Centre.

A CNN team – Arwa Damon, Neil Hannon and Tim Crockett – had got there a few days earlier. They and the activists quickly explained the situation: shelling began every morning at 6.30 and didn't stop until dark. It was relentless. Drones flew overhead watching cars and pedestrians in the street. Getting out of the Media Centre was danger-ous: so was staying in. Scores of civilians were being killed and wounded. The best story was the field hospital but you could go there only when the shelling was concentrated elsewhere, and even then you had to brave snipers positioned on tall buildings on the perimeter of the neighbourhood and run like hell from the car to the building.

Marie Skyped Sean to tell him they were in and safe. Then she and Paul moved to a back room, where they huddled under blankets, Marie with Jim Muir's long johns under her clothes and a black *abaya* she had borrowed on top for extra warmth. Exhausted, she fell asleep immediately.

* * * * *

The shelling started right on cue at dawn. Marie would have slept through but Paul woke her because they had to move to the main room in the centre of the building in case the window shattered. Marie added cold water to the instant coffee she carried – it was better than no coffee at all. They counted incoming shells: forty-six in 3 minutes. Paul noted that the firing was targeted and the Syrian military seemed to have an unlimited supply of ammunition. There was no way he and Marie could move about independently as they had done in Misrata, so they would be reliant on the FSA and the guys at the Media Centre. Abu Hanin, one of the English-speaking activists, told them they should get ready. He would accompany them. As Paul, J-P and Wa'el were preparing to run across the road, a shell landed about 50 metres to their left and they all hit the deck. Brushing off the dust and debris, they ran to an apartment, where Marie and Wa'el interviewed a family, before jumping into a car that careered along the narrow streets, skirting bomb craters and rubble. It began to rain. In her despatch, Marie described the neighbourhood:

Sunday Times, Baba Amr, 19th February 2012
On some streets whole buildings have collapsed – all there is to see are shredded clothes, broken pots and the shattered furniture of families destroyed.

No shops are open, so families are sharing what they have with relatives and neighbours. Many of the dead and injured are those who risked foraging for food.

Fearing the snipers' merciless eyes, families resorted last week to throwing bread across rooftops, or breaking through communal walls to pass unseen.

As the vehicle pulled up under the shelter of a broken balcony, Abu Hanin told them to run the rest of the way to the clinic. A shell exploded behind them and machine-gun fire echoed around. 'Keep moving!' yelled Abu Hanin, and they ran on, passing two rebels carrying a wounded man, his left leg hanging on by a few strands of flesh, until they were pulled into an apartment block. 'We stood in a hallway, bent double as we caught our breath,' wrote Paul. 'Heart thumping, trembling with fear and adrenalin, I found the strength to raise my head and count our numbers. We had all made it.' Then they climbed the stairs to the first floor.

The clinic is merely a first-floor apartment donated by the kindly owner. It still has out-of-place domestic touches: plasma pouches hang from a wooden coat hanger and above the patients a colourful children's mobile hangs from the ceiling.

The shelling last Friday was the most intense yet and the wounded were rushed to the clinic in the backs of cars by family members.

Ali the dentist was cutting the clothes off 24-year-old Ahmed al-Irini on one of the clinic's two operating tables. Shrapnel had gashed huge bloody chunks out of Irini's thighs. Blood poured out as Ali used tweezers to draw a piece of metal from beneath his left eye.

Irini's legs spasmed and he died on the table. His brother-in-law, who had brought him in, began weeping. 'We were playing cards when a missile hit our house,' he said through his tears. Irini was taken out to the makeshift mortuary in a former back bedroom, naked but for a black plastic bag covering his genitals.

There was no let-up. Khaled Abu Kamali died before the doctor could get his clothes off. He had been hit by shrapnel in the chest while at home. [....]

Helping tend the wounded was Um Ammar, a 45-year-old mother of seven, who had offered to be a nurse after a neighbour's house was shelled. She wore filthy plastic gloves and was crying. 'I'm obliged to endure this, because all children brought here are my children,' she said. 'But it is so hard.'

They stayed for several hours in the field hospital. People kept asking why no one was intervening to stop Assad from attacking a neighbourhood full of women and children. 'Where are the human rights? Do we have none? Where are the United Nations?' asked Ahmed Mohammed, a military doctor who had defected from Assad's army. 'We ask all people who believe in God – Christians, Jews and Muslims – to help us!' said a young man who said he had been injured when a shell hit the mosque where he was praying. At dusk it grew safer to move around, so Abu Hanin suggested going to meet some of the women and children where they slept. People emerged from their houses to enjoy a brief respite from the shelling. Marie and company drove for about 5 minutes to another apartment block, and were taken into a cellar. The despatch Marie wrote about it would become her most famous report.

They call it the widows' basement. Crammed amid makeshift beds and scattered belongings are frightened women and children trapped in the horror of Homs, the Syrian city shaken by two weeks of relentless bombardment.

Among the 300 huddling in this wood factory cellar in the besieged district of Baba Amr is 20-year-old Noor, who lost her husband and her home to the shells and rockets.

'Our house was hit by a rocket so 17 of us were staying in one room,' she recalls as Mimi, her three-year-old daughter, and Mohamed, her five-year-old son, cling to her abaya.

'We had had nothing but sugar and water for two days and my husband went to try to find food.' It was the last time she saw Maziad, 30, who had worked in a mobile phone repair shop. 'He was torn to pieces by a mortar shell.'

For Noor, it was a double tragedy. Adnan, her 27-year-old brother, was killed at Maziad's side.

Everyone in the cellar has a similar story of hardship or death. The refuge was chosen because it is one of the few basements in Baba Amr. Foam mattresses are piled against the walls and the children have not seen the light of day since the siege began on February 4. Most families fled their homes with only the clothes on their backs.

The city is running perilously short of supplies and the only food here is rice, tea and some tins of tuna delivered by a local sheikh who looted them from a bombed-out supermarket.

A baby born in the basement last week looked as shellshocked as her mother, Fatima, 19, who fled there when her family's single-storey house was obliterated. 'We survived by a miracle,' she whispers. Fatima is so traumatised that she cannot breastfeed, so the baby has been fed only sugar and water; there is no formula milk.

Fatima may or may not be a widow. Her husband, a shepherd, was in the countryside when the siege started with a ferocious barrage and she has heard no word of him since.

* * * * *

That night Marie emailed Richard.

Darling, a quick note to say that I have made it to the heart of Baba Amr, the neighbourhood under siege in Homs. Under

siege is an understatement. Every building has been hit, and
there is shelling all day. I am cold, wet and muddy but here!
The scale of human tragedy is shocking. [. . . .] I love you deeply.
Mxxxxxxxxxxxx

The news on TV interrupted any relief they felt at having survived the day. CNN was reporting that Anthony Shadid of the *New*
York Times, one of the most thoughtful and perceptive journalists
in the region, had succumbed to an acute asthma attack while
reporting from northern Syria. After trying with no success to
resuscitate him, the photographer Tyler Hicks had carried his body
back across the border to Turkey. 'It hit everyone,' says Paul. 'We'd
all worked with him. He was like an old soldier, he'd been around
so long.' Marie went silent. Anthony's work 'glowed with humanity', she wrote on Facebook. 'He was the best person to shed light
on this strange new Middle East.' She made a Skype call to a mutual
friend, her distress about Anthony's death intensified by the peril
she was in herself.

Then there was more bad news. Arwa Damon, the CNN correspondent, said she'd heard from FSA guys on the street that the Syrian
government was planning a ground invasion of Baba Amr that very
night. Tension rose, as people came and went from the house, talking
in low tones and smoking. The only way out was via the tunnel. If it
was cut by bombing, they would be stuck. Paul knew that Marie
already had a story, and he had pictures, so he felt there was no real
need to remain, but Marie was reluctant to go. 'She was so stubborn,'
recalls Wa'el. In her mind, it was like East Timor: if she left she would
be abandoning the women and children she had met in the widows'
basement. Anyway, the ground invasion might not happen, or at least
not yet. She had a notion that they could stay in the rubble, dressed in
burqas, and report the invasion. Sean Skyped, urging her to leave: she
already had a great story that she could file from the relative safety of
Al-Buwaydah. Eventually Abu Hanin came over and ended all discussion. His group of activists was splitting into two – six would stay in

Baba Amr and become martyrs, while the other six would accompany the journalists out through the tunnel. Everyone should pack their things and be ready to go immediately.

As they climbed into the minibus, Paul, like Marie, felt that they were abandoning the people of Baba Amr. Unlike Marie, he thought they had no choice. Somewhere on the way to the tunnel, the armed escort in the back started shouting at the driver, who backed up at a crossroads. He had taken a wrong turning. Marie leant back in her seat. There was nothing they could do. When told, they got out and walked, Paul by now furious with their escorts, one of whom was wearing trainers with flashing LEDs, like a beacon. The activists chatted amongst themselves, seemingly oblivious to the need for basic security. The trip back through the tunnel was as arduous as it had been in the other direction, followed by a bone-shaking drive to the house of the commander at Al-Buwaydah where they had stayed before. The journey took 24 hours.

Marie walked across to the women's house, where she stayed up all night to write her piece. Her deadline was the next day. She should have been relieved to be in a less dangerous place but she wasn't. In the morning, looking exhausted, her eyes bloodshot, she woke up Paul. The commander had told her that the expected ground invasion had not materialised. Everything was the same as before in Baba Amr. 'We fucked up,' she said. However angry she was about having left, the priority was to file her copy. Neither of their portable satellite terminals was working, which they suspected was because the Syrian government was jamming the signal. Marie would have to dictate her copy by satellite phone, which might take as long as an hour. A security consultant had advised her before she left that she should use the satellite phone only if she were about to move, because the signal was easily traceable, but she had no choice if she was to get her story to London.

Her front page news story was about a veterinarian she had met at the field hospital in Baba Amr, who was using his knowledge of sheep anatomy to treat the wounded. Sean thought that the spread on the inside pages, which started with her description of the widows' basement, was probably the best piece she had ever written. 'She had amazing detail and her whole heart was in this piece.'

The Syrians have dug a huge trench around most of the district, and let virtually nobody in or out. The army is pursuing a brutal campaign to quell the resistance of Homs, Hama and other cities that have risen up against Bashar al-Assad, the Syrian president, whose family has been in power for 42 years.

In Baba Amr, the Free Syrian Army (FSA), the armed force of opposition to Assad, has virtually unanimous support from civilians who see them as their defenders. It is an unequal battle: the tanks and heavy weaponry of Assad's troops against the Kalashnikovs of the FSA.

About 5,000 Syrian soldiers are believed to be on the outskirts of Baba Amr, and the FSA received reports yesterday that they were preparing a ground assault. The residents dread the outcome.

'We live in fear the FSA will leave the city,' said Hamida, 43, hiding with her children and her sister's family in an empty ground-floor apartment after their house was bombed. 'There will be a massacre.'

* * * * *

Marie posted a link to her stories on Vulture Club, a foreign correspondents' Facebook page. 'Getting the story out from here is what we got into journalism for,' she wrote. She made a plea to other reporters not to disclose the smuggling route into Homs, pointing out: 'It is not just for journalists, but it is the only way out for the badly wounded whose only chance is a Lebanese hospital.'

She sent emails to her friends about how desperate Baba Amr was, and started to think about her next trip – maybe Iran? Sean told her that her story had been mentioned in all the newspaper reviews on the radio, Jim Muir had quoted it on the BBC that morning and everyone at the paper thought it brilliant. Richard emailed: 'Fantastic story, My Love. You are truly bearing witness to a terrible event. Your reporting is stunning – amongst your best ever ... I can't tell you how proud I am of you. I worry too.' She called and left a message when he didn't pick up. 'It's kind of madness yesterday. I have to keep moving because I could not get on the internet. Anyway, I'm out of Baba Amr but still in Homs but am being shelled hourly. And I love you.' She emailed Helen Fielding to say she was sorry but she wouldn't make her birthday drinks party.

Plumes of black smoke were rising from Baba Amr on the horizon. The CNN team and J-P were heading to Lebanon, but Marie didn't want to pull out. She felt restless. Marie and Paul explored the possibility of going to Hama, the next city Assad's forces were expected to attack, but it soon became clear that was impossible. Sean suggested they stay put and report the testimony of people fleeing Baba Amr. Marie was still the only British newspaper journalist near Homs, and therefore ahead of the competition. She felt frustrated. The ground invasion hadn't happened, so why had they left? Paul pointed out that they had already done the only feasible story – what could they get that was different? The invasion would surely come within days, if not hours. That didn't satisfy her. She wanted to go back. Feeling listless and unfocused, Paul acquiesced, but didn't feel good about it. Wa'el said he would go if they wanted. It was his neighbourhood after all. Eventually the commander in whose house they were staying agreed to find them transport.

Marie didn't tell Sean she was returning to Baba Amr. Nor did she email Richard or any of her friends. On Sunday, she called Jane Wellesley, leaving no message, and again the following day, this time leaving a message to say she might be out of touch for a few days but there was nothing to worry about. They left just before dusk on Monday the 20th, driving cross-country, until darkness fell and they reached the small house just before the tunnel where they had rested six days earlier. Rebels were hanging about smoking while an elderly couple clucked around, serving sweet tea.

Paul told Marie he had a bad feeling. A nagging voice in his head kept telling him not to return to Baba Amr. Marie asked what that was based on. He shrugged. 'Nothing tangible.' Marie was not to be deterred. If he didn't want to come, she would go alone. She must have known that was not going to happen: to abandon her would have gone against all Paul's training as a soldier, not to mention his loyalty as a friend. How would he live with himself if something happened to her and he had not been there? So he swallowed his fears and they tramped through the mud and climbed over the walls, the same route to the tunnel they had taken before.

Deep in the storm drain, bent over and struggling through the water, they were unaware of what was happening above ground, so didn't hear the massive explosion that ripped through the house where the old man and woman had given them tea. Unbeknownst to them, the rebels had stored several hundred kilos of unstable TNT and C4 plastic explosive in one of the rooms. Something set it off less than half an hour after Paul, Marie and Wa'el left. The old couple, the rebels and many in the surrounding area were blown to pieces.

If they had followed Paul's instinct and aborted the return trip to Baba Amr at that point, they would have still been in the house when the explosives detonated. All three of them would have been killed instantly.

* * * * *

As they shuffled through the tunnel for the third time in less than a week, a stream of people was stumbling in the opposite direction, some borne on stretchers, others walking wounded, victims of snipers and artillery. On the other side it became clear that the situation had deteriorated: explosion followed explosion and the earth shook. They screeched off in a pickup, but were told to stop in the suburb where they had rested briefly on the way in. Marie was on edge, scared but desperate to make it back. Eventually they got into an old Datsun, its shattered windscreen held together by tape, the ignition failing to fire until the fourth attempt. It sped down narrow streets, gunfire echoing all around, the driver hunched down behind the wheel.

'Hey, guys, we're home!' said Wa'el as they drew up in front of the Media Centre, but the activists inside were less than pleased to see them.

'Why have you come back?' asked Abu Hanin.

'We have to witness what's happening and report it,' said Marie.

Wael tried his best to stay detached. 'But I felt sad thinking everything will be ruined and everyone is going to die if this invasion happens,' he recalls.

Marie emailed Richard.

I have come back to Baba Amr and am now freezing in my hovel with no windows.[. . . .] You would have laughed. I had to climb over two stone walls tonight, and had trouble with the second (6 feet) so a rebel made a cats cradle of his two hands and said, 'step here and I will give you a lift up'. Except he thought I was much heavier than I was, so when he 'lifted' my foot he launched me right over the wall and I landed on my head in the mud!

It is so hard to witness what is going on here and I only have words.

I will do one more week here, and then leave. Every day is a horror. I think of you all the time, and I miss you and your body next to mine.

Love you deeply,
Mxxxx

In the early hours, just before the shelling started, Abu Hanin shook them awake to show them a video one of the activists had just taken in the field hospital. On the flickering screen, a wounded baby boy was gasping his last. The medical staff had no way of saving him. A few hours later an activist stumbled into the room, covered in dust, bearing more bad news: one of the best Syrian cameramen, Rami al-Sayed, had been hit by shrapnel and bled to death in the field hospital. Marie and Paul tried to work out what to do. It was too dangerous to go outside. Marie emailed several other journalists. 'I think reports of my survival may be exaggerated,' she wrote. 'In Baba Amr. Sickening, cannot understand how the world can stand by and I should be hardened by now. Maybe not my best move, but so anger making it's worth it.' She emailed Sean as if it were perfectly normal to have returned to the most dangerous place in the world without discussing it with him. 'We have moved to Baba Amr. We would not have covered Srebrenica from the suburbs if we could get in, so here we are.' Her plan, she said, was to report on the defence of the neighbourhood and also the stories of civilians. 'No electricity, no water, very very cold,' she added.

Sean was shocked that she had gone back to Baba Amr without consulting him. He wanted her out, but knew that Marie would dig her heels in if he gave orders. By then news of her whereabouts had spread. The chief press officer at the Foreign Office called Sean to ask how she was planning to get out. Patrick, having heard the news through the journalist grapevine, also rang, concerned that, once again, Marie was in deep danger. Sean began to get calls from TV channels wanting to interview her. 'What we don't want to do is create an incentive for the Syrian army to come looking for you because you're broadcasting about their war crimes,' he wrote to Marie in an email. 'If it's risky I'll tell anyone enquiring that it's not possible at the moment.' Marie knew that the story of the baby who had died in the clinic and the relentless bombardment of civilians wouldn't keep until Sunday. More than that, she and Paul might not survive that long. They wanted to get the story out immediately, but feared that broadcasting live might create a satellite footprint that Assad's military technical teams could use to track them, so they asked Abu Hanin whether the signal would endanger them all further. The activists were themselves doing Skype interviews with Arabic language TV channels. 'Go ahead,' they said. 'That's why you're here.' Wa'el was worried. 'I tried to tell her that writing in the paper is one thing but broadcasting live will make the Syrian regime go crazy,' he says. 'The regime wanted to silence every voice and Marie was the voice of the people of Baba Amr.'

Marie's first interview was with Channel 4 News. Without specifying that she had not been present, she described the video the activist had brought in. 'In the clinic today, if you can even call it that – it's an apartment with two operating tables with a dentist and a doctor – there was a tiny baby, one year old, naked, hit in the left chest. The doctors said we can't do anything and we had to watch the baby's little tummy, desperate for breath, die,' she said. Her interview with the BBC made clear the danger she was in. 'The top floor of the building I'm in was hit last week and the building next to me was completely obliterated,' she said. 'In all the streets I've been on, I've not seen one military target. There simply aren't any, and the wounded and dead I have seen are, I would say, 80 per cent civilians. Of course there are FSA fighters, but it is shelling with impunity and a merciless disregard for the civilians who simply cannot escape.'

She knew that a broadcast on CNN would potentially have the most impact, because it would be seen in the US State Department and White House. 'It's a complete and utter lie that they're only going after terrorists,' she told the CNN anchor, Anderson Cooper. 'The Syrian army is simply shelling a city of cold starving civilians'. When he made the assumption that she had been in the room when the baby died, she did not correct him. 'It was horrific, my heart broke,' she said. 'It's just one of many stories. His house was hit by a shell. Another member of his family arrived later and said the second floor of their house had been hit. Just one piece of shrapnel caught him in the chest.' She had verified the information with the activists returning from the clinic, but broadcasting the video of the baby dying had become more important to her than clarifying that she had not seen it with her own eyes. 'That little baby will probably move more people to think what is going on and why no one is stopping this murder that is going on in Homs every day,' she said to Paul.

* * * * *

In the evening, Marie and Paul sat, wrapped in blankets, thinking about their situation.

'If you weren't getting paid would you still be here?' he asked.

'Yeah,' she said. 'You?'

'Of course,' said Paul.

That was it. Despite Paul's reservations about returning he, like Marie, believed in what they were doing – showing the world the horror of a full scale assault on civilians. Marie, however, took it one stage further – she thought that their presence would make a difference, as she believed it had in East Timor.

'Marie, you've got previous on this,' he said. She laughed.

Sean and Marie had a conversation by Skype. She had done everything she could, he said, and next week's story would be similar to last week's, so what was the point of exposing herself and Paul to further danger? She disagreed. Quietly, behind her back, Paul emailed Sean, saying the single exit route might soon be closed and that Marie's idea of hiding in the rubble was impossible. 'I suspect that Marie's high profile due to this week's material in paper and TV interviews also compromises our safety. The Syrians have an efficient intelligence machine as we know,' he wrote. 'Marie has a brilliant nose for a story but lacks, in my opinion, a general strategic awareness when it comes to military operations.' After another email from Sean, Marie agreed that the following day they would try to get more material and leave that night.

'Hallefuckinglujah,' thought Paul.

And then, just as Paul thought they had an exit plan, the Europeans arrived. Four more journalists had braved the tunnel and the bombardment: Javier Espinosa of the Spanish paper *El Mundo*, the French reporter Edith Bouvier, and two French photographers, William Daniels and Rémi Ochlik. It was great to see friendly faces, but Paul's heart sank: he knew it would be harder to get Marie to leave now that the competition was in town. She emailed Sean. 'A bunch of Euro journalists have piled in!' she wrote. 'I refuse to be beaten by the French!' Others from CNN and Al Jazeera would follow, she thought. 'I suspect, frighteningly, that my report made everyone realise it was possible,' she wrote. She and Paul made plans for the morning. If they got up early, she suggested, before the shelling started, could they go to the field hospital? Wearily, Abu Hanin acquiesced: 5 a.m. would be fine. 'Do you still want to leave now the Eurotrash are here?' Marie asked Paul.

One thing was worrying her – the constant shelling seemed to be making her deaf on one side. Paul took a torch and peered into her ear. 'Stay very still,' he said as he probed with a matchstick. 'You can look now,' he said as he held up the trophy he had extracted. It was the rubber earpiece from the headphones she had been using for the CNN interview. Marie began to giggle. Then Paul. They shook with laughter until one after the other they fell asleep.

* * * * *

That night, as the journalists huddled under the blankets, someone in Khaled al-Fares's informant network told him that she knew the location of the Media Centre. Not only did she have the street and the name of the building's owner, but she was sure there were foreign journalists staying there. Her identity remains hidden, but it is possible that she was a relative of one of the activists. Fares took her to the Homs operations room where General Shahadah was waiting. An aerial photo of Baba Amr was projected on to a screen. With the help of the informant, the general and his men were able to locate their target. In his sworn statement, 'Ulysses' said, 'Al-Fares left the meeting room carrying a large yellow envelope, the type used for intelligence reports.' His instructions: 'Give this to the head of the Computer and Signals section to be verified.' A few hours later, word came back: 'There was a broadcast tonight from the same location.' It was almost certainly one of the broadcasts Marie had made by Skype. At last, General Shahadah had what he wanted. The details were conveyed immediately to artillery units on the edge of town.

* * * * *

Marie tried to wake Abu Hanin at 5 a.m. as agreed but he was sleeping too deeply. They would have to try to reach the field hospital later. Equally exhausted, she crawled back under the blankets and was soon fast asleep again herself, alongside Paul and Wa'el. A couple of hours later, they roused themselves to go to the main room. 'Shit, the snipers will be awake now,' grumbled Marie. 'And so will the French.' As they stumbled in, all their senses were assaulted at once. The deafening screech of a rocket shattered their eardrums. The building shook violently and debris cascaded from the walls and ceiling. Shards of glass from broken windows fell through the smoke and dust. A second explosion hit. People screamed: 'Get out!' Paul's training kicked in: the rockets were getting closer, which meant that the place was being 'bracketed', the artilleryman's tactic of firing to each side of a target, correcting aim with information from a forward spotter or a drone, and firing again. The attackers knew what they were doing. He realised the next rocket would be a direct hit on the house, and a split second later the back of the building exploded with a sickening crunch and the room filled with smoke, dust and a smell of burning. Paul ran to the back room for his camera. Rémi had managed to get his body armour on. Marie had also put on her flak jacket and was pulling something from her bag. 'Get out! Get out!' people were screaming in Arabic, French and English. Edith was paralysed. Should she take her bag? Where should she go? William and Javier were standing against the wall in the main room, Wa'el in the centre.

One of the activists shouted at everyone to run in pairs into the foyer and across the street to a building that had an underground shelter. Wa'el was holding Marie's hand, ready to run, when he realised that Rémi was holding her other hand. He let go. Javier started to run too, but then rushed back to put on his boots. Suddenly it occurred to Paul that they would be more exposed on the street – you can survive an inside wall crumbling on top of you, but not the amount of shrapnel that would be flying outside. 'Don't fucking go out! Don't fucking leave!' he bellowed through the smoke and dust. 'Go back!' shrieked one of the activists at no one in particular. It was too late. A fourth rocket screamed in. Hot metal tore through concrete and wood. Dust choked the air. Wa'el blacked out and Paul felt intense pain in his abdomen and leg.

The rocket exploded at the front of the house just as Marie and Rémi were running through the doorway. It was a direct hit. The impact must have knocked them over instantly as hot shards of shrapnel pierced their bodies. More shells landed, injuring the media activists who had hurtled into the street, and raining rubble and debris on to Marie and Rémi as they lay motionless and mute.

After more than 15 minutes, the attacks ceased and the smoke and dust began to clear. A drone buzzed overhead. Paul, whose leg was badly injured, had managed to staunch the bleeding by applying a tourniquet fashioned from an ethernet cable. He crawled out of the building. Raising his head he could see Marie's belt and blue sweater. Her head was covered by rubble. He knew that she would have been killed instantly by the rocket, but part of him couldn't quite bear to believe it. He reached out and put his hand on her chest. No breath. No beating heart.

* * * * *

EPILOGUE

Exultation is the going
Of an inland soul to sea,
Past the houses – past the headlands –
Into deep Eternity –

Bred as we, among the mountains,
Can the sailor understand
The divine intoxication
Of the first league out from land?

Emily Dickinson

As the surviving journalists made contact with their newsdesks and families, the news filtered out: Marie and Rémi were dead; Paul, Edith and Wa'el injured; Javier and William shocked but unharmed. Sean was on a treadmill in the gym when someone from Al Jazeera rang the foreign desk. As he rushed into the office he tried to convince himself that maybe it wasn't true, maybe she was just injured, but more calls were coming in and everyone seemed to be saying the same thing. He rang Richard.

'I'm very sorry but I'm phoning with the worst possible news. There are reports that Marie's been killed,' he said, following a script he'd been given for breaking bad news. Richard screamed. Sean said, 'I haven't confirmed it yet,' but Richard was already on his computer. 'Jesus, it's on Reuters,' he said and rang off. Soon Jane was on the phone and Marie's other friends, everyone in shock and tears. A few hours later, after the *Sunday Times* had confirmed the worst, Prime Minister David Cameron made a statement in Parliament, saying Marie's death was 'a desperately sad reminder of the risks that journalists take to inform the world of what is happening, and of the dreadful events in Syria'. The leader of the opposition, Ed Milliband, said, 'She was a brave and tireless reporter across many continents and in many difficult situations. She was also an inspiration to women in her profession. Her reports in the hours before her death showed her work at its finest.' CNN went live to Anderson Cooper who had interviewed Marie just a few hours earlier. 'Even though she had been to so many conflicts, she never lost her humanity and her ability to bring that humanity to all of us. That's what made her so remarkable,' he said, sounding shaken. 'Like many in war zones, I think she felt fear but she never allowed fear to stop her from going. That's what makes her heroic.'

In San Francisco, Katrina had just gone to bed and didn't wake when the phone rang, so a friend who was staying answered and woke her with the news. 'No!' she shouted aloud. 'No, no, no, no ...' Cat, in Vermont on a skiing weekend with her children, was also asleep when Sean left a message on her phone, only waking a few hours later when a friend rang to say she had seen a report of Marie's death on CNN. By the time Cat called her, Rosemarie already knew. The six-hour drive back to Oyster Bay seemed endless. Cat kept willing her cellphone to ring and that it would be Marie. *'Oh, Bunny, you didn't believe it, did you?'* By the time she arrived, satellite trucks were lined up outside her mother's small house on the quiet street in East Norwich and reporters were queuing up to interview Rosemarie. After all the years of mixed emotions, her pride in her daughter's achievements always tempered by worry over her safety, Rosemarie decided that no journalist would leave that day without a quote. 'The reason I've been talking to all you guys is that I don't want my daughter's legacy to be 'no comment' ... because she wasn't a "no comment" person,' she said. 'Her legacy is: be passionate and be involved in what you believe in. And do it as thoroughly and honestly and fearlessly as you can.'

* * * * *

In the morning, General Shahadah hosted a celebration in his office. The military officer who had launched the attack was congratulated, along with the intelligence operatives who had helped pinpoint the location of the Media Centre. At around 11 a.m. the head of the General Intelligence Branch 318, Colonel Firas al-Hamed, arrived at the party to say that electronic surveillance had confirmed that two foreign journalists were dead. Having intercepted outgoing calls from Baba Amr asking for help to evacuate both the bodies and the survivors, they knew the names of those who had been killed. According to 'Ulysses', they ate and drank and crowed about their success.

'That blind bitch was Israeli,' said one of the officers.

'Marie Colvin was a dog and now she's dead,' said General Shahadah. 'Let the Americans help her now.'

'Ulysses' says that a few days later, Khaled al-Fares received a reward for his part in the killing of Marie Colvin and Rémi Ochlik: a brand new shiny black luxury sedan, a Hyundai Genesis. 'The car was a gift from Maher al-Assad,' he claims. 'A reward for the successful operation.'

* * * * *

Marie's colleague Hala Jaber was staying with her family in Beirut, grieving for her husband, the photographer Steve Bent, who had died of cancer on Christmas Day. When Sean called to ask if she would go to Damascus to try to retrieve Marie's body and rescue Paul Conroy, she didn't hesitate. 'I thought if the tables were turned, would Marie do this for me?' she recalls. 'Absolutely, yes, she would. Marie wasn't just my colleague but my friend.' She set off by road, still dressed in the traditional black of mourning. Miles Amoore and *Sunday Times* picture editor, Ray Wells, were despatched to Beirut to see if it would be better to get the survivors out via the rebel route.

On arrival in Damascus, Hala called every contact she had, even managing to persuade the Syrian military to negotiate a ceasefire with the FSA to allow an ambulance from the Red Crescent, the equivalent of the Red Cross, to drive to Baba Amr and collect the bodies and the injured. What she couldn't do was speak to Paul directly, because the rebels would have feared that a call from Damascus was intended to locate them in order to launch another attack. She had to speak to the foreign desk in London, which would pass on messages to the team in Beirut, who were in touch with the rebels looking after Paul. To Hala's frustration, Paul, Edith and the others refused to get into the Red Crescent ambulance, believing that they would be detained or even killed once they entered into Syrian government territory. To this day Hala maintains that if the injured journalists had got into the ambulance, they would have been treated well when they reached the government side, but Paul says that the Syrian doctor who accompanied the vehicle warned them that the rescue was just a ruse.

For nearly a week, the injured journalists remained in Baba Amr, trying to work out how to escape. Eventually, with the help of activists, Paul and Javier managed to get back down the tunnel and make it to Beirut. For Paul, with multiple injuries in his leg and side, it was a long, agonising journey. Once he had crossed into Lebanon, he was able to contact Miles and Ray and eventually make it to the British Embassy residence in Beirut. Blocked by fighting, Edith and William had to turn back to Baba Amr. They eventually escaped on the night of 29 February, just hours before the FSA retreated and Syrian government forces retook Baba Amr.

Desperately upset and in shock, Abu Hanin had filmed the bodies of Rémi and Marie. Other activists then took them to a makeshift mortuary and on to a refrigerated truck, but fuel ran out so they buried them, carefully marking the spot and recording it on GPS. Hala showed a senior member of Syrian intelligence a letter from Rosemarie, begging for her daughter's body to be repatriated. The French Ambassador to Syria, Eric Chevallier, was working his contacts to retrieve Rémi's remains. After a few days, a double agent working for both the regime and the rebels disinterred the bodies and reburied them in his garden, from where they were collected when the neighbourhood was retaken by government forces. Two weeks after the attack, the bodies of Marie and Rémi were sent to Damascus. For Hala, identifying Marie was the most miserable task she had ever been assigned, but she was calm and clear. 'I did it for my friend and for her mother, so she could pray over her body,' she says. Hala and the French Ambassador arranged for the bodies to be embalmed and put in coffins, ready to be transported on the last Air France flight out of Damascus before the airline closed its office in the Syrian capital. The two of them sat at the airport, each lost in thought, until the pilot let the ambassador know the plane was out of Syrian airspace.

On 4 March 2012, the body of Marie Colvin arrived in Paris. The next day she was flown on to New York.

Rosemarie, Marie's siblings and Sean were waiting on the tarmac as the coffin, draped in the Stars and Stripes, was lowered into the waiting hearse to be taken to the funeral parlour in Oyster Bay. Marie was home, or at least back to where it had all started. People began arriving from Europe and the Middle East. They held wakes, drank whiskey and swapped stories of Marie's exploits, from her derring-do as a child playing on the hill behind the house to her partying at Yale and her extraordinary achievements as a journalist covering the conflicts of her age. The funeral was held on 12 March, at St Dominic Church where she had worshipped as a child, attended her father's funeral and been married to Patrick. A few months earlier, she and Patrick had made their peace. 'Despite everything she had seen and been through, she kept a kind of innocence and underneath the chic exterior you could always glimpse the eager little Oyster Bay tomboy,' Patrick wrote. 'Time and bitter experience never rubbed away that childlike quality. She was always able to find wonder in things.'

Friends and former lovers, the huge network of people who loved and admired her, from Jerusalem to London and far beyond, assembled. Some of the most important people in her life, including Mickey Maye, Lucien Carr and David Blundy, were dead. Others came even though they hadn't seen her for years, amongst them her early boyfriends Thom De Jesu and Chris Biggart, her teenage accomplice Jerelyn Hanrahan, and Joe McDermott who had given Marie her first job at the Teamsters. A group of Syrian exiles who had never met her turned up to pay their respects. The Yale crowd mixed with friends from Notting Hill and dozens of journalists. There was tension between Richard and Marie's friends and family, who would never forgive him for the pain he had put her through, and who resented his claim to be her partner. Rupert Murdoch sat at the back of the church. Marie was, he said, 'the greatest war correspondent we've had and, I think, probably the best in the world'.

In her eulogy, Katrina described how her friend came, 'trailing clouds of glory and pandemonium'. This was the Marie so many knew: brilliant, brave and always laughing as she failed to find her wallet or turned up late because she was lost. 'You were utterly, sublimely defenceless against the laughter,' said Katrina. 'Marie came by her impracticality honestly, but she fed the aura of *joie de vivre* that wafted around her – it gave cover to another side of her, no more authentic but intensely more private. Here was the tremulous, self-taxing writer, the aspiring scholar of history, the student of prose and poetry, and the fragile woman who would have loved to be happy in love.'

Jane read from the Book of Timothy.

As for me my life is already being poured as a libation, and the time has come for me to be gone. I have fought the good fight to the end; I have run the race to the finish; I have kept the faith.

As pipers played 'Amazing Grace', the mourners stepped out into the sunlight where a knot of Tamils stood silently holding placards and handing out leaflets. 'Yesterday you lost your eye for Sri Lankan Tamils and gave vision to the blind world,' read one. 'Today you lost your life for fellow Syrians and gave teary eyes to the world. Tomorrow you will live forever all over the world in the hearts and minds of the lovers of humanity.'

At the *Sunday Times* there were those who blamed her editors for her death – she should have been taken off the road years ago, they said. There was no coroner's inquest to establish the facts of her death, and they believed Sean and John had encouraged her to take insane risks with little regard for her well-being and, in the end, her life. They regarded as a whitewash a confidential management report that cast no blame. Katrina felt that Marie had never been treated properly for depression and PTSD, nor excessive drinking; she went over and over everything in her mind, trying to work out if there was a point when she or someone else could have intervened. Jane and the Colvin family demurred: Marie pushed herself to extremes, they said, and it was hard to imagine her anywhere but in the conflict zone, 'bearing witness'. She had always refused to obey the rules. No one who knew Marie well believed she had a death wish but even those who loved her questioned her judgement in returning to Baba Amr. She knew it was a bad idea – that's why she told no one before she went.

Paul, who went on to endure more than a dozen operations and sustained permanent physical damage, never criticised Marie for her determination to return to Baba Amr. He believes she thought that her reporting could save people. That sounds like hubris, and maybe it was. The idea that alerting the world might make a difference had been one of her strongest motivators since she had watched the life seep out of Haji Achmed Ali, the young woman killed by a sniper on the 'Path of Death' in the Palestinian refugee camp in Beirut back in 1987. Her life as a journalist coincided with the era of Western human-itarian intervention but, as she knew well, any lingering idealism from Bosnia or Kosovo had died in Iraq. Maybe it was a simple refusal to calculate the odds: she had survived Chechnya and Sri Lanka, could this really be worse? Like Billy Smith, her Jerusalem street cat, she'd had nine lives. On one level she knew it. Some years before, she and a friend had been having a cigarette outside the Frontline Club when someone came up and berated them for smoking. 'Believe me,' Marie had said. 'This is not how I'm going to die.'

Marie's death did not save the people of Baba Amr, nor did it stop the war in Syria. For a few weeks, it concentrated the minds of Western governments, but that passed and the momentum of history resumed. Disillusion and death bred extremism. Some of the activists picked up not only a gun but also a Koran, and pledged loyalty to the jihadist ideology of the Islamic State. Marie's death marked the moment that war corresponding became unacceptably dangerous to many editors and journalists. After she was killed and others kidnapped and beheaded by jihadists, the conflict was mostly filmed and reported by Syrian 'citizen journalists' – brave and skilled without a doubt, but attached to a cause. The attack on the Baba Amr Media Centre was evidence of the extremes to which a ruthless government would go to silence independent eyewitness journalists like Marie.

In 2018, Cat and her two oldest children, Justine and Chris, filed a lawsuit against the Syrian government for Marie's murder. 'Marie was tracked down and targeted by agents of the regime of President Bashar al-Assad as part of a strategy to surveil, capture and even kill journalists to prevent reporting on the regime's crackdown on political opposition,' read the complaint. They hoped that the evidence of the defector 'Ulysses' and others presented to a court in Washington DC would eventually lead to the Syrian President and his associates being prosecuted for war crimes. That, at least, would help them feel that her death had not been in vain.

The last picture of Marie that Paul took shows her, back to the camera, wearing her thick black jacket and jeans, hair pulled into a scrunchie. She is writing, the bright white of her notebook a contrast to the dun-coloured debris of war in the ruined house around her: dirty crumbling walls sprout tangled iron rods, pots and pans are scattered, a green blanket lies on the ground next to crumpled, rusting iron sheeting. It's easy to imagine Marie in her final moments, rushing out of the shattered building in her warm, dark clothes, caught in flight in a freeze frame, forever pushing forwards, notebook in hand.

She never wrote a book, but later that year her best stories were gathered into a volume, *On the Front Line: the Collected Journalism of Marie Colvin,* which served as proof – if any were needed – of her exceptional skill as a reporter and the extraordinary times in which she had lived. Young journalists, especially women, would cite Marie Colvin as a role model, as she had cited Martha Gellhorn and John Hersey. Just as she had carried a battered copy of Gellhorn's book *The Face of War,* now they would carry her book, downloaded on their iPads. After she died, many wrote of how she had taken time to help them in Libya or Iraq, sitting and discussing ideas, critiquing their copy, giving them contacts, even letting them share her hotel room if they had no money. Others recalled her kindness and encouragement when they were interns on the *Sunday Times* foreign desk. It might be too dangerous to get to all the places she had been, but they could still follow in her tradition of focusing on the experience of civilians and the cost of war, remaining sceptical of the charts and cockpit footage military men used to bamboozle reporters. Many up-and-coming journalists were Syrian, Sri Lankan, Egyptian and from every other country where she had reported – just as she had scoffed at the idea that women were less able than men to do the job, so would they defy prejudice.

Marie had always identified with those whose lives she had touched – Palestinian youths, East Timorese refugees, Sri Lankan Tamils and those under siege in Baba Amr. They would remember her not just as a journalist, but also as someone who crossed a boundary to live and eventually die as they did. 'I knew her for a short period but it was a time of life or death, so I saw something in her,' said Wa'el, who survived the rocket attack that killed Marie, and ended up as a refugee in Europe. 'She dreamed of being a voice for the weak, and of a place where war doesn't affect civilians. She wasn't childish or naïve, but she was idealistic. She was a dreamer.'

EPILOGUE

* * * * *

Two memorial services were held in London, one at St Peter's Church in Hammersmith, and the other at St Martin-in-the-Fields, off Trafalgar Square, which was attended by the Foreign Secretary, the head of MI6 and *Sunday Times* readers as well as scores of journalists and friends. Alan Jenkins read 'Reports of My Survival May Be Exaggerated', the poem he wrote upon hearing of Marie's death.

At sunset after the Hammersmith service, Marie's mother, her four siblings, nieces and nephews and her closest friends – Katrina, the two Janes, Alan and Alex – as well as Richard and Ella, took the casket of her ashes to the Thames, as she had requested. Jane Wellesley brought flowers she had picked in her garden. Pink and orange glowed through the grey March clouds as the tide rose. Alan read Emily Dickinson's poem 'Exultation is the Going' and they stepped out on to a pontoon to cast handfuls of ashes and petals over the wide, brown river, as it flowed inexorably to the place Marie loved best in the world: the sea.

* * * * * * *

'Reports of My Survival May Be Exaggerated'
(Marie Colvin, 20 February 2012)

How can you be lying there?
　Immodestly, among the rubble
When we want you to be here
　In some other kind of trouble –

Luffing up, in irons, perhaps,
　Just downstream from the Dove,
Lost in South London, without maps
　Or capsized in love.

What's keeping you? A kind of dare?
　Come back and tell us how you stayed
One step ahead, how you gave fear
　The slip, how you were not afraid –

As we are. Look – here's my idea.
　Come back – this time, for good.
Leave your flak jacket and your gear
　In that burnt-out neighbourhood,

And fly home, via Paris. You'll be met.
　I'll buy a bottle from the corner store,
Like old times. You can have a cigarette.
　Marie, get up off that bloodstained floor!

* * *

Tonight you threw your thin brown arm
Around my shoulders, and you said
   (There was this unearthly calm)
'Can't you take in that I am dead?

   Learn to expect the unexpected turn
Of the tide, the unmarked reef,
   The rock that should be off the stern
On which we come to grief?

   The lies, the ignorance and hate –
The bigger picture? No safe mooring there,
   In Chechnya or Chiswick Eyot.
Those nights I drank my way out of despair,

   And filling ashtrays filed the copy
You would read – or not read – with
   A brackish taste and your first coffee
Contending on your tongue; while Billy Smith,

   My street cat rescued from Jerusalem,
Barged in, shouting, from his wars ...
   As many lives as his – and now I've used them.
I wish I'd made it back to yours.'

* * * * *

Alan Jenkins

SOURCES AND
ACKNOWLEDGEMENTS

This backbone of this book is some 300 journals that Marie kept throughout her life, the earliest from 1969, the latest from January 2012. Some years are missing, presumably lost. Reporting notes are interspersed with personal diary entries, and most – but not all – dated. She also kept appointment diaries, some completed after the event. For permission to quote from these I would like to thank Richard Flaye, the *Sunday Times*, the Colvin family and the executor of Marie's will, Jane Wellesley. Marie wrote down scenes from her life just after they happened, often using direct speech, which I have quoted. Any references to Marie's thoughts come from her journals.

I cannot thank the Colvin family enough for their kindness and hospitality, especially Cat. I would also like to thank the *Sunday Times* for permission to quote from Marie's articles and Bob Tyrer for his assistance. Ray Wells and Annabelle Whitestone of the *Sunday Times* photo desk helped with pictures. Denise Leith kindly let me quote from an interview with Marie she conducted for her book *Bearing Witness: the Lives of War Correspondents and Photojournalists* (Random House, Australia, 2004), while Hugh Hudson and Carine Adler allowed me to use their recording of a conversation with Marie. Richard Flaye, Katrina Heron, Hugh Hudson, Sean Ryan, Alex

Shulman and Jane Wellesley gave me permission to use emails and faxes Marie sent them.

I could not have written this book without Howard Schneider, Dean of the School of Journalism, or the Board of the Marie Colvin Center for International Reporting at Stony Brook University, Long Island, who selected me as their first Visiting Fellow. Jennifer Carlino made all the arrangements and looked after me.

Ray Bonner kindly provided accommodation and encouragement in New York; Jane Wellesley did the same in South Ayrshire. She and Alan Jenkins made helpful suggestions on early versions of the manuscript. My editors at Channel 4 News, Ben de Pear and Nevine Mabro, gave me book leave, and my agent, Felicity Bryan, and my editors, Poppy Hampson and Greg Clowes, provided unstinting support. Many thanks to all.

In Chapter 3, the account of the American raid on Tripoli drew on David Blundy and Andrew Lycett's book *Qaddafi and the Libyan Revolution* (Weidenfeld & Nicolson, 1987). In Chapter 4, I quote from the abstract of a paper by Dr Pauline Cutting and R. Agha, 'Surgery in a Palestinian Refugee Camp' (*Journal of the Care of the Injured*, 1992, Vol. 23, issue 6), with additional information from Dr Cutting's memoir *Children of the Siege* (Pan Books, 1988) and *One Day at a Time: Diaries from a Palestinian Camp* by Suzy Wighton (Hutchinson, 1990). In Chapter 8, I draw on Irena Cristalis's book *Bitter Dawn: East Timor – A People's Story* (Zed Books, 2002) and quote from Sherry Ricchiardi's article, 'Highway to the Danger Zone' (*American Journalism Review*, April 2000). Parts of the last chapter are based on Paul Conroy's book *Under the Wire: Marie Colvin's Final Assignment* (Quercus, 2013) which I highly recommend to anyone who wants to know the extraordinary story of his escape and survival. I also drew on Edith Bouvier's book *Chambre avec vue sur la guerre* (Flammarion, 2012). Details of what was happening within the Syrian regime are taken from sworn testimony in the Complaint against the Syrian Government for the extrajudicial killing of Marie, filed by Cat Colvin and her daughter, Justine, and son, Chris. Thank you to Scott Gilmore of the Center for Justice and Accountability for his help with these documents.

Thank you also to Manuela Andreoni, Suzanne Barry, Hannah Bennett, Antonia Brogna, Ellen Harris and Nicola Shannon who helped with transcription and translation. I interviewed more than a hundred people in the course of my research, several of whom are not mentioned but nonetheless provided essential information and leads, including Huda Abuzeid, Bill Beacon, Nick Birnback, Nora Boustany, Leah Cartmell, Ron Cohen, Lyse Doucet, Donna Fiore, Inigo Gilmore, Val Harper, Sara Hashash, David Jenkins, Ahmad Khalidi, Steve Mufson, Lowell Perry, Henry Porter, Lee Ranaldo, General Sir David Richards, Roxanna Shapour, Colin Storrie, Vera Taggart, Bill Trott, Jess Velmans and Mariann Wenckheim. I must also mention Dima Hamdan, Anna Ridout and Pippa Nairn, who, alongside Jane Wellesley, Lyse Doucet and myself, are working to continue Marie's legacy through the Marie Colvin Journalists' Network, a project to support young female journalists in the Arab World.

Finally, thank you to my partner, Tim Lambon, and my father, Cyril Hilsum, for their support and love.

CREDITS

'Fair Weather', from *The Complete Poems of Dorothy Parker*, by Dorothy Parker, copyright © 1999 by The National Association for the Advancement of Colored People. Used by permission of Penguin Books, an imprint of Penguin Publishing Group, a division of Penguin Random House LLC. All rights reserved.

Extract from 'Elegy', by Seamus Heaney, from *Field Work,* © Estate of Seamus Heaney, and reprinted by permission of Faber and Faber Ltd.

Extract from 'Crazy', Words and Music by Willie Nelson. Copyright © 1961 Sony/ATV Music Publishing LLC. Copyright renewed. All rights administered by Sony/ATV Music Publishing LLC, 4242 Church St, Suite 1200, Nashville, TN 37219. International copyright secured. All rights reserved. Reprinted by permission of Hal Leonard LLC.

Extract from 'El Peligro', by Pablo Neruda, *Fin de mundo.* © 1969, Fundación Pablo Neruda. Excerpt from *Late and Posthumous Poems*, copyright © 1988 by Fundación Pablo Neruda, translation copyright © 1988 by Ben Belitt. Used by permission of Grove/Atlantic, Inc. Any third party use of this material, outside of this publication, is prohibited.

'Reports of My Survival May Be Exaggerated', by Alan Jenkins, from *Revenants* (Clutag Press, 2013). Reprinted by permission of the poet and Clutag Press.

LIST OF ILLUSTRATIONS

All photos and images, unless otherwise stated, are used by kind permission of the Marie Colvin Estate.

Plate Section I

Every effort has been made by the publishers to trace the holders of copyright. Any inadvertent omissions of acknowledgement or permission can be rectified in future editions.

INDEX

382

INDEX

INDEX

INDEX

INDEX